THE OPEN UNIVERSITY GUIDE TO
HEALTHY EATING

IN ASSOCIATION WITH

THE HEALTH EDUCATION COUNCIL
AND THE SCOTTISH HEALTH EDUCATION GROUP

Contents

RAMBLETREE
PELHAM

The Open University Course Team
Joint Course Team Chairmen: Lorna Bailey and
Pamela Shakespeare.
Course Team: Angela Ballard, Joan Carty, Monica Darlington,
Mick Jones, Elisabeth Morse, Derek Prior, Jenny Weaver.

Secretarial support: Gyta Nicola.

Consultants: Frances Abrahams, Mary Bailey,
Dr. Michael Church, Issy Cole-Hamilton, Angela Fisher,
Dr. Godfrey Fowler, Elaine Fullard, Karen Gunner,
Dr. Deryck Lambert, Prof. Geoffrey Rose, Dr. Derek Shrimpton
Hazel Slavin, Jane Thomas, Barbara Webb.

Readers: Dr. John Brown, Dr. Eleanor Carlson,
Issy Cole-Hamilton, Anne Dillon, Dr. John Logan, Dr. Robin
Osner, Maggie Sanderson.
External Assessors: Alan Beattie, Prof. Philip James.
Director of Community Education: Nick Farnes.

First published in Great Britain by
Rambletree Publishing
Chancery House
319 City Road
London EC1V 1LJ

in association with
Pelham Books
44 Bedford Square
London WC1B 3DU.

Healthy eating.
  1. Nutrition
  I. Open University
  613.2   TX353

ISBN: 0-947894-02-0 H.b.
ISBN: 0-947894-03-9 P.b.

Edited, designed and produced by First Editions
(Rambletree Ltd).
Typeset by Presentia Arts, Horsham.
Origination by DS Colour International.
Printed by Redwood Burn, Trowbridge, England.

This book is part of the Open University Community Education
Course on 'Healthy Eating'. Further information on Open
University Community Education courses and packs may be
obtained from the Learning Materials Service Office, The
Centre for Continuing Education, The Open University, P.O.
Box 188, Milton Keynes, MK7 6AA.

Guidelines for Healthy Eating

Today's diet is now known to be an unhealthy diet. It increases our risks of developing heart disease and strokes (cardiovascular disease), certain types of cancer and various disorders of our digestive systems.

Put positively – changing to a healthier diet will give you the reassurance that you are doing all you can, in terms of your diet, to reduce your risks of developing these disorders.

Nutritionists – the experts who study what we need to eat and the links between diet and disease – are now in general agreement as to what makes up a healthier diet.

Over the last ten years an increasing number of reports from around the world, including one from the World Health Organisation (WHO) in 1982, have suggested similar changes towards a healthier diet. In 1983 the NACNE report – produced for the National Advisory Committee on Nutrition Education – reviewed these earlier recommendations and current research findings.

The NACNE report identified what is wrong with today's average diet in Britain and set targets for the changes.

This report was followed in 1984 by the COMA report on *Diet and Cardiovascular Disease,* by the Department of Health's Committee on Medical Aspects of Health.

Both the NACNE and COMA reports came up with essentially the same recommendations. This book is based on these recommendations.

The changes we need to make

The average person needs to:

Eat less fat. Cut down total by 25%, but more from saturated than from unsaturated fats.
Eat less sugar. Cut down by 50%.
Eat less salt. Cut down by 3 grams a day.
Eat more fibre. Increase by 50%.
The overall diet that you end up with, if you meet these targets for more fibre and less fat, sugar and salt, should also ensure that you get enough Vitamins and Mineral Salts.

"What should I do?"

Nutritionists can give general advice. They can also set goals for the average diet of the nation. But these reports, as they stand, do not help the individual to put such changes into practice.

Each person has to decide:
- **How do I measure up to these new targets?**
- **What changes should I make?**
- **What do I need to find out in order to be able to make these changes?**
- **How can I make these changes – and fit them into the kind of life I lead?**

This book aims to help you bridge the gap between what the experts advise and the exact changes you'll decide to make in your own everyday diet.

It's easy to read quickly through this book. But actually *reviewing your diet* will involve you in some hard work that only you can do! This is a workbook: you have to get involved in answering the quizzes, doing the activities and making decisions if the book is to be of any real benefit.

Our testers

During the writing of this book we have been helped by over sixty testers. They tried out the quizzes and activities and told us how we could improve them. They also gave us comments and examples from their own lives to add to this book.

When some of these testers first heard of the changes they should make they wanted an answer to a key question before they were willing to go further:

Will this advice all be changed in the next few years? Well – this advice is only the best that can be recommended at this time. Of course, new research will throw more light on our dietary needs. But there is a general consensus, amongst experts from around the world, that there is sufficient evidence to back these recommendations to the general public.

Looking to the future. There are at least three other areas where research may soon lead to new advice for the general public.

It is likely that the importance of the different types of fibre will become clearer. (see *'Eat more fibre?'*)

Oily fish (eg. mackerel and herring) are now known to contain a particularly beneficial type of polyunsaturated fat. But how much of these fish oils we should – or reasonably could – include in our diet has yet to be worked out.

More detailed advice about the links between diet and cancer should also become available.

Looking at your diet

Our 'diet' is everything that we eat and drink. Of course, what we eat and drink varies from day to day. But it's possible to talk about a typical diet or, for example, an average day's diet. The average person in Britain eats a diet that contains too much fat, sugar and salt, and not enough fibre.

Ordinary people eat food. For example, they see a Ploughman's Lunch as white bread, cheese, butter and pickles. But nutritionists look at the nutrients – substances needed by the body – that are in that food. They see a Ploughman's lunch as a reasonable amount of protein, not much fibre and a lot of fat and salt!

Whilst reviewing your diet and deciding how you can change to a healthier diet you'll need to think, for a while, about the nutrients in your diet. But of course you'll be bearing in mind all the time the other choices and constraints that you also have to consider when deciding what to eat. Sometimes you'll make decisions that a nutritionist wouldn't approve of. But most of the time you'll find you can choose a healthy diet that you can afford, that fits in with the way you live and that you will enjoy eating.

It all adds up

The food we eat and drink provides us with nutrients – the substances the body needs for growth and repair – and with energy to keep our bodies going. This energy is measured as Calories. (This is sometimes written Kcals. because it is a thousandth of the original smaller units – calories with a small 'c'.) You may also sometimes see the energy expressed as Joules – a different way of measuring it that's not, as yet, in everyday use.

How much energy we need to keep our bodies going depends on how active we are and how quickly or slowly our bodies naturally burn it up.

Where *do* we get our Calories?

Saturated fats 18%
Unsaturated fats 20% Including 4% polyunsaturated fats
Sugar 14%
31% Complex carbohydrates (High fibre starchy foods)
Alcohol 6%
Protein 11%

Today's average diet.

Where *should* we get our Calories?

Saturated fats 10%
Unsaturated fats 20% Including 6% polyunsaturated fats
Sugar 7%
48% Complex carbohydrates (High fibre starchy foods)
Alcohol 4%
Protein 11%

The new diet.

Both give the same amount of Calories, but from a different balance of nutrients.

To lose excess weight you need to become more active and/or eat fewer Calories. Fats and sugars are the energy-rich nutrients you should cut down on.

The right amount of Calories: but from the wrong food. Suppose your diet provides you with the right amount of Calories to keep you going. It need not necessarily be a healthy diet in terms of the nutrients it contains. Today, the Calories in the average person's diet come from an unhealthy balance of nutrients. The new, healthier diet provides the needed Calories from a better balance of nutrients.

Charting your diet

As you work through this book you will frequently be asked to consider your own diet. There are many quizzes and activities to help you translate the general dietary advice into what's helpful in your everyday life.

You will need a notebook or file in which to keep a record of your review of your diet. Before you can decide what changes you need to make you will need to know what your present diet is like.

Keep a Starting Point Diary. Don't change your diet in any way. Just keep a record for at least four days, including a weekend. Better still, keep it for a full week. This will make you much more aware of your patterns of eating. It will also provide the answers for some of the activities later on.

Rule up a page for each day with seven columns. Either fill in each time you eat or review what you've eaten at the end of each day. The example, below, shows just one entry. For each time you have something to eat or drink answer these seven questions:

1 What time was it?
2 What did you eat? Give some idea of the amount.
3 Who were you eating with?
4 Where were you eating?
5 How hungry did you feel?
6 What other strong feelings did you have at that time, eg. angry, sad or depressed?
7 How satisfied were you with what you chose to eat?

While you complete this diary, work through the topics in 'Health messages'. These topics will help you look at what you expect from experts. And at how your attitude to taking risks with your health affects how willing you really are to change your diet.

Doing this and keeping your *Starting Point Diary* will make it easier for you to work through the book.

TUESDAY 1 *Time*	2 *What?*	3 *Who with?*	4 *Where?*	5 *Hungry?*	6 *Other feelings?*	7 *Satisfied?*
12.30pm	Ploughman's Lunch: White bread Large piece of Cheddar cheese 2 pats of butter 2 teasps. sweet pickle	Angie, Bill and John	Pub	Yes – didn't have breakfast	Too busy talking to notice	It filled me up – but hardly remembered eating it

Health messages

The bad news
WARNING: The average British diet can harm your health.

The good news
The new advice gives us a blueprint for a healthy diet. It tells us:
● what to change
● how much to change.
This book will help you decide how you measure up and the best way for you to reach these targets.

Responding to health messages
But how do you respond to advice about your health? Do you tend to discard it:-
"So what? These experts are always changing their minds!"

Or query it:
"How can they be certain?"

Or do you see it as irrelevant or unusable:
"Right, I've got the general message. But what on earth, for example, does cut down fat by 25% mean in terms of what I eat?"

How you tend to respond may determine whether you accept or reject the new guidelines for healthy eating.

Taking risks
How do you feel about taking risks? Particularly with your health:
"Life's too short to worry about what you eat."

"Look at Winston Churchill. He lived to a ripe old age doing all the so-called 'wrong' things!"

"We've all got to die of something."

Do you know the risks you take?
Your attitude to taking risks – or avoiding risks – may determine how motivated you are to make changes in your diet.

Taking action
If it's to be easy for individuals to change to a healthier diet there must be changes right along the chain from farmer to what ends up on your plate. This book helps you make the most of the choices open to you at the moment. It will also help you see where other changes must come and how the consumer can speak up.

New advice

*Recent new advice has come from the NACNE and COMA reports.
What are they – and what do they have to say?*

Target	NACNE	COMA	Why the difference?
FATS	**Cut down to** 30% of total daily energy (including alcohol) to come from fats. 10% from saturated fats.	**Cut down to** 35% of daily food energy (not including alcohol) to come from fats. 15% from saturated fats. Recalculated to compare more directly with NACNE this would be: 33% of total daily energy. 14% from saturated fats.	As given in the actual reports there seems to be a bigger difference between the NACNE and COMA recommendations about fat than there actually is. The numbers have been expressed rather differently. NACNE included the Calories from all sources, ie. total daily energy. This counts in the Calories obtained from alcohol. COMA says: Our recommendations are designed to take into account practical considerations in the United Kingdom. We doubt whether the stringent dietary changes which the World Health Organisation recommendation* requires would be implemented by the general population at the present time. *We all recommend such changes for people with increased risk of coronary heart disease.* (Their italics) *NACNE recommendation was same as WHO.*

NACNE: 10% / 20%
Total Fats 30% of Calories

COMA: 14% / 19%
Total Fats 33% of Calories

[Both sets of figures now based on including Calories from alcohol ie. total daily energy]

Target	NACNE	COMA	Why the difference?
SALT	**Cut down by** 3 grams a day.	'Dietary intake of common salt should not be increased further and that consideration should be given to ways and means of decreasing it. We believe that the intake of salt in the United Kingdom is needlessly high. The salt content of many foods makes it difficult for the public to effect an immediate change in intake. (Salt) added at the table or in cooking . . . could be decreased immediately.'	It seems that COMA considers it could only set a target once ways and means of decreasing salt intake can be worked out. It *is* difficult to reach the NACNE target without paying careful attention to avoiding high salt processed foods.
SUGAR	**Cut down by** a half. Only 7% of dietary energy (Calories) to come from sugar.	'Intake of sugar should not be increased further. The Panel notes that restriction of intake of these sugars has been recommended on other health grounds (eg. dental caries)'	COMA is only making recommendations for dietary changes which will reduce cardio-vascular disease.
FIBRE	**Increase from** 20 to 30 grams a day. This will involve an increase in complex carbohydrates (mainly starches which come wrapped up with the fibre) to provide 48% of total energy.	'The panel sees advantages in compensating for a reduced fat intake with increased fibre-rich carbohydrates . . . Otherwise there are no specific recommendations about fibre intake.'	COMA is only making recommendations for dietary changes which will reduce cardio-vascular disease. It does say later in the report 'An increase of fibre intake of approximately 50% would be beneficial in other respects, but the protective effect in relation to coronary heart disease has not been adequately tested.' An increase of 50% would mean 20 grams goes up to 30 grams a day ie., the NACNE recommendation. So COMA and NACNE agree.

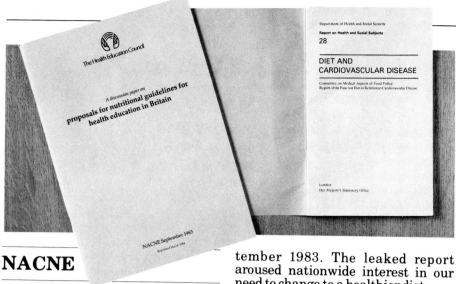

NACNE

Why was NACNE set up? How did it reach its conclusions? The National Advisory Committee on Nutrition Education (NACNE) was set up under the chairmanship of Professor Jerry Morris in 1979. Its task was to identify what is wrong with the diet of the British population as a whole, *including the average typical diet,* and how this could be remedied. It found itself facing conflicting advice as to what was a healthy diet. So the Vice Chairman, Professor Philip James, was asked to set up a working party which would produce a report that would bring together and sum up the recommendations of a series of major reports concerned with diet and health.

The NACNE report said little that was new to nutritionists. It looked for the consensus of opinion amongst the expert reports. Indeed its recommendations were essentially the same as the 1977 Dietary goals for the United States.

What was new?

The NACNE report gave goals and identified just how much the average diet needs to change. It shifted from giving vague warnings like *'it is advisable to cut down on fats'* to giving clear targets: *'In the average diet fats should be cut down by a quarter ie. from 128 grams to 91 grams a day. No more than 30% of the total daily energy requirement (Calories) should come from fat.'*

The clear warning message was that the average British diet was an unhealthy one. Its implications were wide-ranging. It is difficult with the foods available today for the individual to change to a healthier diet. His or her choice is limited. If the whole nation is to change, consumers need a wider choice of healthier foods.

These implications played a part in the long delay in publishing the NACNE report. Indeed the Sunday Times leaked the report's findings before it was finally published by the Health Education Council in Sep-

tember 1983. The leaked report aroused nationwide interest in our need to change to a healthier diet.

Why will the changes take 15 years?

The NACNE report gave both short-term and long-term goals. The report considers that it will take 15 years to reach these long-term goals.

But surely if the long-term goal is good for our health, the sooner it is reached the better? For the individual the answer is undoubtedly 'yes'.

For the nation as a whole it would be unrealistic to expect such a goal to be reached quickly. It takes time for people to get to understand what the new advice is and how to put it into practice in their own lives. But if it is to be made easy for the individual to change, other changes will also be needed. There must be changes along the entire food chain from farmer to the consumer's shopping basket. See *'Who has to change?'*

Surely everyone shares the same concern that the health of the people should come first? In fact the publicaton of the NACNE report led to a great deal of controversy. Not so much over the recommendations, but as to the implications of putting them into practice. The Food Industry could change, but there are signs that they are unwilling to change. Even if they are willing – or political and consumer pressure is used to persuade them to change – it will take time.

The COMA Report

The long-awaited report on 'Diet and Cardiovascular Disease', by the Committee on Medical Aspects of Food (COMA), was finally published by the DHSS in the summer of 1984. Unlike NACNE it is an official government report. Any changes in government policy will be based on it.

It is important to understand how and why the COMA and NACNE reports differ.

The DHSS is often considered to be under pressure from the Ministry of Agriculture (representing farmers)

and the Food Industry to be exceedingly cautious in its statements about the national diet. As it turned out there is much closer agreement than had been generally expected between COMA and NACNE. In some ways the COMA report is more cautious in how practical it considers changes to be. Yet in other ways it goes further than NACNE.

The important difference is, of course, that COMA looked only at diet and cardiovascular disease. NACNE had a wider remit to look at all aspects of diet and health.

Both reports paid detailed attention to the importance of fat and salt in our diet. The detailed differences in what they had to say about fats is considered in *'Cut down on fats?'* Here, in the table left, their main targets are summarised and compared.

What about you?

After looking at what the NACNE and COMA recommendations say you have to make up your own mind what you want to do. Here are some starting points for following up your interests in later topics.

Fats

● Is COMA saying there is no *health reason* for the general population to change to the lower limit? Or is it saying the WHO recommendations are difficult to put into practice at the present time?
● The practical considerations *you* will need to take into account are looked at in *'Cut down on fats?'*
● See *'Your risk factors'* to calculate whether you have an increased risk of coronary heart disease.

Salt

● *'Cut down on salt?'* shows you what steps you *can* take.
● If the general public is recommended to cut down might they not add their voice to demand less salty food?

Sugar

● *'Cut down on sugar?'* looks at the other reasons for cutting down and how you make changes.

Fibre

● *'Eat more fibre?'* looks at the benefits of doing this and how you can make changes.

How certain are they?

The media can distort the message. As what experts say gets passed along a chain towards 'the man in the street' the original message often gets distorted.

Experts: how certain are they?

We need to look at:
- why experts are so cautious
- how the food industry makes selective use of findings
- why health educators often end up making wide generalisations about what to do
- what ordinary people feel about it all.

Many nutritionists have had a scientific training which leads them to set great store by exact, repeatable, scientific experiments. In this type of experiment or trial only one item – say the amount of salt eaten – is varied. Everything else that the people in the trial eat and the rest of their lifestyle has to remain as far as possible unchanged. Two groups, one that made the single change and one that didn't are compared. The trial may need to be continued over several or even many years before any results show up. Large numbers of people have to be involved to overcome the problem that individuals vary as to how their diet affects them.

What do you think the chances are of finding enough willing people and enough money to carry out such trials?

And how can you make people not change their lives in other respects during the course of the trial?

Such trials are really too expensive and too difficult to carry out on human beings with regard to their diet. It might be better for nutritionists to give up attempting to provide answers in this way. They could settle for deciding on the basis of:
- best explanation which fits all the known facts
- no evidence, so far, against this explanation
- explanation accepted by the majority of expert nutritionists.

Getting the evidence

- A few massive trials as described above are under way. One relating lowering blood cholesterol to a decreased risk of heart disease has begun to publish its results. This proves that lowering blood cholesterol does reduce the risk of coronary heart disease.
- It's possible to compare two large populations – even whole nations – which differ naturally in their diet and the amount of various diseases they suffer. The task is to detect

What's your response?

Read through this chain below and for each comment make some notes beside it of your immediate reaction to what it says.

The Scalpel

A diet high in saturated fat is known to be associated with an increased risk of cardio-vascular disease particularly for those individuals whose blood cholesterol is substantially affected by the amount of saturated fat in their diet.
AN EXPERT –

I'd add – 'Evidence, so far, suggests that . . .'
CAUTIOUS EXPERT

I don't think you can go as far as that.
VERY CAUTIOUS EXPERT

OUR ✤ TIMES

A diet high in saturated fat is known to be associated with an increased risk of cardio-vascular disease.

Editor: who wants to shorten the message

There's no mention of the word 'butter'. And we're not going to tell you it's a saturated fat.
THE FOOD INDUSTRY

THE SENTINAL

Fatty diet linked with heart disease.

Editor: who prefers shorts words

possible risk factors. For example, the Japanese have a low fat diet and a low rate of heart disease. Americans – although they are changing now – used to have a high fat diet and a high rate of heart disease. Japanese people living in Hawaii, with an American way of life, eat more fat and have more heart disease than Japanese people in Japan.

In the circumstances you can see why experts tend to make very cautious statements. Rightly, too, they can usually only predict for large groups of people. It *is* possible to say to a person – "if you eat such and such a diet you will reduce your risk of dying at an early age". But what people would like to know is that if they made the change *they personally* would definitely not die before their time. And this can't be done. It's only possible to talk about reducing risks and so improving your chances. There are no absolute certainties.

Health educators

They may find themselves torn between the demands of ordinary people, to give them definite advice, and the demands of the experts, that they should be cautious and not say anything another expert might condemn. In these circumstances it's easy to end up making woolly statements that no expert would disagree with. And which no ordinary person finds helpful in their personal life.

The food industry

Since absolute certainty on dietary issues cannot be reached the food industry is in an ideal position to make selective use of the evidence. They give great publicity to the findings of research – which they often finance – that suggests their products are, after all, good for you. And they seldom reveal any evidence against them. For example, a current butter promotion campaign does not mention in its booklet that butter is a saturated fat. They know, all too well, that the public is beginning to be aware that a diet high in saturated fats increases your risk of developing heart disease.

How people respond

Look back at the comments you noted when looking at the various ways of presenting a health message.

Here is what some of our testers said:

Some were confused:
"I don't understand a word of that."
"Cholesterol — that rings a bell."
"What on earth does 'go easy' mean?"
"These experts are always changing their minds."

Some frightened:
"I've frightened myself reading that."
"My God, I'll never eat fatty foods again — does fish and chips count as fatty?"

Some disregarded the message:
"That's a load of rubbish."
"Uncle George ate all sorts of things and lived to 90."
"Nothing is going to make me give up bacon and eggs."
"So what? You've got to die of something."

Some looked for a magical cure:
"Isn't there some pill or something you can take to protect you from all that fat?"

Some wanted to know what could be done:
"What changes should I make?"
"Why doesn't the government do something about it?"

Some people believe that if they read it in the newspapers it must be true. This topic should help you to read between the lines. And to remember that editors are there to sell newspapers. Sensation and controversy sells newspapers: all newspapers. In July 1984 one of the Sunday papers gave prominent coverage to an opinion that is against the consensus of world experts, the NACNE report and the COMA report. The opinion was stated as a certainty – and probably set health education back several years. Despite protests from key nutritionists and health educators the paper did very little to redress the damage. Was it only coincidence that its' main rival had stolen a march on it earlier by leaking the NACNE report?

DAILY EXPRESSO

Heart attacks are caused by fatty foods.

Editor: trying to make it easier to understand

The Post

IF YOU EAT TOO MUCH FATTY FOOD YOU'LL HAVE A HEART ATTACK!

Editor: Trying to bring the message home to you

THE Moon

EXPERTS SAY – FAT KILLS

Editor: Looking for a shock/horror headline

Go easy on animal fats!
Health Educator: trying not to upset anyone

Changing advice

People often say "Experts are always changing their minds."
What most people would like to know is what are the 'goodies' and 'baddies'.

Over the last twenty years there have certainly been major changes in the advice experts give us about our diet. Before you read further make a note of whether you think the following foods might be thought of as 'goodies' or 'baddies' and why you believe this. Have you changed your mind about these foods over the years?

Potatoes   Cheese
Bread   Milk
Pork chops   Butter
Salt

Old advice

● Cheese, milk, butter, and chops (and other meat) were seen as important sources of protein. It was important to make sure you had enough protein.
● Potatoes and bread used to be thought of as fattening and certainly to be severely restricted if you wanted to control your weight.
● Salt – it used to be thought to be important to make sure you had enough in hot weather or if you were physically *very active*.

New advice

● Today the importance of the fibre that comes packed with the starch in potatoes and bread is now understood. These foods contain respectable amounts of protein, vitamins, and mineral salts. So potatoes and bread might now be seen as 'goodies'. Slimming advice is now changing too. Fats are a more concentrated source of energy (Calories) than starch so the new advice is to concentrate on cutting down fats and sugar.
● Dairy products and meat still contain plenty of protein. But today it's realised that we probably need less protein than experts used to think. More important, dairy products and meat contain saturated fats. And a diet high in saturated fats is linked with an increased risk of heart disease for some people. See *'Cut down on fats?'*

It's easy to get protein from cereal grains, peas and beans, and potatoes. With these it doesn't come wrapped up with saturated fat.

So the one time 'goodies' are now seen to be 'baddies'. However, milk and cheese supply valuable amounts of calcium and there's nothing wrong with protein from animals if only it could be separated from the fat. Skimmed milk is one answer. Low fat cheeses are better than high fat ones. Lean meat from which visible fat is cut off is better than marbled, fatty meat plus a thick wrap-around of fat.

However, the only 'goodness' about butter which is almost entirely saturated fat is the image conjured up for us by some advertisers of fields with buttercups and sunlight.

● Salt – is now considered to be a 'baddie'. Your body actually only needs very small amounts. A high salt diet is linked with an increased risk of high blood pressure for those people who are salt-sensitive. Perhaps only one in five people are salt-sensitive but since we can't, as yet, identify them the recommendation is that we all cut down. See *'Cut down on salt?'*

How do you feel?

Has the advice you've received over the years changed? People often want to stick with the first advice they received. They often want to stick to what they learned in their own home. They are confused, and maybe angry, about having to change things. And if they have been happily tucking into a 'goodie' food that has now been labelled a 'baddie' they are bound to feel frustrated and angry. And possibly frightened too.

It's not really true to say that experts keep changing their minds. The amount of evidence they have on which to base their advice does increase. With more evidence about a wider range of nutrients advice about what foods to eat is likely to change.

For example, when cheese was recommended as a good source of protein it was not yet known that it was important to cut down on saturated fats.

As medicine and dietary advice progresses this will always be a problem. Should health educators hold back on advising the younger generation just because this might also result in the older generation realising that it may be too late for them to benefit from the change?

The lingering annoyance of knowing the advice has changed can make it difficult to accept the new advice.

Maybe that will change too? Yes it may: although there are many more nutritionists today who, on the whole, agree on the main issues.

The fibre story, for example, may be only just beginning. Also, where today blanket advice is given to everyone, for example, to cut down on salt, in future tests may be developed to identify those salt-sensitive people who are particularly at risk.

Are there 'goodies' and 'baddies'?

Not really.

Too much of any food could be bad for you. Equally, a small quantity of any food you particularly love, within an otherwise sensible diet, isn't going to ruin you.

There is no such thing as an absolute 'baddie' or 'goodie' food. 'Moderation in all things' seems like sensible advice. But it isn't much practical use. The new dietary guidelines do point out that the average person needs to cut down on certain nutrients and increase others. It's certainly difficult to make these changes if you don't like certain foods. But there's usually more than one possible way of altering your diet in terms of the actual foods you eat. So you do have a choice.

Some people save up the small amount of butter they allow themselves so that they can smother a baked potato with it or save their salt ration for their boiled eggs. They can make cuts elsewhere to balance it.

The same is true of prawn cocktail, steak and chips and then Black Forest Gateau if they are just what you fancy on a night out. Or if you decide that you don't want to offend someone's feelings at a special meal by refusing at the last minute. (Consider explaining in advance next time why you would prefer something else.) To keep the balance on your healthy diet you would need to cut right back on fat and sugar the next day to make up for it. But at least enjoy it while you're eating it.

Butter – the natural choice?

The COMA report, considering only heart disease, concentrates mainly on cutting down on saturated fats. However, it does also suggest cutting down on total fats to help prevent obesity. NACNE, looking at diet and our overall health, recommends cutting down on all fats, but particularly saturated fats. Saturated fats are found in meat, and dairy products – milk, cream, butter and cheese. Coconut and palm oils are also saturated fats. They are used in the commercial production of many biscuits and cakes – and some margarines.

The butter and margarine industries have long been at war with each other. Neither side tells the whole truth to the consumer. Both seek to convince the consumers that they should eat more of their product. But the truth is that we are recommended to cut down on all of them. But not, of course, cut them right out.

Butter is promoted as 'full of natural goodness' – which is just an advertiser's dream. It's sold by evoking memories of golden childhood years when the sun was always shining. Or, if it was cold and wet, there was hot buttered toast for tea. Butter advertisements do not mention that it is a saturated fat.

Margarine advertisers, however, attempt to trade on the fact that many people vaguely know that they should cut back on butter. Some people think – "If it isn't butter – it must be alright." This is not necessarily true.

The margarine makers don't tell you that the hardening process and the use of fats from other animal sources ensures that all ordinary margarines are also rich in saturated fats.

The margarine companies exploit the fact that many people think that since 'animal fats' are 'baddies', ie. saturated fats, then all vegetable fats must be 'goodies'. They label their products 'made entirely from vegetable oils': but don't say that they use the cheaper coconut and palm oils which *are* saturated fats.

If you want a margarine that is high in unsaturated fats – look on the label for 'High in Polyunsaturates'. Though even these contain some saturated fats, they are likely to have less than the other, harder margarine.

The label 'Mixed Vegetable Oils' is also used by some manufacturers to sell their product. They know the general public tends to think all vegetable oils are 'goodies'. This is not true: so avoid labels which don't say exactly which vegetable oils are used.

'Health education' from the food industry. Many of the food industries, but particularly the dairy products, margarine and sugar industries, today produce health education materials, often for use in schools.

They are expensive, full colour productions and look very attractive. The problem is that they seldom tell you the whole story. You need to be able to read between the lines to work out what they are not telling you.
● Check out any leaflets, and advertisements you come across. Ask yourself what are they leaving out?

Jacket potato and . . .?

Here is the good news: a jacket potato makes a healthy meal. It's high in fibre and, particularly if you eat the skin, will provide you with some protein and vitamins.

But now for the bad news: the butter and cheese shown here are high in fat – and that isn't so good for you.

So what else can you add? Which of these have you tried?
● Low fat cottage cheese
● The new low fat 'cheddar'-type cheeses
● Yoghurt and chives
● Coleslaw
● Baked beans
● Curry sauce

Improving your chances

What happens to your health isn't just a question of being lucky or unlucky. You can improve your chances of 'winning'.

Becoming a skilled gambler

Some people think that health is too important to talk about in gambling terms.

But looking at your health in this way can be useful when considering whether to act on the advice of health experts – particularly nutritionists.

Health experts cannot offer certainties. They can only suggest how you can improve your chances.

Let's look at betting on horses. It is possible to bet on horses in a way that makes it pure chance whether or not you win:
- You could stick a pin in the list of runners.
- Select a name you fancy.
- Choose the jockey wearing your favourite colour shirt.

At the other extreme you can be a skilled gambler:
- Study the horse's form and breeding.
- How has it run in the past?
- Does the 'going', the state of the ground, suit it?

All of these will increase your chances of winning – and reduce the risks of losing your money. But they won't guarantee that you will win. There is no such thing as a dead cert. There are some things you just can't take into account:
- Horses stumble at fences.
- Riderless horses get in their way.
- They may have been 'nobbled' with drugs.
- The jockey may have been bribed to pull the horse back.

Your health. You can choose for yourself whether or not to bet on horses and how often you will do it. You decide how much of your money you will put at risk – what stakes you will play for. And whether you will leave it to luck or take great care in choosing the possible winner.

But what about gambling with your health?

You have everything to win by becoming a skilled gambler!

This book helps you look at the gamble you take with your health when you choose what to eat. It is the quality and length of your life which is at stake.

You can do everything possible to make sure you eat a diet which will improve your chances of staying healthy. This way you can definitely reduce your risks of becoming ill and of dying prematurely.

However, you could eat an unhealthy diet and in the end turn out to be one of the lucky people who suffer no ill effects.

Or you could eat a healthy diet yet still then be unlucky.

Does the way you approach gambling games suggest you are more likely to leave your health to chance? Or is becoming a skilled gambler with your health quite an exciting challenge to you? Can you sum up how you feel about this?

Responding to health messages

If you believe that your life is in the hands of fate or luck you'll probably ignore advice about your health.

For those who believe they can improve their chances there seems plenty of advice available. But it's possible to become an 'informed worrier' rather than taking action to change your ways.

Most heavy smokers are now 'informed worriers'. They know about

the dangers of smoking, but don't give up smoking. They just worry about it. Deciding that you want to make a change is much easier than putting it into practice. People need much more help on how to make changes.

Whose advice do you take?

Whose advice do you take:
A The Media. TV/Radio medical programmes and serious magazine articles?
B Your nearest and dearest. Family and friends and neighbours?
C Vested interests. Health education material, including advertisements, from food manufacturers and health food magazines?
D Personal medical advice. Medical specialists, your GP or health visitor?

Feedback

Group A. The media have their reputation at stake and can afford to buy expert advice. *But* they do have to sell themselves to their audience. To do this they must include dramatic

cases and try to 'scoop' their rivals with rush items on the latest findings. This doesn't always make for a balanced presentation of the findings or experts' opinions.

Group B. Your nearest and dearest can share their own practical 'tips' with you. They can also recount vivid anecdotes that stick in the mind whether or not they give the true picture. This is so powerful that in one study patients were found to discount their doctor's advice if it contradicted this anecdotal evidence.

Group C. Vested interests often make selective use of evidence and use only what suits their case. They often give away free materials and *provided you are aware of any bias* these can be useful. 'Health food' magazines are often financed by the food industry and also rely on their advertisers who want to sell their products.

Group D. Personal medical advice. If a person has symptoms that prove he or she is already suffering the ill effects of an unhealthy lifestyle, then a doctor's warning does seem to be heeded. However, general health advice, offered by the doctor when a patient visits for some unrelated problem, tends to be ignored.

Anecdotal evidence

We tend to believe our own eyes. What we see for ourselves *or* what happened to a friend *or* a friend of a friend... *If they take risks and get away with it then surely we can?*

Also we all know at least one sprightly long-lived person who seems to have taken every possible health risk and survived! Who springs to your mind?

So surely the experts are wrong?

This is not true – but it does seem almost as though no amount of facts, figures or weighty expert opinion can overcome this anecdotal evidence.

Three points may throw some light on this:

1. For every lively 80-year-old, doing everything that's supposed to be unhealthy, who survives, many will have died prematurely. But they will not be around to catch your attention.
2. People disabled by ill health are not prominent in our society. They tend to be hidden away – thus limiting their lives even further – though protecting the rest of us from having to face the reality of such disablement. This is particularly true of severely disabled stroke victims.
3. Many people have a feeling that they are lucky. It's almost a hangover from childhood when we believed in magic. Perhaps all our lives we still look for magical solutions to protect us from harm?

What motivates you?

Which of these motivate you to take more care of yourself?

- [ ] Fear of illness or disability
- [ ] Fear of death
- [ ] A belief that you are morally obliged to guard your health
- [ ] A partner or friend urging you to do it – for their sake
- [ ] The knowledge that others need you to take care of them (eg. partners and children)
- [ ] Someone whose advice you trust suggesting you change
- [ ] Enjoying what's involved in taking care of yourself eg. exercise and good food
- [ ] I'd live longer
- [ ] I'd reduce my chances of a premature death

You may tick all of these: most people tick several of them. It's OK to want to take care of yourself. Some people grow up to believe that they should ignore their own health needs and think only of others. But *you* are important: you deserve to enjoy a healthy life.

What will you do?

Do you find there is a difference between what you know you ought to do and what you actually do? It's a very human failing!

It seems that people often say – "*Yes*, I know what I ought to do – *but...*"

Which of these do you use?
"*Yes – but...*
- I can't
- I know I won't
- I don't feel I can do it
- I don't want to start yet
- It's too much bother
- I'm too busy to do it
- I'll do it one day."

Ask yourself. If you say "I can't": you may have real obstacles to overcome. For example, lack of choice in your shops. The new healthier diet need not be more expensive than the old one. But choosing "I can't" may also be a cover-up. Check back – do any of the others fit better?

All the other responses may be ways of saying "I don't want to do it! (and no-one including me can make me!)."

Or do they serve to help you avoid putting yourself to the test and risking failure?

Low risk: high risk

What counts as low risk? – or a high risk?
Why are health economists more interested in the low risk groups?

What is a 'low' risk?

For example: Heart attacks. Almost everyone's arteries are furred up to some extent. But other factors play a part in determining when – if ever – they become finally blocked and cause a heart attack. If, *as far as is known*, there is nothing about your background and lifestyle that puts you particularly at risk you would be rated by doctors as falling into the 'low risk' group for having a heart attack. This does not mean that you are guaranteed not to have a heart attack. But you would be considered to be at 'low risk'.

Sounds good? Perhaps – but you need to look at it in two ways. There is the 'expert' who calculates the risk and thinks of it as 'high' or 'low' when compared to other risks. There is, however, also the person who faces the risk and what he or she feels about it.

How do you see it? How would you feel about the risk of having a heart attack before you are 60 if the chances were:

    1 in 5
    1 in 10
    1 in 20
    1 in 50
    1 in 100
    1 in 500
    1 in 1000
    1 in 1,000,000?

Make a note of what you feel when you think about these risks. What would you consider to be a low risk?

Our testers' comments showed they saw the key range as between one in 20 and one in 100.
● A risk of one in 20 was rated as high and unacceptable by almost all.
● A risk of one in 50 was considered unacceptable by about half of them and acceptable by the other half.
● A risk of one in 100 was acceptable to almost all of them.

The actual risks. If you are in the 'low risk' group of having a heart attack before you are 60 the actual chances or rate depends on your sex.

For the 'low risk' group of men the rate is about 1 in 16.

For the 'low risk' group of women the rate is about 1 in 50.

It may be important to remind you at this point that heart attacks are not always fatal. Looking back at what you considered to be a low risk how do you respond to this information?

'High risk' groups face a much greater risk of having a heart attack. In certain circumstances this may be as high as one in three. The table below shows you there are some things that can be done to reduce the risk.

Risk of having a heart attack in the next 15 years

Woman, aged 40 and on the pill	1 in 14
Woman, aged 40, on the pill and smoking	1 in 4
Man aged 40, on a bad diet	1 in 8
Man aged 40, on a bad diet, obese and unfit	1 in 3

What are the chances?

Risks are often expressed as the chance of one in something (N) of an event happening.

For example, developing a disease or dying. One in five or one in a million would be extreme examples.

Put in this way risks can tell us what we could expect to find if a large number of people are considered. But there is no way, for example, that someone with a one in five chance of developing a disease can tell for sure if they will be the one whose 'number comes up'. All you could say is that if 500 people were looked at about 100 would have the disease. In real life epidemiologists who study the rates of diseases in large populations usually look at groups of thousands or millions of people.

Avoiding a premature death

"If I make all these changes will I live to be 90? I'm not sure I want to live that long!"

It's not very likely. The real benefit is that if you make all these changes you will be less likely to die before your time. Put the other way round, you will improve your chances of surviving to live out a normal lifespan. Dying before your time – a premature death – is the real tragedy. Any death before the age of 65 is counted as a premature death.

It seems reasonable to assume that if people know they are in the high risk group they will be more motivated, than those in the low risk group, to change to a healthier lifestyle.

What if *you* knew you were in the low risk group? Would you be motivated to change in order to lower your risk even more? A lot depends on your attitude to risk-taking. Some people would: some people wouldn't.

How do health economists see it? To health economists, who count the cost to the nation, the low risk group is of greater interest. They are not interested in the benefit to the individual. They count the number of bodies dead (they also count how many people survive disabled).

The important questions to them are:

● How many people are in the low risk and high risk groups?

● How many dead people will there be at the end from each group?

In Britain they would often be thinking in terms of tens of thousands of people. But to explain their interest in the low risk group it's simpler to look at 100 people.

Supposing that of 100 people 80 fell into the low risk group and 20 into the high risk group.

Remember the low risk group have a one in ten chance of dying in a year. The high risk group has a one in four chance of dying in a year.

First, let's see who will die in the low risk group. Well, there is no way of saying *which* of them will die. They all have a one in ten chance of dying in a year. But you can work out how *many* will die. You might like to try acting as 'fate' – just stab with your pencil at random until you have killed off one in ten of them.

For every ten people one will die so as there are 80 people in the group 80 divided by 10 = 8 will die. Remember 'fate' strikes at random so don't worry about how close or far apart your 'stabs' land.

80 people in
LOW RISK GROUP
one in ten die

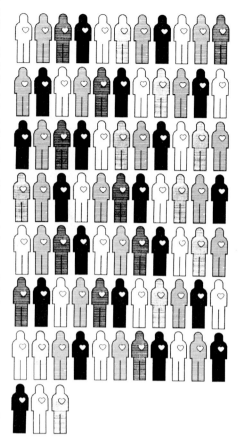

Total Number Dead: 8

Next look at the high risk group. Each person has a one in four chance of dying in a year. For every four people one will die, so as there are 20 people in this group 20 divided by 4 = 5 will die. Again, there's no way of telling in advance which ones will be lucky or unlucky. So stab another five at random.

20 people in
HIGH RISK GROUP
one in four will die

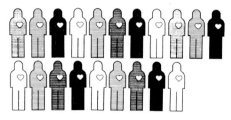

Total Number Dead: 5

Remember health economists are interested in how many die in each group. With groups of these sizes and with these risks there are actually more dead bodies from the low risk group.

From the health economists' point of view the low risk group is more important – they cost the nation more.

Improving the health of the low risk group, so decreasing even further their risk of dying, pays off best.

We haven't used a named disease for this worked example. But this pattern – 80% of the population at low risk and 20% of the populaton of high risk is not unusual.

For the greater good of the nation

The changes now recommended in our diet are, for most people, fairly easy to make. After a while the new diet seems more attractive than the old one for many people.

But some people are faced with having to give up foods they particularly enjoy. They feel their life would be a misery if they had to change. They want to be sure of a substantial benefit if they make the change.

For the good of the nation the low risk group should change. Some experts would argue that it isn't fair to expect the large number of people in the low risk group to change their diet. For each of them there would be a fairly small reduction in the risk they face. But this small reduction for any one person adds up in total to a lot of deaths prevented – and money saved by the NHS.

Don't push the high risk group? If it is seen in terms of cost/benefits to the nation it could be a waste of money trying to persuade the high risk group to change their ways. Of course, the benefit to any one individual can be very high if he or she reduces the risks. But looking at the whole high risk group – because there are relatively few people in it the *total* number of deaths prevented by getting this group to change is small.

This is, of course, a cynical money-orientated way of looking at matters. However someone has to try to balance the nation's budget. The pros and cons have to be discussed.

There is also the point that the main aim must be to prevent heart attacks and strokes. The intensive care needed to help people to survive them is costly. Many of the survivors will also be disabled for the rest of their lives so they, too, will be a cost to the nation.

What about you?

If you belonged to a low risk group:
● Would you make the changes 'for the good of the nation' even though your own risks were only reduced a little?
● Would you feel that even a small reduction in your risks would make the change worthwhile?

Risk factors

Risk factors are the facts about your lifestyle, physical condition and medical history that can increase your risks of developing certain disorders.

Links and causes

These risk factors are known to be associated – or linked – with an increased chance of developing disorders. There are often several risk factors linked with a particular disorder. There isn't usually a simple link. It's not possible to say that any one risk factor is the direct cause of a disorder. The picture is always more complicated than that. There are many steps and cross-links in the chain of events that lead to the full development of the disorder.

Most of the research has been done on calculating risks associated with coronary heart disease and strokes. These two are linked because they are both preceeded by damaged arteries. Perhaps 90% of the adult population has damaged arteries – which are hardened and narrowed by fatty deposits in the inner layers of the artery. There may be no sign of this atherosclerosis until a small clot becomes lodged in the narrowed artery and blocks it. If the clot is in the coronary artery which delivers blood to the muscles of the heart a heart attack occurs. If it is in an artery leading to the brain a stroke occurs.

Of course, not everyone with diseased arteries goes on to have a heart attack or a stroke. Though one in four people in the UK do eventually develop coronary heart disease – angina or a heart attack. It is the main killer in the Western world today.

The important cases are when someone dies prematurely – in mid life when she, or more likely he, might have expected to live another twenty years or more. Most experts would say anyone dying of a heart attack under 65 has died prematurely. In Britain one man in 11 dies of a heart attack before he is 65 years old. Another one of the eleven will have his life severely restricted by chest pain and shortness of breath.

So what can be done to reduce these unnecessary deaths? In America, in particular, these risk factors and what needs to be done about them are being explained to the general public. The risk factors are being reduced and coronary heart disease – the 'Big Killer' – is now dropping in America. It is not yet dropping in the UK which remains very near the top of the league table for rates of heart disease.

Coronary heart disease and strokes

The Three BIG Risk Factors:

1. **Smoking**
2. **High blood pressure**
3. **High level of blood cholesterol**
(Diet high in saturated fats)

Cancer

The picture is being slowly pieced together. Risk factors are usually linked to certain types of cancers. The danger in writing about risk factors, at this time, is that it makes the picture appear too simple. Here are just a few:
● Smoking – the big link is with lung cancer – but it's also linked with other cancers, of the mouth, throat, bladder, kidney and pancreas.
● Diet high in pickled, salted or smoked foods – linked to increase of stomach cancer.
● Diet high in fat and low in fibre – linked to bowel and breast cancer.

How are the links established?

The risk factors have often been identified by comparing large groups of people who are known to have different rates of a certain disorder. The average lifestyle, physical condition and medical history of the people are compared. The question is – does the population with the high rate of the disease differ on any important items from the population with the lower rate? Once a particular item is suspected it's possible to check out other populations for which the same data can be obtained. Sometimes whole nations are compared.

Diet and coronary heart disease

Heart disease has been linked to the amount of saturated fat in the average diet. It's possible to compare the average national diets of different countries. In any one country individual people will differ as to how much fat they eat. But on the whole, for example, people in the UK eat well over twice as much fat as the people in Japan.

At first nutritionists tested out the theory that it might be the total amount of all forms of fat (saturated and unsaturated fats) in the diet that showed a possible link with coronary heart disease.

This didn't produce clear results. Although there was some general trend that suggested the higher the amount of fat in the diet the higher the rate of coronary heart disease, there were some curious exceptions. It was these exceptions that in the end helped to make the picture clearer. Here are the categories the countries fell into:

A	**High Fat: High Coronary Heart Disease** Finland USA UK Canada Denmark Norway
B	**Low Fat: Low Coronary Heart Disease** Japan Greece Yugoslavia
C	**High Fat: Low Coronary Heart Disease** Italy.

THE CORONARY PREVENTION GROUP

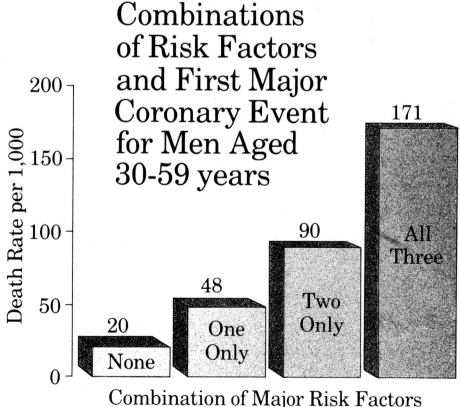

I'll TAKE CARE OF YOU!

Indeed when Finland and Italy were compared the two countries' diets contained similar amounts of fat, but the Finns have almost four times as many fatal heart attacks as the Italians. The UK has only a little more fat than Italy in its diet but has nearly two and a half times as many fatal heart attacks.

Is there something different about the kind of fats the Italians eat? Yes – in the Italian diet fat comes mainly from unsaturated vegetable oils.

The fat in the Finland and UK diets comes mainly from saturated fats – particularly dairy products, milk, butter and cheese.

Now look at lists A and B above. Which group of countries have dairy farming as a major part of their economy? Yes – the North American and Northern European countries of list A.

'Yes but'. It's easy to say there must be lots of other differences that might perhaps account for the different rates of heart disease. What about stress, numbers of cars, – even religion? What's needed is to look at groups of people who don't lead such very different lives.

● One approach led to comparing Italians living in Italy on a typical

Italian diet, with those Italians living in America who had switched to a typical American diet. What would you predict? Yes – the Italians on the American diet had more heart disease than the Italians on the Italian diet.

A group of 'high animal-fat eaters' can be compared with a group of 'low animal-fat eaters'. The two groups can be matched for most other aspects of their life, for example, the same range of age and weight, the amount of exercise they take and how much they smoke. Here the effect of the diet high in animal fats shows up much more clearly.

More links in the chain

● A diet high in saturated fats is linked with a raised level of cholesterol in the blood.
● A raised level of cholesterol in the blood is linked with an increased risk of heart disease.
● However, not every individual with a high level of blood cholesterol eats a high saturated fat diet. The body also makes its own cholesterol and in some people too much gets made. So even if they are on a low saturated fat diet some people may have high blood cholesterol and, therefore, an increased risk.
● Lowering the level of blood cholesterol reduces the risk of developing heart disease.

Multiplying the risk factors

It's not just a question of adding up the risk factors. If you have more than one risk factor for a disease it's often not so much a case of adding up your risks as of multiplying them.

The picture is clearest for the three big risk factors for coronary heart disease: smoking, high blood pressure and high level of cholesterol in the blood.

● If you have only one of these three risk factors your risk of a heart attack or stroke is at least doubled.
● If you have any two of these risk factors your risk is at least quadrupled – four times greater.
● If you have all three risk factors your risk is greater than eight times that of a person with none of the factors.

The chart below from the Boston Medical Centre's Heart Risk Book gives exact figures for a group of men who had various combinations of risk factors. The men were aged 30-59 and the number of 'coronary events', that is angina or heart attacks, as a rate per 1000 people is shown. Note that the men with none of these risk factors were not free of 'coronary events' – they still had a rate of 20 per 1000.

Combinations of Risk Factors and First Major Coronary Event for Men Aged 30-59 years

Death Rate per 1,000

Combination of Major Risk Factors

- None: 20
- One Only: 48
- Two Only: 90
- All Three: 171

Reducing your risks

A few risk factors can't be altered, but many can be changed.
This topic helps you identify the key areas that you may need to change.

Some risk factors you can't do anything about such as your sex, your increasing age or what diseases tend to run in your family.

It could be argued that telling people about factors they can't do anything about only worries them unnecessarily. On the other hand, if people who score high on risk factors that can't be changed don't know this they may not be motivated to change their other risk factors.

However, since adding a risk factor, such as a bad diet, multiplies any other risk it is obviously sensible to reduce any risk factor that you can change.

Your motivation for change

Reducing risk factors is like learning to be a skilled gambler with your health – rather than leaving things to fate or luck.

There aren't any dead certs – but you can make yourself less likely to lose. You *can* improve your chances.

The priority you give to this will depend on what you see as the important things in life. It's amazing how horrified or angry other people – particularly doctors – can be when they see someone not giving top priority to their health.

One of the problems is that you are asked to make changes now for only probable benefits many years later. It helps if there are short-term benefits too to help keep up your commitment.

Over the years

Some people do look back and wish they had paid more attention to a healthy lifestyle when they were younger. But others don't.

Stop and think for a while about how your attitudes to reducing risk factors might vary over your life time. Did your concern about your future health effect your lifestyle?

When you were ten were you thinking about your future – particularly your health – at all? Were you, for example, worried about too many sweets ruining your teeth?

When you were a teenager what did you feel about taking risks with your future health? For example: smoking, riding a motor bike, having sex without using a contraceptive. Did you have any ideals you wanted to live up to? Or was there a key person you wanted to be like? Choose more stages that you've already faced – or are likely to face. How did you – or how do you expect – to feel about your life and your health? For example –

- as a young adult
- as a parent of young children
- at midlife
- at retirement age.

Our testers. Several of our testers said they were more concerned, as adults, about the health of their children and partners. A few said they had moved on to realise that staying healthy themselves was important so that they could look after their families.

There seemed to be some hesitation in taking care of their own health for their own sakes as though it might be selfish or a sign of hypochondria. The Health Education Council obviously needs to continue to press home its message that it is O.K. to 'Look after yourself!'

At the moment where would you place yourself along this scale?

"Eat, drink and be merry for tomorrow we die."

"A frugal life is a long one."

How would you sum up your position?

18

Check out your risks

This test is based on the Michigan Heart Association Test. It will help you work out what are the likely chances of you having a heart attack.

You will be able to see where you can make changes to reduce your risks. The most important point is to work out how to reduce your score.

The test is not designed to be a medical diagnosis. Remember no-one can tell if you will definitely have a heart attack or stroke. Nor can they give you the reassurance that you will definitely not have one. But your score will reveal how you compare with others and where you can improve your chances.

Trying to work out the score may reveal that you don't, as yet, know enough about yourself to work out a total score.

For each risk factor choose the statement that, as far as you know, comes closest to your situation. Write in your score in the box at the bottom of each list.

Factors which can't be changed

If your scores for factors you cannot change are high it is even more important to see which of your other risk factors you should pay attention to. It should give you even greater motivation to look after yourself.

Most people who score high on this section could reduce their score on the 'Factors which can be changed' by an equal amount. Thus evening up the risk.

Your total score for factors which can't be changed. Add up your scores for these factors.

Sex   _____

Age   _____

Heredity   _____

TOTAL   _____

Some doctors would query the wisdom of telling patients about these factors because there is nothing that can be done about them. It would only make them worried. However, today more is known about the other risk factors where risks *can* be reduced. You can make this score less important overall.

So if you do have a high score use the rest of this test to harness your anxiety. Turn it into motivation and energy so that you do look after yourself and get your final total score as low as possible.

Factor which can't be changed	Sex and age/build
	Score
● Female under 40	1
● Female 40-50	2
● Female over 50	3
● Male	5
● Stocky male	6
● Bald, stocky male	7
YOUR SCORE =	

This score takes into account the fact that men have 6 to 10 times more heart attacks than women of child bearing age. After the menopause women's risks increase. Stocky males – particularly if they are bald – have above average risks for men. The reasons for this are not fully understood.

Factor which can't be changed	Age
	Score
● 10-20	1
● 21-30	2
● 31-40	3
● 41-50	4
● 51-60	6
● Over 60	8
YOUR SCORE =	

The special risks of increased age for women have been scored in the first factor.

Eventually, everyone has to die of something. At the moment 1 in 4 people in the UK do eventually develop coronary heart disease.

Factor which can't be changed Heredity
(Count grandparents, parents and brothers and sisters who have had heart attacks or strokes. NB. They need not have died of them.)

	Score
● No known history of cardio-vascular disease	1
● 1 relative with heart attack or stroke over 60	2
● 2 or more relatives with heart attack or stroke over 60	3
● 1 relative with heart attack or stroke under 60	4
● 1 relative under 60 and 1 over 60 with heart attack or stroke	5
● 2 relatives with heart attack or stroke under 60	6
● 3 or more relatives with heart attack or stroke under 60	8
YOUR SCORE =	

You may not know about your grandparents. The chances are that if they lived to a ripe old age there will be family stories about them. Since cardio-vascular diseases are so common many people will score quite high in this section.

Factors which can be changed

If you already have got these factors down to as low a score as possible you should be proud of yourself.

Some risk factors are not included because of the difficulty of measuring them. These include gout, diabetes, low lung capacity for size of lungs, abnormal heart rhythms. Others, such as personality and stress are not fully accepted as risk factors and are almost impossible to measure. Women taking the contraceptive pill particularly if they smoke and/or are over 30 have an increased risk.

Your total score for factors which can be changed. Add up your scores for these five factors.

Smoking ——————

High blood
pressure ——————

High fat diet ——————

Exercise ——————

Weight ——————

TOTAL ——————

Your score for factors that **can't** be changed ——————

Your score for factors that **can** be changed ——————

FINAL SCORE ——————

Your final score

Remember this score is not a diagnosis. It's a device to help you see where you can change to a healthier lifestyle.

If you score

6-11 Your risk is well below average

12-17 Your risk is below average

18-24 Your risk is generally average

25-31 Your risk is moderate

32-40 Your risk is at a dangerous level

41-62 Danger – urgent, see your doctor now.

Factor which can be changed	**Smoking**	
	Score	
• Non-smoker	0	Most people know that smoking is linked with cancer. It is also strongly linked with increased risk of cardio-vascular disease. Add 1 to your score if you inhale deeply and/or smoke the cigarette right down to the butt. Women on the Pill and smoking add 2.
• Cigar and /or pipe	1	
• 10 or fewer cigarettes a day	2	
• 20 cigarettes a day	4	
• 30 cigarettes a day	6	
• 40 cigarettes a day	10	

YOUR SCORE =

Factor which can be changed	**High blood pressure**	
	Score	
• Upper reading 100	1	If you have recently passed an insurance company medical your blood pressure is likely to be below 140. If you have no idea – get it measured. Ask your GP or the nurse at work if there is one. It is an important thing to know in order to take care of yourself. If you do score high it's extra important to cut down on salty foods – watch carefully your weight and the amount of exercise you take. There is more about high blood pressure in 'Cut down on salt?'
• Upper reading 120	2	
• Upper reading 140	3	
• Upper reading 160	4	
• Upper reading 180	6	
• Upper reading 200 or more	8	

YOUR SCORE =

Factor which can be changed	**High fat diet** (high level of cholesterol in the blood)	
	Score	
• Diet contains no animal fats (blood cholesterol below 180 mg)	1	Foods which contain animal fats are meat (not just the visible fat), dairy products (cream, ordinary milk, hard and cream cheeses and butter), sausages and meat pies, pastry and many cakes. The average person in the UK today would score 4 in this section! If you have kept a food diary you may be able to answer this now. If not 'Cut down on fats?' shows you how to check on the fat in your diet. It would be more accurate to use your blood cholesterol level to work out your score. You are unlikely to know your blood cholesterol level, but you can ask your doctor how to get this done.
• Animal fats 10% (blood cholesterol 181-205 mg)	2	
• Animal fats 20% (blood cholesterol 206-230 mg)	3	
• Animal fats 30% (blood cholesterol 231-255 mg)	4	
• Animal fats 40% (blood cholesterol 256-280 mg)	6	
• Animal fats 50% (blood cholesterol 281-300 mg)	8	

YOUR SCORE =

Factor which can be changed **Exercise**

	Score
• Intensive exercise. work and recreation	1
• Moderate exercise work and recreation	2
• Sedentary work and intense recreational exercise	3
• Sedentary work and moderate recreational exercise	5
• Sedentary work and light recreational exercise	6
• Complete lack of exercise	8

YOUR SCORE =

Sorry – housework using modern labour-saving devices counts as sedentary work.

The exercise needs to give your body plenty of movement and be just energetic enough to make you fairly breathless (but not gasping for breath).

Moving your muscles creates a greater demand for oxygen in the blood and makes more work for your heart and lungs. Regular exercise of this kind strengthens the heart muscles.

Brisk walking is excellent. So is running up stairs, jogging, disco dancing, skipping, swimming and cycling.

If you do this type of activity three times a week for at least 20 minutes count this as moderate recreational exercise.

Factor which can be changed **Weight**

Look at the height/weight charts, below. Run a line across from your height and vertically from your weight. Mark where the two lines cross. Give yourself the score in that section but add two more if you are overweight or obese *and* under the age of 40.

Score zero for more than 5lbs underweight if you also 'eat like a horse'. You may be taking a lot of exercise or naturally need to eat a lot because your body has a high metabolic rate.

However, score 2 if you are more than 5lbs underweight but take little or no exercise and only keep your weight at this level by 'eating like a sparrow' and virtually starving yourself. Here the risks of being overweight are only calculated for cardio-vascular diseases. Remember your risk of developing diabetes and joint problems is also increased.

What do you think? There are three points you should now consider:

• The whole country has a notoriously high rate of heart diseases and strokes. The UK is almost top of the world league table. The national average risk needs to be – and can be – changed. So is being at average risk good enough for you?

• Which are the most important changeable risk factors for you?

• This is only your 'final score' for now. You can change your lifestyle and re-check your score at intervals to monitor your progress.

Stop for a while and make some notes for yourself

• How did you react to your individual scores as you worked through each factor?

• What about your final score?

• Which factors *should* you be doing something about? Which **will** you do something about?

• Do you need to:

a Check your scores more accurately? Ask your doctor to check your blood pressure or blood cholesterol level, or come back after reading 'Cut down on fats?'

b Find out more about how to make your desired changes?

• What exactly are your plans? And when will you start?

Our testers

Of the ten testers who scored 18 or more (ie. average risk or above):

• Two were first going to get their doctor to check their blood pressure or blood cholesterol level.

• Eight were definitely planning to make changes. Most were planning to reduce two or more of their risk factors.

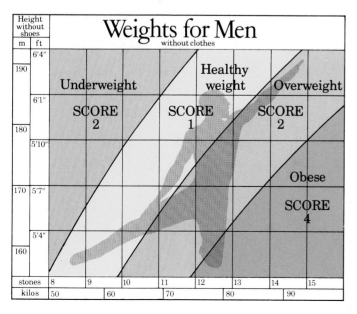

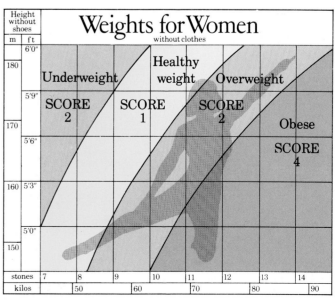

Never too late?

*Supposing you've been eating what is now known to be an unhealthy diet.
Is it too late to change? Has the damage already been done?
It's difficult to get clear answers on these questions.*

Dietary advice for the nation

Concentrating on the younger generation. At the time when the recommendation to cut down on saturated fats was receiving great publicity a well-known expert suggested on a TV programme that by the age of 20 arteries were already damaged. The implications seemed to be that only the younger generation was worth bothering about. This is not the whole story. Indeed, dramatic results, in terms of reduced mortality from coronary heart disease, have shown up. For example, in Norway where high risk middle-aged men have changed to a healthier diet and given up smoking.

Certainly the younger generation has everything to gain. They are a group the older generation are prepared to fight for. Emphasising the needs of the young is a powerful lever on the consciences of farmers, food manufacturers, caterers and politicians – and parents.

Local authorities responsible for school meals, and therefore able to offer huge profitable contracts, could exert moral and financial pressure on their food suppliers to supply better balanced meals. Indeed the provision of high fat, sugary, low fibre meals in schools should provoke outcries from the Parent Teacher Associations. So should school tuck shops.

Getting everyone to make the changes. On the other hand, some health experts are convinced that you need to give exactly the same dietary advice right across the board to everyone, regardless of age.

Their reasons for doing this are:

● It keeps the message simple.

● Since making the changes certainly won't harm anyone, then everyone – whether or not they would benefit from them – might as well make them. This is an unnecessarily cynical approach. There is a good deal of evidence from USA, Canada, Belgium and Finland that middle-aged *and* elderly people do benefit from changing their everyday diet to one which is healthier.

- It may take nearly a generation for most of the population to change eating habits.
- As it is the adult population who has 'the strongest consumer voice', it's important that they want to make the changes. They can put pressure on the government and the food industry to provide a wider choice of healthier food.
- By making the changes the older generation acts as a role-model for younger people.

Fortunately there *are* personal benefits for the older generation. Making changes will prevent further damage. And in some cases may reverse existing damage.

Where do you stand?

Would you make a change that might not benefit you very much?

Why would you do this? Most of our testers said they would for the sake of their children and partners.

How about fighting for other people?

Write down in your notebook how you now feel – at your age and in your circumstances – about changing your diet.

Special groups

Babies

- Solid foods should not be introduced before three to six months. There may be a link between early introduction of protein foods and the development of allergies.
- Salt and salty foods should be avoided. This may avoid the child coming to prefer salty foods.
- Sugar and sugary foods should be kept low. Once the teeth start to arrive sugary food that stays in the mouth over a long period of time such as rusks or dummies dipped in syrup are likely to lead to tooth decay.
- Skimmed milk should not be used for bottlefeeding.

Young children

- Since children like to copy their parents it's important for parents to be seen to be eating a healthy diet.
- A high-fibre diet may provide more food than a child with a small appetite is prepared to eat. It is better not to force the issue. Seek advice from a health visitor if you are concerned about your child's diet.
- Children need milk to supply the calcium they need. It would be best if this could be skimmed or semi-skimmed low-fat milk.

- A low-sugar diet – particularly avoiding sticky sugary snacks between meals – will help minimise the risks of tooth decay. So does using a fluoride toothpaste and brushing the teeth properly.

Teenagers

This is probably the group who has most to gain by changing to a healthier diet. But they may be the least likely to make the changes.
- They are at an age when health risks that only show an effect in middle or old age seem unimportant.
- Their pattern of eating – more snacks and 'takeaways' – can make it difficult to obtain healthy food. Snacks which are low in fat, salt and sugar but high in fibre need to be easily available.
- Teenage girls in particular may go on restricted diets to keep their weight down. They are likely to give up starchy foods and so have a low-fibre diet.

20 to 40 year olds

It's well worthwhile for this group to make changes.
- Women in this group are the people most likely to decide to change their pattern of eating. They may also change their partner's diet.
- Some women fear that giving up smoking – the most important health change of all – will lead to them putting on weight. Most 'giving-up smoking' leaflets explain that this need not happen. But preventing weight gain does usually involve switching to a healthier diet.
- Parents of young children have to think about the example they set their children, how to teach them what makes up a healthy diet, and how to put pressure on the school to provide good food.
- If sugary foods do not reduce your appetite for the healthy food that you need to eat *and* you are not over-weight, there may not be much point in cutting down on sugar.

40 to 65 year olds

Some people in this group will already have warning signs that they are showing the ill effects of a poor diet.
- Cutting down on salt is extra important if you already have high blood pressure. So is getting your weight down.
- Many years of a high saturated fat diet will almost certainly have furred up your arteries. But further damage can be prevented and the risk of a clot blocking the narrowed arteries be reduced if saturated fats are cut down.

- Weight tends to rise at this age. Cutting down on all fats – which are Calorie-rich foods – will help to keep weight down. Keeping your weight down by eating like a sparrow may be unhealthy. In adult men it has been shown to be linked to an increased risk of heart disease. For everyone it's probably better to take more exercise to allow you to eat more food whilst still keeping your weight down.
- It's never too late to gain the benefits from switching to a high-fibre diet.

Elderly people

Elderly people tend to lose weight from their muscles. With a low weight they don't need so much food to keep their body working. It's difficult in these circumstances to eat a sufficient variety of foods to ensure a good supply of vitamins and mineral salts. You can eat a perfectly good diet even if you do only need 1000 Calories a day to keep you going. But it does mean paying extra attention to eating nourishing foods. Unfortunately living alone, illness, apathy and misery can all too easily lead to just living off tea and toast or biscuits.
- Remaining as active as possible helps to prevent weight loss from the muscles and keeps your appetite up.
- It's not too late to make a gradual change to a high-fibre diet and this is quite the best way to help deal with any increasing problems with constipation.
- Reduced income, and possibly eating on your own, can make you less likely to eat a varied, healthy diet. Getting Meals on Wheels – or, better still, going to an OAP's lunch club may help. So might taking turns to cook for each other with a neighbour.

What will you do?

Just reading this topic will not help. You may need to decide to take action. Look back through the special groups that are relevant to you and your family.

First of all think about yourself: What strikes you as being particularly important for you to
- change?
- make sure you keep up?

Is there anything you need to find out more about in order to do this?

Are there other people you wish to help? Your children, or parents, friends or neighbours. What can you do to help? Can you do it on your own? Or do you need to contact special groups?

Who has to change?

This is a topic to start you thinking about the implications of the new dietary guidelines. It isn't just the individual who will have to change.

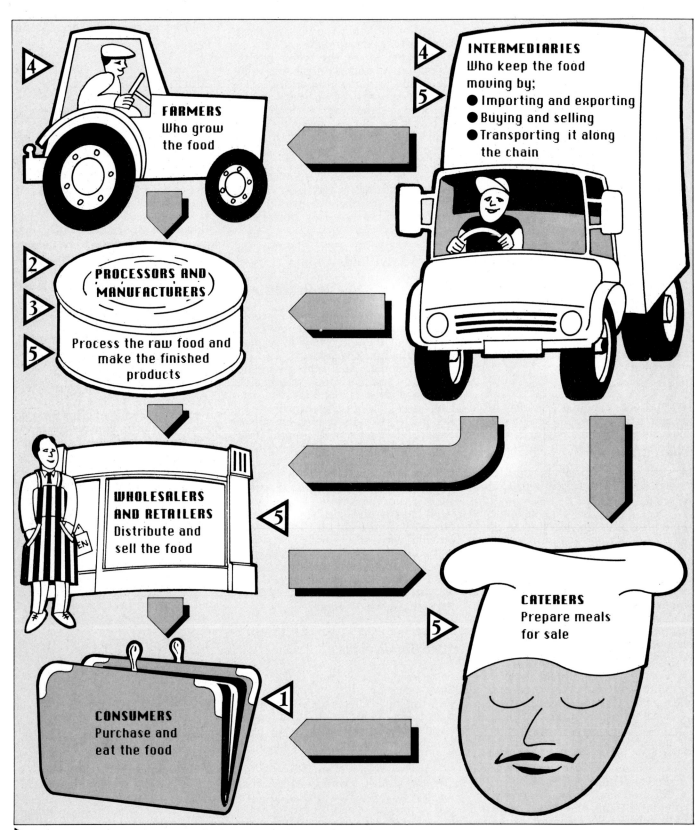

▷Points at which pressure can be brought to bring about change.

This topic cannot give the answers – though it does point to ways forward. At least it will make you more aware of the complex changes needed. Then you can add your voice to the demand for such changes.

From farmer to your plate

This diagram, left, shows the food chain along which the food passes from the farmer to the consumer.

At the moment there is too much food in this chain that is high in fats, high in sugar, or high in salt.

Or it has been refined during processing so that it has little or no fibre, although the original product the farmer grew was high in fibre. There could easily be more wholegrain, high-fibre foods in this chain. But the consumer doesn't seem to want them.

Passing the buck?

Our diet is not as healthy as it could be and changes need to be made. What's to be done? To start you thinking – how would you answer these questions?

Blame. Who along the chain would you blame? Who might the people who work at each of the stages in the chain blame?

The farmers might blame the _____

because _____

The manufacturers –

The retailers –

The caterers –

The consumers –

And who do you think the government might blame?

But does playing the 'Blame Game' help?

These may seem provocative questions that encourage people to blame others. But little encouragement is needed. This *is* what happens when changing the national diet is discussed.

On the whole our testers suggested that everyone puts the blame one step back along the chain.

It may be that who the government 'blames' depends on which political party is in power. In addition, government departments don't always agree. They may represent very different interests. Personal interests and financial or political interests don't always agree. Do farmers want to avoid having heart attacks? Do politians want to avoid having heart attacks?

What do you think these people have to say to each other?

Strategies for change

Where might it be easiest to start the changes? Perhaps you consider that the whole chain has to change? From what you know already can you suggest at least one change that could be made at each of the stages? What change could the government make?

Deciding what changes should be made – who should make them – and how they can be brought about – is a complicated issue.

However, there are a variety of strategies that can be used to put pressure for change at different points in the food chain. The points at which these interventions can be made in the food chain are shown by numbered arrows in the diagram opposite.

1. Help people change to a healthier diet.
This can be attempted through health education and promotion, advertising, and labelling the ingredients in foods. It doesn't have a high success rate. And is sometimes used to put 'blame' and responsibility on the individual who may have a limited choice.

2. Supermarkets use their strong purchasing power to demand better foods from the manufacturers.
Responsible chains are responsive to consumer demands and do have enough power to 'frighten' the food industry. Some supermarkets carry 'own brand' ranges of low sugar tinned fruit and jams, high-fibre breakfast cereals, and 'high in polyunsaturates' margarine.

3. The government, as the largest national caterer, sets a good example and uses its purchasing power to demand better food from the manufacturers, wholesalers and retailers.
Government controlled institutions cater for people in schools, hospitals, prison, the armed services and in the canteens for civil servants. They should set an example in providing good food. The purchasing power they have over the food industry is enormous. A few health authorities are already setting a good example.

4. Government manipulates the prices received by producers in favour of better food.
This can be a matter of international politics. The Common Food Policy of the EEC needs to be changed. At the moment it works in favour of producing dairy products and sugar. The changes that are being proposed are done for economic rather than health reasons. Subsidies, quotas, import taxes can all be used to adjust prices.

5. The government changes the rules and regulations in favour of better food.
At the moment regulations are aimed at guarding against dangerous additives and checking on hygiene. But controls on ingredients, processing and advertising could be aimed more positively at encouraging good food to be produced and promoted.

Playing the 'Blame Game' . . .

Playing the Blame Game – particularly when done by the media – can raise the general public's awareness of the issues and get at the consciences of those who must make the change.

● This can sometimes work with the government – who depend on votes for their power. Voters can put pressure on their MPs particularly at election time.

● Local bad publicity for retailers can sometimes work. They have to face their customers who can, if they wish, usually take their custom elsewhere.

● Media exposure of manufacturers who try to hide what goes into their products can sometimes have quite dramatic results.

. . . can be counter productive

Playing the blame game can also harden the opposition – who might otherwise have willingly co-operated in making the changes.

Since changes must be made it's better to have the co-operation of the farmers, manufacturers and retailers. Farmers and managers in the food industry don't want to have heart attacks. They want to know what to do to improve their own health.

You may be cynical about whether their concern extends to the consumers of their products. But they can also see the way the wind is blowing. They realise that there is now virtually a worldwide consensus amongst experts as to the major dietary changes that need to be made. Even though they may continue to publicise the findings of the few who disagree.

The Food Business is wealthy and full of talented managers who are perfectly capable of making changes. Or – they can use their energies to fight rear-guard actions to impede change. Powerful interests like the Sugar Industry and the Dairy Board are fighting back. We may even see the Butter Council and the Margarine Industry getting together to oppose the NACNE recommendation to cut down on fats!

Rewarding the good? Perhaps the media can be more effective by rewarding good practice? Publicity for the manufacturers and shops who offer low fat, salt or sugar products is money in the till and makes them feel good. The ordinary viewer gets good consumer advice. The publicity also brings to the attention of their competitors that such changes can succeed.

Blaming the consumer. Food manufacturers and retailers often complain that they only supply what the customer wants.

The Blame Game has also often been played by the government. It blames the individual for not taking more care of his or her health.

'Under the guise of allowing freedom of choice it supports those who promote products that can contribute to our ill-health. It's usually to its own advantage to do so.

If it believes in freedom of choice why doesn't it:

● See that people are well informed about the health risks they face? (Much more needs to be spent on health education).

● Ensure that an equally wide range of healthier products are available?

Leaking the NACNE Report

Crusading journalism can reach millions of people. It can also draw the nation's attention overnight to an issue.

Consider the leaking of the NACNE report. Its findings were 'leaked' in the *Sunday Times* before it was published. The report made a front page story with sensational headlines.

This was taken up by TV, Radio, magazines and several other newspapers.

Now you have read this topic sum up the pros and cons, as you see it, of this leak. Who gained from it? Were any of the changes discussed in this topic made easier? In what ways may it have set back the chances of such changes coming about?

You might like to imagine what went on in the heads of the people who leaked it, the journalist who made the 'scoop' and the editor who decided to put it on the front page. What about the first reactions when it was printed of – the Chairman of the NACNE working party that produced the report, the Department of Health and Social Security, and all the links along the food chain? Suggesting that the nation is eating an unhealthy diet and that changes need to be made is no easy matter.

Cut down on fats?

We get too many of our Calories from fats. The average person needs to cut down on total fats by nearly a quarter. The NACNE report recommends that we should cut down on all fats from our present day 38% of total daily energy (Calories). NACNE sets the target at 30%. The COMA figures, recalculated to compare exactly with NACNE, sets it at 33%.

Put another way – at the moment four out of ten of the Calories we eat come from fat. We need to get it down to three out of ten. The target for fats is expressed as a percentage of the total daily energy we need. If we count up all the Calories we get each day from food and drink, including alcohol, no more than 30 to 34% of these should come from fats.

But what does that mean for an individual in terms of grams of fat a day? This has to be worked out according to how active you are and how fast or slowly your body burns up energy (Calories).

Fats can do more damage than just loading us up with Calories. Some types of fats – the saturated fats – are linked with damaged arteries and an increased risk of angina, heart attacks and strokes.

Again, both NACNE and COMA agree that we should cut down particularly on saturated fats.

Where does all the fat come from? Around 60% of it comes from meat products and dairy products. It's these two groups that provide most of the saturated fat and where most of the cuts should be made. Indeed COMA actually suggests we should slightly increase the amount of polyunsaturated fats we use.

How much do we need? Two tablespoonfuls a day of a polyunsaturated fat would provide us with all the fat our body actually needs! The cells of our body need small amounts of certain fatty acids. Also certain vitamins are dissolved in fat.

However, we do like cooking with fat. It makes food crisp or shiny. It also makes food slippery and easier to swallow. But we don't need a lot of fat to achieve this.

Cutting down on fat can be easy. Understanding *why* we should do it and *what* the labels mean is not so easy.

What are fats?

'Cut down on fats' – sounds easy enough. But understanding why we should cut down and what the labels mean is more difficult.

What we commonly call 'fats' and 'oils' are both fats. 'Fats' in the everyday sense are solid at room temperature and oils are liquid. But this doesn't apply if you live in the tropics where, for example, butter at room temperature is a liquid. Nor in colder countries where coconut oil and olive oil are solid.

Whatever you call them they all count as fats and we need to cut down on them. Unfortunately, we need to know much more if we are to understand *why* we should cut down and *what* the labels mean.

Saturated and unsaturated fats

These are the key groups to understand. The difference lies in their chemistry (see below).

All fats are a mixture of saturated and unsaturated fatty acids. Which group they are put in depends on which type they have most of (see chart right).

Saturated fats are linked with an increased risk of coronary heart disease. We need to cut right back on these.

However, both types of fat provide us with large amounts of Calories. We all get too many of our Calories from fats and need to eat more high fibre food instead.

Saturated fats

Saturated fats are found mainly *but not entirely* as animal fats in meat – beef, lamb, pork, suet, lard and dripping – and dairy products – milk, cheese and butter.

The two main exceptions are coconut and palm oil. These are both vegetable saturated fats. It's important not to think that all vegetable fats or oils are O.K. Advertisers exploit this confusion. Coconut and palm oil are used a great deal in the manufacture of cakes and biscuits.

Hydrogenated or hardened oils are also saturated. In the manufacture of margarines liquid oils are hydrogenated – saturated with hydrogen – to make them hard enough to spread. The harder the margarine the more saturated, hardened oils it contains.

Unsaturated fats

There are two groups:

● **Monounsaturated fats.** These are rich in monounsaturated fatty acids. Olive oil is the best known of these. They are not bad for the heart – they have a neutral effect on arteries and blood.

● **Polyunsaturated fats.** These are rich in polyunsaturated fatty acids. These may actually lower the level of cholesterol in the blood and, possibly also, undo some of the damage done by saturated fats.

Most polyunsaturated fats are vegetable oils from seeds and nuts. Special, soft margarines which are labelled as high in polyunsaturates are also polyunsaturated fats.

Fish oils as they occur naturally are also polyunsaturated fats. Once extracted, refined and hardened for use in margarines they become saturated fats. Oily fish such as herring, mackerel, salmon and trout, contain a type of polyunsaturated fat that is positively good for your heart.

One small difference . . .

The structure of the molecules of saturated and unsaturated fats differ in one small, crucial way. It's amazing that this one small difference can be so important for our health.

A fat or triglyceride. Chemists call both saturated and unsaturated fats 'triglycerides'. A triglyceride has three fatty acids attached to a substance called glycerol. Its structure could be shown like this:

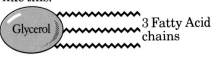
3 Fatty Acid chains

It's the fatty acids that hold the key to the crucial difference.
A fatty acid. This is basically a long chain of carbon atoms.
The crucial way they differ is in how the carbon atoms in the chain are linked to each other.

● All the carbon atoms in the chain may be joined together by a single link or bond. A small part of this chain could be shown like this:

Carbon atoms in a chain linked in this way also have two atoms of hydrogen linked to them. In more detail they could be shown like this:

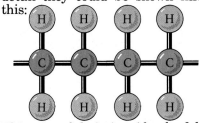

This type of chain is said to be full up – **saturated** – with hydrogen. It is a **saturated fatty acid.**

● Sometimes the carbon atoms in the chain are linked by a less stable, double bond. It could be shown like this:

In this case the carbon atoms linked by the double bond only have one atom of hydrogen linked to them:

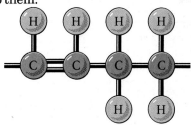

This type of chain is not full up with hydrogen – it's **unsaturated**. It is an **unsaturated fatty acid**. If the fatty acid contains one double bond it's called a **mono-unsaturated fatty acid.**

If it contains two or more double bonds it's called a **poly-unsaturated fatty acid.**

All fats contain mixtures of these three types of fatty acids. Depending on which they have most of they are called saturated fats or unsaturated fats. Unsaturated fats may be monounsaturated or polyunsaturated. (See chart, opposite).

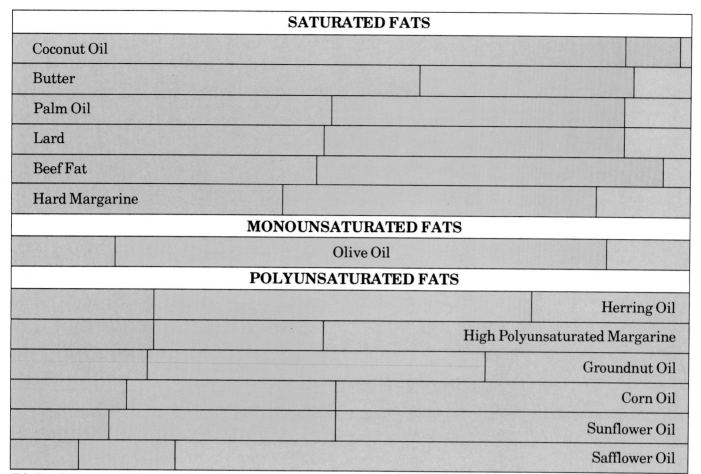

SATURATED FATS		
Coconut Oil		
Butter		
Palm Oil		
Lard		
Beef Fat		
Hard Margarine		
MONOUNSATURATED FATS		
Olive Oil		
POLYUNSATURATED FATS		
		Herring Oil
		High Polyunsaturated Margarine
		Groundnut Oil
		Corn Oil
		Sunflower Oil
		Safflower Oil

Pink – Saturated fatty acids.   Orange – Monounsaturated   Green – Polyunsaturated fatty acids.

'Cis' and 'Trans'

Ever heard of 'cis' and 'trans' fatty acids? If you've looked closely enough at the labels on polyunsaturated margarines and oils you may have seen 'cis' mentioned. New regulations may require the minimum level of 'cis' fatty acids to be stated on labels in the future.

What's the difference? When oils are hardened to make margarine, most of the unsaturated fatty acids are converted into saturated fatty acids. But some of the remaining unsaturated fatty acids are changed into a 'trans' form. These 'trans' fatty acids seem to have the same effects on our bodies as saturated fatty acids do. So the COMA report recommends that they should be counted in with saturated fats.

In the natural 'cis' form of fatty acids the long chains of carbon atoms are fairly straight. But in the 'trans' form the long chains have distinct kinks and tend to be folded up. In this form they are more solid at room temperatures.

Harder margarine, and the hydrogenated vegetable oils used in the commercial production of biscuits, cakes and pastry, are often high in the 'trans' fatty acids. Polyunsaturated margarines have low levels of 'trans' and high levels of 'cis' fatty acids.

Switch to polyunsaturated fats?

The NACNE report felt unable to recommend this mainly because the first COMA report (1974) was quite specifically against it. NACNE did acknowledge that in making major cutbacks on saturated fats there probably would be a switch to polyunsaturated fats.

However, the recent COMA report (1984) does cautiously recommend a small increase in polyunsaturated fats. It suggests an upper limit of six % of the total dietary energy to come from polyunsaturated fats.

Polyunsaturated fats, especially those from oily fish, may offer some positive protection against heart attacks and strokes. They may lower the level of cholesterol in the blood – so that the artery walls may not become so rough. Also, they may make the blood less likely to clot. This means that, even if the artery walls are rough, a thrombosis (which causes heart attacks and strokes) is less likely to occur.

Research began on fish oils after it was realised that Eskimos, who eat large amounts of oily fish, almost never die of heart attacks. We are now recommended to eat more oily fish, such as mackerel and herring. More exact advice may soon be available.

Advanced level labelling

The labelling on margarines can be most confusing:

● First of all ignore any labels about 'low in cholesterol'. That's a red herring – any margarine that's made entirely from vegetable oils can use this label. It's more important to know if it counts as polyunsaturated fat.

● Remember, a polyunsaturated fat has a high proportion of polyunsaturated fatty acids in it. The higher the better (see chart). Advertisers often use the word 'polyunsaturates' when more correctly they should use the words 'polyunsaturated fatty acids' (as in 'High in Polyunsaturates' on a margarine label). This type of margarine is a polyunsaturated fat: it contains a high proportion of polyunsaturated fatty acids.

● To clarify all this, new legislation may require all margarines claiming to be 'High in Polyunsaturates' to use a new label. They may be asked to state the minimum amount of linolenic and linoleic fatty acids, in their naturally occuring 'cis' form, that they contain. Linolenic and linoleic are the two most important polyunsaturated fatty acids.

New targets

What do the new targets mean in terms of how much fat you can eat?
What benefits can you expect?

According to NACNE, the average person gets 38% of his total daily energy (Calories) from fats. Total daily energy is worked out by adding up all the Calories from everything you eat and drink, including alcohol.

The NACNE report sets the new target at 30% and the COMA report sets it at 33%. In some ways the difference reflects how quickly the two reports felt the food industry could change. But for the individual trying to decide there's little in it.

Most of the cuts should come from saturated fats. They now provide, on average, 18% of total energy. They should be cut to 10% (NACNE) or 14% (COMA).

TOTAL DAILY ENERGY

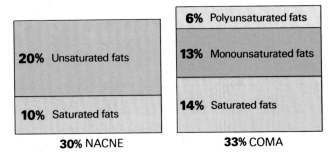

20% Unsaturated fats	**6%** Polyunsaturated fats
	13% Monounsaturated fats
10% Saturated fats	**14%** Saturated fats
30% NACNE	**33%** COMA

*COMA figures recalculated to include alcohol for direct comparison with NACNE.

Our testers tended to go for the NACNE target. One pointed out that *"It doesn't matter to the individual. But it does matter to food manufacturers who want to go for the minimum possible recommended change"*.

But remember, too, that even if you don't reach the target any change would be better than nothing.

"Even if I know many grams of fat I eat I still can't work out the percentage of energy they provide. I'd have to count up the Calories in absolutely everything I eat!"

We agree. The way in which the targets are stated aren't much practical help in everyday life.

How much you should eat depends on how many Calories you need to keep you going each day without gaining excess weight.

As you probably know, some people can eat like a horse and not gain weight. These people are said to have a high metabolic rate – they use up Calories very quickly and need a lot to keep them going. Other people with a low metabolic rate gain weight whilst eating far fewer Calories. There's a lot of individual variation.

● If you are overweight work out your target but then cut down by an extra 20 to 30 grams a day. This will help you lose one to one and a half pounds a week.

● If you are eating a diet that maintains your weight at an acceptable level then set your target as below:

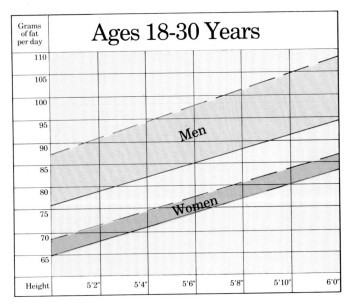

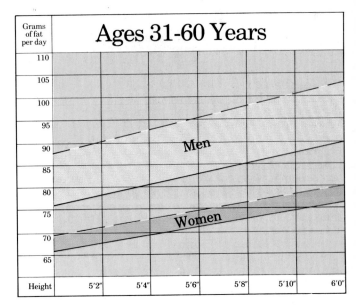

1. Use the left hand chart if you are 18-30 years old.
   Use the right hand chart if you are 31-60 years old.

2. Men – look at the light green band.
   Women – look at the dark green band.

3. Follow a line up from your height until you reach your band, then across to the left hand margin to read off your daily fat allowance. The lower limit of the band is for those who engage in only light activity. The upper limit is for those who are moderately active.

You may choose to eat less than the target if you wish.

Reduce your risks of heart disease

For the average person the NACNE target means cutting saturated fats down by nearly a half. Most experts would now agree that there is strong evidence to show that cutting down on saturated fats can reduce the risks of coronary heart disease. The earlier such a change is made the better.

A diet high in saturated fats can cause the level of cholesterol in the blood to be raised. This, in turn, leads to the arteries becoming clogged with fatty deposits. Damaged arteries like these can lead to heart attacks and strokes. It is now thought that as many as 90% of 40-year-olds in Britain have diseased arteries. The damage begins to show up in childhood.

Not everyone who has diseased arteries ends up with coronary heart disease – angina, heart attack or sudden death. But one in four of us does eventually end up with coronary heart disease.

It is estimated that diseased arteries account for a quarter of a million deaths from heart attacks and strokes each year in Britain. Britain is now top of the international league of countries for the proportion of people dying from coronary artery disease.

The fats and coronary heart disease picture has already taken 50 years to piece together. Other countries, particularly America, have already begun to change their diets. Their rate of coronary heart disease is dropping.

Other risk factors. A diet high in saturated fats is only one of the risk factors for coronary heart disease – though it may well be the most important. Risk factors determine how likely you are to develop a disease. The other two main risk factors for coronary heart disease are smoking and risked blood pressure.

Overweight and lack of exercise also play a part. So, too, do some factors you can't change – your sex, age, body build and family history of heart disease. 'Risk factors' and 'Your risk factors' go into this in much more detail.

Damaged arteries

● Doctors became suspicious when, while doing post-mortems on heart attack victims, they looked inside the arteries and found them hardened and clogged with patches of fatty, fibrous tissue. This fatty tissue is now called atheroma and the disorder is atherosclerosis, which means hardening from atheroma.

● Atheroma results in the smaller arteries becoming narrowed and furred up. The rough lining may crack which can cause the blood to clot (a thrombosis). Or because the wall is weakened it may give way and blood leaks out (a haemorrhage). If the arteries taking blood to the muscles of the heart develop atheroma (coronary artery disease) this can lead to angina, heart attacks or sudden death. Atheroma in the arteries leading to the brain can end up causing strokes.

Blood cholesterol

Cholesterol is essential for the normal functioning of every cell in the body. Only a small amount is needed. It is carried to the cells by the blood. But many people's blood contains far more than is needed. The higher the cholesterol in the blood the more atheroma develops. The risk of coronary heart disease is much increased. For example, a 40-year-old man with high blood cholesterol level is as much as three times more likely to have a heart attack than a 40-year-old with normal blood cholesterol.

Saturated fat in the food we eat can stimulate the formation of cholesterol. Around 30% of the cholesterol in the blood comes from saturated fats and cholesterol in our diet. The liver itself makes the rest. It is only the 20-30% coming from the diet that can be altered by cutting down on dietary cholesterol. Changing the diet can also reduce the formation of cholesterol by the body itself. Cutting down on saturated fats is the most important step.

Control your weight

Weight for weight fats provide more Calories than proteins or carbohydrates. So cutting down on Calories can seem much easier on a low-fat diet.

Some of the Calories lost when the fats are cut down will need to be offset by Calories from the increased starchy fibre (eg. wholemeal bread and potatoes) you are recommended to eat. But it is still fairly easy to achieve an overall reduction in Calorie intake and so lose weight.

The body only actually needs a little fat a day. Two tablespoonfuls of oil a day would be enough to keep you topped up. So if you are trying to lose weight there's no harm in cutting down to well below the recommended target. See the diagram (left) to work out *your* target.

Losing weight on a healthy diet. Cutting down on fats – since it is also good for your heart – is now the recommended way of losing weight. Cutting down on sugar will also help.

Do you need to lose weight?

About one in three adults in Britain are overweight. More men than women are overweight. However, more women than men say they want to lose weight!

The longer you have been overweight and the more overweight you are the greater the risk of dying early. Use this chart to check your weight against your height. If you fall into the obese band you are more than 20% overweight and it is very important for you to cut down. If you are in the overweight band, then the younger you are the more important it is for the sake of your health for you to cut down. This is particularly true if you have a family history of diabetes or high blood pressure.

Take more exercise. You'll almost certainly need to increase the exercise you take so that your body burns up your food faster.

Right weight: unhealthy diet

"I'm not overweight: so I must be healthy!" This is not necessarily true.

You can be the right weight, but still eat an unhealthy diet. Whatever your weight – too much saturated fat is bad for your heart. Too much sugar, and salt, and too little fibre can also be bad for you.

Overweight: healthy diet

It's certainly better to be overweight on an otherwise healthy diet than overweight on an unhealthy diet.

Changing to the new healthier diet where you cut down on fat, sugar and salt, and eat more fibre is a step in the right direction. It is also a diet for life – enjoyable to eat and easy to stay on. Once you are used to this diet try the effects of cutting down even further on fats and sugar.

Changing to a lower fat diet

It's difficult with fats to count up how much is in your present diet.
It's more helpful to check how you measure up against a target diet.

The new diet

The diet given below is taken from the American MR FIT project. (MR FIT stands for the Multiple Risk Factor Intervention Trial.) It was designed to provide about 33% of the total daily energy requirements from fat for a middle-aged man. This would be 80-90 grams of fat a day. If *your* target is lower than this go for the lower limits in groups two and three.

You may have a shock when you check yourself against this target diet. It may be consolation – though not a reason for giving up – to know that more than 80% of the people in Britain eat more fat than is recommended.

Where's the fat?

In today's diet well over half the fat comes from meat and dairy products. And these fats are saturated fats.

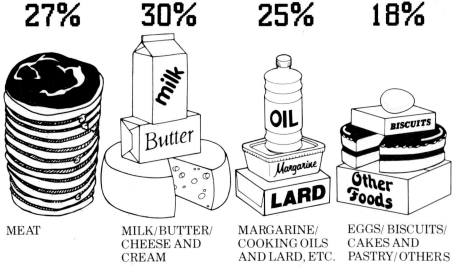

27%	30%	25%	18%
MEAT	MILK/BUTTER/ CHEESE AND CREAM	MARGARINE/ COOKING OILS AND LARD, ETC.	EGGS/ BISCUITS/ CAKES AND PASTRY/OTHERS

Your target

MR FIT programme. Diet to provide 33% daily energy from fat.

Food group	Daily ration	Comments
Fish, poultry, lean meats and low fat cheese	6 oz or less	Chicken and turkey should have skin removed. Lean meat only with all visible fat cut off.
Skimmed or semi-skimmed milk, low-fat yoghurt and low-fat cheese	2 servings (1 serving = 1 cup = 8 fluid oz)	Go for skimmed milk if it's important to keep your total Calories down.
Polyunsaturated margarines and oils.	2-4 level tablespoons. Use at least 2 tablespoons – they provide the essential fatty acids your body needs.	Includes those used in frying, salad dressings, and in baked goods, ie., biscuits, cakes and pastry. American diet recommends cutting out butter. You might wish to retain, say, 1 tablespoon of butter as part of the allowance. But keep nearer the lower limit if it's important to keep your total Calories down.
Eggs	2 or fewer *per week*	1 egg contains the equivalent of 1 teaspoon of fat! American diet also aims to keep cholesterol low.
Meatless meals	As often as possible	Protein doesn't have to come mixed up with fat from meat. Allowance of meat is probably only enough for one meat meal a day.

Steps towards your target

Food Groups	Level 1: STOP AND THINK	Level 2: GETTING BETTER	Level 3: NICE GOING
Chicken, turkey and fish	Eat less than once a week	Eat chicken, turkey or fish 1-2 times per week	Eat chicken, turkey or fish 3 or more times per week.
Meat	Eat red meat 2-3 times a day, lean or high-fat	Eat red meat once a day, lean meats only	Eat red meat 2-4 times a week, lean meats only
Dairy products	Use whole milk	Use semi-skimmed milk – 2% fat	Use skimmed milk
	Use ice cream	Use low fat yoghurt and frozen low-fat yoghurt	Use fruit ices
	Eat only high-fat cheeses (eg. Cheddar)	Eat a combination of high fat and low fat cheeses.	Eat only low fat cheeses (eg. cottage cheese, mozzarella and ricotta).
	Use cream	Use semi-skimmed milk and plain low-fat yoghurt	Use skimmed dry milk powder and low-fat yoghurt
Cooking oils and spreads	Use butter, shortening or lard for cooking or eating	Eat polyunsaturated margarine and use polyunsaturated oils for frying	Use corn, sunflower or safflower (polyunsaturated) oils and margarines in eating and all cooking
Baked goods (biscuits, cakes, pastries and pies)	Frequently eat baked goods and desserts	Use low-fat commercial baked goods and desserts or modified homemade baked goods and desserts	Use baked goods and desserts with negligible fat (ie. angel-food cake, non-fat milk puddings, etc.)
Cheese biscuits, crispbreads and snacks (eg. crisps)	Frequently eat high-fat cheese biscuits and snacks	Use low-fat commercial cheese biscuits, crispbreads and snacks or modified homemade cheese biscuits and snacks.	Use no-fat homemade and commercial cheese biscuits, crispbreads and snacks only.

On the way

The NACNE report considered it would take 15 years for the average national diet to reach this new low level. We are not suggesting that any one individual will take this time to make the change! But don't put yourself off by making too drastic a change too suddenly.

The second chart, adapted from *Eating for your Heart's Content*, the Minnesota Heart Health Project, should provide encouragement to make small but steady changes. Try making the changes one at a time and a step at a time. Circle where you are now for each item on the chart. Then set yourself a date for when you will check up on your progress.

The other topics in this chapter will provide more detail as to why these changes should be made. They will help you make informed choices as to what you want to eat.

Hidden fats

These diets assume you aren't going to be eating sausages, luncheon meat, liver sausage, salami, paté and meat pies. These meat products are very high in fat – most of it saturated – and it doesn't show up on their labels.

They also recommend that in general you stick to homemade biscuits, cake and pastry and use low-fat recipes as far as possible. When these are commercially made they are often high in fat. And again it doesn't show up on their labels.

With all this hidden fat it's difficult to keep track of how much you are eating. More information on their labels would enable you to chose, if you wished, to count in small portions of them in your fat controlled diet.

Our economic policies and farming system produce too much milk and butter, and too fatty carcases. Surplus milk fat and meat fat make cheap fillers for meat products and certain baked goods. So there is every incentive to keep adding this 'hidden' fat to our food.

Better labels and better policies

A list of ingredients is not good enough.
We need to know how much of the different nutrients a food contains.

"Why not just say how much of each nutrient a food contains?"
This can be done by calculating the percentage weight of each nutrient. For example, a hundred grams of double cream contains 48 grams of fat. That's to say it has 48%, by weight, fat. A hundred grams of grilled pork sausage contains 25 grams of fat – 25%, by weight, fat.

This is a scientific way that enables the fat content of different products to be exactly compared.

"But I don't eat a hundred grams of sausages! How much fat is there in a sausage?"
This isn't as accurate, but a typical grilled pork sausage contains nine grams of fat. Now we are measuring by servings. You know how many sausages you've eaten. So if you usually eat three sausages as part of a meal they would give 27 grams of fat.

But what about a serving of double cream? How big is a serving? How would you measure it?

It is possible to ask a lot of people and work out a typical size serving – but people vary a great deal as to what they count as a serving of cream. What's probably a typical serving – say a third of a small pot – would provide 30 grams of fat.

"These are all weights but NACNE and COMA talk about percentage of total energy — particularly for fats."
Yes – this takes into account that different people need different total weights of food to keep them going. Some people are very active and need to eat a lot of food – others just seem to be able to eat like horses and not put on weight. Both these types need more energy (Calories) to keep their bodies going. They are said to have a high metabolic rate. Less active people and people who naturally have a lower metabolic rate need less food to keep them going.

The recommendation is that, *however many or few Calories you need* only 30 to 34% of them should come from fats.

New guidelines for labels?

The DHSS's COMA report emphasised the need for better labelling and the government is, at this time (1984), consulting widely. At the International Nutrition Conference in Canada in 1984 the experiences of the various countries who do use food labelling revealed that it is a confusing and complex field. When information is provided it is often in a form that is difficult to understand. It's not always easy to use the information to decide what to buy. With most systems it's still possible for some manufacturers to slant the information to put their products in an unfairly good light.

Our greatest need is probably to know more about the fat content of food – particularly the saturated fat. However there will undoubtedly be pressure from the milk and meat industries to label just total fat rather than identifying saturated fats separately.

"Suppose all foods were labelled with the percentage of energy provided by the fat in them? Then I could make sure that, however much food I need to eat, the percentage energy from fat averages out at around 30%."
Many nutritionists would like to see labels giving the energy provided by the different nutrients as a percentage of the total energy in the food. These labels are also much more useful in at least two other ways:

● They ignore the weight of water in a product. There are no Calories in water.

● They bring out the difference in terms of Calories of, say, a gram of fat and a gram of protein or sugar. There are far more Calories in a gram of fat than in a gram of any other nutrient.

Let's look at how the weight and percentage energy content compare for double cream

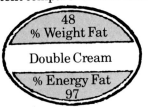

How would you answer these questions?

1. If you wanted to sell cream which label would you prefer?
2. Which would you chose if you wanted to help people keep to a diet in which their daily total of fat from all the foods eaten averages out at 30-34%?
3. If you were worried about eating too much fat would you conclude that you should never eat cream?

Answers 1. % weight. 2. % energy. 3. No: but you could really only afford it as a special treat when you could make up for it by cutting down somewhere else. By doing this your total daily energy from fats would still average out at around 30%.

The chart, below, gives both sets of figures for two groups of food in which there is a good deal of hidden fat.

Product	FAT % by weight	FAT % Energy
Grilled pork sausage	25	71
Luncheon meat	27	78
Liver sausage	27	78
Salami	45	82
Plain digestive biscuit	20	38
Cream sandwich biscuit	26	46
Shortcrust pastry	32	55
Madeira cake	17	40

Better policies

Farmers within the EEC produce too much milk and butter. They also produce meat carcases which are too fatty.

Butter mountains and milk lakes

Even with today's high fat diet surplus dairy products are building up. This will be made much worse once people start cutting down on fats. Already the increasing demand for semi-skimmed and skimmed milk is leading to more of the skimmed off fat going into the butter and cheese industries – and into animal feeds!

What happens to the surplus? *As you read this section ask yourself: 'Does anyone seem to be considering people's health when making these decisions?'*

Storage costs are high and there is little point in storing surpluses unless supply is likely to decrease or demand increase. Some surpluses, particularly surplus liquid milk, just have to be thrown away.

The EEC often has to cut its losses and sell cheaply. Cheap surplus butter has found a market in Russia. To protect the retailers and farmers it cannot be allowed to flood the home market and upset the price structure. Though in the last few years some has been available as a special Christmas treat. Who needs saturated fats as a Christmas 'present'?

As part of the intervention to cut down the surplus, cheap 'Intervention Butter' is made available to institutions within the EEC. Schools, hospitals and prisons can all benefit. It keeps their running costs down.

Dried milk fat and some butter is also sold cheaply to manufacturers of biscuits, cakes and pastry. Dried milk fat mixes easily with the other ingredients in the food processing. It provides bulk and a buttery flavour – both good selling points. No wonder there is little incentive to food manufacturers to cut down on fats for the sake of the health of the consumers.

A step in the right direction? The EEC is now imposing restrictive milk quotas on dairy farmers. This was not done for health reasons, but because of the surplus butter mountain and milk lake. These quotas were imposed too abruptly and caused a great outcry. Better forward planning would have made them more acceptable. But in the past British dairy farmers have done well out of subsidies, which were designed to protect the smaller, mixed-economy farmers on the Continent.

For health reasons it would help if subsidies were used to encourage the breeding of cows which give a lower fat, higher protein milk.

The Milk Marketing Board and the Butter Council still spend millions encouraging us to eat more saturated fats.

Fatty carcases

There's hope here too:

● Present regulations encourage farmers to produce fatty animals. They specify the minimum quantity of fat on a carcase if it is to be accepted for human consumption. These could be changed so that they penalise fatty carcases. This has already happened in Norway.
● Research will need to be continued on breeding animals that are naturally leaner.
● Restrict feed intake so animals grow more slowly and lay down less fat.
● Slaughter earlier – before fat is laid down.
● Grass-fed cattle have only half as much saturated fat as grain-fed cattle. So farmers need to be encouraged to leave cattle out to grass longer or to feed grass silage.

Enraged consumers

A better labelling system for meat content might lead to an outraged demand from consumers for less fatty meat products. Retailers, particularly the powerful supermarkets which can really make the food manufacturers and farmers jump, would pass the complaints on. At the moment the term 'meat' on a label can cover up a nasty mess. 'Meat' does not mean just lean meat and should certainly not be thought of as protein. 'Meat' may legally contain the proportion of fat normally found on the animal. It may also contain any edible part of the animal. Feet, ears, tails – even finely ground up bone in some cases.

It would be better if *lean meat* content was labelled. Though even this would include some fat. Ideally, the fat content should also be given.

Dairy products and meat

Almost one third of the total amount of fat we eat comes from dairy products. Nearly another third comes from meat. It's all saturated fat.

Dairy products

Butter is almost 100% saturated fat so there is nothing to be lost – from the nutritional point of view – from cutting it out. Though if you like it there's no reason why you shouldn't include it as part of your small daily ration of saturated fat. However, milk and cheese also provide some of the protein and quite a large amount of the calcium we need in our diet. But must we eat them with such a lot of saturated fat in them?

The bottom of the milk

Milk *is* an important source of calcium. (There are other ways of getting protein.) Some people's diets might become deficient in calcium if they cut down on drinking milk. So how can we retain the benefits of milk without the disadvantages of all that fat?

A simple solution is to pour away the cream from the top of the milk. The bottom of the milk contains far less fat and is much better for you.

Unfortunately, milk is sometimes homogenised so that the cream doesn't separate off at the top.

Why can't the dairies take the fat off for us? In fact they can do this and in response to increasing consumer demand semi-skimmed and skimmed milk is now quite widely available.

We first asked our testers about this in late 1983. They said they could buy low fat milks in some supermarkets, but not many of their milkmen delivered it. Within a year most found their milkman would deliver *if they asked for it.* But it wasn't widely advertised.

Even if you haven't, as yet, decided to try using a semi-skimmed or skimmed milk keep an eye open for it in the shops and ask your milkman if he can deliver it. If your milkman doesn't have it you might tell him where you can get it locally so that the dairy will realise they have competition. Make a note of the various types available, their fat content and their price.

Changing to low-fat milk

Is it worthwhile? Well, 17% of the saturated fat in our diet comes from milk. By switching just to semi-skimmed milk you could cut this by half. You would be well on the way to reaching the new target for fats. In fact for many people it may be difficult to cut down enough on fats if they don't switch to low-fat milk. Fortunately, once they get used to the different taste, many people find this a fairly simple change to make and keep up.

What about you? Some people think that semi-skimmed or skimmed milk tastes unpleasant. Often they have only tried the long-life (U.H.T.) variety. This milk is heated to a high temperature to make it keep longer on the shelf. Any U.H.T. (Ultra Heat Treated) milk – skimmed or not – has this same taste. Fresh, pasteurised, semi-skimmed or skimmed milk tastes much more like the silver top most people drink.

Look back at the notes you made about what's available locally and choose which milk you will try. Put it in a jug and try it on someone else in tea or coffee! Do they notice the difference? Can you tell?

Since it's so much better for your health would you be prepared to try it for a whole week to see if you get used to the taste? Or keep it for general use, but also buy full-fat ordinary milk for special occasions?

How much fat?

Check this table for the fat content of the milk, cream and yoghurt you use:

Dairy product	% by weight fat
Gold top (full cream) milk	4.8
Silver top (full cream) milk	3.8
Low-fat (semi-skimmed) milk	2.0
Skimmed milk	0.1
Single cream	21.0
Sterilised cream	23.0
Whipping cream	35.0
Double cream	48.0
Natural low-fat yoghurt	1.0
Natural full-fat yoghurt	4.0

When some of our testers looked at this table they asked:

"Why all the fuss? Milk doesn't look as though it has so much fat in it?"

One problem is that we drink such a lot of it. The average person in the U.K. drinks four and a half pints a week. So it all adds up.

Another problem is the way in which the amount of fat is expressed.

Let's look at low-fat, semi-skimmed milk.

It has 2.0% by weight of fat in it. That's to say 100 grams of semi-skimmed milk contains two grams of fat. But there is a lot of water in milk. Also fat, compared to protein or carbohydrates, is energy rich ie. weight for weight it's higher in Calories.

If we look at the amount of energy (Calories) the milk contains and express the fat content in terms of the percentage of total energy (Calories) in milk provided by the fat this works out to be 36%.

So even the semi-skimmed milk is higher than the 30% recommended by the NACNE report. However, it's a big step in the right direction.

Cream

Many people only eat cream as an occasional treat. If you are using it two or more times a week consider switching to single cream *or better* – natural full-fat yoghurt – *or best of all* – natural low-fat yoghurt.

Coffee whiteners and cream substitutes

Coffee whiteners can be spooned as a dry powder into coffee or tea. Watch out! Don't let their labels mislead you. The vegetable fats they contain are almost entirely highly saturated ones – often coconut oil. Use skimmed milk powder: it is much lower in saturated fats.

The same is true of imitation 'cream' toppings – they too are made from saturated vegetable fats.

Cheese

Almost all cheeses are high in saturated fat. Some are higher than others. By all means switch to a low fat cheese for everyday use. Or buy such a strong flavoured cheese that you'll need to use less of it. But the main message is that we need to be careful about how much cheese we eat.

Labelling the fat content. There's a great deal of confusion here. British cheeses, as yet, are not required by law to have their fat content labelled. Some manufacturers, particularly of the new 'Cheddar-type' lower fat cheeses, do label the fat content.

French cheeses must be labelled – but on a different basis to that used in Britain. French cheeses are labelled with fat content calculated on a *dry weight* basis ie., not counting the water in them. Have a look at some of their labels. A camembert may state, for example, '40% matières grasse'. They all appear to be very high in fat.

On the more commonly used *wet weight* basis including the water, ie. in the form in which it's actually eaten, French cheeses, on the whole, contain less fat than British ones.

Type of Cheese	% Fat by weight in natural product
Cream cheese	47
Stilton	40
Cheddar	33
Brie	27
Camembert	27
Edam	25
Processed	25
Low-fat 'Cheddar type'	17
Cottage cheese	4

Cutting the fat from meat

Twenty seven percent of the fat we eat comes with our meat. Most of it is saturated fat.

Visible and invisible fat

Take a look at the meat in your fridge or on your plate. There's probably some fat you can see on the outside. That's easily cut off. But there is an almost equal amount of invisible fat closely wrapped up with the protein in the lean part of the meat. What can be done about this?

● You could eat smaller portions of meat. Compare your average helping to the one shown in the diagram which is the average size portion of steak recommended in a famous American Coronary Heart Disease Prevention project.

● You could switch to meats that contain less fat. Eat less beef, lamb and pork. When you do eat these choose from steak, sirloin, topside and lean stewing steak; and trimmed chops, roast leg and loin, and unsmoked ham. Mince, *with as much fat as possible drained off during cooking,* can be fairly low in fat.

● Eat more turkey and chicken which contain less fat. The fat they do have is less saturated. Rabbit, venison and game are also low in fat, if you can afford them. With turkey and chicken consider using recipes in which you don't use the skin. Much of the fat they do have is just under the skin.

Deliberately hidden fat?

At the present time all the spare fat – including that which the consumer refuses to buy with a joint – is put to good use and profit. It goes into mince, sausages, luncheon meat, meat pies and other processed meat products. Along with this fat go odds and ends from the rest of the carcase.

Eat as little as possible of luncheon meats, liver sausage and patés, and meat pies and sausages rolls (fatty meat plus fatty pastry). A single portion will provide a large amount of your daily ration of fat. (See table, below).

With sausages. *If you must eat them,* grill them slowly so some of the fat drains away. They will still be high in fat because the rusk in sausages soaks up a lot of it.

With mince. After the initial browning allow it to cool down and then pour off the fat before finishing off the dish. Mince is a great place to hide fat. You drain off a lot of your money with the fat, but the mince is then reasonably lean.

Meat product	Grams of fat
1 portion of pork pie	28
1 thick, grilled pork sausage	9
1 beefburger	11
1 'quarterpounder' beefburger	22
1 slice liver sausage	6.5
1 slice luncheon meat	6.5

Eat smaller portions. Do you know what three ounces of cooked lean meat looks like? It's not always possible to weigh it out. But a half-inch-thick portion of steak would be this size:

Low fat, high protein

We need to switch from high fat, high quality protein foods to those with low fat, high quality protein.

Saturated fats tend to come wrapped round or mixed up with proteins. Meats, milk and cheese are mostly high in saturated fats as well as protein. Which foods are low on fat, but have high quality protein?

Getting enough protein?

In the past, when there was concern as to whether people were getting enough protein, foods such as milk and cheese were recommended because they are high in protein. But two things have changed since the 1940s. First, the average British diet now contains enough protein – some nutritionists would say more than is necessary. Secondly, a diet high in saturated fats is now known to be linked with an increased risk of coronary heart disease.

If you cut down on fatty meats such as beef, lamb or pork and on high fat cheeses and creamy milk – then you will also cut down on protein, certain minerals like iron and some of the B vitamins. To make up for these you can eat more:

● Chicken and turkey
● Fish
● Low fat cheeses and yoghurt
● Pulses (peas and beans), wholegrain cereal products, including rice, wholemeal bread and potatoes.

Just cutting down or cutting out meat, without making up for it elsewhere, will give you an unbalanced diet. Your diet will need to be replanned.

Protein from plants

Your diet probably already gives you quite a lot of protein from plants. White or brown bread and potatoes are quite good sources of protein.

The trouble with suggesting eating more proteins from plant sources is that it may still conjure up images of cranky vegetarians eating nut cutlets or soya meat substitutes.

Fortunately, cookery magazines and TV series have done a great deal to change this image. There are now many good vegetarian cook books. They are full of delicious recipes and are often based on cuisines which have always been mainly vegetarian.

You don't have to become a vegetarian. Though there is increasing evidence that a vegetarian diet based on a wide variety of foods, *and not high on cheese and eggs,* is a very healthy diet.

It's often possible, particularly in stews and casseroles, to cut down on the meat and add various beans to a dish. This way you end up with as much protein but much less fat.

Grains and pulses

Both grains and pulses contain high proportions of proteins. Eaten together they meet human requirements more exactly than either alone. Forget the very old fashioned notion of plant proteins being second class.

Grains. These are the seeds of cereal crops. They include wheat, rice, corn (maize), oats, barley, rye, millets and sorghums. Almost every country in the world bases its' diet on one or more of these staple foods. The grain is easy to store. It can be eaten as whole grain or else made into bread, pasta and noodles, pancakes and tortillas, and porridge and other breakfast cereals.

Pulses. These are the seeds of plants from the Legume family (peas and beans). They are sometimes called legumes.

There are probably more than a hundred different kinds of peas and beans eaten around the world.

Have a look in your local wholefood shop or if there isn't one try a health food shop or large supermarket. What can you find? Try cooking one kind that's new to you. Most pulses need soaking before cooking. They sometimes need long cooking. A pressure cooker saves time. Don't use a slow cooker as the temperature does not get high enough. Some beans – the ones that have brown, red or black skins – have substances in their skins which can occasionally cause severe stomach upsets if they are not cooked properly. Take care:

● Throw away the water they have been soaked in.
● Don't eat them raw after they have been soaked.
● *Boil* them for at least 15 minutes.

What's in your shops? Supermarkets are gradually stocking a wider range of pulses. But wholefood, Asian, West Indian and Cypriot stores are good places to look.

Here's what we found in a small wholefood shop in Bletchley: kidney beans, haricot beans, dried peas, lima beans, chick peas, mung beans, aduki beans, borlotti beans, and green, brown and red lentils.

A happy coincidence?

Many traditional meals around the world have dishes based on the whole grains – and their products – and pulses (peas and beans). Meat and cheese are used in small quantities to flavour or garnish the dishes.

- Rice and dhal (lentils) in India.
- Pasta (wheat) and peas or beans in Italy.
- Tortillas (corn meal) and kidney beans in Mexico.
- Rice and soya bean products in China.
- Burghul (wheat) and chick peas in the Middle East.
- Millet and groundnuts (peanuts) in Africa.
- Beans on toast (wheat) in Britain.

In addition to containing proteins from plants, and therefore little saturated fat, these meals are also high in fibre. They were developed long before there were nutritionists around to explain why they are good. Is it just a happy coincidence? Or was it that those who ate these well-balanced meals thrived – and the traditional meals were passed on?

Learning new recipes. If you want to switch to eating more proteins from plants, watch out for magazines which often have dishes from other countries, try out the dishes in restaurants, or borrow cookery books from the library. There are some particularly good Middle Eastern and Indian cookery books. In many cases these dishes contain small quantities of meats – watch out that cookery editors or restaurants haven't dressed them for Western tastes with too much meat.

You may find – or could ask for – local evening cookery classes on vegetarian, high fibre, or Asian dishes.

Filleting a flat fish

(1)

(2)

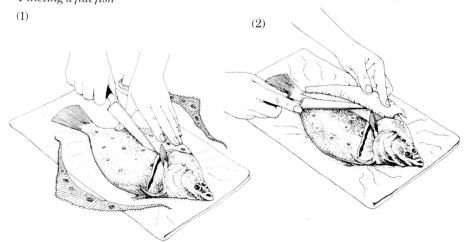

Switch to fish?

The polyunsaturated fats in fish are now known to be particularly good for you. White fish, such as cod, haddock, whiting, coley, sole and plaice are low in fat. Herring, mackerel, salmon, tuna, pilchards and sardines are high in fat.

Less fish is being eaten today than in pre-war years. The amount per person has fallen from 11.99 kilograms a year in the 1930s to only 6.9 kilograms in 1982. That's an average, today, of one serving a week.

The only boom in the fish industry has been in fish fingers. Many of today's children will never have eaten fresh fish.

Here's what some people say about why they eat little or no fish. How many do you agree with?
"It's not easy to prepare."
"I can't get fresh fish where I live."
"It's too expensive."
"It makes the whole house smell."
"I don't know how to cook it."
"My kids don't like the taste."
"I'm worried about all the bones."

Why has eating fish declined so much?

It's not a straightforward story because the factors are all linked together.

If the fish is too expensive or not available in the shops then it's not bought and served up in the home. Over a period of time people get used to not eating it – and a new generation of cooks don't know how to cook it or how to avoid filling the house with fishy smells. So fewer people ask for fish, which leads to fish becoming too expensive and less of it being available in the shops . . .

On top of this fishermen have suffered more than many from political and economic changes. Quota restrictions in traditional fishing grounds have taken their toll. Many trawler owners have gone out of business.

The industry could change. Fish can be chilled, rather than frozen. This gives a fresher taste. Supermarkets could use modern counters to keep fish fresh and not smelly. Fish farming on our rivers and waterways could increase the numbers of fish available and make supplies more reliable. At the moment it is mainly high priced fish like trout which are farmed for the restaurant trade.

The consumer could change. Take a look around your local shops to see what fish you can find. Can you get what you want? If you can't, why not ask the shop keeper, fishmonger or supermarket manager? Keep an eye open for different fish recipes and try these when you find the fish available.

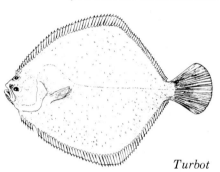

Turbot

Cooking fish

Fish can be baked or grilled. Frying in breadcrumbs or batter increases the fat, so on the occasions that you chose to eat fried fish try to check that the oil used is a polyunsaturated one.

To keep the smell right down find recipes to cook fish by baking in a covered dish or wrapped up in foil packets. Or you can buy special 'boil in the bag' plastic bags that you put the fish into and then cook in boiling water. This way the fish is really cooked in its own steam and is delicious.

Lining the grill pan with foil, though it costs a few pence, makes washing up more pleasant after grilling fish.

Happy to stick with fish fingers? Grill rather than fry them: frying adds an extra 1.5 gram of fat and an extra 9 Calories to each fish finger.

Each fish finger contains:

	Grilled	Fried
• Protein	3.5 gms	3.5 gms
• Fat	2.0 gms	3.5 gms
• Carbohydrates	50 gms	50 gms
• Calories	53	62

Grilled fish fingers with peas and large chunky chips or oven chips make a fairly well balanced meal. Much better than sausages, or hamburgers, or meat pies.

Spreading and cooking

It can be quite easy to make the fat we add at the table go further.
Changing the way we cook will help too.

Do you usually:
- Spread butter or margarine on bread and toast?
- Put butter or margarine on vegetables?
- Fry food?
- Use recipes in which some ingredients are first browned in fat, eg., casseroles and stews?
- Bake pastry, cakes and biscuits?

These are all areas in which it's relatively easy to cut down on the amount of fat used. Or at least avoid using saturated fats.

How far will it go?

You can help to cut down on fat by spreading the fat you do use more thinly. During the war fat was rationed. Fat intake dropped to the level recommended today.

A week's ration of butter or margarine was two ounces. Try sticking to this ration yourself. Take the spread that you normally use – butter, margarine or low-fat spread – and measure out 2 oz (or 55 grams). Put the fat in a separate container and use it every time you want to add it to vegetables or spread it on bread. How long does it last? If you don't manage to make it last the whole week, try again. How can you make it go further?

Here is how some of our testers got on:

"I weighed out the butter allowance. It looked quite a lot. But I used it in under two days. I talked about this to someone who suggested using a soft margarine because it went further. The second time around I did better. I found that I could sometimes cut out the margarine altogether."

"I did some lateral thinking and decided to cut my slices of bread thicker — so there were fewer slices to spread the butter on."

"I remembered what my mother used to say about spreading it thick and then scraping it thin. It amazed me how much I could scrape off!"

"I put the margarine on only one slice of the bread for sandwiches."

With this approach you can cut down on the amount of fat you use. Some of our testers' families turned this approach into a competition.

If you do cut down in this way you might decide that since you now use so little of it you may as well stick to butter, even though it is a saturated fat.

However several of our testers could only manage to spread the fat further by using a soft margarine or a low-fat spread.

Low-fat spreads

These may contain butter or margarine. The important point is that they have had extra water beaten into them and so contain far fewer calories. They need to be kept in the fridge but are easy to spread. Using these you can cut down on fat. This is because much of what you spread is water. Of course, you may not like their watery taste.

At the moment there are no low-fat spreads made from high polyunsaturated margarines. So all low-fat spreads contain saturated fats.

Soft margarines

These, too, spread more easily than butter. It's important to check that their labels say 'high in polyunsaturates' or give a minimum level of polyunsaturates. Margarines that are not labelled 'high in polyunsaturates' are high in saturated fats. Manufacturers of these do not say this on their labels.

Margarines high in polyunsaturates are better for your health if you are thinking in terms of reducing your risk of coronary disease. However, it's important to remember that butter and all types of margarine are high in calories. They will both damage your health if you eat too much and become overweight.

With cooked vegetables . . .

Many of our testers said they didn't like melted margarine on hot vegetables. Some said that, come what may, they would still stick to using butter.

You may find that adding extra flavour with parsley, chives, mint, pepper or nutmeg may help. Or try steaming vegetables to retain more of their natural flavour.

Cooking with fats

If you cook for yourself or a family think about the times when you add fat in cooking. Frying and browning the meat for casseroles and stews adds fat. Making pastry, cakes and biscuits also often uses a great deal of fat.

Think about the meals you might prepare in a typical week. Make a list of all the frying you do and the type of fat you use. Make a second list of all the pies, tarts, puddings, pastries and biscuits you cook. Again note down the type of fat you use in each recipe.

As you read through the rest of this topic review your list and think of ways in which you could:

● Cut down on the total amount of fat used *and*

● Avoid using a saturated fat ie., switch to a polyunsaturated fat.

Cutting down on fat

Which of these can you try?

Grilling rather than frying. This way you don't add extra fat. Or try dry-frying in a non-stick pan.

Using non-stick pans. Some people still add too much fat with these.

Go on – trust them. Or convince yourself by test cooking pancakes or an omelette with almost no fat in the pan.

Taking excess fat off. Fried food can be drained on kitchen paper. Also you can blot the surface of a cooked dish with kitchen paper or a special brush designed to soak up the fat.

Leave fatty casseroles in the fridge, if you have time, then most of the fat will come to the top and be easy to remove. Then reheat to serve.

Omit browning in fat. When making casseroles try leaving out this stage. You may still like the final flavour. Or dry-fry in a non-stick pan, adding a little water at the end to dissolve the flavours from the pan.

Find lower-fat recipes. Sort through magazines to look for recipes for pastry and cakes which use less fat. Or experiment for yourself. It's difficult to produce a low-fat pastry so you may conclude that you will need to cut down on how much pastry you use. Instead of meat pies serve bread with casseroled or stewed meat. Instead of fruit pies you could try the filling topped with crunchy breakfast cereals or wholemeal breadcrumbs.

Switching to polyunsaturated fats

Remember the aim is still to cut down the total amount of fats used. However, at least by switching to polyunsaturated fats you do cut down on the saturated fats.

What do you use in cooking? Take a look at the cooking fats and oils in your larder and fridge. Look carefully at the labels. What do they tell you about the kind of fat it is?

If you use hard fats they are unlikely to give you any information about what kind of fat they are. Which food manufacturers will voluntarily tell you bad news about their products? These hard fats are all saturated fats. Butter, lard (pork), suet (beef), and dripping are all saturated fats. So are the processed white cooking fats and hard margarines which are made by hardening, ie. making saturated, fish and vegetable oils.

If you cook with oils watch out for those labelled just 'Vegetable Oil' or 'Mixed or Blended'. These almost certainly contain saturated vegetable oils.

Most of the polyunsaturated vegetable oils will be well labelled. These include soya, sunflower and corn (maize) oil. Groundnut oil is less rich in polyunsaturates but still much better than hard cooking fats.

Frying with polyunsaturated fats

Frying with polyunsaturated vegetable oils is easy. They don't splutter, unless the food you put in them is wet. And they can get hotter without burning so they produce crisply fried, less oily food.

However, continued use of the same oil for deep frying is not recommended. Reheating of these oils, particularly if they contain small particles of food, can alter the nature of the polyunsaturates. Be sure to strain the oil you use and throw it away as soon as it becomes cloudy or darker – perhaps after three or four uses.

Baking with polyunsaturated fats

Polyunsaturated margarines can be substituted for butter in cakes, biscuits and even pastry. Indeed polyunsaturated vegetable oils (which are even richer in polyunsaturates than the margarines are) can also be used. Specially modified recipes may be needed. Watch out for these or write directly to the manufacturers to ask for recipes.

Chips with everything?

Many people adore chips. Asking them to give up chips might put them off changing to a healthier diet altogether!

All chips *are* fatty: but some contain less fat than others. If you want to choose a healthier chip first check what sort of fat it's fried in. It should be fried in a polyunsaturated vegetable oil rather than a saturated fat, eg. dripping or lard.

Next go for the least fatty type:

● Home cooked chips, which can be drained on kitchen paper and eaten at once, are less fatty than shop-cooked chips. These shop-cooked chips are often kept warm in a heap and they gradually soak up even more fat.
● Large thick chips soak up less fat than small, thin chips.
● Straight chips soak up less fat than crinkle cut chips, which have a much larger surface area.
● 'Oven cook' frozen chips end up with less fat in them than ordinary fried frozen chips.

'Best chips' are therefore home-cooked, large, straight chips. These should be fried in sunflower, safflower, soya or corn oil.

Next best chips are large-cut oven chips.

A frying start

It's a scandal that so much fatty food is offered to school children at lunch time. The damage to their arteries starts in childhood.

Today's school dinners . . .

Be it school dinner, packed lunch or a takeaway from a local shop, the chances are that there is a lot of fat in what a child eats at midday. A two year study of 11- to 13-year-old boys and girls in Newcastle showed they were eating far too much fat and sugar. 40% of all their food energy came from fats and 21% from sugars.

School dinners are now often served in a self-service cafeteria. The children pay only for the foods they choose – not for a complete meal. The aim is to provide quickly prepared, cheap food with little waste that is popular with the children.

At Naseby School in Birmingham, the children carried out a survey of school meals.

- The children preferred chips, sausages, beefburgers and fish fingers.

- Vegetables – especially boiled ones, were mostly wasted.

- Little attempt was made to cater for groups other than meat-eating children of Anglo-Saxon origin.

- Chicken was not used at all because of risks of Salmonella poisoning. This was a local authority guideline.

- Fish was not often used because the children didn't like it – except for fish and chips and fish fingers, which have fat added during frying.

After completing their survey they talked with the head and the school meals service. Significant changes were made. They included more fresh fruit, salads, vegetarian and Asian dishes.

Packed lunches

A lot of parents give their children packed lunches. This can be a way of reducing fat. But not necessarily. Cheese sandwiches, sausage rolls and crisps are often packed. These are all high in fat. For example, a lunchbox of a round of cheese sandwiches (21 grams of fat), a packet of crisps (7 grams) and an apple (no fat) adds up to 28 grams of fat. Add a slice of cake and the total goes over 40 grams.

. . . tomorrow's heart attacks

It's bad enough that school children learn to prefer fatty foods. But what is now realised to be much worse is that even at this age their arteries begin to be damaged.

Little or no health education about choosing a healthy diet is given in many schools. And actual positive harm is done by the amount of fatty food that is offered to them.

Changing to a healthier diet at any age can bring benefits. But starting off on the right lines in childhood is best of all. All parents want to do the best for their children. But many do not know how to make their voices heard in what can be seen as a political scandal.

Changes in school dinners

With cuts in spending in the 1970s and 1980s, Education Authorities had to look to their budgets. The priority was to keep teachers and maintain buildings and equipment. Among the budgets pared to the bone in most areas was school meals.

Some education authorities tried to end school meals altogether. But the law demands that meals are available for children who want them. So some kind of service had to be provided.

During and after the war there was a national policy for school dinners which laid down what percentage of the daily minimum requirements should be provided by a school dinner. As standards of living rose it was decided to drop these requirements. The cafeteria system today includes too many fatty foods and too few healthier alternatives. With the new understanding of a healthy diet new policies are needed.

Speaking out

It's well worth putting pressure on your local education authority. Write directly to them or better still get a group of parents, possibly via a parent-teacher association to approach them. You can also ask a parent school governor to raise any of these issues.

- Ask what nutritional policy they follow in deciding what will be served at school dinners.

- They may have a definite policy. If they don't have one suggest they approach the district health authority. The health authority should include advice about standards of school meals in their food and health policy statements.

- Remind the education authority that they have strong purchasing powers. For example, the ILEA (the Inner London Education Authority) spends about £25 million a year on food. They should lay down nutritional requirements as part of the specifications for caterers and food suppliers who wish to tender for school meals contracts.

- Suggest to the head teacher that a local community dietician be invited to talk with parents, staff and school meal service organisers.

- Enquire from the headteacher or at parents' evening what part teachers are playing in helping pupils choose a healthy combination of foods.

- For primary schools suggest that they help the children choose wisely by discussing the day's menu in class.

- Ask your child to bring home copies of the school menus – these are decided well in advance – so that you can talk to your children about the choices they have.

- Arrange for a display of typical dishes from the school's canteen for a parents' evening. This is particularly useful for the open evening for new pupils and their parents.

It can be done

The New York Schools Project has a large budget for school meals. It insists on buying food that meets modern nutritional standards. The food must be high in fibre and low in fat, sugar, salt and additives. If the food supplier doesn't keep up to these standards he loses the school meals contract. Food from these suppliers is also allowed to carry an 'Approved by the New York Schools Project' label. So outside sales have also increased.

Cut down on salt?

WARNING

The NACNE report recommends that the daily intake of salt should be reduced by three grams a day.

It's difficult to calculate the *average* daily intake of salt. Estimates vary from about nine to 12 grams. This average includes both sexes. However, men do eat more salt than women. Bearing all this in mind, the NACNE report concluded that everyone should be recommended to cut down by three grams a day.

But how much salt do you actually need? The minimum amount estimated to be needed by the body (mainly for the effective working of the heart and the nerves) is half a gram.

So you can cut down by more if you wish. However it's difficult to avoid having to buy processed foods with a great deal of added salt. The NACNE report considered that recommending a lower goal would 'necessitate major changes in food manufacture and marketing.'

To help you work out what is involved in cutting down we have taken the target for daily intake as six grams. This is the lower estimate of average daily intake (nine grams) minus the recommended cut (three grams). This is still higher than the 1982 WHO (World Health Organisation) recommended five grams a day. If all the salt in the food you eat in a day could be measured by the level teaspoonful your limit (six grams) would be one and a quarter teaspoonfuls.

Why cut down? If the whole population cuts down this would 'substantially lower the prevalence rate of hypertension, and therefore the mortality resulting from this disease and associated pathology' (NACNE Report). That's to say we expect there would be fewer people with high blood pressure. And fewer people dying from heart disease, strokes and kidney failure which are linked to high blood pressure.

"Will cutting down definitely help me?" It will lower your risks of developing high blood pressure. Some people are salt-sensitive and for them it is particularly important to cut down. *But* the trouble is that you can't tell if you are salt-sensitive until the damage is done and you have developed high blood pressure.

The current theory is that cutting down on salt reduces the amount of potentially harmful sodium in the diet. Sodium is one of two elements which with chloride form salt: the chemical name for salt is sodium chloride. Because we get at least 95% of our sodium from salt in the diet, we usually talk about salt intake rather than sodium intake. However, you may see the sodium content of foods listed as milligrams (mg) of sodium per 100 grams of the food. Your daily limit would be 2,400 milligrams (ie. 2.4 grams) of sodium.

Salt and high blood pressure

High blood pressure increases your risks of having a stroke, a heart attack or heart failure. Have you had your blood pressure checked recently?

Lowering the national average salt intake will reduce the number of people with high blood pressure. In time this will lead to fewer deaths from diseases associated with high blood pressure.

For salt-sensitive individuals cutting down on salt will reduce the risk of developing high blood pressure.

If there is already a high blood pressure the low salt diet should help bring this down. On hearing this general advice most people want to know the answer to two questions:
● What is high blood pressure and why is it dangerous?
● Will cutting down on salt work for me?
Unfortunately there is no way of knowing if you are sensitive to salt – until you know you already have high blood pressure. You may decide to cut down anyway to be on the safe side. 'Should you cut down?' will help you decide if it might be particularly important for you to do so.

Blood Pressure

With each heartbeat a pressure wave passes down the artery as blood is pumped out from the heart. The highest pressure – systolic pressure – occurs shortly after the blood is pumped from the heart into the large blood vessels. The lowest pressure – diastolic pressure – occurs when the heart is relaxed and being filled by the blood returning through the veins.

A systolic pressure of 140 and a diastolic pressure of 90 is usually spoken of as "140 over 90" and written as 140/90.

During the course of the day, blood pressure changes constantly for everyone. Strenuous exercise raises blood pressure, so does stress. However, it's only when blood pressure is continually raised that a person can be said to have high blood pressure. A doctor would probably want to measure your pressure on three separate occasions to check this out.

How is blood pressure measured?

Having your blood pressure measured is simple. It can be measured with a sphygmomanometer, one part of which is a rubber bag enclosed in a fabric cuff. This cuff is wrapped around your arm and a squeeze bulb is used to pump air into the cuff which is connected to a pressure meter. A stethoscope is used to listen to the pulse in the arm. As the air from the cuff is slowly released the pressure in the cuff falls until the blood is able to surge past the cuff. At this point a pulse is heard as each pressure wave surges down the artery. This first reading, when the pulse is heard, is the systolic pressure. The air in the cuff is then further released until the pulse cannot be heard. The sound ceases when blood is flowing continually through the artery. This second reading is the diastolic pressure.

It's quite possible to use a machine yourself and measure your own blood pressure.

What's normal? It is difficult to say precisely when the level of blood pressure should be described as high rather than normal. However, generally it's now defined as mild high blood pressure when the diastolic pressure (the low measurement) is between 90 and 105, moderate between 105 and 120 and severe when it exceeds 120.

There is really no such disease as 'low blood pressure'. Except in rare situations, like shock or heavy bleeding, the lower your blood pressure is the better.

You need to have your blood pressure checked regularly – about once in every two years – in order to detect the beginnings of high blood pressure. One third of our testers had not had their blood pressure checked in the previous two years. All said they would like to have regular tests. Some didn't like to bother their doctors.

Ask your GP to measure your blood pressure or watch out for screening clinics which may be held at health centres or at work. If there is an occupational health nurse where you work, ask if she will organise a screening clinic so that everyone can have their blood pressure measured. Whoever measures your blood pressure, ask them to tell you what it is and keep a record of it yourself.

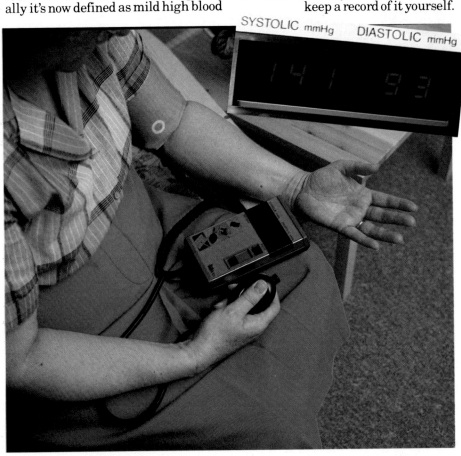

The risks of high blood pressure

The large Framingham Study in the USA showed that people with untreated high blood pressures are:
- three times more likely to have heart attacks –
- seven times more likely to have strokes –
- four times more likely to have heart failure –

than people with normal blood pressure.

Heart attacks are not, as is often thought, "the quick way to go". They may be prolonged, painful and result in disablement rather than death. Strokes may leave people severely disabled with paralysis and speech disturbances rather than killing them.

In terms of the overall cost to the nation, caring for the large number of people severely disabled by strokes is a more expensive 'item' than the intensive coronary care units required for heart patients.

Hardening of the arteries – atherosclerosis – develops because the high pressure makes the blood vessels thick, rigid and twisted. A blood clot (thrombosis) is more likely to develop inside these damaged vessels. Problems are most likely to arise from damaged blood vessels of the heart, brain and kidneys.

When high blood pressure is controlled by drugs the outlook is much better. Many of the complications can be prevented, but existing damage cannot be undone. Some of the drugs used to control blood pressure, particularly since they almost always need to be taken for the rest of your life, have potentially worrying side effects. So it's best to do everything possible to avoid having to take them.

What causes high blood pressure?

In between five and ten percent of all cases the high blood pressure is caused by kidney or gland problems, or rarely by drugs, including the contraceptive pill. It's difficult for a doctor to decide how much effort should be made to determine if a particular case falls into this group. And even if a definite cause is determined there may be little that can be done about it. The patient then ends up on the same drugs as they would have been prescribed without the tests.

For the remaining 90 percent or more of cases there is no known cause of the raised blood pressure. This doesn't mean that there *is* no cause; just that doctors haven't discovered it yet. However, plenty of research is

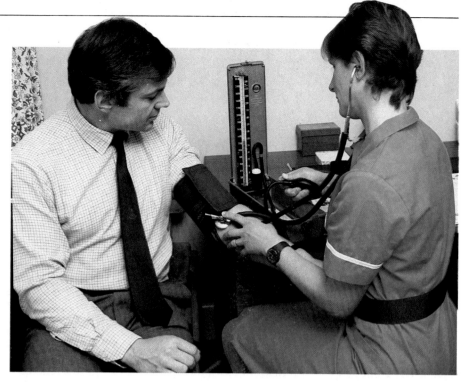

going on and it is now generally thought that there is no single cause, but rather a collection of linked risk factors. The most important risk factor is now strongly suspected to be the salt level in the diet.

How is salt involved?

Sodium, one of the two constituents of salt is known to be essential to the maintenance of correct blood volume and blood pressure – it influences the passage of water in and out of the body's cells.

The amount of salt we consume, however, provides much more sodium than our bodies need. The question is does this surplus of sodium affect blood pressure?

It seems likely that most people's kidneys efficiently handle the sodium and all the excess is excreted. However, some people's kidneys seem to work differently. Their efforts to get rid of sodium into the urine also result in sodium passing from the blood into the cells of the walls of the blood vessels. The cells of the walls of the small blood vessels play a part in controlling blood pressure. When the sodium passes into them they swell up. This makes it more difficult for blood to flow through these small blood vessels and so the blood pressure rises.

However this is only one theory and is only part of the story. Further research should make the relationship between salt intake and raised blood pressure more clear.

It's thought that this salt-sensitivity is inherited. However, apart from a known family history of high blood pressure, which gives us clues, we can't tell if we are salt-sensitive until a blood pressure check

reveals we already have high blood pressure.

What's needed is a test that could be done to check if someone is salt-sensitive so that the diet could be changed before the damage is done. Research continues on this. Meantime the recommendation is that everyone should cut down on salt – which certainly won't do them any harm – in order to make sure the salt-sensitive people are protected.

What's the evidence?

Comparing one country with another. Countries with low salt intake have little or no high blood pressure and blood pressure does not tend to increase with age.

Those with high salt intake have more cases of high blood pressure. And the blood pressure does rise with age.

However, populations with low blood pressure also tend to have other things in common. Perhaps the most important may be a high potassium intake, which may protect against the effect of sodium.

Changing the amount of salt in the diet. Investigations which have tried to relate salt intake to blood pressure have not always been successful.

Best results were obtained when a group of people who were guessed to be salt-sensitive, because their parents were known to have high blood pressure, were compared with a group of people who were guessed to be unlikely to be salt-sensitive, because their parents were known definitely not to have high blood pressure.

The salt-sensitive group showed good reductions of blood pressure when they cut the salt in their diet.

Should you cut down on salt?

If you are salt-sensitive, cutting down on salt may reduce your risk of developing high blood pressure.

Eating less salt may reduce the risks of getting high blood pressure – a preventative measure.

It would be very important to do this if you are salt-sensitive and cannot get rid of excess sodium in your blood. However, you can't tell for sure if you are one of the lucky ones who can cope with a high salt diet. So if everyone cuts down on salt, some people will have changed their diet without really needing to.

Unfortunately the stakes in this risk-taking are too high to think of it as a game. Who wants to risk taking twenty years off their life – which is what eating a high salt diet might do if you *are* salt-sensitive.

However, if you do take the risk, regular blood pressure checks, to detect the early stages of raised blood pressure, will become even more important.

How could you decide?

What you decide to do will depend on:
● what you know of the medical risks
● what your attitude to risk-taking is.

It may also depend on how easy you think it is to make the change. How to make the change is followed up in *'Making changes'*. Most people who decide to cut down find it fairly easy to do so.

Your risk factors

It would be possible to draw up, from a medical point of view, a list of priorities for what's worth worrying about.

It seems sensible to think first about the 'biggest' killer – coronary heart disease and strokes.

Risk factors are the physical conditions or life habits that are believed to increase one's risk of developing certain diseases. The three big ones are:

Smoking   linked with lung cancer, certain other cancers, chronic bronchitis and coronary heart disease – particularly heart attacks.

High blood pressure   linked with kidney failure, but particularly with coronary heart disease and strokes.

High level of blood cholesterol   caused in part by high level of animal fats in the diet and linked with coronary heart disease and strokes.

'Smoking' and 'high blood pressure' together are particularly risky.

Giving up smoking is probably the most important single change you could make because it is linked to other diseases, particularly cancer, as well.

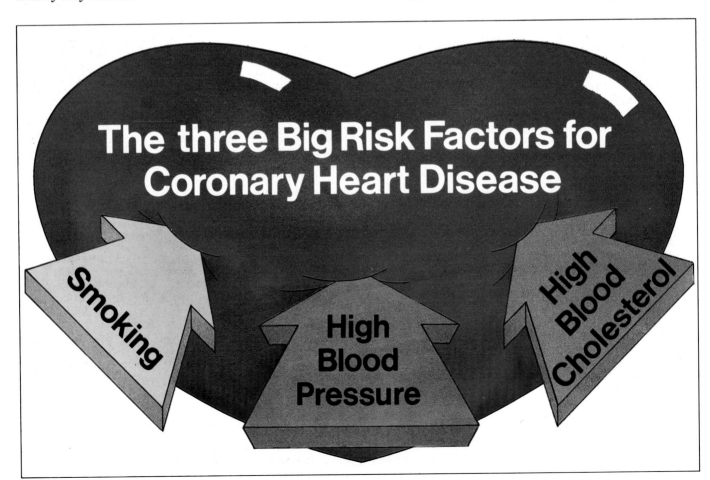

The three Big Risk Factors for Coronary Heart Disease

Smoking

High Blood Pressure

High Blood Cholesterol

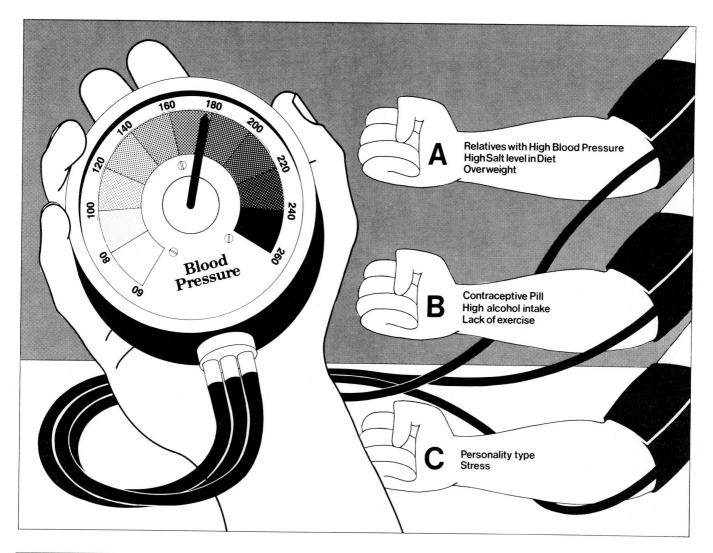

High blood pressure

High blood pressure – the focus of this chapter – in turn has risk factors linked with it which make a person more likely to develop it. Exactly how these risk factors lead to the development of high blood pressure is not yet fully understood. They can be put into three groups:

A Those about which there is general agreement and which many people have.

B Those about which there is general agreement, but not many people have.

C Those for which there is little hard scientific evidence, but which many experts suspect some link will be established. These affect many people.

These links are shown – in a simple way – in the diagram above. Other cross-links and possible additional links could be shown. But it's important to concentrate on the main links first.

Group A. These are important risk factors. There is an inherited tendency to develop high blood pressure and you can't do anything about that. However, at least it gives you advance warning that you are one of the people for whom it is particularly important to cut down salt and keep your weight down.

Overweight, particularly where this is linked with lack of exercise, increases your risk. Getting your weight down can make your life better in many ways – you feel more energetic, it's easier to join in physical activities, and your joints aren't being damaged by an excess load.

Group B. The contraceptive pill may raise your blood pressure, but once you come off the pill your blood pressure should drop. Women who already have a higher risk because they have the other risk factors may want to think particularly carefully about using the pill. But, of course, most women regard an unwanted pregnancy as a risk they don't want to take.

If you are on the pill get your blood pressure checked regularly. You may also decide to pay particular attention to getting your other risk factors down. It's the combination of smoking and taking the pill that seriously increases the risks.

As regards 'high alcohol intake', you do not have to be an alcoholic to be at risk. Drinking in moderation is thought to be O.K. This is generally taken to mean, for a man, half a bottle of wine and two pints of beer a day. Women seem to be slightly more easily harmed by alcohol so they should set a lower limit.

Group C. Stress and personality type are difficult to measure in any really scientific way.

You may hear high blood pressure called hypertension. It's not a good term since it suggests to many people that it's caused by high tension or stress.

Everyone needs some stress to keep them stimulated. Some people thrive on stress. Most people could easily learn to cope with the stress in life. Problems seem to be more likely to arise when the type of stress and their type of personality lead a person to feel almost permanently discouraged with little or no hope for the future.

Some people would argue that telling people about risk factors increases the stress in their life. How do you feel about 'ignorance is bliss'? Would you rather not know or would you prefer to know so that you can plan how to reduce your risks?

How worried are you?

How worried are you when you look at the evidence that links a high salt diet with an increased risk of developing high blood pressure?

Your worries

It's possible to give yourself a 'worry rating' to get a picture of how concerned you are over the risk factors that apply to you.

Filling in the chart opposite will help you work out how worried you really are. The previous 'Risk factors' section should have helped you work out the risks you face. Logically, the more risk factors that apply to you, the higher your worries might be expected to be. But this isn't always so.

Who worries about what?

Some people worry a great deal about certain risk factors and yet ignore other risk factors that their doctors consider they should be worried about. They may be particularly worried about something they have seen someone close to them experience. Or about something that seems especially tragic or painful. Or risk factors may be such a part of what they think is their 'normal' life that they couldn't imagine being able to make a significant change.

A third group seems to worry about everything, sometimes even give the impression they need to have something to worry about. Their worries often swamp them because they don't know what they can do about them. Our aim is to help people make their own decisions, but always to offer practical help as to how such changes can be made.

Working out your 'worry rating'

Look at each square on the game board opposite. If you think the risk factor applies to you put a tick. For each risk factor you tick score your worry rating as shown.

Consider Part 1 first. If you tick smoking then, realistically, you should tackle this first as it is so important. If you don't score three for this think carefully about why you feel you don't 'believe' the evidence or why you feel you will be the 'lucky' one who can get away with it.

Part 2. Where you score a high 'worry rating' it will be important to find out more about that particular risk factor to help you decide what to do about it. Your first step could be to discuss this with your doctor. In some cases you may find that you do not need to be so concerned. In others finding out more will help you plan a course of action that will help reduce both your worries and your risks.

In this section we follow up only the high salt factor.

What do you now want to do?

Your worry rating scores and the comments about risk factors should help you decide what, if anything, you want to do.

Certainly the easiest change for many people to bring about is to reduce salt intake. If you do happen to be susceptible to salt it's an insurance policy. If you aren't then you won't have done any harm and you'll soon have a greater taste for the actual flavours of foods. If you are high risk for other factors, then cutting down your salt isn't the only way of lessening risk.

Sum up how you feel

Looking back through the topic and how you filled in the chart, try to write down how you feel about these risks and what you would like to do about them – particularly about the salt in your diet.

Here's how Viv and Hugh viewed the topic and the action they decided to take.

Viv is fairly fit as she cycles to the school where she works three miles away. She's not overweight and she doesn't smoke. The only risk factors which Viv ticked were the family history one (her mother is being treated for high blood pressure) and eating plenty of salt. Viv is concerned about her health and worried about getting high blood pressure. She'd scored both ticks at three, and reading the comments only confirmed her concern. Viv decided that she'd make a big effort to gradually decrease the amount of salt she uses at the table and also in cooking for her family. She also decided to try to find out more about how much salt the processed foods she buys contains – so that she can cut down there as well.

Hugh is 50. At a recent check-up his doctor told him he had high blood pressure and started him on drugs for it. Hugh is nearly a stone overweight, smokes five cigarettes a day and loves salt on his food. Hugh scored smoking and overweight at 2 and salt intake at 0. He's prepared to try and give up smoking, and to try and lose the stone in weight. However, as he pointed out *"I'd like the food I do eat to be tasty and I'm just not prepared to give up salt. I'm not particularly bothered by the risk involved"*.

Where do you stand? Look at the following comments and see which are closest to your own reactions to this topic.

- I'll definitely reduce the salt in my diet as much as possible. ☐
- I'd rather not be 'hung up' about what I eat, so won't change my current habits. ☐
- I'll think before I add salt to my meals. ☐
- I don't feel my current intake of salt is a risk to my health. ☐
- I'm more worried about other risk factors than salt intake. ☐
- I'll work on the other risk factors rather than salt. ☐
- I ought to change, but I really don't think I could. ☐
- I think I'll try to lessen each risk factor I've ticked just a small amount. ☐

If you decide any risks you are taking worry you, then write down what you are going to try and achieve and come back to your chart occasionally to check how you're getting on.

If your chart shows you to be taking serious risks and you aren't concerned then presumably you think one of the following:

- It won't happen to me (**it might!**)
- It may happen to me and I am prepared to take the consequences (**are you?**)

You may find it helpful to read the section 'Who worries about what?' again.

PART 1 START HERE

CORONARY HEART DISEASE RISK FACTOR
SMOKING

If you smoke this is probably the most important change to make.

Applies to me ☐ Worry rating ☐

CORONARY HEART DISEASE RISK FACTOR
HIGH BLOOD PRESSURE

If you have high blood pressure follow medical advice. All other risk factors become more important.

Applies to me ☐ Worry rating ☐

CORONARY HEART DISEASE RISK FACTOR
HIGH CHOLESTEROL LEVEL

You may not know your cholesterol level. A diet high in fats from dairy products and meat makes high levels more likely.

Applies to me ☐ Worry rating ☐

TOTAL WORRY RATING

 A FACTORS   **B** FACTORS   **C** FACTORS

☐ ☐ ☐

TOTAL FOR **C** FACTORS ☐

 C FACTOR HIGH BLOOD PRESSURE
PERSONALITY TYPE

Hard, pushy, time-watching, aggressive personality.

Applies to me ☐ Worry rating ☐

 C FACTOR HIGH BLOOD PRESSURE
STRESS

Continuous high everyday stress.

Applies to me ☐ Worry rating ☐

TOTAL FOR **B** FACTORS ☐

 B FACTOR HIGH BLOOD PRESSURE
HIGH ALCOHOL INTAKE

Applies to me ☐ Worry rating ☐

 B FACTOR HIGH BLOOD PRESSURE
CONTRACEPTIVE PILL

Particularly important if you are over 35 and/or you smoke.

Applies to me ☐ Worry rating ☐

 B FACTOR HIGH BLOOD PRESSURE
DIABETES

All other risk factors become more important.

Applies to me ☐ Worry rating ☐

SCORING YOUR WORRY RATING

0 No concern at all.

1 Occasional concern (i e when you read a newspaper article or see a T V programme about this issue).

2 Moderate concern, think it might be a good idea to do something about it.

3 Frequent concern, worry and think about it a lot.

PART START 2 HERE

 A FACTOR HIGH BLOOD PRESSURE
RELATIVES WITH HIGH BLOOD PRESSURE

Can't alter this. But if 'Yes' other factors, particularly salt, are important.

Applies to me ☐ Worry rating ☐

 A FACTOR HIGH BLOOD PRESSURE
HIGH SALT LEVEL IN DIET

You can make a difference by changing – read the rest of this chapter.

Applies to me ☐ Worry rating ☐

 A FACTOR HIGH BLOOD PRESSURE
OVERWEIGHT

Particularly important if due to diet high in animal fats.

Applies to me ☐ Worry rating ☐

 A FACTOR HIGH BLOOD PRESSURE
LACK OF EXERCISE

Important if also overweight.

Applies to me ☐ Worry rating ☐

TOTAL FOR **A** FACTORS ☐

Where's the salt?

You add salt at the table and in the kitchen. But some foods are naturally salty or have salt already added.

It's reckoned that most of us get through the equivalent of one and three quarter teaspoonfuls (nine grams) of salt a day one way or another.

The average man has been shown to have a higher average daily intake than the average women. This doesn't seem to be because men prefer saltier food! It's more likely to be because the average man weighs more than the average woman. In general a larger body needs more food to keep it going. Since so many foods contain salt, the more food you eat the higher your salt intake.

The NACNE report recommends that everyone, regardless of sex and weight, should cut down by three grams a day. In some ways this is the simplest, general recommendation to make.

But this is not particularly helpful to the individual trying to decide what is best for him or her to do.

An adult actually needs less than half a gram of salt a day. This small amount is vital for the proper functioning of the body. In particular, the beating of the heart and the passage of signals along the nerves depend on it.

We suggest that to make working things out easier you check how you measure up against a goal of six grams a day. (The World Health Organisation (WHO) has been suggesting a goal of five grams since 1982 – so the NACNE report should not have come as a surprise.)

A target of six grams a day would allow you the equivalent of one and a quarter teaspoonfuls of salt.

The salt in your diet

This topic will help you get a rough idea of how much salt you do eat.

It's the sodium in the salt – and other sodium-containing substances – that can be bad for you. Watch out when reading articles about diet and check whether they are talking about the amount of salt or the amount of sodium. One and a quarter teaspoonfuls of salt (six grams) contains 2.4 grams (= 2,400 milligrams) of sodium.

Tables showing milligrams of sodium are really only useful for comparing the amounts of sodium in different foods. (*The Salt Counter*, by Michael Wright [*Pan*], gives full lists.) It isn't necessary for healthy adults to keep such a close watch on their diet since it doesn't matter if you cut down well below the goal of six grams of salt (2,400 milligrams of sodium). But some people, particularly those with kidney problems, may be recommended to count milligrams of sodium – a tedious job.

Nearly all the sodium we consume comes from the food we eat. There are four main sources of it in our diet:
● Salt added to foods at the table.
● Salt added to foods during preparation or cooking at home.
● Salt and other sodium containing substances added to foods processed by manufacturers.
● Naturally salty foods. Many foods naturally contain salt. There is more salt in foods of animal origin than of plant origin. Shellfish are particularly high in salt because they live in sea water.

Where else? Less than 1% of our average daily intake of salt comes from drinking water. A number of medicines either prescribed or bought over the counter contain sodium, although these are unlikely to add much to the daily intake. However, the regular use of some non-prescription drugs such as antacids, laxatives and health salts based on sodium salts, could result in a moderate increase in sodium intake. Some health shops even sell salt tablets.

Adding salt at the table

Even when we eat food chosen and prepared for us by others we do have control over how much salt we add. But how often is the decision a conscious one? How many of us automatically add salt to a meal without tasting it first? (One in three of our testers did!)

A study of people's salting habits found out that 60 out of every 100 people added salt to their meals, and of these 60 only about 15 tasted their food first. Watch for a few days, at home and when you eat out. Watch people trailing round a canteen looking for a full salt cellar. Are the people you watched similar to those in the survey?

The same study found that more salt was added when people were presented with a salt sachet, less from a shaker on a table, and less when it's only available from a shaker at the serving counter. The study also found the amount of salt added was directly related to the size of the hole in the shaker. Furthermore, if people found the shaker's hole too small they tried to make the hole larger with sharp instruments such as forks.

The paper plate activity

How much salt do you add to your food? The next time or few times you sit down for a meal, cover the meal with a paper plate the same size, or better still an ovenproof glass or transparent plastic plate so you can see the meal. Sprinkle your normal amount of salt for that meal on the plate and then check it and measure it on a teaspoon. If you use about an eighth of a teaspoon that's more than most adults actually need in an entire day to stay healthy.

If you do this for each meal in the day you can get a rough idea of how much salt you add to the food on your plate in a day. Another way to check would be to keep a salt cellar for your own use. Weigh it one Sunday morning and then reweigh it the next Sunday morning to find out how much you've used during the week. Divide your answer by seven to find how much salt you add *in your own home* to your meals each day.

By the way – do you find you add more salt to some foods than others? Most of our testers said boiled eggs and chips.

Adding salt during cooking and preparation

Salt is commonly added to many different foods when they are cooked or prepared at home. Sometimes it plays a crucial part in a recipe, such as in pickling, or when it's added to vegetables before cooking to create a certain flavour. Most people add it to vegetables during cooking rather than after so that it blends better with the other flavours. Incidentally, when it's added to vegetables in cooking, as well

as increasing the sodium content of them, it also removes a lot of the potassium which naturally occurs in vegetables.

Sometimes salt is supposed to affect the quality and texture of the finished products such as cakes and bread. Some home economist teachers still teach children that added salt improves all baked foods!

The 'salt in the hand' activity

Instead of adding salt directly to the food you are cooking and guessing the amount – as 50% of our testers did – pour it into your hand to see just how much you are adding, then measure it. You may be surprised by how much salt you are adding.

Also check on how much you add when a recipe says that a certain amount of salt should be added. In fact, the addition of salt is usually optional anyway. But when an amount is specified, or a pinch of salt suggested how often do you just guess and shake salt directly in the bowl or pan? Shake the same amount onto your hand and see just how much it is.

Unless you cook all your own meals it's difficult to estimate just how much salt in your diet is added at the cooking stage.

Sodium in manufactured foods

Salt and other sodium-containing chemicals are added to many foods during processing and manufacturing. Recent findings suggest that

additions provide most of us with something like 70-80% of our sodium intake. So most of us can't cut down enough on salt just by avoiding adding salt at the table or in cooking. We also need to look carefully at the salt in processed foods.

Salt and other sodium compounds are added for a variety of reasons which we examine in another topic. Whatever the reasons, processing may increase sodium content enormously.

Look at the label

In Britain it's usually difficult to work out how much sodium foods contain. It's rare to find any information on salt or sodium content.

On most foods the label just gives a list of ingredients. Some don't have any information at all. Ingredients are listed according to their weight in the product recipe from most to least.

Listing by weight makes salt come well down on the list. This can give quite the wrong impression even when the actual weights are given.

You don't, for example, ever need to compare the weight of salt with the weight of fat in a food.

You do need to have some idea of how much of your desired total salt intake that food will provide. Ideally for those who want to keep a careful check the label should state the amount by weight of salt or sodium in 100 grams *or* in a typical serving (which should be defined). At the very least it would be helpful to know if experts would rate the food as high, medium or low in salt.

However, the government does not

seem to be considering making it compulsory for food labels to give this information. (Most American and some European products do give this information.)

Check how many items in your kitchen cupboards are labelled as containing sodium. It should start to give you some idea of how difficult it is to avoid sodium. Do any give the exact amount?

Any ingredient which includes the word soda, sodium or the chemical symbol Na contains sodium.

The following list is a start:

Salt, baking powder, baking soda, brine, soy sauce, monosodium glutamate, bicarbonate of soda, sodium benzoate, sodium bicarbonate, sodium sulphite, sodium hydroxide, sodium cyclamate, sodium alginate, sodium propionate.

Look out too for words such as 'in brine', cured, smoked, kippered or self-raising.

Eating naturally salty foods

If you have a highly developed taste for salt and like it on your food, you'll probably also like naturally salty foods. Buying and eating these is entirely a matter of choice. It is an area where we do have control. The chart in the next topic will help you become more aware of what counts as high salt food. It lists both naturally salty and processed foods which are high in sodium.

Some of our testers felt quite depressed when they first saw it. Many of the high items surprised them. However we have not given you this chart to make you feel there's hardly anything you can eat. You don't have to cut out salt – only cut down. The chart is only to help you become more aware of which foods have high levels. When you choose to eat them just keep a closer check on the other food you eat that day.

You will also see, later, that you can use the chart to lead you to find lower sodium alternatives for the items that do worry you.

Examining the chart will also help you see why the NACNE report considered that setting an even lower goal would seriously upset the food industry.

Sea Salt tastes different. It's not as highly purified as ordinary salt and does contain traces of other minerals. Choose it if you prefer the taste, but remember there is nothing healthy about it. You will still need to keep a check that you are not eating too much of it.

Making changes

If you decide to cut down it's much easier to reduce your salt intake gradually. You won't notice small changes so much.

Remember you weren't born with a preference for salt. You learned it and you *can* unlearn it. Foods may seem slightly bland to begin with, but you'll probably find your taste will soon adjust. You may even find yourself wondering why you used to eat such salty food before.

How easy you find some of these is going to depend on your way of life; for instance, it will make a difference whether you shop and cook for yourself.

You could take one step at a time. Steps 1 and 2 may be the easiest to make, but you will certainly need to move on to step 3. Most of our testers thought that step 4 would be easy and enjoyable.

Step 1 – Less salt at the table

Because you control it, it's probably easiest to reduce the amount of salt you use at the table.

● Always taste your food before you salt it.
● Try one shake of salt cellar instead of two.
● Keep your salt shaker in the cupboard. Then you'll have to take an active decision to get up and get it.
● If you are eating out and are given a sachet of salt be careful. Perhaps pour a little of it onto your hand before you add it to your food.

If you eat with family or friends, remember they may not wish to reduce their salt intake, so banning the salt cellar from the table may provoke angry scenes!

Help yourself

Use things other than salt to go with your food.

● There are commercial salt substitutes, usually potassium chloride. Not everyone thinks these are adequate substitutes. Some people find them bitter. Anyone with a heart or kidney condition should seek their doctor's advice before switching to salt-substitutes – as they can be dangerous in these circumstances.
● Be careful about switching to commercial sauces, pickles and relishes. You may find by doing this you are adding as much salt as ever and in some cases things such as sugar.
● Use herbs and spices to give extra flavour. You can add them to vegetables, casseroles and salads and salad dressings. For example: mint or dill when boiling peas and beans; oregano and basil with tomato dishes; parsley and chives for decorating and flavouring many dishes.

Step 2 – Less salt in the kitchen

● Reduce the amount of salt you add when cooking rice, cereals, pasta, noodles, potatoes and other vegetables. Use the 'salt in the hand' activity from 'Where's the salt?' to monitor your progress. Remember too, if you use vegetable water to make your gravy, that the less salt there is in that the less salt there'll be in the gravy.
● Cut down the salt in recipes you use frequently until you've got it down to half or less. Look for recipes with little salt, or use half what a new recipe suggests and see if the result is acceptable.
● Think about how much sodium the individual ingredients in a recipe already contain. You may not need to add any salt if you're using smoked or cured fish or meat, dehydrated or canned soup, cheese or canned vegetables.
● Think about sodium when you're planning meals. If you have a high sodium food, choose a low sodium food to go with it. If you plan a high sodium meal make the rest of the meals that day low in sodium.

Don't go overboard with salt reduction if you cook for others. Suddenly cutting out salt could have them all reaching for the salt cellar.

Step 3 – Eat less of high sodium foods

This activity will help you decide which of these high sodium foods:

- You wouldn't dream of giving up.
- You could easily cut down.
- You would like to find low sodium alternatives for.

First look through the table and make your own list of high sodium foods which you eat at least once a month. Underline the ones that are very high.

Don't worry about items like the lobster you eat once a year – you should be so lucky! Nor the black pudding you only eat when visiting your parents.

Next go through your own list and cross out any food you could easily give up.

Find your favourites. Make a – hopefully short – list of your favourite salty foods. Remind yourself that you do *not* have to give these up. Enjoy them when you eat them. Just cut right down on other salt the days you eat them.

Finally from your first list make a new list of foods that you eat most days. Our testers' lists had bread, biscuits and breakfast cereals; butter and margarine; and various salty flavourings eg. stock cubes, Marmite, Bovril and soya sauce.

For some items on this list, particularly bread, their fibre makes them important to your healthy diet. So, unless you bake your own bread – and

most of our testers just couldn't fit this into their busy lives – you have to count the salt in bread as part of your inevitable daily intake. Incidentally the Health Education Council is putting pressure on bakers to provide a lower salt loaf. So keep an eye open – in case they succeed.

Most breakfast cereals contain moderate to high amounts of added salt. Our testers found three – Puffed Wheat, Shredded Wheat and Mini-Wheats – that don't have added salt. Other manufacturers are likely to cut down over the next few years.

If you find you frequently use tinned vegetables you can look out for the Del Monte 'no salt added' range or switch to frozen vegetables which contain very little.

Most of our testers said they had to use processed rather than fresh vegetables on many occasions – so this can be a real problem.

High sodium foods (over 250 mg per 100 g of food). Those set in bold are very high in salt (over 1000 mg per 100 g of food)

Vegetables

Baked beans (in sauce), Dahl, Tinned carrots, Tinned peas, Tinned new potatoes, Crisps, Tinned sweetcorn, **Instant potato** (before cooking).

Dairy products, oils, egg and cheese dishes

Dried milk, Butter (salted), Cheddar type, Edam type, Parmesan, Cottage cheese, Cream cheese, Cheese pudding, Cheese soufflé, Macaroni cheese, Pizza, Quiche, Scotch egg, Low fat spread, Margarine, **Camembert, Danish blue type, Stilton, Processed cheese, Cheese spread, Omelettes, Scrambled egg, Welsh rarebit.**

Nuts

Salted peanuts, Peanut butter.

Beverages, juices, alcoholic drinks

Cocoa powder, Horlicks, Rosehip Syrup.

Fish, shellfish

Dried salt cod, Bloater, Kipper, Pilchards (tinned), Salmon (tinned), Sardines (tinned), Tuna (tinned), Crab, Lobster, Scampi, Whelks, Tinned crab, Fish cakes and fingers, Fish paste, Kedgeree, **Smoked cod, Smoked haddock, Smoked salmon, Prawns, Shrimps, Cockles, Winkles.**

Fruit

Olives in brine.

Sugars, preserves, confectionery

Golden syrup, Toffees.

Adapted from Selora chart

Meat and meat products, poultry, game

Tinned minced beef, Silverside (salted), Tinned stewing steak, Tinned lamb, Stew, Kidney (fried or stewed), Chicken liver (cooked), Corned beef, Stewed steak in gravy, Faggots, Haggis, Liver sausage, Frankfurters, Beefburgers, Brawn, Meat paste, Cornish pasties, Pork pie, Sausage roll, Steak and kidney pie, Beef steak pudding, Beef stew, Bolognese sauce, Curried meat, Hotpot, Irish stew, Moussaka, Shepherd's pie, **Bacon, Gammon, Ox tongue (cooked), Ham, Luncheon meat, Chopped pork, Tongue, Jellied veal, Black pudding, Salami, Beef sausages, Pork sausages.**

Sauces, pickles, soups

Brown sauce (bottled), Cheese sauce, French dressing, Mayonnaise, Onion sauce, Salad cream, Tomato sauce, Tomato purée, Savoury white sauce, Cream of chicken soup, Chicken noodle soup, Minestrone soup, Cream of mushroom, Oxtail, Tomato soup, Vegetable soup, Curry powder, **Piccalilli, Sweet pickle, Tomato ketchup, Baking powder, Bovril, Marmite, Oxo cubes, Salt.**

Cereals, biscuits, cakes, puddings

Custard powder, Self-raising flour, Porridge, Spaghetti (tinned in sauce), Bread (all), Special K, Weetabix, Cream crackers, Wheat crispbread, Digestive, Ginger nuts, Sweet biscuits, Shortbread, Water biscuits, Madeira cake, Rock cake, Sponge cake, Pastry, Scones, Scotch pancakes, Cheesecake, Dumplings, Sponge pudding, Suet pudding, Yorkshire pudding, **All-bran, Cornflakes, Rice Krispies, Oatcakes.**

Step 4 – Balancing sodium with potassium

It has been suggested that the balance between sodium and potassium in the body may be what affects blood pressure, rather than just the amount of sodium.

So, as well as reducing your sodium intake, you might like to increase your potassium intake. Fruit and vegetables are particularly high in potassium. If the sodium-potassium balance is important then eating a couple of the following each day will enhance the effect of cutting back on salt.

Potassium rich foods

Apples	Beans
Apricots	Brussels Sprouts
Bananas	Cabbage
(very high)	
Dates	Corn on the Cob
Grapefruits	Peas
Oranges	Peppers
Prunes	Potatoes
	(very high)
Raisins	Radishes

Remember that boiling vegetables in salt water reduces their potassium content.

The COMA Report on *Diet and Cardiovascular Disease* (1984) recommends that doctors should encourage their patients who take certain types of diuretic tablets to make sure they eat enough potassium rich foods. Diuretics (sometimes called water tablets) help the body get rid of excess water. In doing this the body also loses sodium and potassium.

If you take diuretics discuss this with your doctor. Two commonly prescribed diuretics are Lasix and Aprinox.

What you buy

You do have some choice. With the increasing awareness of the need to cut down on salt a wider choice of less salty foods should become available.

Choosing a meal

Many of us eat out on special occasions and as part of our regular routine. Then we have even less control over the sodium content of our food. When you are eating out for a special occasion you'll probably decide there are more important things than thinking about salt! But it's the more everyday food you eat out that can be very salty and offers you very little choice.

Look now at the following list and by the side of it put how many times you have eaten in any of these places in the past seven days.

School/work/institutional canteen_____

Coffee bar _____

Fast food chain (eg. Wimpey, MacDonald's) _____

Takeaway (eg. fish 'n' chips, Chinese)_____

Sit down restaurant _____

Public house_____

Wine bar _____

● The salt content of food often varies from dish to dish, so choosing between different items available on the menu allows you some control over the sodium intake.
● As well as differences between dishes, there are large differences in the sodium content of food from different places. A 'fast food' cheeseburger with processed cheese, relishes, and pre-salted chips will contain much more sodium than fried haddock and chips with vinegar but no salt.
● Some restaurants by the nature of their cooking style provide very high sodium food – for instance, a Chinese meal may contain 12 grams of salt and Japanese food may be even saltier.

Now think of one of the meals you've eaten recently when you've been out. Use the sodium content chart in *'Making changes'* to work out whether it was a high sodium meal or not.

Do you think the meal you've just thought about is typical of your eating out patterns? Think about some of the other meals you've eaten out recently. Do you tend to eat out where you are likely to get food which has a high sodium content?

Consumer action. Tell the manager if you decide not to go back to a place because the food is so salty. But check out occasionally because new management, customer pressure and so on can all lead to changes in catering facilities.

It's more difficult if it's a place, like a works canteen, where you have to eat. You could try forming an action group to persuade them to provide options on the menu where no extra salt has been added.

In pubs most of the snacks are salty. This suits the publican because they give you a thirst. But ask if they can also stock, for example, mixed nuts and raisins or unsalted peanuts.

A checklist for eating out

● Check the menu to see if some dishes are less salty.
● If you can't tell, ask serving staff whether salt is added or whether they use processed goods with added salt. If the serving staff don't know check with the management or the cook.
● Choose a dish that isn't prepared in advance and ask if they will cook your portion without added salt.
● Ask them to put gravy or sauces on one side of the plate. Then you can check how salty it is before it covers your food.

Finally you have the option to take your own food. A picnic for a family outing rather than eating at a hamburger fast-food place. A packed lunch to work – and be prepared to fight for the right to eat your own food in the canteen.

Cost and effort

Cutting down on salt may mean more work for you. Many people end up eating quite high sodium foods because they're easier to obtain. Processed foods in particular often need little preparation and keep for a long time. Buying fresh food and doing home cooking can be more expensive and time consuming.

Buying salt-free food may be more expensive too, until manufacturers are persuaded to use less sodium. But if

enough people buy it when it is a little more expensive, the price will come down, because manufacturers, realising there is a market, will compete with each other.

Buy lower sodium alternatives

This chart should help you start thinking about switching to lower sodium alternatives. Remember it is the sodium in the salt that is harmful. In this table the sodium content of 100 grams (g) of the food is given in milligrams (mg). The NACNE report target would be no more than 2,400 mg sodium a day.

The figures are given to help you see the substantial savings you can make in many cases by switching to lower sodium alternatives. In other cases, eg., pickles and stock cubes, they should serve to remind you to use only small quantities of them.

Compare the items across the columns.

When you use the table remember that some food isn't readily available or is expensive. These are marked on the table.

Expensive and at present only from health food shops.
**All breads should count as high — but you've little choice. Hopefully pressure on the bakers will lead to them cutting down on salt.*

***Remember, most people eat smaller quantities of the strongly flavoured cheeses. So if you are comparing the size portions you eat you might find you were only eating 20 grams of Danish Blue (=284 mg Sodium) but 100 grams of Cottage Cheese (=430 mg Sodium).*

Where do you shop?

Where you shop may affect how much salt you eat in your diet.

Where do you buy your food from? Think about the shopping you've done for food in the past seven days and make a note of:

- which shops
- how often
- which factors affect what they sell.

Consider how many customers the different types of shops have. Can they shift the fresh fruit and vegetables fast enough to make it worthwhile to stock such perishable food? How much freezer space do they have? Or do they mainly stock tinned and packaged foods?

It may not be the range of food they offer which determines whether you shop there. How easy is it to reach them? When are they open?

Here's what one of our testers said about the shops:

Corner shop *"I usually pop in about twice a week. It's cramped and has only got a tiny freezer. Most of the stuff is tinned — I know it's got a lot of salt in it, but I'm often in a hurry and it's very handy."*

Local small supermarket *"Has quite nice fruit and vegetables — I don't add salt when I cook them now. It always has the same kind of things — nothing special."*

Large supermarket (in nearby town) *"I go here once a week when my husband can take me. It's crowded there and I can't buy — they won't keep — enough fruit and vegetables for the week. They do have a wide range, though, and their own stuff is always a bit cheaper. They do have some 'no salt added' tins of vegetables."*

Switch to lower sodium alternatives.
The figures are averages for that kind of food unless a particular brand name is given.

Higher		Lower
Salted butter 870	All margarines 800 / Low-fat spread 690	Unsalted butter 7 / Vitaquell margarine* 2.4
Crumpets Mother's Pride 820	Hovis 580	White and Wholemeal bread** 540 (still high)
Danish blue cheese*** 1,420	Cheddar type cheeses 610	Cottage cheese 430
Potato crisps 550	Instant potato (made up as directed) 260	Boiled potatoes 3
All Bran 1,530	Cornflakes 1,160	Ready Brek (Instant porridge) 23 / Shredded Wheat 8
Canned garden peas (drained) 230	Peas (frozen and uncooked) 3	Peas (fresh and uncooked) 1
Sweet pickle (Commercial brand) 1,700	Pickled onions (Haywards) 700	Homemade tomato chutney 130
Bacon (back, fried) 1,910	Ham (tinned) 1,250	Pork (lean) 76
Kippers (baked) 990	Pilchards (tinned in tomato sauce) 370	Mackerel (fresh) 130
Fish cakes (frozen) 480	Fish fingers (frozen) 320	Cod (fresh fillets) 77
Beefburgers (cooked) 880	Stewed steak with gravy (canned) 380	Lean beef 61
Roast, salted peanuts 440	Peanut butter 350	Peanuts (raw) 6
Bovril stock cube, 12,400	Oxo cube (beef) 10,300	Bovril (undiluted) 4,800 / Natex (undiluted) 388
Salt 38,850	Typical low sodium salt substitute 19,415	Soy sauce 7,340

55

Changing the food industry

The pressures are building up. The American food industry has shown that it can be done. With more consumer demand our manufacturers could at the very least provide us with more choice.

Home use: commercial use

Salt (sodium chloride) is used in industrial food processing partly for the same reasons that it is used in the home.

- It contributes to the taste of food and enhances the flavour.
- It acts as a preservative, where it slows down or prevents the growth of undesirable micro-organisms.
- If a certain concentration of salt is added it helps desirable processes, such as fermentation.
- Other sodium-containing chemicals are also used. Sodium bicarbonate is a raising agent. Sodium benzoate and sodium nitrate are preservatives. Monosodium glutamate is a flavour enhancer. Sodium nitrate regulates how acidic a food is. Vitamin C is often added to foods as sodium ascorbate.

The processing methods were developed before high levels of salt were thought to be potentially dangerous. Present processing methods are geared up to use salt, but they could be changed.

Condiments

Salt is often used as a preservative and to improve the texture and taste in condiments such as sauces, dips, salad dressing and mustard. Pickles are by their very nature often a salty garnish to what otherwise may be a dull dish. Almost all cultures have traditional pickle recipes. People take their recipes with them when they move around the world. Were certain types of pickles an important part of your early family life? Do you still make homemade pickles? If so, check the recipes for how much salt they use. You could probably cut down the amount of salt, particularly if you keep the jar in the fridge once opened.

Shop bought pickles are often so salty that you may find them unacceptable once you've begun to cut down on salt. Perhaps you could experiment with other, newer types of pickles and sauces that are coming into the shop.

'Life' brand, low sodium foods available in health shops include Tomato Ketchup, Brown Sauce, Worcester Sauce and Mustard. 'Natex' makes a low-salt Yeast Extract (1000 mg sodium per 100 g). Check with a health food shop for other low-salt alternatives.

Tinned vegetables

Salt has been traditionally used for pickling. In addition, many tinned vegetables are in a salt solution, which is intended to be discarded. Some processing methods may also involve salt: for instance, peas are sorted by floating in brine before canning.

Del Monte now produce 'no salt added' tinned peas, carrots, green beans and sweet corn. Some supermarkets now stock the range alongside their ordinary range. Keep a look out for them. At the moment they cost a few pence more, but provided enough people buy them now the 'own name brands' will also market them and this will probably bring the price down.

Bread and breakfast cereals

The bread situation is a disgrace. Pressure from the Health Education Council is being put on bakers to cut down the salt in bread.

In bread manufacture, salt improves the mixing of dough, and controls the fermentation rate of yeast to produce a uniform quality. But they should be able to overcome these problems in other ways.

Salt is commonly added to breakfast cereals to enhance their flavour. This is particularly true for bran-rich cereals. The NACNE report, whilst suggesting that people should eat more fibre, does not recommend *added* bran as a way of doing it. Wholegrain breakfast cereals with low or no added salt include Shredded Wheat, Puffed Wheat, Mini-wheats, Cubs and Ready Brek.

Dairy products

Salt is used as a preservative in butter – salted butter keeps twice or three times as long as unsalted butter.

Virtually all cheeses are high in

56

salt: it is used in the expulsion of whey, to develop a firm texture.

It also controls the rate of growth of cheese-making bacteria and inhibits the growth of unwanted micro-organisms. Blue cheeses are highly salted. This allows the growth of the blue salt-tolerant moulds, while inhibiting bacterial growth.

Processed cheese and cheese spreads contain sodium phosphate and sodium citrate to give texture and firmness, and to act as a preservative.

Meat products

Cured meats, such as bacon and ham, are very high in sodium. Salt, sodium nitrate and sodium phosphate flavour, colour and preserve the meat.

Salt is also used to bind smaller bits of meat into a large ham; it alters the protein structure and acts as a binding agent.

Sodium polyphosphates are used in hams and frozen poultry; they help water retention, and thus texture.

With canned or vacuum-packed meats, the absence of air allows the organisms responsible for the rare but dangerous disease botulism to grow. Using sodium-containing preservatives means that less heat is required for safe canning.

Fish

To flavour and preserve it, fish is treated in brine before smoking.

Sodium polyphosphates help the binding of small bits of fish into fish fingers and fish steaks – but not all fish fingers are made in this way.

Supposing they cut down ...

Generally, the salt content of processed foods has declined over recent years, but very slowly. However, in the USA where there is a more vocal consumer demand for low salt products a wider range is available. They are reaching a point where a 'no salt added' label is a positive selling point.

The main fear seems to be that consumers wouldn't like it – and sales would not be high enough for the products to be kept on the market.

Certainly cutting down on salt in sauces and pickles would require a major change in the recipe. Low salt versions do not taste the same. You could try some of the limited low/no salt products available. These are generally sold through health shops – which adds to their slightly cranky image. And they are on the shelves with products that no reputable nutritionist or health adviser would recommend. They should be available to all of us at our usual shops.

Some British manufacturers say that there is not enough evidence to link sodium with high blood pressure, and anyway a reduction in sodium intake would only be recommended for a minority. They say that picking out sodium on labelling suggests that it is more important or dangerous than other food components. And that it is difficult to measure the sodium content reliably in some foods; for

instance, how much salt sticks to a crisp? They also say the cost of voluntary labelling would cost 1% of the product price.

Consumer action

If you feel that your shopping choices and eating out choices do not provide you with enough choice for your preferred eating patterns you may want to take consumer action.

This would mean finding like-minded people who can work together to demonstrate there is a demand; communicating what you want and arguing your case.

For example, if everyone on your street reliably wanted fresh fruit and vegetables, the corner shop would stock them. If 'low salt' products were fast sellers in the supermarket, the management would keep stocking them. If a restaurant kept on being asked for low salt meals, they'd eventually provide them.

But often 'everyone' doesn't suddenly decide to demand a particular thing. However, a good many people may well buy it once it's there. If you want different things to be available in your local shops, or your work canteen, then it can be more effective to form a consumer action group to provide the appropriate pressure.

You may already belong to a group that has an interest in healthy eating. A group 'voice' is so much more powerful than the individual. Your group could make its opinion known to individual shop keepers, supermarket managers and food manufacturers – the address may be on the product or ask the shop manager. Ask them what the sodium content of their product is. Don't settle for it's 'low' or 'average' as an answer.

Ask, too, why sodium is essential in the manufacturing process. Forestall their answer of 'people like it that way' by pointing out that you are looking for alternatives to their products. You could also ask them what percentage of a person's daily limit of sodium is provided by a single average portion of their product. Working it out might make some manufacturers ashamed of themselves.

● **Your local MP.** Try asking a specific question like *"Is there any reason why a particular change could not be made?"* or *"What committees are considering certain topics and what are their recommendations likely to be?"* These types of questions mean he has to ask around to find the answer and may get him personally interested in the issue.

Finally make what you find out available to other people. Many groups have newsletters, and local papers are usually keen to report local consumer action.

A good start?

Do food manufacturers care more for your baby than you do? For most adults cutting down on salt certainly won't do any harm and may do some good. But it's important for all babies not to be given any extra salt.

Why babies don't need salt

There are three main reasons for this:
- Their kidneys can't cope with much salt before they are eight months old.
- Even when babies reach an age when their kidneys can cope with a little added salt it's not a good idea to give it to them. They have not acquired a taste for it at that age, there's no reason for you to add it – you won't be depriving them of something they like. It has been suggested that a high salt intake in infancy may lead to increased susceptibility to high blood pressure in later life. *But* the evidence for this is only from experiments on animals.
- We learn to like salt – particularly if we associate salty food with pleasant situations and rewards. So it helps not to teach babies and young children to like salty foods.

Can you remember?

When you were a young child do you remember particularly liking:
- putting the salt in the boiled egg?
- Marmite 'fingers' on toast?
- Twiglets?
- packets of salty snacks?

Marmite came top of our testers' fond memories. One man even told us of how he still likes the way the salt makes your lips tingle if it gets on them. Other testers mentioned hot buttered toast with Marmite to cheer themselves up when they come in cold on winter evenings.
Because we enjoyed them when we were little:
- It's difficult for us to cut down on salt now we are older.
- We are still tempted to have them if we want to give ourselves a little reward or if we are feeling a bit down.
- We expect our children to enjoy them too. As parents we want to be 'good' to our children in the same way as our parents were.

Commercial baby foods

The British Nutrition Foundation recommends that no sodium should be added to commercial baby foods, and recently the sodium content in some foods has indeed been cut back.

However, some parents taste these foods – find them too bland and then add a little salt to improve their flavour!

Milk

For babies. Cows' milk contains three times as much salt as human milk.

Babies' kidneys can cope with human milk, but unmodified cows' milk has too much sodium for them in the early months. Milk powders made especially for babies have had some of the sodium taken out. So provided you don't add an extra scoop to the bottle to make the milk look creamier, bottle-fed babies will not get too much sodium.

For adults. The table shows the sodium content for various milks. If dried and evaporated milks are mixed up with the recommended amount of water they have the same sodium content as fresh milk. The trouble is that they are often used straight in their concentrated form.

Some people add two or more teaspoonfuls of skimmed dried milk to a cup of coffee in order to make it look creamy. This adds at least 50 mg of sodium to the cup. A powdered vegetable fat milk-substitute adds less sodium, though the fats in it are no better than cream if you are anxious to cut down on saturated fats.

Evaporated milk is often poured on desserts as an alternative to cream. But it has more sodium than cream has. Natural yoghurt has less, so could be used as an alternative.

Sodium content in milligrams (mg) in 100 grams (g) of food	
Human milk (1 month after birth)	14 mg
Whole cows' milk	35-90 mg
Skimmed cows' milk	52 mg
Dried skimmed milk (powder)	550 mg
Evaporated milk, unsweetened	180 mg
Fresh single cream	42 mg
Vegetable fat milk-substitute	146 mg
Natural yoghurt	76 mg

Cut down on sugar?

• The NACNE report recommends that the amount of sugar in the average British diet should be reduced by 50%.

• Half the sugar in our diet comes from what we add ourselves in cooking or at the table. The other half is added by food manufacturers – mainly to cakes, biscuits, sweets and drinks. Today less packet sugar is being bought. But food manufacturers are adding more sugar to processed foods – mainly in the form of glucose syrups. A smaller amount, not included in the calculations, occurs naturally in milk, fruit and vegetables.

• The new target reduces the average amount of sugar to 20 kilograms a year. On a daily basis this would work out as eight and a half teaspoonfuls for an average man and seven and a half for an average woman.

• Half should be cut from our main meals and the other half from the sugary snacks so many of us enjoy.

• *"But sugar is good for you — it gives you energy."* So does everything else you eat! The trouble is that to an expert 'energy' just means Calories – and too many of these make you fat. However, to the ordinary person 'energy' suggests an image of being 'full of energy' – always on the go without getting tired. And it's this meaning that advertisers exploit.

What is sugar?

Our diet must provide the energy to make our bodies work.
Sugar provides energy – Calories – and nothing else.
That's why it is sometimes called an 'empty food'.

Does sugar give you energy?

Our diet must provide energy to make our bodies work. But what does the word 'energy' conjure up for you? Do you think of oil, coal and body fat and other forms of fuel or do you think of someone who looks full of zest and vitality? When you say "I haven't got the energy", you probably mean "I feel tired and I haven't got the will or the motivation". You will certainly not be having a shortage of body fuel, for even the slimmest person has some stores of energy – ie. body fat – somewhere about their person.

When nutritionists use the term 'energy', they mean fuel energy, not the feeling of vim and vigour. In this context all foods supply fuel energy. This energy is measured in units called Calories. The foods which supply most energy are those which are fattiest. A gram of fat provides nine Calories. A gram of protein, starch or sugar provides four Calories. The interesting thing about manufactured sugar is that it is about the only food that provides energy, ie. Calories *and nothing else*. That's why it is sometimes called an 'empty food'.

The sugars in natural foods do come wrapped up with minerals, vitamins, fibre and starch. You are unlikely to be eating too much if your only source of it is natural foods – fruit, vegetables and milk. When extracted and manufactured sugars are added to other foods in our diet then we often end up getting much more than we need.

What's in a name?

Sugar is a general term for several different things. Look at the different sugars in the picture below and make a note, with your reasons, of any which you think might be better for you.

White sugars. Chemically pure, no other nutrients apart from sucrose.
Brown sugars. Slightly less refined than white. Different, 'dirtier' flavour, minimal amounts of minerals and vitamins.
Honey. 20% water, 75% fructose and glucose, minimal amounts of minerals and vitamins.
Syrups, treacle, molasses. Concentrated solutions of sugar containing 70% water, some contain significant amounts of calcium and iron.
Glucose syrups. Combination of simple and more complex sugars made from starch and much used by the food manufacturing industry.

Many of our testers thought that brown sugar was better than white and that honey had something special about it.

The truth is that they are all sugars – offering nothing but empty Calories and the risk of dental decay. The amount of minerals and vitamins in some of them is so small that you would have to eat vast quantities of the sugar to get a reasonable amount.

Perhaps you tend to link brown sugar with wholemeal bread and goodness? And honey conjures up images of bees and flowers and some kind of magical ingredient promoted by 'health food' advertising.

From a nutritional point of view all sugars are the same. But do you like the taste of some of them better? Or do they remind you of happy childhood occasions? Although they are certainly not nutritionally better for you they may count as one of the pleasures in your life.

Manufactured sugars

Manufacturers can make different kinds of sugars – xylitol from wood, sorbitol from glucose (often used in diabetic foods because it is more slowly absorbed), mannitol from seaweed, glucose syrups from a mixture of simple and more complex sugars made by a chemical process from starch. Glucose syrups are used in the food manufacturing industry and you'll see them on food labels.

Check the label

The sugars we purchase for use in the home are only half the story. An equal

amount of sugar in our diet comes from manufactured foods we buy.

If you start looking at labels on tinned and packeted food-stuffs you may be surprised to see how many foods contain sugar.

Check your kitchen cupboard or spend some time in a supermarket checking labels and identifying manufactured foods that contain sugar. Any name ending in -ose will be a sugar. Look out for any of these terms – they all mean sugar:

Sucrose, Dextrose, Glucose syrup, Glucose powder, Lactose, Maltose, Fructose.

Is it bad for you?

Saying that sugar doesn't contain much that's good for you is not the same thing at all as saying that it's bad for you.

As you read the following summary of some of the evidence about sugar, think about how you react to it. If you feel personal concern about any of them it is worth examining how much – and how often – you eat sugary foods.

Dental decay

The DHSS report *Eating for Health* admits that the UK has a poor record in dental health ...

"Throughout the world the incidence of dental decay in children is related to the consumption of sugar ... sugar taken between meals in whatever form ... is especially harmful — it is the misuse of sugar which causes harm. It would not be as harmful if taken in moderation at meal times."

As far as children are concerned, if milk teeth are not properly preserved the second teeth may not come through in the right places and will be more likely to decay. Soft, clinging foods eaten frequently lead to dental decay. Teeth are commonly coated with a soft layer of bacteria called plaque. If you chew a disclosing tablet (available from chemists) you will see the plaque shown up as a bright pink. Brush your teeth thoroughly to make the pink – and the plaque – disappear.

The bacteria in plaque produce acid if they have sugars and starch to work on and the acid eats away the tooth enamel. Most of the damage is done in the first few minutes after eating sticky things because acid production is at its highest then. So even if you do sprint to the bathroom to brush your teeth every time you eat or drink, the chances are the damage will have been done before you get there!

Teeth can in fact cope with small amounts of damage. Saliva in the mouth helps to neutralise the acids and fluoride in toothpaste helps strengthen the tooth enamel. So, if sticky or sugary foods are only eaten

at mealtimes and the teeth are thoroughly brushed to remove plaque, then the mouth should be able to cope. But, if soft, clinging foods like cakes, biscuits, crisps, sweets and sugary drinks are eaten between meals, then acid is produced too frequently for the teeth's natural defences.

Weighing up the evidence. Sum up for yourself – and your family if you have one – what you want to do to reduce the risk of dental decay.

Overweight

If you have a 'sweet tooth' it's easy to end up eating too much of foods that have added sugar in them. Being overweight greatly increases your risk of developing late-onset diabetes. It's also linked with increased risk of gall bladder trouble, high blood pressure and, because of the extra weight they must bear, damaged hip and knee joints.

Weighing up the evidence. Since being overweight is itself a health risk, it's best to keep an eye on your weight and avoid becoming overweight. Eating too many 'empty Calories' in sugar isn't advisable. You should remember, too, that all types of fats are high in Calories.

Losing weight if you are already overweight can be best achieved if, as well as keeping an eye on how many Calories you eat, you can speed up the rate at which your body burns up the food you eat. Taking additional exercise is part of the answer. Avoid very strict or fad diets. They may help you lose weight, but you will almost certainly regain it all. And the regained fat may be even more difficult to lose. Look out for books and magazines which explain the new approach to slimming, including the need for increased exercise.

Blood sugar: high and low

You probably know people who claim that sugar 'gives them energy'. It's true that a little sugar *can* give temporary lift to those whose blood glucose has run low – but this is rare. Most people's metabolisms – unless they have some metabolic disorder like diabetes or have taken excessive exercise or are ravenously hungry – are normally quite efficient at keeping a good balance of glucose in the blood. For most people, therefore, it's more likely to be the break taken to have a bar of chocolate that does them good rather than the sugar.

For those whose blood glucose really has run low then bread or a baked potato have been shown to have a more 'instant' effect than sugar!

How much and how often?

You may need to cut down on the total amount of sugar you eat for your general health. And – for the sake of your teeth – how often you eat it.

The NACNE report suggests that the average amount of sugar in the diet should be reduced by 50%.

With this amount the daily allowance of sugar from manufactured foods and added at home works out as *equivalent to* eight and a half level teaspoonfuls for an average man and seven and a half for an average woman.

How do you measure up?

Some people eat much more than the national average. Others eat very little sugar indeed. If you are going to measure how much sugar you eat, one of the difficulties that you face is that you don't know how much sugar manufactured foods contain. The label will only state whether or not it contains sugar. However, you can develop some working rules to help you work out how much sugar you eat.

For some people there are parts of their diet where the amount of sugar can be measured with some accuracy. Keep written notes of all the activities you do in this topic: these will help you later if you do decide you want to cut down.

The jam jar test

This will help you measure how much sugar you add to drinks and meals. Take an empty jam jar and every time you spoon sugar into a drink or on to a cereal, stewed fruit or other dish put the same amount into the jam jar. Do this for several days including a weekend day. Then weigh the sugar in the jar and divide it by the number of days you've been keeping a tally. A level teaspoon is five

grams, and from this you should be able to work out how many teaspoons of sugar you add in an average day.

Remember you have to include the sugar in the food cooked at home or purchased ready-made when seeing how you compare to the suggested target of eight and a half or seven and a half level teaspoonfuls a day.

How do you feel about how much sugar you eat after doing just this jam jar test?

The recipe test

If you have home-baked cakes and desserts, look at the recipes you use. See how much sugar is used for various cakes and puddings. Think about how many portions could be made from each recipe and divide the amount of sugar in the recipe by the number of portions. This will give you some idea of how much sugar is contained in each portion.

Sugar content of prepared foods

The list right gives you some idea about how much sugar there is in various foods. It shows the weight of average portions of the food, roughly how many teaspoons of sugar per portion, and whether this rates as a high, medium or low sugar content.

• High content is 20% or more sugar (ie. 100 grams of food contains 20 or more grams of sugar).
• Medium content is 10-20% sugar.
• Low content is less than 10% sugar.

Food (Average portions) usual measure	Level tea-spoons of sugar	Sugar content
1 teaspoon sugar (5 grams)	1	High
1 scoop ice cream (50 grams)	2	High
2 teaspoons jam	2	High
2 teaspoons sugar-reduced jam	1	High
Slice plain cake (50 grams)	3	High
1 doughnut (32 grams)	1	Medium
1 semi-sweet biscuit (15 grams)	¾	High
Small tin tomato soup	2-3	Low
3 teaspoons tomato ketchup	¾	Low
Small tin baked beans (200 grams)	2	Low
Tinned peaches in syrup (120 grams)	6	High
Tinned peaches in apple juice (120 grams)	2	Medium
1 fruit yoghurt (150 grams)	2½	Medium
2 tablespoons muesli (30 grams)	1½	High
Small bowl All-Bran (30 grams)	1	Medium
1 Shredded Wheat (22 grams)	Trace	Low
1 tube Polo mints	2	High
1 Mars bar	5	High
1 tube Smarties	4½	High
1 glass glucose drink	7¾	Medium
1 can 'Coke'	7	Medium
1 glass Ribena	5	High
1 glass orange squash	2½	High
1 glass orange juice (100 mls)	2½	High
Large glass sweet sherry (60 mls)	1	High
1 pint of beer	2½	Low
1 cup Ovaltine (3 tsps)	1	High
1 cup drinking chocolate (3 tsps)	2½	High

Sometimes magazines and newspapers have articles giving the sugar content of foods. You could collect these to add to your information. Watch out to see if they give the amount of sugar in an average portion or serving, *or* as the amount in 100 grams of the food. However, don't get too obsessive. You are not trying to cut out sugar completely.

How big is a portion?

Check what you mean by a portion. Look through the table. Did any of the standard portions given seem small to you? Watch what you take by way of slices of cake, helpings of pudding, dollops of sauce. If you are doubtful about what average portions are, check in slimming magazines; these frequently show reasonable portions of lots of different sorts of food. Check how often you take the largest portion on a plate. Check how often you finish up leftovers without counting them.

Check what you mean by a spoonful. Is it level? Or is it so heaped you couldn't move it without spilling it? In this topic we have been referring to level teaspoonfuls.

● A good general rule is the higher you think the sugar content is in a food, the smaller a reasonable portion is.

It all adds up

Find some scales that weigh in grams. Maybe you can borrow some or would like an excuse to buy new scales anyway.

Ideally you would need to do this activity each day for a week. But even one or two days should confirm for you whether you are way above the recommended target – or already below it. Only one of our testers was below it. Make a guess beforehand of what the sugar you eat will add up to.

During the day you will need to keep a note of:
● how many level teaspoonfuls you add to drinks and food.
● what you eat and drink that contains sugar and how big the portion was. Ideally weigh each portion. Or check out later on by weighing something similar. In some cases you will have to guess.
● At the end of the day add it all up. Use the table here. You will need to match what you eat or drink to similar things in the table.

High sugar content foods contain *at least* 20% sugar and frequently more, so count at least 20 grams = four teaspoonfuls for every 100 grams of food. If you are in doubt assume there's more rather than less sugar.

It's probably a good idea to assume that savoury, tinned, frozen and manufactured foods labelled as containing sugar should be taken into account. So add one teaspoonful to your total if you've had some today.

What have you decided? If you are eating the average diet of today your total could well be around the equivalent of 16 teaspoonfuls of sugar a day. Possibly very much more!

Take a while to sum up how you feel about the amount of sugar you eat. And how you now feel about cutting down to the recommended target.

What have you learned about your pattern of eating that surprised you?

Which foods do you now think you will have to keep a special check on?

How often?

When it comes to dental decay the key question is "how often do you eat sugary foods?"

Each time you eat something sugary the teeth are left with a sticky coating. In a few minutes the bacteria feeding on this produce the acid which eats into the enamel. If this happens more than three times a day enough acid is produced to do serious damage.

So sucking sweets off and on all day – or sipping sugary drinks – or eating a sweet biscuit every ten minutes is the worst possible pattern for increasing your risks of decay.

You have to be honest with yourself. If necessary keep a diary for a few days to check out how often you coat your teeth with sugar by eating sugary foods or drinks. This is particularly important for children under seven. Decayed teeth can cause trouble for the second set. Some babies teeth are damaged by sucking rusks and syrupy drinks within the first year. So, if you have children keep a diary for them too.

Regular cleaning is important, but it's difficult to clean teeth thoroughly. Fortunately most toothpastes now contain fluoride. This plays a part – particularly with children – in reducing dental decay.

What have you decided? Bearing in mind the present state of your teeth and your pattern of eating, do you plan to do anything differently? What about your children (if you have any)? Does setting a good example to children have to be taken into consideration?

Why is our diet so sugary?

*As a nation Britain is eating less sugar.
But we are still amongst the top consumers.
Why is this?*

"Sugars would hardly be present in the diet at all except for lactose in milk and fructose from fruit and honey, were it not for the liberal use of sucrose, both alone and in jams, tinned fruit, cakes, biscuits, ice cream and other processed foods." (Ministry of Agriculture, Fisheries and Food, 1970).

Added sugars

Today we eat less sucrose, but extra sugar is slipped into our food in the form of glucose syrup by food manufacturers. In 1965 the average person in the UK ate 49 kg sugar. By 1983 this was down to 42.7 kg.

During this time the amount of sucrose consumed dropped by more than this, but at the same time manufacturers were adding more glucose, in the form of glucose (or corn) syrups, to their products.

The total of 42.7 kg per person for 1983 is made up of 36.7 kg sucrose and 6.0 kg of glucose syrups.

When we think about the sugar we eat it's easy to identify the white stuff we spoon on.

However, there is far more sugar hidden in our food that's not so easily counted.

In 1983 if you were an average person you would have spooned out 16.7 kg from packets of sugar. The rest – 26 kg – would have been mainly in cakes and biscuits, sweets and chocolates, and sweet drinks.

One thing is for sure, almost everyone needs to cut down to reach the suggested target of 20 kg a year.

'Sugar' on the label

Lactose, fructose, glucose (glucose or corn syrup) and sucrose are all sugars. But when the label says 'sugar' the manufacturer is only obliged to tell you how much sucrose is in the product. So glucose syrups, which are used a great deal, are not counted.

It is thought that the consumer can only think in terms of the kind of sugar (which is sucrose) that comes out of packets.

Better regulations are needed as to what should be labelled and what should be counted as 'sugar'.

Manufactured foods

What are we eating that gives us the extra 25 kg of sugar a year?

● A lot of people now eat manufactured cakes and biscuits rather than making them. A bought cake usually contains less fat and more sugar than a home-baked one.
● More soft drinks, including squashes and fizzy drinks and more fruit juices are being drunk. These are all high in sugar.
● A wider range of chocolate bars and other sugary snacks are being manufactured.
● Sugary desserts, in packet form or already made up, are popular.

All of these give us sugar in quick, easy form. Easy to buy and serve. And easy to eat quickly with nothing much to slow us down. At least when we ate sugar in jam sandwiches, homemade cakes, rice puddings and so on, it came with some fibre and starch to slow us down and satisfy our hunger more.

Unsuspected sugar

We expect some foods to be sweet. Fresh fruit is naturally sweet.

Tinned fruit in a heavy syrup bears little resemblance to the original fruit. Just remind yourself, try eating a peach and then a slice of tinned peach in heavy syrup. They don't have much in common. But at least you do expect peaches to be sweet anyway.

However consider the following: Many manufacturers seem to believe that the customer likes sugar in savoury foods. Indeed our taste buds would probably complain if our baked beans or tomato ketchup didn't contain sugar. We'd think there was something *missing*. In fact something which is largely unnecessary is *added*.

The British Sugar Bureau's *Sugar It!* teaching materials for schools explains that:

"Sugar is used in foods like baked beans to bring out the flavour of the beans and their sauce. Sugar softens the acid taste of savoury sauces, like salad dressings and mayonnaise."

Indeed the slogan used with the *Sugar It!* material is *"The Indispensable Ingredient!"*

Find the sugar

Check through your store cupboard to see which tins, packages and bottles of savoury foods contain sugar.

You may also like to look at more items next time you are in a supermarket.

Were you surprised to find sugar in any of these foods?

Our testers. The sugar added to tinned vegetables generally came as a surprise. Soups and tinned meats came next on their lists.

Manufacturers say they provide what the public wants. Your shopping list exercise should therefore give you some sort of picture of 'what the public wants' . . . Can it really be the case that the public wants sugar in so many things? Isn't it just that they are used to it and have never been offered any alternatives?

What *Which* found (February 1979) *"In a quick look round a supermarket, we found sugar listed as an ingredient in these savoury foods (though not in all brands); tins of processed and garden peas, potatoes, sweetcorn, butter beans, baked beans, kidney beans, spaghetti, pease pudding, frozen peas, several dried and tinned soups, macaroni cheese, ravioli, casserole mixes and sauces, coleslaw, savoury rice, mixes, mayonnaise, salad cream, salad dressings, mustard, stock cubes, lasagne, peanut butter, breakfast cereals, savoury biscuits, chopped ham and pork, luncheon meat, corned beef, beefburgers (tinned), cured ham, liver and bacon paté, liver sausage."*

Can all these foods really need sugar to improve the flavour? Or do manufacturers work to a rule of 'when in doubt – sugar it'?

Just a little bit . . .

These savoury foods may not contain a great deal of sugar. But it does all add up. Also, many people are unaware of the sugar and so don't know what they are eating.

However, you may feel it is important for you to choose to eat some of these foods because:
- It's your favourite food.
- It makes other more nutritious foods taste better.
- It also provides a good source of fibre.

What do you think?

Are we addicted?

How sensitive are you to sugar in your diet? If you don't have a sweet tooth or have been able to wean yourself off sweet things, the average sugary diet may set your teeth on edge and probably induce nausea.

An experiment

Caution. Do not do this experiment if you are diabetic.

The purpose of this experiment is to help you become much more aware of sugar in your diet. One tester refused to try this because she had spent a long time breaking her craving for sugary foods and didn't want to trigger it off again. However, most of our testers had a go at it, but some found that just imagining day one in vivid detail worked as well.

Day one. Take much more sugar than usual. If you don't take it in hot drinks, add a couple of spoonfuls to each drink. Put enough on cereal to leave a sludge in the bottom of the dish. Only eat tinned products containing sugar. Have honey-baked meat. Eat at least three big chocolate bars and two sweet sticky desserts. At the end of the day be sure to clean your teeth extra carefully. Write down what you ate and your feelings about it, put

it in an envelope, seal it and put it away for a few weeks.

Day two. Go back to your normal pattern of eating. Write down everything you eat. Put your list in an envelope, seal it and put it away for a few weeks.

Day one should give you some idea of what it's like to eat way over the recommended limit of 55 gms of sugar per day. For some people it's a normal day's intake. Such people have lost much of their sensitivity to the taste of sugar.

Tune up your taste-buds. The more sensitive you are to sugar the less likely you are to eat it without thinking.

If you want to increase your sensitivity to sugar then try for one month to reduce your sugar intake by eating fewer sweet foods. Then try your day two menu again. At the end of the day check what you originally wrote about your day one experiment. If you are becoming more sensitive to sugar then some of your comments should now apply to your day two menu – second time around!

Here is what some of our testers said about day one:
"I enjoyed the actual eating, but felt sick, sluggish, bloated and totally unattractive all day — and guilty."

"I felt sick and my teeth felt as if they were covered with fur."

"Nauseated. I could not go back to spooning the sugar in. It has taken me a lot of hard work and perseverance to kick the habit. The thought of that sickly, cloying taste put me off. Not even for you could I do this."

A sweet tooth

Nutritionists say we don't need sugar. But maybe you feel you need it to give yourself a treat or cheer yourself up?

Whether or not we are born with a liking for sweet things, most of us soon learn to like sugary food. Our language and everyday life keep reinforcing the idea that sugar should be on our list of all things nice.

I don't want to cut down!

It is difficult to see why you should cut down on sugar if you:

- are naturally slim – *and*
- have false teeth – *and*
- are not a diabetic (but remember if you are overweight you are more likely to develop late-onset diabetes in middle age).

Even if you cannot tick all of these it may still be difficult for you to decide what to do. It's very much a question of weighing up the evidence *and* your attitudes to risk-taking before you can reach a personal decision you are happy with. Some people settle for becoming much more aware of how much and how often they eat sugary foods. When they do positively choose to eat sugary foods they relax and enjoy them! If you do this, try to avoid eating sugary foods on more than three occasions on one day. And have them as part of the meal. This helps to keep dental decay down. So does thorough cleaning with a fluoride toothpaste and regular visits to the dentist.

Perhaps you'd like to cut down on sugar or have already tried and failed and come to the conclusion that you're weak-willed? Wherever you are in your attempts, it is worthwhile remembering that throughout our lives there are pressures on us to eat sweet things.

Born with a sweet tooth?

It has been suggested that in the dim distant past the sweet taste of sugar helped people to detect what was good to eat. In natural foods sugars came packaged with minerals, vitamins, fibre and starch.

However, sugar can now be extracted from plants, mainly sugar beet and sugar cane. This commercial sugar only provides extra calories when added to our food.

Perhaps we have inherited a sweet tooth from our ancestors who lived off wild fruits and seeds. However a sweet tooth today, far from helping us to survive, can now lead us into over eating – and to the dentist!

Learned in childhood

We don't know for sure yet whether babies actually inherit a liking for sweet things. They certainly do become keen on sweet things very quickly. Breast milk is very sweet and so is the amniotic fluid in the womb, which the baby swallows. And it seems that the more opportunity small children have to eat sugar the more they learn to like it.

Even if parents don't give their children sugary foods they will soon see other children eating sweets and biscuits. And they will want to be the same as them.

A survey of children's lunch boxes has shown an almost identical pattern of contents – a packet of crisps, a chocolate biscuit, a small sandwich (usually cheese or ham) and a piece of fruit.

Restricting sweet foods in early life may have little long term benefit when sugar is an important part of our culture. They will discover it sooner or later! But it does have a short term benefit when children's teeth are difficult to clean. It may seem like a losing battle, but it's one worth fighting.

Sugar is sweet and so are you

If children like sugar anyway, it can only reinforce their liking if they are given it for being good, for being ill, for being liked, or for being hurt. It says you're nice, you've done well, you were brave. Sugar also says this to adults: – thank you for the dinner, happy birthday, get well soon, I like you. The sentiments are full of goodwill and if the reward or gift is frequently sugar it comes to be associated with good too.

If you have children of your own you'll probably be familiar with all this. If you need to have your memory triggered about your childhood or you thought it was only *your* children, you might find it revealing to:

- Watch children at the supermarket checkout where there are sweets.
- Go into a street corner shop and look at the wide variety of cheap sweets and who buys them.

You should quickly build up an idea of their preference for sweet things. You may, too, become concerned about the ethics of advertisers and the sellers of sweets. Are they justified in saying they are only providing what the customer wants?

Every day in every way

Advertising slogans slip off the tongue as easily as chocolates and sweets slip onto it. *And all because the lady loves . . . with less fattening centres . . . helps you work, rest and play. Take a break, take a . . . . . . is just enough to give yourself a treat.*

But how much notice do you take of them? What do you feel when you see them?

- Does your mouth begin to water?
- Do you think I haven't had a . . . for a long time?
- Do you find yourself imagining the taste of . . .?
- Are you tempted to buy any of the sweets you've seen advertised?
- What else?

Make your own chart to analyse your response. We have filled in this chart (right) with comments from our testers.

Which situations make you most want to eat sweet things? Many of our testers could resist adverts and sweet displays, providing they didn't have children with them. In restaurants they definitely gave in when the sweet trolley arrived, though they did say they counted it as a special treat. Going to buy bread and encountering cream cakes seemed to provide almost overwhelming temptation.

Once a sweet tooth . . .?

Being aware of the hold sugar has over you is a good first move towards changing your intake. People learn to see sugar as a treat, a reward, a gift or a comforter. They also learn the habit of eating it at certain times. Fortunately, what you have learned can be unlearned.

Choosing to change. Below are some sentences. Replace italicised words with something that doesn't involve sugar.

- When I go to a restaurant I have the *sweetest, stickiest* desserts.

- When I give small presents they tend to be *chocolates*.

- When I'm feeling sorry for myself I have a *chocolate bar*.

- When it's my teabreak I usually have a *chocolate or a doughnut*.

- When my children have been good I give them *chocolate drops*.

Next think of some more situations which you have learned to connect with sweet things. Write down what the sweet things are 'saying' in that situation. What else could convey the same 'message'?

Remember we aren't talking about not having treats and comforters – just not overdoing sugar. Say each sentence to yourself several times. If it sounds OK, try putting it into practice once or twice. When it feels OK doing it a couple of times, you are beginning to unlearn your ideas about sugar.

Situation	Makes me feel –	Puts me off	Not interested	I want it
Adverts on TV	If I'm watching after dinner they don't affect me.		✓	
Looking at magazines	The full colour pictures start me off.			✓
Supermarket sweet displays	I try to shop without my two children – I can pass by when I'm on my own.		✓	
Newsagents sweet displays	Not usually interested, but do buy at railway stations.		✓	
At the cinema	I wouldn't buy anything myself, but I like it when my husband buys me chocolates.			✓
In a restaurant	When the sweet trolley is wheeled up close to the table, I give in.			✓
In a works canteen	Whole atmosphere puts me off food.	✓		
In a cake shop	These are paradise.			✓

" The tube is so trying why not . . . "

" Show her you love her "

" There's going to be a scene if you don't buy me for your child . . . "

" Eat me while you're reading the newspaper "

" You've had a hard day. Go on – reward yourself "

Getting informed

As a consumer you can, under your own steam, do some useful survey work about what's available to you in the shops.

You can locate information that is available and decide what you need more information about. You can reach your own decisions bearing in mind the factors that are important to you. As far as sugar is concerned this might mean for one particular food:

- Looking at the range available.
- Checking labels.
- Writing to manufacturers for more information.
- Weighing up the cost of going further afield than your local shops to get what you want.

This topic looks at how Nancy examined certain baby foods and matched her findings against her requirements. But you could do the same type of survey on other foods.

Why look at baby foods?

This type of survey can be done for all sorts of foods. We've chosen baby foods for several reasons:

- Some babies' teeth decay almost as soon as they come through. Young children, below the age of seven, are most vulnerable to dental decay. So keeping down the number of times their teeth are coated with sugar – which provides a meal for the bacteria causing dental decay – is most important. (Rusks are often chewed off and on throughout the day.)

- A taste for sweet things can easily be developed. This makes it difficult for them in later life to cut down on sugars for themselves.

- Babies need adults to speak up for them.

In addition this case-study provides an example of how – apparently in response to consumer demand – a 'reduced sugar' product is brought out. But it isn't all it seems to be – although at the present time it's all perfectly legal.

Andrew's rusks

Nancy's baby, Andrew, is eight months old. She is keen to cut down, or remove, all added sugar from his diet. She usually avoids manufactured baby foods and makes as much of his food as she can, taking care not to give him a taste for sugary food. But she does buy rusks from time to time.

Nancy decides to take a close look at the ingredients of the various rusks on sale the next time she goes to the shops to see how much sugar they contain. On her way round she looks at the various packets, makes a note of as much as she can and compares the information when she gets home. She redrafts her notes in the form of a small table.

Nancy is concerned about the sugar content of the food she gives her children, but at the same time her housekeeping is limited. So she looks at the information she's collected (February 1984) to see whether she can find products that are sugar-free and of a reasonable cost.

Check the table yourself. Do you think there's enough information for Nancy to make the decisions that are important to her?

> Most manufacturers don't put the quantities of ingredients included in their food on the label. However, by law the nearer the beginning of the list the larger is the amount of the ingredient.

Which rusk?

Here the decision is difficult. Nancy had hoped to find out more information about the actual quantity of sugar in the various products.

The only completely sugar-free rusk is the Bickiepeg brand. But these rusks not only cost a great deal more than the others Nancy found, but they're different in shape and intended for a rather different use. Bickiepegs are small (about $2\frac{1}{2}''$ long) and very hard with a hole in one end so you can thread a piece of cotton ribbon (provided) through. Then you attach the Bickiepeg to the child's clothing, so he can't drop the rusk.

All the other rusks are larger, of a more biscuit-like type and can either be held in the hand or mashed up with milk. They all contain sugar, but one of them is labelled 'Low Sugar Rusks', so she assumes that this contains less than the others which don't say how much they contain. However, even the 15% sugar the Farley's Low Sugar Rusks contain seems pretty high to her.

Nancy said *"I still don't really know what to do — I'm not sure I understand about the sugars. Andrew doesn't seem to like Bickiepegs so much — they are expensive and I don't think they look very nice. But I'm worried about his teeth more than anything else — so perhaps it had better be Bickiepegs."*

She decided to find out how much sugar was in the two types of Farley's rusks. They said their Original Rusks contain 30% sugar and the new Low Sugar Rusks contain 15%. Nancy was amazed at that 30%. However, she felt reassured about the new Low Sugar Rusks and decided to switch to them.

Nancy's chart

Name	No of	Weight	What the label says about sugar	Price
Bickiepegs	9	28.35 grams	"Sugar-free"	45p
Boots Choc Chip Toddler Rusks	12	200 grams	Sugar is second after flour in a long list of ingredients	48p
Boots Rusks	18	300 grams	Sugar is second after wheat flour in list of ingredients	58p
Farley's Original Rusks	18	300 grams	Sugar is second after wheat flour in list of ingredients	62p
Farley's Low Sugar Rusks	18	300 grams	Sugar is second in ingredients list after mixed flours. Claims it is 15%	62p

Doing it yourself

If you are concerned about sugar in manufactured foods you may well wish to think about doing similar sorts of surveys.

- Looking at the amount of sugar in breakfast cereals or jams.
- Seeking out 'no added sugar' versions of the many savoury foods listed as having sugar added.
- Comparing the amount of sugar in fizzy drinks, squashes and fruit juice – and alcoholic drinks too if you like.
- Comparing the sugar in different yoghurts.

You might also be concerned to check which shops carry them, and who offers them at the best price.

Again the type of survey could look at more than sugar content. How much fat is in the food? Has salt been added? Is it high in fibre – and what does high in fibre mean?

Finding out more. If you feel you *cannot* make a satisfactory decision on the amount of information you've collected from labels, then you need to do more research – write to manufacturers, see if shops are prepared to find out for you.

Asking for improvements. If consumers don't make their feelings known producers will justifiably continue to say the current situation is what the public wants. You can choose to take public action, though, to be honest, this won't necessarily get instant results.

- Asking managers of local stores if they'd stock low/no sugar versions of the food you are concerned about.
- Writing to shops or to manufacturers at national level – you can get their address from the manager of your local shop.
- Joining with other people to make your demands more public.
- Lobbying the government.

And all for a carton of yoghurt or a jar of jam? It's not really just about them at all. As an individual you can only choose to buy from a very limited low or no sugar range of alternatives, or you can choose not to buy. Neither of these are very satisfying choices. If you want greater choice in the long run, taking part in public action of some sort is a useful contribution to make.

Changing the pattern

Make it easier for yourself: plan ahead. That way you can avoid having to fight the temptation that's on the plate in front of you.

You need to know what your pattern of eating *is* before you can change it. You also need to consider what comes before the final decision point when you must decide whether or not to put that sugary food into your mouth.

Your own pattern of eating

Keeping a diary will enable you to check your pattern to see:

- Whether you have a choice or if it's made for you.
- What counts as a 'normal' pattern.
- What other reasons determined your choice.
- Whereabouts along the chain of decision points that led up to your finally eating the sugary food you could have made a different decision.

Keep a diary of the sugary foods you eat for three days like the one shown on the opposite page. Don't change your pattern of eating – you are trying to get a quick 'snapshot' of your everyday pattern. Write it up as you go along – or bring it up to date at the end of each day. But do not fill in columns 5, 6 and 7.

At the end of the three days – review your diary

- **In Column 5** tick if you had a choice when you ate the food. Put an X if you didn't. You will need to work out a different strategy in advance if you are to cut down the number of occasions when you have no real choice but to eat the sugary food.
- **In Column 6** tick those items you would normally eat. Put an X beside any you consider you wouldn't normally eat and a brief note as to why this was an exception.

Does the number of Xs surprise you? Many of our testers were surprised. They had discovered that they kept on making exceptions. *"Just this time", "I had to accept it so as not to hurt her feelings", "It was a reward for fighting my way round the supermarket", "Everyone else was eating it".* For some, 'exceptions' were normal! What they actually ate bore little resemblance to what they would have said they normally eat.

You have to be honest with yourself. If your pattern contains many exceptions it should alert you to repeat this diary exercise occasionally once you have started making changes. Then you can check if your real pattern of eating matches your desired one.

The difficult times may be when you were eating sweet things because you felt under stress, unloved, anxious or depressed. This often applies to sugary snacks. If this might be an important category for you, keep another diary noting how you felt just before you chose to eat. What would you have liked at these times even more than something sweet? Do you need to stop studying how to eat better; at least for a while, and pay attention to other problems in your life?

You probably need to decide, perhaps in advance, what special occasions you really will make exceptions for. Our testers mentioned birthday cakes, things their children had cooked for them and presents given to make up quarrels.

Decision points

After reading this section you should be able to go back and fill in column 7. Write in *what* different decision you could have made to avoid ending up eating what you did.

The shopping list

Making a shopping list and sticking to it can help you avoid too many impulse buys.

Try to write down the quantity of sugar, jam, biscuits, etc. you will buy. 'One jar of jam' – will help you avoid

taking the cherry *as well* as the strawberry jam.

What would happen if you bought one packet of sugar or biscuits rather than two?

Do you need to add new items? For example, sultanas to use instead of sugar to flavour porridge. More fruit to replace sugary snacks for taking to school or to work.

As you think about the other decision points you may find you need to make changes in your standard shopping list.

You could keep your shopping lists to prove your pattern changes!

At the shops

Whether or not you've made a shopping list – have another think:

● **Buy less.** Could you buy less sugar, jam, honey, etc? How long could you make a bag of sugar last?

● **Buy a lower or no added sugar brand.** Do any of the brands have a lower sugar content? Our testers found two main supermarket chains with own-brand tinned fruit in fruit juice instead of syrup. They also found own brand 'no sugar added' muesli. Breakfast cereals surprised some testers. Even the alternatives to the sugar or honey-coated versions they normally used often contained added sugar. They had to read the labels carefully to find the two or three types with no added sugar.

One supermarket has a particularly good range of own brand sugar-reduced jam. However, some testers liked it so much that they ended up eating much more of it so didn't make any saving on the sugar!

Natural yoghurt – you could add chopped fresh fruit later – is widely available.

Sugar-free peanut butter was found in a health shop. So were sugar-free baked beans and tomato ketchup. These last two were also low-salt – but they were more expensive.

● **Buy something different.** When you reach out to buy something sugary consider: What am I buying this for? *When* will it be eaten? What would be nicer to have instead? For example, fruit instead of biscuits or chocolate for snacks at school or at work. Or fruit – fresh or tinned in juice – instead of ice-cream or sticky puddings.

● **At the pay out.** Some of our testers said that seeing the sweets at the pay out did two things:
a) Their children wanted them.
b) They wanted them – it had been harassing going round and they deserved a treat.

Too late? Maybe this time. Next time, decide in advance on an even better reward. If it's to be food you could even make it the first thing you put in your trolley!

● **Try different shops.** By shopping around you may increase your choice. Some supermarkets, health food shops and so on do make efforts to provide a greater choice although you may have to pay more to do without so much sugar in some foods!

One of the best ways to locate low/no sugar sweet foods is at slimming counters. But that suggests people wanting such food are 'special cases' and that added sugar is normal. But since no one *needs* added sugar there aren't any special cases.

Patterns of eating diary

Tuesday 14th September

Time	Sugary Food	Where ?	Who with ?	Choice ?	Normal?	A Different Decision ?
7.30	Sugar on Weetabix	In Kitchen	Alone	X	✓	
10.15	Chocolate Biscuit	At work	Workmate	✓	X	
12.40	Lemon Meringue Pie	Café near work	With 2 friends	✓	X	

Planning menus

- **Plan ahead.** Or at least keep a list of meals as you go along. This way you can put your plans into action. Can you serve sweet dishes less often?

- **Watch the overall balance.** When you choose to serve sweet food, where else can you cut down that day.

- **Keep a record.** Put a star (*) beside new, less sweet dishes that turned out to be a success so that you can remember to serve them more often in future. Keeping your menus will help you prove that you really are putting your plans into practice.

Cooking

In cooking sugar adds flavour but it also adds bulk. This may be important in cakes and biscuits.

- **Look out for specially adapted recipes.** Slimming magazines are a good source of these.

- **Alter your own recipes.** Try cutting the sugar down to a half. Is the flavour still OK? Cakes may have a firmer texture but do you still like them?

- **Try substituting artificial sweeteners.**

- **Use alternative flavourings.** Adding dried fruit, eg. sultanas to porridge, or spices, eg. cinnamon to stewed apples, may mean you need to use little or no added sugar.

At the table

Try to alert yourself so that you make a more conscious decision when you add sugar to help yourself to sweet dishes.

- **Adding sugar.** You might like to try rationing or monitoring the amount of sugar you add to your drinks and your food.
Rationing involves deciding in advance how much you will 'allow' yourself. Put it out on the table and see if you can make it last a week. Try allowing yourself 28 level teaspoonfuls a week ie., an average of four a day. (Remember total daily intake should be about eight and that includes what is already in the food.) Or work down to it if that strikes you as terrible. If you want to *monitor* the amount of sugar you add, use your own sugar bowl. Fill it up and weigh it on a Sunday morning. Use what you want during the week and weigh it the following Sunday morning. If you

want to convert to teaspoonfuls 5 grams = 1 teaspoonful; 1 oz = 5½ teaspoonfuls.
You can check out on honey or jam or marmalade in the same ways.

- **Helping yourself.** Spooning out a smaller serving is a pretty obvious way to cut down. Cutting cakes and pies into more pieces, eg. eight instead of six, cuts down on portion size. But watch out you don't end up having two slices to finish it up!

Grabbing a snack

Most snacks are grabbed on the spur of the moment.

- **Try to plan ahead.** This way you are less likely to succumb to temptation.

- **Stock up on a wide range of low sugar or alternative snacks.** This leaves you scope for a spontaneous decision. You can still grab a snack – but hopefully a healthier one.

Eating out

Here you may have a limited choice. Or – particularly if you are in someone else's house – you may not want to offend or hurt other people's feelings.

- **Check the menus.** Look at restaurants, work canteen menus etc., then decide to:
a) go somewhere else
b) take some of your own food
c) ask them to serve something different.

Commercial cakes look light and attractive: extra sugar adds bulk and texture.

- **Refuse without offence.** Saying 'No' without hurting feelings is an important skill to acquire. Rehearse in advance what you will say.

- **Warn the cook** and say what you do like.

Giving presents

What must the present say? It doesn't have to be said with sweet things. Be inventive.

Changes into practice

Do you like a general onslaught – to make a massive change? Some people enjoy this *and* get away with it.
Most people manage better with a step at a time. They like to try it out and check that it's working before taking the next step.
Now that you are aware of the chain of decision points that end up with you actually eating the food, you can choose where you will make a start. Too often, people – some of our testers included – see changing their diet as just having the will-power to say "No" to the sugary food that's before them. This really isn't the best approach – unless you've learned to like punishing yourself.
Real will-power is not about gritting your teeth and resisting temptation. It's to do with using your wits, becoming skilled at decision making and choosing more enjoyable foods – or other activities.

The food industry must change too

Manufacturers find that sugar is a particularly useful aid in processing many foods. Let's look at why it's used and what the alternatives are.

Sweetener

Many people now prefer less sweet food and this trend should continue. However, a large number of alternative sweeteners both natural and artificial are being developed and investigated. Before any of them go on the market they have to pass a good many safety tests that the government sets up.

One new sweetener which has gained acceptance recently for use in food in the UK is aspartame, which is two hundred times sweeter than sucrose (commercial sugar). Talin, another sweetener which is two to three thousand times sweeter than sugar, has now been approved for use in medicine and may be permitted for more general use in future.

Adding bulk

This is probably the most important use of Polydextrose, a new bulking agent which can replace sugar in frozen cakes and sweets. This could reduce the energy intake you can get from eating, say a cake, by 50%. But it is three or four times more expensive than sugar to make.

Preservative

Sugar is used as a preservative, particularly to stop moulds growing, in both canning and freezing foods. However, canning and freezing methods have improved – and it may be just habit to add so much sugar. Certainly when the demand arose it was found that jams with half the traditional amount of sugar in them could be made. Now that opened jars can, if necessary, be kept in a fridge, moulds are also far less likely to grow once it has been opened.

Improves texture

Sugar speeds up the working of yeast and helps ensure a well-risen dough. But the amounts used for this are hardly important enough for it to be the major focus for change.

It also lightens cake because it traps air between the fat-coated sugar crystals. Without so much sugar

Artificial sweeteners

These have an intensely sweet taste – and only a little needs to be used. They are useful if you want to cut down on Calories and avoid tooth decay – but still want a sweet taste. They are much used in making soft drinks.

Saccharine. In use for over a hundred years. Thought by some people to have an off-putting bitter aftertaste. But very cheap.

Aspartame. Sometimes called Nutra-sweet it is sold in the UK as 'Canderel'. Newly permitted sweetener without a bitter aftertaste.

Acelsulfaine K. Another new sweetener. Will probably be mainly used in foods and drinks. Can be bought as tablets – has a slight aftertaste.

Talin. The third new sweetener. 2000 times sweeter than sugar but a natural product. (It's extracted from a West African fruit.) Trouble is that it has a delayed sweetening action. You may only notice the taste after you have swallowed the food! May be able to be adapted for use in manufactured foods.

Can you have too much? Artificial sweeteners have to be approved for safety by the Food Advisory Committee. But could you still use too much of them? Although most people consume relatively small quantities it is possible that some people drinking large quantities of artificially sweetened squashes and fizzy drinks might drink over the recommended limits. The only area for possible concern might be small children, especially when they are thirsty in hot weather.

Sprinkling them on your food. Artificial sweeteners are sometimes mixed with bulking agents so that you can sprinkle them on your food. Watch out – because in most cases the bulking agent is some kind of sugar! However, as you don't have to add so much you would only end up with a few extra calories.

commercial cakes would certainly not look so large and light. This may be a feature that the consumer must learn not to demand. After all, delicious homemade cakes, particularly with traditional recipes, tend to look flat and solid – and it doesn't seem to matter. Alternatively, food technologists could develop improvements on Polydextrose.

Mouth feel

This is a food manufacturer's jargon term meaning the pleasant feel in the mouth that we get from sweet foods and drinks. It's partly taste and partly the syrupy feel.

This is all part of the intangible virtues promoted by advertisers that seem to appeal to a need we have.

But people are gradually coming not to rate it above their health.

Pressure to change

Inertia, good profits from existing high sugar products, and no competition make it unlikely that the industry will change quickly.

There *are* alternatives to sugar that have the same sorts of characteristics. Manufacturers *can* provide a reasonable substitute. But sugar and corn syrups are cheap, which is a big plus point for manufacturers and as yet consumers haven't really complained a great deal.

Downfall of the sugar industry?

"This is the house that Jack supports . . ." What if the average consumer did eat less than half the amount of sugar he now eats?

Supposing . . . everyone made the change more-or-less overnight? Would this bring about the downfall of the sugar industry? And what if it did?

Any answers?

This diagram looks at the main groups which would be affected. How you look at these groups will depend on your political viewpoint and the values you hold dear. And also how much you tend to sympathise with or blame people who have problems.

Whose point of view?

Read through the notes about each group and then write down how you would feel about the shrinking demand for sugar *if you were:*

a) The chairman of Tate and Lyle.
b) A worker on the shop floor at Tate and Lyle.
c) An East Anglian sugar beet farmer.
d) A Mauritian sugar cane cutter (almost their whole economy depends on sugar).
e) The owner of a sweet shop.

Who do you feel sympathy for? Who would you blame? Might any of these people's health be damaged by the changes?

Planning for change

The NACNE report recognises the need for the food industry to be fully informed and also "envisaged these overall changes being achieved over a period of 15 years in order to allow sufficient time for industrial adjustments to occur."

Of course this supposes that the food industry will accept that a consensus of opinion does now exist that these changes need to be made. It also assumes that the powerful sugar interests won't fight back by putting pressure on the government, in particular the DHSS, or through advertising and educational materials.

There are already good examples of the food industry rising to meet the challenge. As these examples become more widely known and supported by the consumer other manufacturers will follow suit.

Use it for something else? There seems little else to do with sugar except eat it. However, research is going on into turning it into other substances that do have a commercial use. Perhaps the most promising is the work in Brazil where sugar is converted into alcohol which is then used to fuel motor cars!

Third world sugar countries
Economy now dependent on growing a single cash crop – sugar.

Sugar processors
Powerful big business. Tate and Lyle and British Sugar process almost all sugar in Britain.

Sugar beet farmers
Particularly in East Anglia. Although a quota is imposed by the EEC they are at present guaranteed a good price.

Cake, biscuits and sweets and soft drinks manufacturers
Already looking at artificial sweeteners and bulking agents as alternatives.

Supermarkets
Have power to influence food industry.

Cornershops
May be heavily dependent on sweet sales. Often represent life savings investment of the owners.

EEC
Already allows sugar mountain to build up. So cut back in consumption would make this much worse.

British government
Sugar industry has MPs who keep their interests in mind. Department of Trade and the Treasury on their side because of the extra jobs and revenues linked to the sugar industry.

World market
Sugar market is in any case unstable because EEC dumps cheap sugar (at below true market price).

Eat more fibre?

The NACNE discussion paper on the British diet is mostly about cutting down. Eat less fats, sugar and salt. Fibre is the odd one out. We need to eat *more* dietary fibre.

"It is recommended that the intake should be increased to an average of about 30 grams dietary fibre per day for adults."

At present we only eat about 20 grams a day. So the average person needs to eat half as much again. But where will the fibre come from? The answer is from cereals (grains), pulses (peas and beans), fruits and vegetables.

"Cereal fibre in particular should be increased because it is more effective in increasing fæcal weight than fruit or vegetable fibre."

Cereals are most important. We need to eat more foods made from wheat, oats and rice – bread, pasta, crispbreads, breakfast cereals, porridge and rice dishes. These foods keep our bowels on the move and help prevent constipation. A diet high in fibre is also linked with a lower risk of other disorders of the digestive system and of heart disease and certain types of cancer.

Dietary fibre refers to the fibres naturally present in the foods we eat. Adding extra fibre – usually bran – is not the answer. The Royal College of Physicians in its report on dietary fibre recommends that *"people eat foods which are closer to the natural grain, vegetable or fruit than the highly processed and refined products which now form a large part of our food."*

In most countries where the traditional diet is high in fibre-rich foods it is also low in fats. Altogether a healthier diet.

Fibre-rich foods

*We are recommended to eat more of the foods that are naturally rich in fibres –
whole grain cereals, peas and beans, and fruit and vegetables.*

Dietary fibre, or bulk or roughage as you'll sometimes hear it called, doesn't have a single, simple definition. It has been described as *"the part of plant food that passes through the small intestine (bowel) completely undigested and reaches the large intestine (bowel) intact."* It absorbs water in the large bowel.

Fibre isn't a single, simple substance – it comes in various forms. In natural fibre-rich foods it also comes closely mixed up with other complex carbohydrates.

It's a good idea to eat a variety of fibre-rich foods. They fall into four main groups.

Cereals

Most cereals, particularly whole grain cereals (as in wholemeal bread and brown rice), are good sources of fibre. They provide the kind of fibre that works in the gut keeping it working smoothly and efficiently. For this reason they are very good at relieving constipation.

Peas and beans

Peas and beans – pulses – are rich in gums and mucilages which play a part in controlling the level of sugar in the blood. They may prove to be an important part in the diet of diabetics.

Root vegetables

Root vegetables – potatoes, carrots, parsnips, turnips, swedes – are high in fibre and starch. Potatoes provide a reasonable amount of protein and vitamin C.

Fruit and leafy vegetables

Leafy vegetables would include cabbage, lettuce and spinach. Since they are mainly water they are much more

dilute sources of fibre. But this is an advantage for slimmers as they are also a dilute source of Calories. So they fill you, provide you with some of the fibre you need, and don't make you fat.

Some fruits are particularly rich sources of pectin which may play a part in reducing cholesterol in the blood.

A fibre-rich diet

The overall pattern of diet is important. A fibre-rich diet is one where plenty of fruit, vegetables, whole grain cereals, pulses and beans are eaten. The key words are plenty and variety.

The fibre-rich foods take longer to chew which helps you feel you've eaten a lot. They are bulky and help fill you up so that you don't have room for too much fatty food. And the food stays longer in the stomach so you don't feel hunger pangs so soon.

In countries where the traditional diet is high in fibre it is also low in fat and sugar. The overall balance of this type of diet is much healthier. And it's this type of diet that we are now all recommended to eat.

Just adding fibre, in the form of bran, to the typical Western diet that's high in fat and sugar isn't enough. The diet still remains unbalanced – and unhealthy.

Slimming diets

Have you ever tried to slim? Many slimming diets concentrate on cutting down on carbohydrates. The pity is that a lot of high starch foods contain fibre. So these diets are also low-fibre diets.

When you have been dieting, which of these foods did you cut out?

● potatoes
● bread
● beans
● rice
● breakfast cereal
● pasta

Many slimmers add some fibre from vegetables and fruit to their diet. But they cut out fibres from cereals and beans. These are the most concentrated forms. You would have to eat a whole lettuce to give you the same amount of fibre as a portion of beans, a couple of slices of wholemeal bread or a bowl of breakfast cereal.

Many slimmers also get constipation. Changing to a diet that is low in fibre-rich foods – particularly cereals – blocks you up. There isn't enough bulky food inside you to keep your bowels working. Indeed it has been suggested that the ill effects of straining when you're constipated produce some of the side-effects of obesity.

If you have a weight problem, eating fibre can help. Look for a diet that has plenty of whole grain foods, beans, vegetables and fruit. They have low sugar and fat content so you don't get concentrated doses of energy. You still have to watch the Calories and take exercise, but you needn't feel so hungry.

What about bran?

When many people think of fibre they think of bran. There has been a great deal of advertising to promote bran and bran enriched foods. Some of our testers felt that only bran would do as a source of fibre.

Bran is the outer layer of cereal grains – it is a rich source of the fibre lignin. Wheat bran is the outer layer of wheat which is removed when white flour is being prepared.

Added bran is not the answer

A low-fibre diet high in refined foods or foods naturally low in fibre, such as meat, dairy products and sugars, does not have a healthy balance. Such a diet is also high in fat and sugar. Adding one or two tablespoons of bran will not turn a bad diet into a healthy one.

Adding bran can relieve constipation – but the rest of the diet can still be poor. It is better to relieve constipation by eating more ordinary fibre-rich foods rather than add bran as a supplement.

Raw bran contains phytate, a substance that makes it difficult for the body to absorb certain minerals – calcium, zinc and iron – from the food. Some phytate is destroyed if bran is cooked. Also when combined with yeast in the leavening process to make bread even more of the phytate is destroyed. So you don't need to worry about the phytate present in bread made from wholemeal flour, which is milled from the whole grain of wheat including the outer bran layer.

Promoters of bran would argue that although it contains phytate most people have more than enough calcium, zinc and iron in the diet so that the reduction caused by the phytate doesn't matter.

Special groups. Anyone who is not absorbing quite enough calcium, zinc or iron and who then supplements their diet with bran, particularly raw bran, may be risking their health.

Groups who are known to be at risk are:

● **Asians** whose diet tends to be deficient in vitamin D. Their traditional bread, chapattis, are unleavened and so the phytate remains in their diet. Added bran may make matters worse. However, since most Asians' diets are on the whole rich in fibre there should be little reason for anyone to wish to add bran.
● **Elderly people** who have a reduced ability to absorb calcium. They tend to suffer from constipation and may therefore add bran to their diet.
● **Women with heavy periods** who need plenty of iron in their diet.
● **Pregnant women.** There is some concern that a zinc deficiency in the mother's diet may have something to do with babies who are a low weight (though not premature) at birth. Since pregnant women suffer from constipation they may be tempted to add bran to their diet.

The inside story

What happens to fibre as it passes through the gut? It used to be thought of as just 'roughage' that served little useful purpose.

Most of the fibre we eat eventually comes out again. But while the fibre passes through our digestive system it can be doing a great deal of good. Some of the fibre is digested by the normal bacteria in our intestine. This digested fibre provides chemicals which seem to be needed for the health of the lining of the bowel.

A low-fibre diet can cause trouble in two ways. Firstly, the small amount of actual fibre in the diet causes trouble in the bowels, and may affect some other body processes. Secondly, a low-fibre diet is usually high in other foods, particularly fatty and sugary foods, that aren't good for you in large quantities. Here it is the overall balance of the diet that is poor.

What goes in . . .

In the mouth. The more fibre-rich food you eat, the more work you do eating it. Besides being bulky and therefore satisfying for that reason, fibre is more work to eat. It gives you more chewing to do, which is satisfying. In addition, more chewing creates more saliva, which is good for your dental health.

You can test for yourself how fibre-rich foods take more chewing. Do these experiments on separate occasions, or you'll be so full by the time you get to the last one you won't really be able to tell!

● Take one wholemeal sandwich and one white bread sandwich with identical fillings and time how long each one takes to chew.
● Eat a peeled orange and compare the time taken to drink an equivalent amount of orange juice.
● Eat an apple and then the equivalent amount of stewed apple.

Usually the more fibre in a food the more chewing is necessary and the more time that takes. Drinking a glass of orange juice is only a second's work, eating an orange takes a few minutes.

In the stomach. Food slides down your oesophagus – the tube leading to the stomach. Here it mixes with digestive juices which begin to break down (digest) the food. The food is in your stomach for one to two hours. Low-

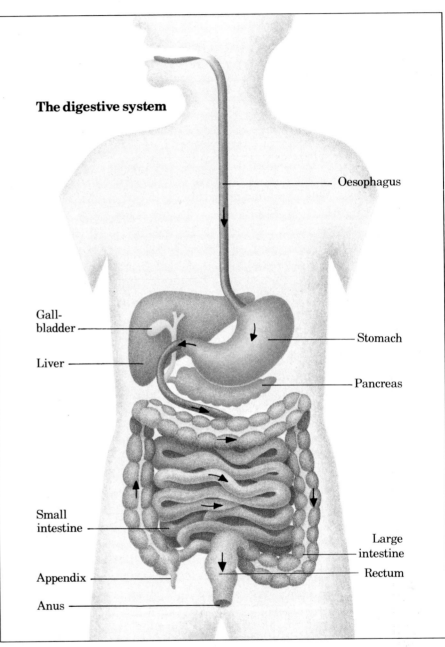

The digestive system

Oesophagus

Gall-bladder

Liver

Stomach

Pancreas

Small intestine

Large intestine

Rectum

Appendix

Anus

fibre food stays for a shorter time – and this can result in you feeling hungrier sooner.

In the small intestine (bowel). The food passes on from the stomach into the small intestine where the process of digestion continues. If the food is high in fibre, particularly those from peas and beans, the food will be a thick sticky mixture. If it is like this then the absorption of sugar into the blood stream is slowed down. There isn't a sudden flood of sugar into the

blood. A sudden rise in blood sugar increases the demand for insulin which puts a strain on the pancreas which produces it. This may be particularly important for diabetics.

It's also thought that the pectin type fibre from fruit and vegetables may hold onto the cholesterol in food and also trap the cholesterol which is being lost naturally in the bile. The fibre seems to prevent some of the cholesterol being absorbed. So this might play a part in preventing heart disease.

Large intestine

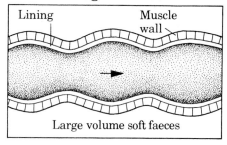

Lining   Muscle wall

Large volume soft faeces

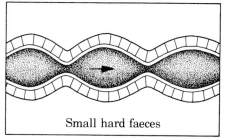

Small hard faeces

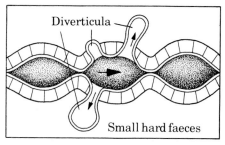

Diverticula

Small hard faeces

In the large intestine (large bowel or colon). The remains of the food now move on into the large intestine. The fibre has not been digested and now plays an important part. It mops up waste products which are then rapidly passed out in a bulky stool instead of lingering in the bowel where they may be absorbed into the blood stream. This may be particularly important if any carcinogens – substances capable of triggering off the development of cancer – are present. The fibre holds on to the water like a sponge and doesn't allow too much of it to be absorbed into the body through the wall of the large intestine. Some of the fibre is digested by the bacteria to produce special substances which may prevent the lining of the colon being affected by carcinogens. With a high-fibre diet the stool remains moist and bulky. It's easy for the gut to squeeze it along and get rid of it. If there is too little fibre too much water is taken out and the remaining fæces (stools) are small and hard.

Hard work

It's difficult for the muscles in the wall of the large intestine to push hard fæces along. And this can cause problems.

The regular muscle contractions of the bowel wall that squeeze the fæces along can become upset. The squeezing can become irregular and the muscle can tighten into a painful spasm. This condition has several medical names – irritable bowel syndrome, irritable colon or spastic colon. Whatever its label it is usually improved by eating a high-fibre diet. When the bowel muscles have to squeeze extra strongly, to move the hard fæces along, the increased pressure can lead to weak points in the bowel all stretching out into small balloonlike pouches. The medical term for these pouches is 'diverticula'. *Diverticulitis* means inflammation of these diverticula.

It's also thought that hard fæces may play a part in the development of appendicitis. A small lump may become trapped in the appendix. Appendicitis follows if the blocked appendix becomes inflamed.

A constipated person has to strain to pass a stool. This straining makes pressure inside the abdomen build up. In turn, this increased pressure is thought to play a part in causing piles, varicose veins and hiatus hernia.

...must come out

The way to check if you are eating enough fibre is to check what comes out.

It's funny that doctors and patients often have trouble talking to each other about this. Medical people use terms like fæces and stools or ask questions like 'How often do your bowels move?'

It's a topic often joked about in everyday life but difficult to write about in a way which doesn't either sound coy or offensive.

What about you?

The key question is 'What are your fæces (or stools) like?' We suggest you use your own word everytime you see these terms. Our testers' usual words were: shit, poohs, crap, number twos, business and jobs. Whatever you call it you need to have a good look at it.

When you think of fibre the word roughage probably comes to mind. Yet your bowels would be more likely to call it smoothage. The effect is not like a pan scourer. Just the opposite. A good stool is three-quarters water because the fibre acts like a sponge.

Think about times when you have enjoyed a trip to the toilet. Has passing a stool (put in your own favourite word) actually given you pleasure? If it has then the chances are that you are getting plenty of fibre. For most people passing a lot quickly and without pain makes for a happy visit to the smallest room.

Of course we are not referring to the satisfaction and relief that a constipated person feels after successfully straining for some time. Straining is bad for you. Laxatives are now seldom recommended by doctors. They might suggest bran as a temporary measure to get you going. But the aim should always be to increase the natural high-fibre foods in your diet.

Your aim should be to get food to pass quickly through your body and for your stools to be moist and bulky.

It's not just uncomfortable to be constipated. Possibly harmful waste products hang about for that much longer. So a fast passage is good.

You might like to check the transit time of the food through your gut by eating a meal containing a food that tends to pass through in a recognisable form. Sweetcorn or beetroot are good ones to try: but they do not always show up. You may know from past experience which foods tend to pass straight through you. These make a good marker to use.

In one experiment schoolboys were given a harmless plastic marker to swallow with one meal. It took anything from one day to a whole week for the marker to pass right through them.

You might like to consider how you would measure up to these average figures:

	Transit time
Europeans	70 hours
Vegetarian Europeans	43 hours
Rural Africans	35 hours

You could also check whether you speed up after changing to a high-fibre diet.

Incidentally the average weight of stools passed was: Europeans 100 grams, Vegetarian Europeans 180 grams, Rural Africans 400 grams. We don't suggest you need to weigh your stools. The satisfaction test is probably as good as any.

Too much wind

If you shift to a high-fibre diet you may have a little trouble if you make too rapid a change or eat large amounts of pulses. 'Beans means farts' – is all too true for many people. Not everyone reacts in this way – and it may not bother you even if you do. *But* for some people it could be very painful, too. You can minimise the amount of wind you get by making the change slowly so you get the chance to get used to the high fibre. If you cook your own dried peas and beans, throw away the water you soak them in and cook in fresh water. You might like to try, too, the commonly accepted idea that eating yoghurt at the same meal as pulses helps. Certainly Middle Eastern and Indian dishes often combine pulses and yoghurt – so there's a long tradition of eating this combination.

Is it just a fad?

The advice to eat more wholefoods was often ignored because it was being recommended by people considered to be 'cranks'.

It has long been suggested that whole foods (high in fibre) are better for you than refined foods from which most of the fibre has been removed. The debate sometimes gets focussed on Brown Bread versus White Bread.

It's certainly true that there was little hard evidence to back the advice. 'Eat more whole foods' has often been considered 'cranky' advice. And some of the people backing it did so with religious zeal.

Even today, with increasing medical evidence to back it, the recommendation to eat more fibre seems more likely than other recent dietary advice to be dismissed as cranky.

A campaign against refined foods

For many years dietary fibre or roughage, as it was then called, was looked upon as an indigestible waste product. Most nutritionists were interested in other aspects of food.

In 1956, surgeon Captain T. L. Cleave campaigned against refined foods from which most of the fibre had been removed. He thought that what are now called 'Western diseases' or the 'diseases of affluence' were linked in various ways to the refinement of carbohydrate or the so-called 'civilised diet'. His cause was later taken up by such people as Denis Burkitt and Hugh Trowell, doctors and missionaries in Africa. They went out to try and help reduce the death rate from tropical diseases.

The death rate was indeed high from tropical diseases. However they found that there were far fewer instances of 'Western diseases' – cancer of the colon, coronary heart disease, varicose veins, piles, diabetes, obesity, gall stones, diverticular disorders, appendicitis and hiatus hernia. Burkitt and Trowell suggested that this was possibly due to the difference in diet, and particularly to the amount of fibre eaten in developing countries.

People in rich countries eat on average only 15-20 grams of fibre each day compared to 40-60 grams of fibre in the developing countries of Africa and Asia. Critics of the 'eat more fibre' movement say that the difference could be caused by any number of

things. Lifestyles in the third world countries are so completely different from ours. For example, we have less exercise, more pollution . . .

Dr Denis Burkitt, a leading expert on fibre, has a simple answer to the critics. Many of the 'western diseases' are related to what happens during digestion. So why not start looking at what we feed into our digestive system?

Interest in the function of fibre in the diet has since become considerable. The old view that it was merely the cell walls of plants that just went through the body undigested began to be questioned.

What's the evidence?

The fibre story all hangs together in a logical way and fits the evidence that's available. But it's difficult, as with many areas of diet and health, to do experiments to prove it.

Also it is virtually impossible – and probably unethical – to make large groups of people deliberately eat a low-fibre diet for perhaps 10 or 20 years to prove, under experimental conditions, the ill effects of a low-fibre diet.

Certainly doctors recommend a high-fibre diet to help avoid constipation, irritable colon and diverticulitis. Many people gain almost instant benefit from eating more high-fibre foods. It's a satisfying change to make and they pass on the good news.

Recent evidence suggest that these are longer term benefits. Experiments have shown the link between pulse fibres and blood sugar levels.

The gums and mucilages in fibres from peas and beans (pulses) help to slow down the uptake of glucose into the blood stream so that there isn't too sudden a surge in blood sugar.

Other experiments on pectins in the fibre from fruit and vegetables suggest that they bind on to cholesterol in food and so reduce the amount that gets into the bloodstream. (High levels of blood cholesterol are linked with increased risks of coronary heart disease.)

It is now recognised that fibre comes in different forms and works in different ways.

The Royal College of Physicians summed things up in a report on fibre: *"It seems that added fibre may increase the weight of the stools; alter the transit time through the intestines; lower muscle tension in the colon; alter*

the activity of bacteria in the bowel; modify the absorption of fats, sugars, minerals and bile acids, influence the appetite and absorb toxins. Effects such as these could tip the scales between health and disease but long-term studies are needed to establish the true role of dietary fibre in maintaining health."

Advice from 'cranks'?

The advice to eat more fibre-rich whole foods has, in the past, come from people labelled as 'cranks' – because of their own beliefs.

Who were these 'cranks'?
● Seventh Day Adventists with their unusual religious beliefs and strictly controlled way of life.
● Vegetarians – labelled the 'beards and sandals brigade'.
● Health food 'freaks' with their emphasis on the need for vitamin and mineral supplements and the 'magical' virtues of honey.

In time the eating of 'whole foods' was itself considered cranky.

What's cranky? There are fashions and fads in foods and there are usually some groups of people whose attitudes to food are seen as extreme by others. At the moment the establishment has taken up the case for fibre, but years ago a concern with it might have been seen as cranky.

What do you see as cranky?
● eating brown bread
● adding bran to cereal
● being a vegetarian
● being a vegan (a vegetarian who eats no dairy produce)
● insisting on only eating unrefined foods
● refusing certain foods for religious reasons
● eating certain foods to cure ailments
● taking vitamin tablets
● taking laxatives
● baking your own wholemeal bread

Obviously there are no right answers. You probably thought of other attitudes to food that you consider decidedly odd. Crankiness is very much personally defined and it's partly related to the fashion. It's rather unlikely that the many people who eat brown bread nowadays would be branded cranky.

However, as you read these pages, it's worthwhile keeping a note of any paragraphs or subjects, that when you initially read them the first thing that comes into head is 'that's cranky'. Ask yourself why you thought that. Read on and make your own mind up based on the evidence. Changes in eating habits are partly achieved by being open-minded to new evidence.

Breakfast cereals

Breakfast cereals may have been invented by so-called cranks. But today millions of people enjoy them.

In the United States the Seventh Day Adventists were already experimenting with cereal-based foods in the 1850s. In 1900 Helen G White, a leader of the Seventh Day Adventists, proclaimed *"the cereal food business is one of the Lord's own instruments"* and she ordained that the Adventists eat a vegetarian diet.

From these foundations for dietary reform came Henry D. Perkey, who invented Shredded Wheat, and John H. Kellogg, physician in chief of the Seventh Day Adventists Institution at Battle Creek, Michigan. Kellogg invented the forerunners of Corn Flakes, Rice Krispies and Bran Flakes. He also lectured on the value of whole cereal foods and advocated the use of bran for constipation.

To begin with breakfast cereals were marketed as health foods – 'natural and biologic'. As they gained more popular appeal brand names like Elijah's Manna were dropped. By 1911 there were over 100 brands of cornflakes. In Britain breakfast cereals also became very popular particularly since they were easily prepared. What started off as 'religious whole food' ended up by becoming an everyday part of the nation's breakfast.

Today breakfast cereals are big business. To increase sales many new types, often with a great deal of added sugar or honey are on the market.

However those made from the whole grain, without sugar or salt added during their manufacture, are excellent sources of cereal fibre.

Indeed without eating some sort of breakfast cereal, it's difficult to include enough cereal fibres in the diet. Bread and rice are the other two usual sources.

But of course you don't have to eat them at breakfast time. They can make useful snacks. Or be used as a crunchy addition to fresh, tinned or stewed fruit to make them into what seems more like a 'pudding' at the end of a meal.

Getting enough fibre?

How can you tell if you are getting enough fibre? What is 30 grams of fibre in terms of the everyday food you eat?

You may have any number of reasons to eat more fibre-rich foods:

● To reach the NACNE recommended average national target of 30 grams of fibre a day.
● To help with constipation, irritable colon or piles.
● To reduce your risk of bowel disease.
● To eat a diet containing fat and sugar without feeling hungry.
● To find a diet to help control your weight.

Whatever your reasons, finding what is enough of a change is important. Getting it right needs a bit of trial and error. There are plenty of different ways of getting enough so you can work out which you prefer.

A rough check

You can check your present diet to get a rough idea if you are getting enough.

At the end of a day check the following table and circle any of the foods mentioned that you've had a reasonable helping of during the day. If you've had more than one helping of any food, note down how many helpings you've had.

A	Wholemeal bread, brown rice, fibre-rich breakfast cereal, wholemeal pasta, pies etc. cooked with wholemeal flour, bran.
B	Peas, beans (any kind of beans), nuts, dried fruit.
C	Potatoes, carrots, parsnips, turnips, swedes, etc.
D	Spinach, cabbage, celery, lettuce, tomatoes etc., apples, bananas, pears, oranges, etc.

If you've eaten four to six helpings of food from groups A and B then your diet probably contains a reasonable amount of fibre.

If most of your fibre intake was in groups C and D (and particularly if most of it was in group D) then you'd have to eat an awful lot of these foods to reach the national average target of 30 grams a day. Salads have been described as packaged water. To get 30 grams of fibre you would need to eat about 60 servings of lettuce (1 oz each).

Making this rough check may surprise you. Some of our testers felt disappointed that they weren't getting enough fibre from all the salads and fruit they were eating. Though of course these do provide valuable vitamins and minerals. Some concluded they would have to go back to eating breakfast in order to get enough fibre from cereals.

The other problem with such a rough check is that it talks of 'reasonable servings'. Did you have trouble in deciding what that means? Or do you suspect other people's 'reasonable servings' might be huge or tiny by your standards?

Now you might like to go on to make a more accurate assessment of the fibre you eat *or* go on to look at some ways to get 30 grams of fibre.

Food	Portion	Fibre
*Wholemeal bread	1 slice	2.6 grams
*White bread	1 slice	0.8 gram
*Bran enriched bread	1 slice	1.8 grams
(*Bread values are based on large loaf, medium sliced bread)		
Ryvita crispbread	1	1.2 grams
Digestive biscuit	1	0.8 gram
Plain biscuit	1	0.3 gram
Pastry	Small square	0.5 gram
Wholemeal pastry	Small square	1.7 grams
All Bran	1 cup/bowl	7.5 grams
Bran Flakes	1 cup/bowl	4.2 grams
Cornflakes	1 cup/bowl	1.9 grams
Puffed Wheat	1 cup/bowl	2.5 grams
Porridge	1 cup/bowl	1.4 grams
1 Shredded Wheat		2.7 grams
1 Weetabix		2.2 grams
Brown rice	3 tablespoons* (2 oz)	2.5 grams
White rice	3 tablespoons* (2 oz)	1.4 grams
Spaghetti	3 tablespoons* (2 oz)	0.8 gram
Wholemeal spaghetti	3 tablespoons* (2 oz) (* = dry weight)	6.0 grams
Baked beans	4 tablespoons	8.7 grams
Peas (frozen)	3 tablespoons	10.8 grams
Potato (boiled)	1 small	0.6 grams
Cabbage (boiled)	3 tablespoons	2.5 grams
Sweetcorn	2 tablespoons	2.8 grams
Banana (peeled)	1 medium	3.4 grams
Apple (whole)	1 medium	1.5 grams
Orange (peeled)	1 medium	2.4 grams
Prunes (stewed)	1 bowl	7.0 grams
Dried apricots	1 oz	7.2 grams
Dried raisins	1 oz	2.0 grams
Peanuts	1 oz	2.4 grams
Hazelnuts	1 oz	1.8 grams
Lettuce	Small serving (1 oz)	0.5 gram
Tomato	1 average size (2 oz)	0.9 gram

Adding up the fibre

How many grams of fibre did you eat today? The table, left, gives the fibre content of portions of a range of foods. You can use it to make quite an accurate count.

Make a list of the foods that you have eaten as meals and snacks today. Look through the table and check which of these are on your list. Estimate how much was in each portion of high-fibre food that you had. Then work out the grams of fibre that you ate.

If you really want to know how much you are eating then you will need to look at what you eat for several days. After a while you should get better at spotting the fibre so you will have a good idea of the foods that give you the recommended 30 grams.

Some of our testers were annoyed to discover that the salads they had been eating were giving them such small amounts of fibres. In fact several of them who had rated themselves as eating plenty of fibre-rich food found they fell short when they added it up. What about you?

Today the average person in the UK eats about 20 grams of fibre a day. But there is a wide range: some people only get through six grams, others eat 80 grams of fibre a day.

The recommended average intake is 30 grams. You may eat more – but some people become bloated and uncomfortable if they do so.

Counting up the portions

The photograph on this page shows how much of various foods would give the recommended 30 grams of fibre. (From top left) 37½ slices white bread, 13½ Weetabix, 8 portions broccoli, 25 crispbreads, 4 bowls Allbran, 4oz dried apricots, 1 large can kidney beans, 1.8 cans baked beans, 4 bowls stewed prunes, 11½ slices wholemeal bread, 11 Shredded Wheat, 12½oz peanuts, 6½ large jacket potatoes.

Of course you don't have to get it all from one source! In fact it's better if you don't.

Mix and match. Two Weetabix, a small tin of baked beans, a jacket potato, two slices of wholemeal bread and 1oz of dried apricots, for example, that's 30 grams of fibre in all.

Keep a look out for recipe books that give the fibre content of various dishes. Some Calorie counters and magazine articles give you fibre charts. Packages of high-fibre food often carry dietary information so you can check the fibre that you are eating.

What comes out?

You can check whether or not you are eating enough fibre by keeping an eye on what you pass in the toilet. If you regularly pass, *without any straining,* a soft bulky stool then your fibre intake is OK.

As you switch to a higher fibre diet you'll probably find that food passes through you more quickly. Some of our testers mentioned that they found their new high-fibre stools much more satisfying to pass. One tester said that although he went to the loo more often he stayed for less time.

Some of our testers had obviously mistaken the runny, loose stools that a high salad and fruit diet can give you for the soft, bulky high-fibre stool. They soon noticed the difference when they ate more bread and cereals.

Bread

Eating more bread is one of the easiest ways to increase your fibre. But is there much difference between brown or white bread?

Do you know the fibre content of the bread that you usually eat? Are there other breads with more fibre that you could try and like? A move from white to wholemeal could make it much easier to reach 30 gram fibre target. What kind of bread do you like?

When it comes to the bread that we eat, taste is often the top consideration. Some people love home-made wholemeal bread. Others wouldn't touch it with a barge-pole and prefer white sliced.

What kind of bread do you prefer to eat? Look at the different loaves shown below. In the box beside the name of the loaf, mark

*   if you eat this regularly
✔ if you've tried this and wouldn't mind eating more
?   if you've never tried it.

Now try to sum up why you prefer the types of bread you regularly eat. Leaving aside cost and availability, what kind of bread do you like?

When you've finished this topic check those breads you've ticked or put a question mark by. Are they higher in fibre than those you regularly eat? How do they measure up to your description of the kind of bread you like?

Granary bread. This has whole, unmilled grains of wheat added to the dough. These are the crunchy bits. Apart from these grains the fibre content varies according to the recipe. Most are medium fibre. ☐

White bread. A typical white loaf has only about one third of the fibre of a wholemeal loaf. This is the lowest in fibre. ☐

Wholemeal bread. This uses all of the wheat grain. It is sometimes called wholewheat or Graham bread. High in fibre. ☐

Bran enriched white bread. This has added bran. Not all of this bran is from wheat, however. Most brands of enriched bread tell you the amount of fibre. A typical brand of enriched-white bread has about three-quarters as much fibre as a wholemeal loaf. ☐

Wheatgerm bread. This is made of white flour with added wheatgerm and some bran. A popular brand has a little more than half the fibre of wholemeal bread. ☐

Wheatmeal bread This has a mixture of different flours. The Government is planning to ban the use of this label. Its bran content can vary. Some can be quite high in fibre, others medium to low. ☐

The miller's tale

The key to understanding about the fibre in bread is flour. How the flour is processed is all important. The wheat that is the main ingredient can be treated in many ways. Some get rid of bran, the outer fibrous coat of the wheat grains. Some leave all the bran in the flour. Others take it out and then put some or all back.

Stoneground flour

In this the whole grain is ground up together so the flour produced is a 100% wholemeal flour. Stonegrinding is the traditional way of milling wheat. Two large round mill stones are used to break up the grains. The top stone revolves and ridges on its surface shear the grain apart. The result is a coarse flour with all of the components of the wheat. It is a well tried way of making flour, but its coarse texture tends to make a slightly heavier loaf.

Roller milled flour

In this more modern process giant rollers crush the wheat. By sieving the results in between trips through the rollers, three bits of the wheat can be separated.

1. Bran – the outer fibrous coat of the grain – the high-fibre part.

2. Wheatgerm – the part of the grain which could grow into a new plant.

3. Endosperm – the starchy part that will provide food for the germinating new plant.

These three components can be used separately or recombined to form a variety of flours.

Wholemeal flour. Here all three components are recombined. If the flour is labelled 100% wholemeal then everything is put back.

White flour. May be made entirely, or almost entirely, with the starchy endosperm part of the grain.

Brown flour. Contains fibre somewhere between that of white and wholemeal flour. May also have brown colouring added.

Special mixes. Various quantities of the wheatgerm and bran can be mixed back into white flour. Hovis, Allinson, Windmill are examples of trade names of these special flours. Hovis flour for example has added wheatgerm, but less bran than wholemeal.

I still prefer white bread!

Since switching to wholemeal bread is such an easy way to increase the fibre in your diet it does tend to be pushed down people's throats by health experts.

The danger is that people can get to feel guilty if they don't eat brown bread – or to feel that white bread is positively bad for you.

It would be more accurate to say white bread is good for you, but wholemeal bread is even better. White bread contains fibre, but you would have to eat three slices of white bread to get the fibre that one slice of wholemeal could give you. You would get more starch that way. Rather than eat such a lot of white bread it would be better to switch to eating more wholegrain cereals – or, dare we say it, brown rice!

It isn't just the taste that leads people to choose to eat white bread. Here are some reasons people have given us for choosing white bread.

Which of these reasons account for why you eat white bread – if you do?

Times are changing. Sales of wholemeal bread have increased rapidly over the last few years. So the cost should come down and wholemeal bread become more widely available. It is already available sliced in some supermarkets. So keep looking around if you gave reasons A, B and C for choosing white bread.

Bakers encouraged by the government have been experimenting with additives to produce a lighter texture. In future they will be able to continue to use ascorbic acid (vitamin C) as a lightener in wholemeal bread. Again the major supermarkets already stock this bread.

These points have been emphasised in case you base your objections to wholemeal bread on the heavy, difficult to slice loaves that used to be the only kind available.

Thinking this through should also enable you to feel positive about the times you choose white bread!

	Which of these reasons account for why you eat white bread – if you do?	
A ☐	**Cost –**	"It's a few pence cheaper – and it all adds up."
B ☐	**Sliced –**	"I can keep an eye on how much I'm eating."
C ☐	**Availability –**	"It's the only type my local shop sells." "If I run out I can usually find a local shop with white, sliced bread."
D ☐	**Softness –**	"I associate this with posh food." "I haven't got many teeth." "I don't like chewing away at hard wholemeal bread."
E ☐	**Texture/ flavour**	"It isn't so crunchy as wholemeal." "It makes better sandwiches." "It lasts longer without going mouldy." "It makes better toast."
F ☐	**Variety –**	"It comes in all shapes and sizes."

Fibre league table

For more exact information this table gives the average loaf's fibre content.

100g of Bread	Fibre (g)
Wholemeal	8.5
Granary	6.0
Typical Bran-Enriched White	5.7
Brown	5.1
Wheatgerm	4.8
White	2.7

Counting the Calories? Slimmers might like to note that one gram of fibre comes wrapped up with 86 Calories in white bread but with only 33 Calories in wholemeal bread. So if you are trying to limit your Calories whilst increasing your fibre, consider wholemeal bread.

More bread = more salt?

A problem that remains is that bakers by tradition have always added a lot of salt to bread. We are already recommended to cut down on the salt we eat.

So if you increase the amount of bread you eat in order to get more fibre you should consider paying special attention to cutting down on the amount of salt you add to your food and the amount of salty processed foods you eat.

Bakers could make good bread without as much salt and it is to be hoped that increasing awareness of the need to cut down on salt will lead to a change.

Home baking. The only way to be sure your bread is low in salt is to bake it yourself. If you have the time then it can be a satisfying activity as well as providing a healthier product.

Shopping

How easy is it for you to buy fibre-rich foods in the shops? Remember a diet rich in fibre consists of plenty of wholegrain foods, fruit and vegetables.

You will need to look at both choice of foods and at how constant and reliable supplies of fibre-rich foods are in your shops. Wholegrain foods and pulses and beans, could make an important contribution to a fibre-rich diet *at most meals*. So you need to be confident you can buy them regularly without any bother.

What's available?

Survey your local shops, ones you generally use, plus any local health food shops you know of.

First of all see what fibre-rich foods are available on one visit to your shops. Make a list of what you see on your visit to the shops and check whether you are able to buy a sufficiently large variety of these foods to supply you for a few days.

● Can you buy wholemeal bread, brown rice, wholemeal pasta, wholemeal flour easily? Is the labelling of such products good enough for you to make an informed choice? If you buy your bread from a baker's, can you find out from assistants or the management what sort of flour is used in their bread?

• Can you buy pulses – beans, peas, lentils – and dried fruit and nuts? Do you have a choice of dried, tinned and frozen versions of these foods (where applicable)?

• Can you easily buy a variety of root and green leafy vegetables and also a variety of fruits that are fresh and appetising and not looking sorry for themselves?

The next few times you go to the shops check your list and see if there's always the same variety and a regular supply. For instance, does wholemeal bread tend to run out? Is wholemeal pasta a standard line in your supermarket?

Special foods?

We are recommended to eat more of the *naturally* fibre-rich foods. We don't need to switch to 'added fibre' foods.

However fibre is now fashionable and bran, in particular, is promoted as a 'magic' ingredient. Today there is plenty of publicity for products which are outside the range of naturally fibre-rich foods we've talked about. Check them carefully when you see them.

Look at the labels

Watch out for products that say 'bran enriched', 'added fibre' or just 'bran' on them. These may not be made from the whole grain. Adding bran to a product is not the same as providing a whole grain fibre-rich product.

A better fibre-rich diet can be achieved without such additions and more cheaply.

Misleading labels. Some manufacturers who draw attention to the high-fibre level of their products do not mention the high sugar or salt content. Added bran breakfast cereals, in particular, need salt and sugar to help make them eatable.

Of course, naturally fibre-rich breakfast cereals made from the wholegrain cannot use the label 'added fibre'! So they may not catch your attention.

Since there is as yet no definition of what counts as 'high-fibre' even this label can be misleading. For example 'high-fibre' or 'bran enriched' white loaves do have more fibre than plain white loaves. But they may not be as high in fibre as wholemeal loaves.

Special shops?

Having examined your local shops including health food shops, from the point of view of wholegrain foods (as opposed to 'bran added' foods), does your supermarket or your health food shop provide you with a better choice? Is there a whole food shop in your area?

Health food shops

Look carefully at the 'health' foods you find. Are they wholegrain or are they more faddy, 'extra vitamins', supplemented with wheatgerm, ginseng and so on?

If you want an 'enriched', 'supplemented' diet all well and good. But a fibre-rich diet can be achieved without such additions more cheaply and more effectively.

It seems odd that 'health' should be a specialist area of food marketing. Ordinary healthy eating is not a fad. And it is to be hoped that supermarkets can provide people with the food they need for a healthy diet. Health food shops do tend to be more expensive and they can make you anxious too, because of all the supplements that seem to be good for you. It's a bit like reading a medical dictionary when you discover all sorts of ailments you think you have.

Whole food shops

These concentrate on selling whole grains and their products eg. wholemeal flour, semolina, pasta, oat flakes, and a wide range of beans, peas and lentils, and also dried fruit and nuts. They provide a good range and you can often buy large quantities much more cheaply.

Avoid buying from open sacks. They make the shop look 'earthy' and attractive. But they can also attract insects and mice. The risk of products becoming mouldy unless the premises are well ventilated and kept at an even temperature is also increased.

Another advantage of packaged grains and pulses is that they will also probably have been picked over and cleaned before packing.

Wholefood shops are often run by people who are committed to trying to keep prices low. But large supermarkets who now stock a wide range of grains and pulses can undercut them.

Asian, West Indian and Cypriot Stores

These have always been a good source of grains and pulses, almost all of which come pre-packed. If you want to try out new recipes using grains and pulses they also sell the other ingredients you need!

Storage

Fibre-rich foods are bulky foods in more senses than one. Bags of rice, lentils, porridge oats, etc. – boxes of breakfast cereals – cabbages, carrots, apples and oranges – these are all bulky objects to pack in your shopping bags, carry home and store.

If you have to go to special shops you'll probably want to stock up on some of them.

Fruit and vegetables. Today many houses don't have a cool larder and although most fruit and vegetables keep up to a week in the fridge, there isn't room for much to be stored. Frozen vegetables are a good standby if you have a freezer. Storing in a wooden box in an outside unheated shed or garage works well in winter.

Dry goods. Keep these in closed containers. If possible they are best kept outside the kitchen if it tends to get steamy, as moisture tends to make them go mouldy.

Bread. Wholemeal bread tends to go mouldy sooner than white bread. This is because almost all white bread has mould inhibitors added to it to increase its shelf life. If you are not going to be able to eat it up quickly it's a good idea to cut a wholemeal loaf in half and store one half in the freezer.

Throw out mouldy foods. Some moulds have been linked with serious liver disorders. Not enough is known about the risks from eating mouldy food so don't take chances – throw it out. If you have good storage conditions you probably won't have any problems.

Watch out, too, for cereals and crunchy bars that say they don't have added preservatives. That sounds like a good selling line, but they should also have 'eat before' or 'best before' dates on them. They are fine provided you eat them before they go mouldy.

When choice is limited

What about when you have to eat outside your own home?
Is your choice limited?

You do have some choice when eating in cafés, restaurants, canteens and takeaways. But in schools and hospitals there may be little or no choice.

A good example?

"Hospitals are still bad offenders in not providing a diet with a generous fibre content." Sir Francis Avery Jones, Consultant Gastroenterologist.

You would think that hospitals, which exist to help people towards health, would set a good example. It seems particularly important that they offer a nutritionally sound choice of foods since people in hospitals really don't have any alternatives – they can't get up and leave if they don't like the food.

Here is an account of one woman's experience when she went into hospital to have a hysterectomy.

"After my operation, I thought I'd never be allowed out. You see, they want to send you home as soon as possible to save money. The booklet they sent me before I went in said 'Come prepared for a stay of ten days to three weeks'.

"However after the operation, which was on a Monday, they said 'we want you out by the weekend — but you can't go home until we know your bowels are working'.

"Well, of course, cutting you open for the operation seems to slow your bowels up and they can take a bit of time to start up. When the menu came round to choose what meals you want I looked for fruit and vegetables and even more importantly brown bread and cereals. There was hardly anything with fibre in. And as I was used to eating a lot of fibre at home, my bowels just gave up.

"They gave me laxatives and an enema that felt like an exploding firework, but I just didn't go.

"In the end my husband smuggled in some brown bread and some dried apricots for me. These — and the newspapers I sneaked into the loo to read so I could feel more relaxed — did the trick.

"I was reading about the Argentines launching an Exocet missile at the time when my bowels finally worked! At least that gave me a laugh, though I didn't find any of the rest of my experiences funny."

This is a typical menu in this particular hospital.

MENU

Cream of Chicken Soup

Slice White Bread

★ ★ ★

Battered Cod

Chips

Grilled Tomatoes

★ ★ ★

Tinned Peaches

Custard

★ ★ ★

Coffee

Reading this case-study triggered our testers into giving us many more examples. These included women in post-natal wards and elderly people in long-stay hospitals.

What do you think this woman was being offered? Was she:
- offered what was good for her?
- offered what was cheapest?
- offered what she usually eats?
- offered what *she* wanted?
- offered what people generally want?
- offered a menu based on modern nutritional theories?

There was very little fibre on the menu. It was high in fat, sugar and refined processed foods. Probably it was quite cheap. Probably it was based on ideas about twenty years old. Or even on the old notion of 'bland food for invalids'.

And what else happened? She was set a task and told she couldn't leave hospital until she had achieved it, probably making her anxious. She wasn't given any easy assistance (why give people enemas when you can give them wholemeal bread to eat?).

The Royal College of Physicians panel working on dietary fibre thought that all who are responsible for public catering should take the lead in offering consumers a wider choice of white, brown or wholemeal breads. Indeed a few health authorities do – most notably Brent and Wessex.

But clearly this hospital, as a public caterer, was not taking the lead. And while she was in hospital this woman couldn't really do anything except receive the smuggled food her husband brought her. Asking for different food where there are mass catering facilities is not going to reap instant personal results.

What might she have done? After she came out of hospital she could have gone to her local Community

Health Council and asked them to take up the issue of menus with the hospital. Better still she could have asked them to take up the wider issue of hospital catering in the whole local area. An account of her experiences would have been useful to them and so would a run down on the menus she was offered.

Drawing the District Health Authority's attention to the fact that Brent Health Authority has shown that a healthier diet can be provided at no extra cost, might provoke them into reviewing their catering, rather than just saying a healthier diet would be too expensive.

And the excuse that people won't eat different food has also been disproved in hospitals where it has been tried.

Taking action

Hospitals. If these are issues that interest you, ask your local Community Health Council (CHC) whose remit includes representing the views of the general public about hospital services, to find out what's being served in your local hospitals. If you have had similar experiences to this woman tell your CHC. Your local Health Authority should have a clearly defined policy about the nutritional balance of the diet they provide in their hospitals and be prepared to explain this to the general public.

Schools. In the same way the Catering Officer should be able to explain your local Education Authority's policy about school meals. You can ask directly or perhaps better still go through your Parents' Association or the Parent Governors on the school's board of governors.

Inviting your local Community Dietician or Community Physician to a Parents' Association to discuss the new dietary guidelines may help raise interest in what's available as school meals. You can contact them via your local Health Authority.

Eating out

There are several ways to provide yourself with some choice when you eat outside your home. Here we are dealing with choosing to eat a fibre-rich diet. However, if you are able to find ways of doing this you'll also be well on your way to cutting down on fats and possibly added sugars too.

You could:
● Avoid where possible eating at places where you consider the choice of food appalling.
● Make a habit of going places where there is a good choice.
● Make the best of limited choice when that's what you've got, by having a clear idea of what you're looking for and what you're looking to avoid. Don't use limited choice as an excuse.
● Make your voice heard if you desire a greater choice. The British are notorious for putting up with poor service.

Examine your choices. Compare your works canteen with local sandwich bars/takeaways/restaurants/cafés.

Do they:
● Offer wholemeal or brown bread sandwiches?
● Always have potatoes on the menu?
● Frequently have pulses and green leafy vegetables on the menu?
● Offer a choice of fresh fruits as well as cooked desserts?

Certainly some advances are being made. Sandwich shops will often make brown bread sandwiches. Some burger chains now offer a wholemeal bun for their quarter pounder burger. As long as they have customers for their new wholemeal fibre-rich lines, caterers will almost certainly continue to offer them.

So if you've got a better choice than your current eating arrangements then do opt for it.

Cheating?

Consumer action and speaking out rarely get instant results. And if you are concerned to improve the quality of your eating out now, then you might consider cheating. Cheating is unlikely to get things altered in the long run but, together with speaking out, may lead to a more reasonable diet!
● If you have to go into hospital or on to an aeroplane or otherwise put up with periods of institutional eating – ask in advance, if possible, to have vegetarian food. Institutional vegetarian meals are at least as good and frequently better than other institutional catering.
● If the catering facility allows it (and watch out for 'You can only eat our food on our premises' notices), then take a wholegrain portion of your own food to add to the basic component of a meal. For example, take your own wholemeal bread to add to a canteen stew.

Making your voice heard

You may have grumbles and grievances about fibre but not know what to do about them. Who should you talk to?

If you want to make your voice heard more loudly then consider these suggestions:

Takeaways. Write to the headquarters pointing out features you like in other similar places (eg. a wholemeal bun in a fast food chain, Calorie values of meals in menus).

Cafés and restaurants. Take a party of like-minded people along and all ask for high-fibre variants on the menu. If possible go back once a week. Write and tell the Manager you were surprised when you found high-fibre foods were not generally available.

Works canteen. Enlist the help of your union. You could get your local Community Dietician to come and talk. You could try inviting the Catering Manager out for a drink with work colleagues who hold the same views as you. Better still, get the Catering Manager and Community Dietician together for talks – it's already worked well in some companies.

Work through a group

Join a local consumer group or consider asking other groups to which you belong to look at the new dietary guidelines.

Many groups will find it easy to persuade local managers of food stores or restaurants to come and talk to them. Community Dieticians and Physicians will also come along. Perhaps you could get them together at a 'Food Forum' session.

The groups' activities can often be reported to local newspapers and this raises wider interest. Your paper might invite the Community Dietician to suggest health-conscious choices from the menus of local restaurants.

The paper might be interested in any consumer surveys you do. A lot of people think that consumer surveys and action are well worthwhile. Manufacturers can always say ' That's what the public want' until someone begins to say that it isn't. Several major supermarket chains have said that the growth in their fresh food market has less to do with their own marketing strategies than with realising what the customer wants.

The consumer can win

Certain minerals and vitamins have had to be added to bread as a health measure since the last war.

In 1983 the government decided that the nation was now sufficiently healthy and it was no longer necessary to add them. However, their proposals met with opposition and they changed their mind as this item from *The Guardian* (28.3.84) shows:

A U-turn over what goes into bread

By Rosemary Collins,
Agriculture Correspondent

The government has changed its mind over its proposals, published almost a year ago, to change the legal composition of bread.

It had intended to end the requirement that bread manufacturers should add certain vitamins and minerals to white bread, and to allow the addition of flour improvers to hitherto unadulterated wholemeal bread.

Yesterday the Ministry of Agriculture announced that the proposals have been dropped because of the overwhelming weight of public protest which they aroused. "At the end of the day this is a democracy, and we have had many complaints about the original proposals that we have had to recognise the weight of public opinion," a ministry spokesman said.

Adding vitamins and minerals to white bread was a Second World War health measure, and the government's technical advisers were firm last year in insisting that it was an unnecessary procedure these days. But there have been vigorous protests, chiefly from organisations concerned about the diet of elderly people who often live on tea and toast, and for whom white bread forms an untypically high proportion of their food intake.

The only surviving part of last year's proposals remains the banning of the term "wheatmeal", which ministry scientists regard as meaningless. They are afraid that consumers may have believed that "wheatmeal" bread was marginally more nutritious than "brown" bread – a false assumption.

Under the revision of the bread and flour regulations, the only permitted additive to wholemeal products will be vitamin C. Major bakeries welcomed last year's proposal to allow a wide range of flour improvers in wholemeal bread, because they felt it would enable them to make lighter and longer-keeping loaves.

But in order to clarify a confused situation the government intends to make it compulsory for all the ingredients of wrapped bread to be printed on the wrapping, and for shops selling unwrapped bread to display a list of ingredients prominently alongside the loaves.

[Handwritten margin notes:]

Government has changed its mind

The weight of public opinion must be recognised

Some groups are still at risk – and do need the added nutrients

'Wheatmeal', as a term, to be banned

Only one permitted additive to wholemeal bread

Labels on bread and in shops

At the end of the review

You've now come to the end of this review of your present day diet.
What changes have you decided to make?
What's the overall pattern of your new diet?

A new pattern?

Working through this review will have helped you work out how you measure up to the new targets for a healthier diet. Along the way you've been asked to sum up the changes you are now committed to making.

Now you have to get them all together and build a picture of the kind of foods *you enjoy eating* that fit this new diet. You have to switch from thinking about the nutrients in your diet – the fats, fibres, sugar and salt – to choosing what foods you will eat.

But before you go on . . .

Write yourself a letter. It will help you put all your ideas together and sum up the changes you want to make and how you feel about making them. It will also be there for you to read later on so that you can review your progress and renew your motivation.

What would you say in a letter to someone you know well if you were describing how you had got on doing this review and the changes that you now want to make? Take as much time as you need to write this letter – it will be of great help to you. If you like, address the envelope to yourself and put the date – perhaps three or six months time, or next January 1st – on which to open it and reread it.

We asked our testers to write such a letter. This example, from a middle-aged woman may help to get you started. She probably wouldn't be rated as 'typical' – each person is individual. Everyone has to consider how they measure up to the new targets and what changes, if any, they wish to make. They need to bear in mind the new information they now have and how their personal attitudes to risk-taking and caring for their health affects the decisions they make.

Only you can write your letter. Be honest with yourself: Margaret isn't living up to all the high standards nutritionists set but she is on the way . . .

> Dear Margaret,
> I've finished that review at last! Here's what I think:
>
> **Fats.** I eat more than the average person. I've switched to sunflower oil for cooking. I'm dithering about whether to eat butter or marg. I'd like to cut down on meat and high fat cheeses and cream so that I could go on eating butter. I don't eat pastry and only cakes occasionally. I've switched to skimmed milk – I hardly notice the different taste now. But I still love oily salad dressings.
>
> **Sugar.** I was definitely below average for this. But now that I eat a whole grain breakfast cereal, which I don't like without sugar, I may be eating more. I now have about nine teaspoonfuls a day. So I'm trying to cut down on sugar elsewhere.
>
> **Salt.** My big success: I've cut right down on the salt I add *and* the salty foods I buy. I decided to allow myself olives and a kipper sometimes – and I do eat them – but they taste so salty now! I told my GP I was doing this and now I don't have to take one of the two types of drugs I have for high blood pressure.
>
> **Fibre.** We eat wholemeal bread. My family likes rice and pulses (one of my daughters is vegetarian and she helped us get more interested.) I eat plenty of fruit and veg. Reckon I get a good 30 grams of fibre a day. I've concentrated on these rather than eating more potatoes because they tempt me to use a lot of butter on them.
>
> I notice the difference when visiting my family or having to eat out a lot – I get constipated. But now I take some high-fibre emergency rations with me.
>
> I'm sure I'm eating a healthier diet but to be honest I'm eating too much of it. I'm still overweight. I *know* I use too much oil in cooking and have too big helpings!
>
> I feel better about being overweight on a healthier diet but there are many good reasons why I should lose weight. I'm taking more exercise, but I've lost weight before only to put it on again. Any weight I do attempt to lose is not going to be by strict dieting.

To remind you

Remember the average person is recommended to:

* Eat less fat. Cut down total by 25% but more from saturated than from unsaturated fats

* Eat less sugar Cut down by 50%

* Eat less salt Cut down by 33%

* Eat more fibre Increase dietary fibre by 50%

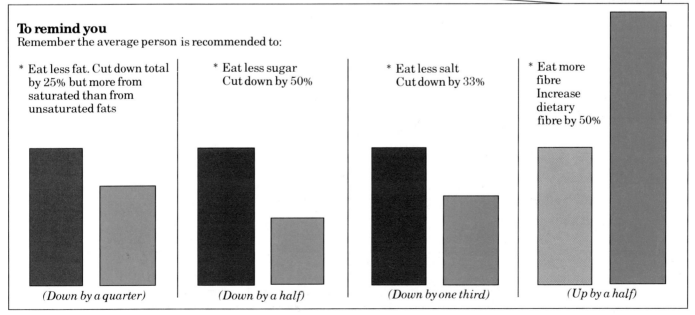

(Down by a quarter) *(Down by a half)* *(Down by one third)* *(Up by a half)*

Eating 'real food'

Ordinary people think about food not nutrients! What foods will you eat on your new, healthier diet?

Ordinary people and nutritionists

Ordinary people eat food. Nutritionists look at the nutrients – substances needed by the body – that are in that food. It's often difficult for ordinary people to make use, in their everyday life, of the advice nutritionists give. And it sometimes seems that nutritionists forget that people want to enjoy the food they eat. There's more to food than just eating it to stay alive.

As you worked through the review did you at some point – like several of our testers – think *"Sod it! What can I eat then?"* This is likely to happen when you are reviewing your diet in terms of its nutrients – the fats, fibres, sugars, etc. After all, very few people think in terms of eating nutrients. They eat food – and they want to enjoy their meals.

One meal: two ways of seeing it

You decide to have a 'Ploughman's Lunch'. Perhaps you are at home, or eating at work or eating out in a café or pub. It's easy to prepare and fairly cheap.

What a nutritionist sees: This chart shows the nutrients in this food:

Ploughman's Lunch	Weight (grams)	Fat (g)	Fibre (g)	Salt (mg sodium)	Energy (Calories)
Large chunk of white bread	70	1.2	1.9	378	163
2oz Cheddar cheese	60	20.0	–	366	244
2 pats of butter	14	11.5	–	122	103
2 teaspoons of pickle	17	–	0.3	289	22.7
Totals		32.7	2.2	1155	532.7

What is in a Ploughman's Lunch?
Have a look at this picture. There's:
● A fairly large piece of Cheddar cheese
● A large chunk of white bread
● Two pats of butter
● Two teaspoonfuls of sweet pickle

A nutritionist could tell you:
● A Ploughman's Lunch is high in fat. It would give the average person about one third of the recommended daily target for fat. The fat is a saturated fat, the type we should all cut down on particularly hard. So if you have the Ploughman's Lunch you'll have to be careful about how much fat you eat in your other meals during the day.

● It's very low in fibre. You'd need 13 times that amount to reach your daily target. You could include more fibre if the bread is wholemeal. Otherwise you'll have to eat an enormous amount of fibre at other meals.

● It's very salty. The bread, cheese and pickle are all quite high in salt. Many of the foods we buy are high in salt. It can be quite difficult to cut down. Better take extra care not to add salt at the table or in cooking for the rest of the day.

What will you decide? You might decide – "O.K., now I know how I can balance out my diet over the rest of the day, I'll still choose the Ploughman's Lunch". That's fine – if you do make the other changes.

Or you might decide – "Bearing in mind what I shall eat the rest of the day – there's too much salt and fat, and too little fibre. What could I eat instead?"

By comparing the nutrients in a wide range of meals a nutritionist can work out what fits more nearly into the 'new diet'. One alternative would be Chicken and Salad. You could have: a large chunk of wholemeal bread (90g), two pats of polyunsaturated margarine (14g), two slices of chicken breast with the skin removed (60g), a half a tomato, two large lettuce leaves and a tablespoon of sweetcorn.

This would look more on your plate than the Ploughman's Lunch, but would give you half the fat (most of it the healthier polyunsaturated fat), half the salt, and three times the amount of fibre.

If you had this as a salad you might prefer to have one tablespoon of mayonnaise or salad cream on the salad instead of the margarine on the bread. This wouldn't make much difference.

Or you might prefer to have it made up as a large sandwich.

What can I eat, then?

Most people don't want to spend the rest of their lives counting up the amounts of different nutrients in their diet, even if some nutritionists would like them to. Unless you have to keep to a strict diet on the advice of your doctor we would urge you not to go on doing this. By all means review your diet occasionally – you could always work through the activities in these materials again.

Once you've an idea of how much of the various nutrients are enough, it's better to get on with life and enjoy your meals.

Stop thinking about nutrients. Proteins, fats, sugars, starches, salt, fibre, vitamins and mineral salts.

Start choosing from 'Real Foods'. Choose mainly from a wide variety of
● Lean meat, chicken, turkey, game and fish.
● Skimmed milk, low fat yoghurt, low fat cheeses.
● Bread, rice, pasta, potatoes, whole grain breakfast cereals, porridge.
● All sorts of peas and beans (pulses).
● All kinds of fruit and vegetables.
● Enjoy the real taste of foods – without the salt. Or liven them up with herbs and spices.

Choosing a wide variety

You *could* eat a low fat, low sugar, low salt, and high fibre diet by eating just a small range of foods.

But it's much healthier to eat the same type of diet, but with a wide range of foods.

Vitamins and mineral salts. You won't need to check on individual vitamins and minerals if you eat a wide range of foods from the recommended diet. You should ask your doctor to refer you to a Community Dietician for advice if you are worried about getting enough vitamins and minerals. In certain, special cases you may need to pay extra attention to these. However, most of the anxiety about 'getting enough' is caused by misleading advertisements and articles that promote 'health foods' and 'health shops'. Your body doesn't need expensive supplements – eating a varied diet is good enough.

It's unlikely that this will dissuade people who psychologically need 'health supplements'. They feel better when they take them. So what's the harm in that? Nothing, if you can afford them and you are very careful not to exceed the stated dose. Too much can be bad for you and some can be near the recommended maximum.

Their appeal is often to the part of us that wants a 'magic cure' – quick and easy – which doesn't require us to review our whole diet.

Keep a sense of proportion: save your worry to motivate you to make the key changes. There is little point in worrying about getting enough vitamins and mineral salts if your diet is already laden with saturated fats and salts.

Avoid 'Good' and 'Bad' labels

It would be incorrect to start labelling foods as 'bad' or 'good' in *themselves*. After all, too much of anything may have a bad effect. Margaret (on page 91) seems to be having too much oil, bread and rice – they are providing more Calories than she needs.

Equally, a single helping of any one food, within the overall target you've set yourself isn't 'bad'. Though we have helped you check that your diet is not full of one-off – 'just this time' – exceptions.

Many people like to save up the butter they allow themselves for their baked potatoes. Or the very small amount of salt to use on their boiled egg. Or the small amount of sugar to put on their plain wholegrain breakfast cereals. Of course, they could use something else if they wished: but

they chose not to. There's a world of difference between choosing to do something and doing it without thinking about it.

Plan – if you choose – to include your favourite foods in your diet. Margaret is working out how to keep the butter she loves in her diet by cutting down even further on fatty meats and cheeses. However, again like Margaret with her olives and kippers, you may find that after a while on the diet you don't fancy your old favourites so much. Several of our testers mentioned that once they had got used to eating less fat treating themselves to their favourite cream cakes made them feel sick.

Labelling certain foods as 'baddies' can also make them particularly tempting and rebellious. Hence the great success of the 'Naughty but nice!' campaign to promote cream cakes.

Change your self-image

If you see yourself as: *"I'm the kind of person who adores chocolate* (or whatever). Or – *who can't resist cream cakes. But I've given them up"*.

Then – you may face a lifetime of temptation or get fed-up of having to cut back elsewhere to be able to include them in your healthier diet.

You might like to try changing your self-image. Tell yourself – and imagine yourself behaving as if –

"I'm the kind of person who takes care of their health. I eat plenty of — (name all the healthier foods you enjoy). *I take care not to eat too much chocolate/cream cakes* (or whatever). *In fact I don't really like their taste now"*.

Killing a craving. Or go further. Train yourself positively to dislike certain foods. But only do this if you really want to – not because someone else urges you to. And don't attempt it when you are under a lot of stress which may increase your longing for 'comfort' foods. Try eating too much of these foods until you begin to feel sick or queasy. Tell yourself *"I feel sick if I eat these"*. Or use your imagination – but choose a time when for some other reason you are off your food. Imagine you are eating the food and it makes your stomach turn. Sounds too gruesome? Well, you don't have to go on with all these vivid pictures. After a while you will find that *without thinking about it* you won't want to choose these foods so often.

Planning your meals

You need to eat more of some foods than others. The 'Healthy Diet Pyramid'
thought up by the Australian Nutrition Foundation
is one way of showing this.

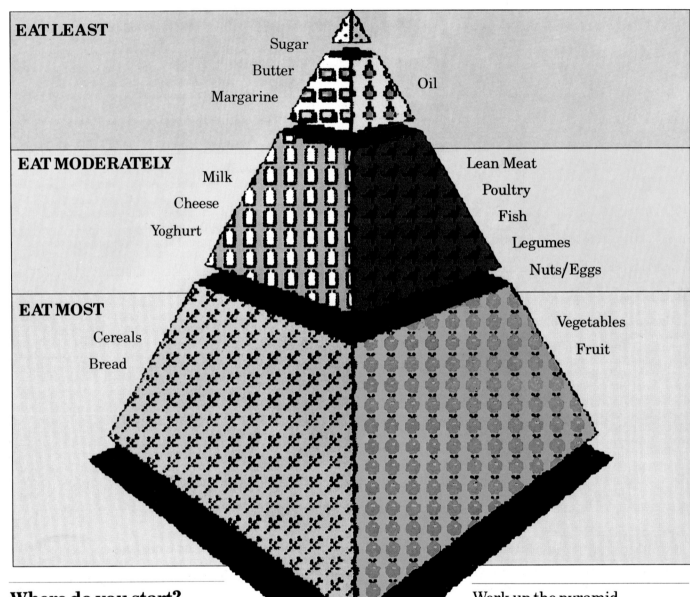

EAT LEAST

Sugar
Butter
Margarine
Oil

EAT MODERATELY

Milk
Cheese
Yoghurt

Lean Meat
Poultry
Fish
Legumes
Nuts/Eggs

EAT MOST

Cereals
Bread

Vegetables
Fruit

Where do you start?

What will you eat for your next meal or for next Sunday lunch? When you plan a meal which ingredient do you think of first?

Most people think of the meat or fish (ie. the protein) first, then the potato, bread, rice or pasta. And finally the vegetables.

Restaurants and cafés take the same approach. You start by ordering the meat or fish and then what goes with it.

In most Western countries the protein component comes first. This is partly because of publicity about the protein being the most important part of the meal. It may also be because your status and wealth are reflected by the cost of the meat or fish.

"I'll have the venison, sauté potatoes, brussels sprouts with chestnuts and cranberry sauce".

"I'll have steak, chips and a side salad".

"I'll have sausages, mash and peas".

Work up the pyramid

You should find it easier to plan healthier meals if you switch from *"Meat and ..."* to choosing the staple, high fibre, starchy food first. *"Staple and ..."* could be *"Potatoes, bread, rice or pasta and ..."*

Next think of the vegetables and finally, choose from the second layer of the pyramid.

Within the second layer, which will provide protein, consider smaller helpings than you usually have. Or have a small helping of meat plus peas or beans. Or choose vegetarian.

Your aim should be to use as little as possible from the top of the pyramid.

Vanishing staples?

Most people would probably say that bread and potatoes are our main staples in the UK. However:

● We now tend to eat less starch, dietary fibre and vegetable protein than we used to and more animal protein.

● We seem to have moved towards snack eating. One survey recently suggested that most people tend to have one or two meals a day and four or five snacks. This might well make cooked staples much more difficult to integrate into a 'snack' diet.

● Many people cut bread and potatoes out of their meals in the mistaken belief that they are bad for you. Because potatoes are high in carbohydrates they have been seen as 'baddies', especially for slimmers.

Are staples vanishing from your diet or have they already disappeared?

Write down what you've eaten for the last three meals and three snacks that you remember. Did the meals contain a large serving of potato, bread, rice or pasta? What about the snacks?

Some suggestions

When you are planning meals or snacks think *"Staple and ..."* If you find the idea of one staple as the major ingredient in a meal daunting – use two to provide the majority of the food.

Bread and ...
● Use thicker slices so that you don't use extra butter.

● Toast with a topping eg. baked beans, sardines, or grilled tomatoes. No need to butter it.

● Sandwiches with a moist filling so that they don't need butter. Include tomatoes or spread low fat cheese to help stick the sandwich together.

● To eat with stews and casseroles to mop up gravy.

● Pitta bread, filled with kebabs and salad as a takeaway snack.

Potatoes and ...
● Most people like 'potatoes and fat' – chips, roast potatoes, buttered new potatoes and creamy, buttery mashed potatoes!

So watch out for this temptation.

● Baked potatoes – good because you can eat the skins too. It's tempting to add butter. Invent additions that 'lubricate' without adding too much fat, eg. coleslaw, yoghurt and chives, cottage cheese, gravy. They are often

available as takeaway snacks with a huge range of fillings to choose from.

● Mashed topping eg. shepherd's pie or as a substitute for fatty pastry over a pie filling.

● Added to casseroles and stews, perhaps with other root vegetables or pulses. This way you can have less meat, but the dish still seems satisfying.

Pasta and ...
● Many supermarkets as well as Italian shops now sell fresh pasta. It tastes much nicer. You can buy wholemeal pastas too.

● Double the pasta and half the meat. This will be more like the traditional Italian meals. Or use tomato or mushroom or spinach sauces instead of meat.

● Use cold pasta as part of a mixed salad.

● Noodles are pasta! Try takeaway noodle-based dishes from Chinese restaurants.

Rice and ...
● Wholegrain rice served with pulses makes a high fibre and high protein meal. For example, rice and peas, rice and lentils, rice and kidney beans.

● Rice puddings – but try using skimmed milk and raisins rather than full-cream milk and sugar.

● Rice and curries. Well known and popular. Available from Indian takeaways. Easy and interesting to

cook for yourself, now ingredients and recipes are widely available.

Changing recipes

You can approach the new diet in two ways.

1. Adapt your present day diet. Stick as far as possible to the dishes you know and enjoy, but alter them a little so that they provide a healthier diet.

2. Change to new dishes. Experiment when eating out or trying new recipes from magazines and cookery books. Build up a range of new, healthier dishes that you enjoy eating.

Which approach do you prefer? Perhaps a bit of both? However most people like to continue to eat their old family favourites, however adventurous they may be about new foods.

Adapting favourite recipes

In the Minnesota Heart Health Programme, aimed to reduce coronary heart disease, there is a scheme whereby families can get their favourite recipes checked out or modified. It's very popular.

You could experiment with adapting your recipes:
You can change ways of cooking – look for ways to boil, grill, braise and stew rather than frying or roasting. Look for ways to substitute ingredients so that you get less fat, sugar and salt, and more fibre.

Ingredient	Possible substitute
● Butter	Equal quantity of sunflower margarine. Or slightly less of corn oil or sunflower oil. (When making pastry and cakes keep ingredients and utensils as cold as possible.)
● Whole milk	Skimmed milk
● Cream	Plain yoghurt
● Mayonnaise or salad cream	Half and half with plain yoghurt or seasoned plain yoghurt (eg. garlic, lemon juice or chives).
● Oily salad dressings	Seasoned plain yoghurt
● Egg	Two egg whites or 1 egg white, a teaspoon of sunflower or corn oil and a little skimmed milk.
● Sugar	Try cutting down. Texture of cakes is altered, but you may still like them. As a sweetener substitute raisins, eg. in porridge and rice puddings.
● Plain white flour	Wholemeal flour.
● Mince or cubed meat	Use half quantity of meat and top up with beans, peas or root vegetables.
● Salt	Usually makes no difference, except to taste, if you omit it. For flavouring, substitute herbs, spices, or lemon juice.

You could cook them differently

● Grill rather than fry
● Steam vegetables rather than sauté.
● Omit browning meat and vegetables before making a casserole, etc.

● Make casseroles, stews and mince well in advance. Put in the refrigerator for a few hours so that fat will congeal on top and can be thrown away.

Read on

This is a guide to sources of information and recipes which will help you to change to a healthier diet.

Reports

- **Coma Report – Diet and Cardio-vascular Disease.** (1984). Committee on Medical Aspects of Food Policy. DHSS, Report on Health and Social Subjects No. 28, HMSO.
- **NACNE Report** (September 1983). A discussion paper on proposals for nutritional guidelines for health education in Britain. Prepared for the National Advisory Committee on Nutrition Education by an ad hoc working party under the chairmanship of Professor W.P.T. James. Available free from the Health Education Council, 78 New Oxford Street, London, WC1A 1AH.
- **Coronary Heart Disease Prevention – Plans for Action** (1984). A report based on an interdisciplinary workshop conference held at Canterbury, September 1983. Pitman.

Reports NACNE consulted

These reports are all major government or academic reports.
- DHSS (1978 and 1979) Report on Eating for Health, HMSO.
- DHSS (1974) Report on Health and Social Subjects No. 7. Diet and Coronary Heart Disease, HMSO.
- The Royal College of Physicians and British Cardiac Society (1976) Report on Prevention of Coronary Artery Disease.
- The Royal College of Physicians (1981) Report on Medical Aspects of Dietary Fibre.
- DHSS (1979) Report on Health and Social Studies No. 15. Recommended daily amounts of food energy and nutrients for groups of people in the United Kingdom, HMSO.
- DHSS (1981) Report on Avoiding Heart Attacks, HMSO.
- WHO (1982) Report on the Prevention of Coronary Heart Disease. World Health Organisation.
- The Royal College of Physicians (1983) Report on Obesity.

Explaining the NACNE Report

- **Diet 2000.** Dr Alan Maryon-Davis with Jane Thomas (1984). *Pan.* How to eat for a healthier future. Based on the revolutionary NACNE report.

- **The food scandal.** Caroline Walker and Geoffrey Cannon (1984) *Century.* What's wrong with the British diet and how to put it right.

Slimming

You need to do more than just cut down on the calories:
- **Dieting makes you fat.** Geoffrey Cannon and Hetty Einzig (1983). *Century.* A paperback version is also available (1984). *Sphere.* Looks at why 'yo-yo' dieting – a repeated pattern of rapid weight loss followed by rapid weight gain – can upset your metabolic rate so that subsequent dieting becomes even more difficult. It also explains why exercise may be even more important than a slimming diet for controlling your weight.
- **Fat is a feminist issue** and **Fat is a feminist issue 2.** Susie Orbach (1979 and 1984). *Hamlyn Paperbacks.* Examines social and psychological aspects of body image and weight control. Second book has detailed suggestions on how to overcome such personal problems.
- **F-plan diet.** Audrey Eyton (1982). *Penguin.* Explains how to lose weight on a fibre-rich diet. Does not take into consideration the salt content of the food and in some cases the foods are suprisingly high in sugar so not altogether suitable for a long-term healthy diet.
- **F-plan calorie and fibre chart.** Audrey Eyton (1982). *Penguin.* Fibre content details are useful even if you do not want to lose weight but do want a high fibre diet.
  When looking at slimming diets check that they are low fat, low sugar, low salt and high fibre. Choose slimming diets on which you can eat a wide variety of ordinary foods. Avoid slimming diets that concentrate on a limited range of foods or exotic ingredients. They may well provide an unbalanced diet if used for longer than a few days. Even more important they don't teach you to eat a healthy, well balanced, varied diet that you can keep to for the rest of your life.

Cooking

Some new cookery books give the nutrient content of their recipes. This makes it much easier to check, for

example, that you are not cooking too many high fat dishes or to find higher fibre versions of your favourite recipes. Some magazines, particularly *New Health,* also give nutrient contents for their recipes.
- **The high-fibre cook book.** Pamela Westland (1982). *Dunitz.* Recipes for good health.
- **The diabetics' diet book.** Dr Jim Mann and the Oxford Diabetic Group (1982). *Dunitz.* A new high fibre eating programme. Written for diabetics, this book led the breakthrough to a new approach to a suitable diet for diabetics. As diabetics also need to watch their weight these delicious recipes are also helpful to non-diabetics as well.
- **Cooking for your heart's content.** The British Heart Foundation Cookbook (1977). *Arrow.* Provides a wide variety of recipes, low in saturated fats. Recipes are also calorie counted. However, watch out for the salt – it could often easily be cut down.
- **Modified diets.** Jill Leslie (for the British Nutrition Foundation). Sainsbury's Food Guides, No. 5. Provides helpful background information for those whose doctor or dietician has advised them, for medical reasons, to go on special diets.

Vegetarian and ethnic cookbooks

Not all vegetarian cookbooks provide recipes that match up to dietary guidelines. Avoid those that use large amounts of eggs, cheese and butter. Many well-balanced vegetarian dishes come from countries where the traditional diet is vegetarian.
- **Sarah Brown's vegetarian cookbook.** Sarah Brown (1984). *Dorling Kindersley.* Shows just how delicious vegetarian dishes can look.
- **Eastern vegetarian cookery.** Madhur Jaffrey (1983). *Cape.* Well-known for her TV series and book on Indian cookery. She makes the recipes sound tempting and easy to cook. This book covers the whole of the East.
- **Vegetarian dishes from the Middle East.** Arto der Haroutunian (1984). *Century.* The up-dated paperback edition is a practical cookbook that is also interesting to read.

PART 2
PATTERNS OF EATING

Patterns of Eating

A new set of guidelines for healthy eating has now been produced. Two recent reports have developed these guidelines – the NACNE report from the National Advisory Committee on Nutrition Education, and the COMA report on 'Diet and Cardiovascular Disease' by the department of Health and Social Security's Committee on Medical Aspects of Food. Basically the guidelines suggest that as a nation we should cut down on fats, particularly saturated fats, sugar and salt, and eat more fibre-rich foods.

Putting it into practice

These guidelines are an exciting development in the field of nutrition and if we can implement them in our lives, many of us can look forward to having a much healthier diet than we have at the moment.

However, for many of us it's quite a challenge to put into practice changes that can mean altering habits and attitudes that have been learned over a lifetime. Needless to say, eating spills over into a whole host of other events and situations in our lives. *Patterns of Eating* helps you look at the new guidelines for healthy eating in relation to your life as a whole. You'll find the guidelines mentioned in most topics you read. They have been highlighted in the text as a checklist to remind you.

It is possible, of course, to make some piecemeal changes. For instance, for an individual changing to using semi-skimmed milk from whole milk is a very positive change to make and yet it doesn't involve a major social upheaval. It just means the colour of your coffee is slightly different! But other changes may mean re-examining your attitude to food and eating and how they fit into your life as a whole.

Patterns of Eating helps you build up this wider picture of both your individual attributes and the sort of factors that affect us all.

National and regional trends. Such trends in food consumption affect us as individuals. We don't buy food in isolation. We have to go out and buy what's available. This may be a very different selection depending on where you live, and who you are. For instance, the vast selection of family packs of food is for many single and elderly people no choice at all in practical terms.

So how we deal with eating as individuals is affected by such seemingly simple things as not being able to buy small sizes. Generally, such factors may be just a passing annoyance. But once we start to examine our pattern of eating with an eye to change then they come to be seen as more significant.

Food is not just fuel

For many people food and eating serves all sorts of purposes – much more than keeping us alive and healthy.

Food can be a source of enjoyment – eating with other people, preparing and sharing special meals. It can be a comforter providing ourselves with the attention and love that might not be available from other sources. Offering food to others can show love and the bonds between us and them. But it can also be a way of expressing power over others.

Food helps us organise our time. Meals and snacks break up the day. Food is time-consuming too – you need to shop for food and prepare it. And of course, it can be a problem if you haven't got much money or you don't know how to eat healthily or you become obsessed about it.

Food is something that involves us all, even though everyone's experience of it is unique. We all have views and opinions about it. And it can be quite a revelation hearing what other people have to say about the subject. During the preparation of *Patterns of Eating* all the draft materials were read by various testers. A lot of their comments have been included in the final material.

Table talk

For many of the questions we ask in the text there are no absolute right or wrong answers. It's what's right for you that's important. Our testers' comments will frequently give you something to compare your own views against. Certainly other people's views are useful in helping you to become clearer about your own. So don't just read testers' comments, talk to friends and colleagues. Find out what they think. It's a lively area of debate!

The team writing the material went through a stage of almost non-stop talking about food and eating. Testers' comments led to major discussions. Every meal and snack became a subject of interest. Parents, partners and children were all tackled on their opinions. When it comes to views and opinions, rather than nutritional facts, what everyone has to say is valid.

We hope you find that you have the same sense of exhilaration as you work through *Patterns of Eating*. Look at the new guidelines for healthy eating in terms of your whole life. Your pattern of eating involves far more than the food itself. There are lots of activities in the text that should help you examine the strengths and weaknesses of your own pattern. Before you try any major alterations, can we suggest you go through the whole book? When you've built up a complete picture of your eating pattern you'll be in a better position to make considered and effective changes. Remember too, to give yourself a pat on the back for your strengths. Hold on to them and build on them.

Don't rush into change. It's worth taking time over something as important as a healthy pattern of eating.

A different diet?

Everyone's pattern of eating is unique. The stage you've reached in your life, the experiences you've been through, the tastes in food you've acquired, your body shape and weight, your emotions, finances and relationships are all important factors in your experience of eating. Put together they are what make your pattern of eating yours and yours alone.

However, there are national, regional and social class patterns in food consumption. As a nation we now eat too much fat, particularly saturated fat, sugar, salt and not enough fibre. And we have moved towards different styles of eating too in the past few years – more snacks, fewer meals.

How do all these things affect you? This chapter helps you make some connections between your own pattern of eating and some of the national food trends. The chapter also considers a variety of different eating patterns and whether some groups of people have special problems when it comes to food. You'll also be asked to think about whether other people's eating patterns help to throw any light on your own.

Changing lifestyles

The way we live our lives affects our diet.
Changing lifestyles may mean changing patterns of eating too.

"When I think back to my early days, many of them as a child before the war, the idea that any 'foreign' dishes should come from my mother's kitchen was absolutely unthinkable.

"We had two kitchens then — one up and one down. The bottom kitchen was reserved in all its flagged glory for clothes washing in the old set pot (which on occasions doubled as a ham and pudding boiler), but it was in the upstairs kitchen that the most impor-

tant work was done, and to come into that top kitchen at the end of the baking day was a moment I waited for each week.

"There, spread out on scrubbed whitewood tables, would be white loaves, brown loaves, tea cakes, scones, Sally Lunns, twists, plaits, oven bottom cake, deep custards, apple pies, cheesecakes — all the trappings, in fact, of a typical Yorkshire baking day.

"First home got first cut at the oven

bottom cake; split open and spread liberally with home made butter and dark treacle before being sandwiched together and swilled down with a huge mug of tea. How well that tasted, particularly when it was a bit scorched."

(These mouthwatering memories were written by Michael Smith and appeared in *Yorkshire Cooking* by Shirley Kaye — produced by the Halifax Courier in the late 1960s.)

Changes in your life

Ah, those were the days! This description is a very personal one. Many people, at that time, would have had different experiences of food from the one quoted. But it does conjure up a picture of one very definite pattern of eating in the past.

For everybody many things have changed over the years – such as domestic routines, family sizes, cooking styles and the different kinds of food available. These changes can be seen in terms of the nation as a whole, but they are experienced by us as individuals.

So what have people's experiences of these changes been? How do we personally experience current trends in patterns of eating? What do we understand by them? What do they mean in terms of our own lives?

The foods of childhood

What are your fondest childhood memories of food? On a separate piece of paper quickly write down a list of foods you loved when you were little.

Our testers. Some of the foods our testers mentioned were ... tinned tomatoes with bread to mop up the juice ... cheese melted in milk under the grill ... boiled egg with soldiers ... jam with cream on ... mashed banana with sugar and milk ... freshly baked currant tea cakes ... cold meat with salad ... Weetabix with golden syrup. One tester commented, *"We were too large a family to be able to afford to have Weetabix as a breakfast cereal, but it was looked upon as a special treat with syrup on."*

Now write a list of your current favourite foods. How does it compare with your childhood favourites?

The British Nutrition Foundation carried out a survey on *Eating in the early 1980s.* They found that:

"... people felt that there was an adventurous stage between the eating conservatisms of childhood and old age; that as one grew up one's taste tended to change from sweet to savoury ..."

Think of three adjectives which would describe the sort of food you had a taste for in your childhood. Our testers used a whole variety of words. Words which cropped up on several occasions were 'sweet', 'stodgy', 'soft', 'bland'.

Would the adjectives you've chosen describe your tastes now? Try choosing three adjectives to describe the sort of food you have a taste for now. How different are your two sets of adjectives?

Eat up your greens!

What other foods do you remember being given as a child – apart from the ones you loved? Jot down another list and include the foods you really didn't like very much.

Your list may well have included foods that your parents thought were good for you. Or it may show mainly the foods your parents could afford. But such foods will have been a part of your family's eating patterns too, as well as the treats.

Try talking to your parents or other people of their generation. Talk to your grandparents too, or people of their age. Ask them to tell you about foods they enjoyed in childhood. And ask them about foods they were given because they were 'good' for them. Did they know why these foods were supposed to be 'good' for them? As one man, now in his 60s, said of his mother, *"Her aim in life was that we should all have cheeks like dumplings and plenty of flesh all over. For her that's what healthy children were. So we were given lots of food that did make us plump."*

New guidelines for healthy eating

> The new guidelines for healthy eating are that we should eat: less fat, less sugar, less salt, and more fibre.

Ask parents and grandparents whether they think they now eat more fats, sugars and salt than they did when they were young. And do they eat less fibre?

Has your childhood pattern of eating changed? Did you use to eat fewer fats and less sugar and salt than you do now – and more fibre?

Compare eating experiences. Look at the lines below. Put one cross on each line where you think your eating habits are *now.* And put a circle on the same line where you think your eating habits were when you were a child. Ask the people of different generations you've talked to to do the same. Write their initials on the crosses and circles they've marked on the lines.

|————————————————|

Lots of fibre   Very little fibre

|————————————————|

Lots of salt   Very little salt

|————————————————|

Lots of sugar   Very little sugar

|————————————————|

Lots of fats   Very few fats

Look particularly at the circles on each line. How do the childhood experiences of food for parents and grandparents compare with yours? Hopefully, this should help you begin to pick up a picture of how patterns of eating do change over time.

Food for families

Of course, the whole story of the foods you ate in your childhood is not just told in their taste. Your memories will be coloured by what sort of events meals were and who was there. They may have been ordinary family meals or special occasions.

Think about meals in your childhood. Can you recall meals that were particularly important, in some way, as family events? It may be easier to remember special meals. Jot down a few lines using these questions to help you:

- Was the valued meal a special occasion?
- What foods were served?
- When and where were such meals eaten?
- Who did you eat the meals with?
- Were there special rituals attached to these meals?

Special meals. Here are two people's accounts of special meals in childhood.

"Sunday tea with visitors, friends and relatives. It was always a delicious salad with cold meat, stewed fruit and trifle and cake. We ate it about 4.30 in the dining room, just before church, around a large table. There was always a beautiful tablecloth and the silver shone."

"Sunday breakfast. I never heard of anyone else who did this, but we always had pork pie, cold pressed meats — brawn, faggots and so on — with lots of crusty bread and big cups of tea. We always had it in the kitchen, the whole family. We had one of those wood burning cookers and in the winter it was always a lovely, warm, comfortable meal."

For some people such memories have an effect on some of their present day patterns. As one person said, *"I occasionally cook childhood foods for my husband now. He tends to look back with regret saying how good it all was. Of course, he forgets how well he looks now, when he's no longer on a diet of stodgy, greasy foods."*

These pictures not only show images of food, but images of households, families and how they deal with food. Of course, memory can build up images and both these accounts are quite nostalgic, but they are also both strong memories.

Some memories may be more mundane.

"My valued meal was Sunday lunch, my mother and us children. My dad was usually still at the pub."

Changing

People not only change their tastes in food and their patterns of eating over the years. Their situation changes too. This isn't always just a matter of growing up or moving into different social settings. Often matters of national change affect them too. For instance, the way we organise our families and households may well be different now. This, too, has an effect on our eating patterns.

Look at this quote from the 1950s. It comes from *Rose Buckner's Book of Homemaking* (Odhams Press).

"I think the nicest welcome home to a husband and family is for them to open the front door and smell something they like cooking, see a nicely set table and a good, warm fire, that's home. You, the housewife, are the only one who can make this picture come true."

What do you think this statement is about? Is it to do with practical aspects of catering? Or is it expressing a desirable role for a woman to play?

Do you think most people would agree with that statement today? Have times changed?

Whatever people may desire in patterns of family eating, it's affected by the real situation they find themselves in. What about the wife who

works and comes home at the same time as everyone else? This picture of the warm welcome for the family, by the housewife who's been preparing food all afternoon, will be difficult to achieve! It may not even be considered desirable in many families. Roles in families are changing.

Changes?

What other things have changed? Think about some changes in *the way* you eat, that have happened during your lifetime in the households that you have lived in. Don't worry about changes in the actual food so much. Concentrate more on things connected with your lifestyle.

Write down five changes which have been significant for you.

Our testers. Here are some of the changes our testers mentioned in their lives. How do they compare with yours?

"We used to eat at regular times. Now eating seems to take place at any old time when people are hungry."

"When I was a teenager I passed the bulk of my wages over to my mother and had all my meals with the family. My own teenage children rarely eat with us. They eat out a lot."

"One of my mother's main tasks in life was feeding the family. Her day was organised around getting breakfast, mid-day meal and dinner. I fit feeding the family around my jobs, which means they often get their own food."

"We used to sit down at the table together every evening. Now we tend to eat in easy chairs with trays perched on our laps while we're watching television."

"The rituals of a meal are often not carried out today, for instance, laying a tablecloth and putting out table napkins. It sounds a small thing, but I think it means people are more rushed than they used to be."

"We get food onto the table a lot faster than when I was little. It's possible to prepare it a lot more quickly."

"I don't know whether it's just a phase I'm going through, but because I live by myself I just eat what I want. Often I don't eat meals at all."

"I was brought up in a very working class household in the Midlands, where we had regular, and I mean regular, meals. We always had tea at 6.00pm, when the news started on the radio. Now we never eat till 8.00pm. I don't suppose that's got much to do with living in London, but it's probably got a lot to do with my having moved into different circles because of my education and marriage."

New trends

Of course, some of the significant changes are to do with personal changes in people's situations – living alone instead of living in a family, moving to a different part of the country, getting married. However, read the following paragraphs. Some of them are about general trends which may affect eating patterns. Some are about widescale changes in eating patterns themselves.

Check your own list of significant changes. Which of the widescale changes do you recognise as having occurred at an individual level? Which ones have made no appearance in your life at all?

Working mothers. A greater proportion of women with dependent children are now working than a generation ago. In a 1980 study of women and employment, the Office of Population Censuses and Surveys found the following:

● In 1959, seven % of women whose youngest child was under five were working part-time. By 1979 the proportion was 24%.
● The same story for women whose youngest child was between five and ten. In 1959 19% of them worked part-time, by 1979 that proportion was 45%
● And again, for women whose youngest child was between 11 and 15 ... in 1959 30% of them worked

part-time, in 1979 this had increased to 47%.

Family patterns. According to materials collected on social trends in Britain, only one third of all households now contain Mum, Dad and one or more kids. Another third are couples with no children, or whose children have left home. In the last 20 years the number of people living on their own, mainly those over retirement age, has doubled – they now make up over one-quarter of all households.

Meals and snacks. Recent research by the British Nutrition Foundation has suggested that meals are less important than they used to be. In the day before being asked questions by the researchers it was found that four % of adults surveyed had had no meal, 48% had had one meal, 27% had had two meals and 21% had had three or more meals.

Eating and drinking now seems to be an activity that goes on fairly evenly throughout the day, from 6.45 in the morning to midnight. In any hour during this time about one third of adults are eating or drinking something.

This is how the British Nutrition Foundation researchers summed up their findings. They reported that the figures "... *make one wonder about the much used phrase 'between meal eating'. The reality seems to be that meals are things that occur between snacks!*"

So it seems that the day is no longer regulated by meal times by many people. Styles are changing.

Yet more changes?

Think again about the current guidelines for healthy eating. As a nation we eat too much fat, too much sugar, too much salt and not enough fibre.

If you want to change that balance you need to think more generally about how eating fits into your life, as well as about the foods themselves. The idea of deliberate change in your eating habits may seem difficult, but in some ways personal patterns of eating do change a lot. You may have experienced the following changes:

● Your tastes will almost certainly have changed. Your eating as a child may have been very different from your eating now.
● Your own, special circumstances will have changed. There have been changes in your lifestyle which have affected your eating patterns from childhood to adulthood – perhaps going to college, getting married and having your own children, or living by yourself.
● You may have been part of wider, national changes. Households and ideas about organising eating have changed – fewer meals, more snacks, more flexible eating styles.

Food trends

What we eat as a nation and how we eat it changes through the years. What do these changes mean for us as individuals?

Watching a film made 20 years ago you can't help noticing how much life has changed. It doesn't seem so long ago, yet look at the different clothes, different hairstyles, different cars. We even talked differently. Do we eat different foods now too? Have food trends changed as obviously as trends in other areas of life?

This topic looks at how changes in food trends can be seen in our individual diets – in other words, what's on our plates!

Two days in Bill's life. This is a record of what Bill, aged 30, ate yesterday and his memories of the sort of food he would have eaten on a typical day 20 years ago.

7.30 tea in bed (with wife)... 8.15 muesli, brown toast and marmalade, black coffee (in kitchen on own)... 10.30 black coffee, two chocolate biscuits (with workmates)... 11.15 black coffee (at desk)... 1.00 half pint bitter, toasted cheese sandwich and chips (at pub on own)... 3.30 tea and chocolate bar (at desk)... 5.30 apple (on bus)... 6.30 pint bitter, crisps, peanuts (in pub with next door neighbour)... 8.30 takeaway pizza (at home with wife)... 10.30 brown bread, tomato sandwich and black coffee (while finishing painting back bedroom).

And 20 years ago.
7.45 cornflakes, sugar, milk, white bread, bacon sandwich, toast, marmalade and tea (in kitchen with mum)... 10.45 school milk (in playground with friends)... 12.30 stew, mashed potatoes and swede, sponge pudding and custard (in canteen with friends)... 4.15 tea and bun (in kitchen on own)... 5.30 sausages, chips, white bread and butter, tinned fruit and evaporated milk, cake, tea (in dining room with family)... 9.00 Ovaltine and biscuits (in living room with family).

Bill's changes. There are some big changes here. Some of them are to do with growing up. Bill isn't eating his mother's food and school dinners any longer. But what he ate yesterday and the circumstances he ate it in, show some signs of changes in food habits that are national rather than individual in origin.

Look back over the two days Bill recorded. Twenty years ago he ate fewer snacks and more meals. Yesterday his eating fitted round his other activities more than it did when he was a child. You will see that he had a foreign takeaway. That was his only 'proper' meal, but he did eat or drink nine times. Twenty years ago muesli wasn't popular, brown bread and crisps not so popular and foreign food not so generally available.

Change and you

How has your own diet changed over the past few years? Try asking yourself these questions and make a note of your answers. The questions deal with the last 20 years, but you may want to look at just five years ago instead, or maybe 10 or 15 years ago. This will depend on your age and memory!

- What was your favourite meal when you had just left school or left your parents' home? Has it changed?
- Do you have the same breakfast now as you had 20 years ago?
- Do you eat more sugar than you used to?
- Do you eat as much meat as you used to? Has the sort of meat you eat changed?
- Do you eat as much bread and potatoes as you used to?
- Do you eat as many fats as you used to?

Our testers' comments.

"I used to eat lots of white, crusty bread and butter. Now I only eat brown bread, usually wholemeal or granary."

"I used to eat a cooked breakfast, now it's cereal and toast."

"There have been few changes in my diet, as I grew up in a family who all enjoyed fresh fruit and vegetable dishes and stone-ground breads."

"I've given up frying foods altogether. Now instead of frying I always grill."

"I have stopped eating stodgy puddings such as dumplings."

"My favourite meal when I left home was Sunday roast and jam roly-poly. And it still is!"

But even if our favourite meals remain the same, things certainly have changed in lots of ways.

Times change

Below is a list of things that were common a generation ago. On the right are three examples of present day alternatives. Fill in the rest of this column.

Include your own personal changes. Also add any general changes that you've noticed. What other examples can you think of?

A generation ago	Present day alternatives
Rice as pudding	Rice as vegetable
Pasta meant macaroni cheese	Spaghetti and sauce
No snacks	Commercially produced snacks
Fresh fish	
Fresh or canned peas	
White bread	
Boiled sweets	
Lard for frying	
Butter	
Fish and chips as takeaway	
Deep fried chips	
Soup at start of meal	
Custard on all puddings	
Steamed, boiled or baked puddings	
Sugar	
Salad as lettuce and tomato	
Chicken for special occasions	
Fruit meant apples or oranges	

Of course, there are all sorts of answers – changes are personal to each one of us. But several of our testers pointed to a greater use of vegetable oils and of margarine than 20 years ago. And, also, to a greater use of frozen food and fewer puddings.

In doing this exercise yourself you will probably have recognised that many of the changes you've noted have not been unique just to yourself. Your friends may have made the same changes. Or perhaps you'll have seen them happening wider afield. There are all sorts of reasons why such changes come about in the national diet.

Availability. A dramatic example of how the availability of food affects food trends is provided by the effect of the Second World War on food supplies. Transport problems meant citrus fruits and bananas were almost unheard of. Rationing limited eggs, butchers' meat, bacon, milk, fats, cheese and sugar. We all ate more bread and vegetables. Overall this was a healthier diet.

Since the war, there has been a huge increase of all sorts of food from all sorts of places. Ease of transport and methods of chilling mean food can be brought from all over the globe. There is now a great variety of foods on offer.

Other changes. Storage facilities affect the kind of food we eat. We used to keep food in cold stores and larders. Now we have fridges and freezers. We can have fish fingers and ice cream all the time. The techniques of canning, freezing and chilling mean we can have all sorts of foods that are out of season. On the other hand, light, warm, modern houses are not particularly suited to storing sacks of potatoes and carrots.

Convenience versus nutrition. The trend in food habits seems to be towards a more casual, more snacking style of eating. Much of the food we eat on these occasions is bought ready prepared. For those who want to be less involved in food preparation this is probably good news.

In a recent article it was quoted that 65% of the food we eat as a nation we buy ready prepared. Much of this food contains things that we could do with eating less of – fats, salt, sugar. Of course, it also often contains nutrients that we do need. Soft drinks, crisps and other snack products have rocketed in consumption since the 1960s. Convenience desserts, such as fruit yoghurt, contain a lot of sugar.

So when we eat ready prepared food we eat the salt, sugar and fats that go into them. And the move towards 'snacking' seems to mean an increased consumption of these foods in our diet. You can, of course, cook a ready prepared convenience meal too. However, when you cook a meal from scratch you have much more influence over what actually goes into it. And it's therefore easier to bring your own cooking into line with current health recommendations – you can't really change a ready prepared meal. But 'snacking' can mean flexible eating – and fits well with life today. However, it is worth thinking about what increased snacking and the use of ready prepared food means to our diet.

Then and now

What type of changes in our consumption of various foods has taken place over the years? Below are some comments about changes relating to some of our major food stuffs.

Bread. The consumption of bread has been going down steadily. In the mid 1860s rural workers each ate nearly 12lb of bread a week. By 1980 each person, on average, was eating just under 2lb of bread a week. There were big drops of consumption of bread after both world wars. And after the Second World War bread was rationed. This decline is probably the most marked of all changes in food patterns.

Sugar. The total consumption of sugar has remained the same for some time. But that total disguises two major changes. We now add much less sugar to our food and drink. However, manufacturers are adding much more of it to food, particularly as glucose syrup, in manufactured foods we buy.

Potatoes. We don't eat so many potatoes. Even in 1960 we were eating an average of 3½ lbs a week. By 1980 the average weekly consumption was more like 2½ lb. But although we eat fewer potatoes in their plain, unadorned form, we do eat more chips and crisps than we used to do. And eating potatoes in this form introduces more salt and fat into our diet.

Meat. Meat eating has shown a steady increase in consumption until recently. In 1900, among working class people, each individual ate an average of just under 1½ lb of meat a week. In 1970 the average person ate nearly 2¼ lb a week. These figures are dropping slightly. In 1980 we were eating on average one ounce a week less. This change sparked off the British Meat Campaign.

Milk. There was a sudden rise in our milk consumption during the Second World War. During the war the figure shot up to four pints of milk per person a week – previously it was under two pints. This was in part due to the introduction of the Welfare Foods scheme. The consumption of milk has stayed at this high level ever since.

Fats. The actual amount of fats that we eat has gone down. In the 1960s and 1970s we each ate 12 ounces a week – in 1980 this figure was down to 9.7 ounces. But we now eat less carbohydrates – bread and potatoes – so our diet is less bulky. This means that we actually eat less food, pound for pound, than we used to. The percentage of fat in our diet has increased. We may eat less of it, but it's a bigger proportion of our total diet.

Fruit and vegetables. In the past fruit and vegetables were often grown on allotments and so it was difficult to estimate how much people ate. Since figures have been available fruit consumption has been increasing but not vegetables.

When you read about these national changes you need to bear in mind people's personal circumstances – the money that they earn, or don't earn, the job they have, their regional and class background. *All* these things contribute to the sort of diet they have. The *national* picture doesn't pick all of this up. Historically, such differences have always existed but more specialised breakdowns give a feel for these variations.

Variations

Not everyone made the same changes. It often depended on what social class people were in and which part of the country they lived in. Regional and social class variations in eating continue now.

There are considerable variations across the nation in consumption of different types of food. Some of them are not easy to explain. A recent British Nutrition Foundation survey *Eating in the early 1980s* noted that 23% of Midlanders eat gravy in any day compared with the national average of 16%. Only five % of Scots eat gravy in any day. Quite a difference!

The BNF survey showed up some substantial differences in response to the question 'What did you eat yesterday?' Bear in mind that the survey was done in the winter. Here are some results for what people ate 'yesterday':

Soup
- 14% of people in the UK ate soup.
- 43% of Scots ate soup.

Poultry
- 14% of people in the UK ate chicken.
- 20% of social classes A and B (that is upper middle class and middle class) ate chicken.

Brown bread
- 24% of people in the UK ate brown bread.
- 35% of social classes A and B ate brown bread.

Londoners queue for their bread in 1946

• 19% of people from social classes C2 and D (that is skilled working class and working class) ate brown bread.

It's reassuring to learn that 85% of the people asked in the survey drank tea yesterday! Some things are truly national it seems. But there are significant differences in lots of foods. Why?

Looking at wholemeal bread

Suppose you are poor, busy, with plenty of worries, no transport and a family to feed. What kind of bread are you looking for?

• Cheap – because every penny counts.
• Sliced – no sharp knives needed, so children can help themselves.
• Bread is the original convenience food – you can walk round with it and it's ready in an instant.
• Familiar texture and flavour – important if you are busy and worried, you don't want any more battles on your hands than you have already.
• Readily available – if you've got no transport then the corner shop is the easiest daily option.

In the early 1980s wholemeal bread was more expensive, compared to white bread, than it is now. It was only available unsliced. It had for many people a dense, unfamiliar texture. It wasn't widely available in great quantity. Is it any wonder that certain sections of the population weren't likely to seek it out?

Times change. Today in the mid-80s all this has changed. Wholemeal bread comes sliced, wrapped, it's light in texture and has far more outlets – including corner shops. In five years' time this trend will probably show up very significantly on the statistics.

Prices and standard of living

What food we buy depends on how much it costs and how much of our income we are able to spend on it. There have been big changes in the past one hundred years. At the end of the 19th century one family of five, in rural Dorset, spent 65% of their income on food. And that wasn't counting the fact that they had their potato ground which provided them with their staple vegetable. In 1913 the percentage of weekly income that a working class family would spend on food was 60% or even more. Families like this, spending so much of their income on food, still weren't well fed and some were suffering from the effects of malnutrition.

In 1968 low paid families with three or more children were reported to be spending 50% of their disposable income on food.

How much of the money you actually receive each week do you spend on food – in other words, what proportion of your disposal income? A quarter, a half, a tenth? Our testers mentioned that proportions from about one quarter to two thirds of their income was spent on food. One tester said that it was approximately half of her pension money.

Doing without

Some foods that we eat regularly we see as being essential to us. We go on buying them even if the price goes up. When the price of less essential foods goes up, we think we can do without them. However, what we see as essentials do change over time. This quote comes from 1913:

"Potatoes are an invariable item. Greens may go, butter may go, meat may diminish almost to vanishing point before potatoes are affected." (So says Mrs Pember Reeves in a book by Rowntree and Kendall *Round-about a £1 a week*.)

Would you say this was true today? Certainly at times during the past 20 years or so, potatoes have been seen as real villains. The same with bread. We don't eat nearly as much as we used to. What you have on your plate today and the proportions of the various foods may differ from 20 years ago.

Where would you make changes? Say you're shopping for a meal for a special occasion. Perhaps your shopping list would look something like this:

2lb	topside
3lb	potatoes
1lb	carrots
1lb	frozen peas
1	medium cauliflower

Work out what you think the cost of these various items would be. Now imagine that all the items on the list were £1 per pound more expensive.

What changes would you make?
• Would you stick to meat even though it's more expensive?
• Would you go for cheaper cuts?
• Would you think twice about vegetables?

Make a list of the substitutions you would make.

Of the people who tested this exercise one person suggested cutting out two vegetables, several people opted for cheaper meat, often meat that could be casseroled along with vegetables. Others decided they'd look for cheaper vegetables. Only one person

said she'd substitute a vegetarian meal.

For a few days try sizing up the various foods you have on your plate. What would you be prepared to cut out? What for you are the real essentials on your plate? Does the food on your plate represent the recent national trends – plenty of meat, fats, salt, sugar, not very many fibre-rich foods? Or are you already trying to move towards the new guidelines?

A matter of taste

Various health education campaigns and the concern with slimming have made most people familiar with terms like protein, calories, vitamins, minerals and carbohydrates. Publicity about cancer and heart disease may have made other terms familiar – such as cholesterol, saturated fats, polyunsaturated fat and fibre. Other terms are becoming more common because of the public and consumer interest in what our food contains – emulsifiers, monosodium glutamate, etc.

Even if we do know about healthy foods, we don't always put our knowledge into action. Taste, convenience and the pressures of family, friends and lifestyles may well play a big part in determining what we eat as well as our ideas about nutrition.

> In the current guidelines for healthy eating we're recommended to eat: less fats, less sugar, less salt, more fibre.

Think now about the personal changes to do with food that you've examined in this topic. Have any of the changes in eating that you've noted in your life contributed towards a healthier pattern of eating for you? This was one of our tester's reactions:

"I loved sugar when I was little in all its' forms — golden syrup was my favourite. When I was 15 I thought I was fat, so I stopped taking sugar in my tea. Then I began to find other things rather sweet. I began to form a taste for savoury food. Now I don't have sugar if I can help it, mainly because of all the stuff I've read and heard about sugar and tooth decay."

It may be difficult for you to change the proportion of your income that you spend on food. But you can change the proportions of various foods on your plate. Reducing meat, increasing staples, increasing vegetables, using meat as a flavourant are changes on the plate that mean moving away from recent national trends. They are ways of moving towards the current recommendations for healthy eating. Let's hope they do become national trends.

We are all individuals

Everyone's pattern of eating is individual.
And the new recommendations for a healthier diet need to be considered
in relation to what actually goes on in people's lives.

> As a nation we eat more sugar, salt and fats than we need and not enough fibre rich foods.

As an individual, you may feel that circumstances are against you in any moves *you* want to make towards eating more healthily.

If you are the main caterer in your household you may find yourself concerned with several people who have very different approaches to eating. This will have implications for the way you tackle your task of catering. It may also affect your own eating. On the other hand, if you are in charge of your *own* catering – for example, living by yourself or living in a household where everyone caters for themselves – it could be your lifestyle which affects your patterns of eating.

This topic looks at a variety of things that may affect eating patterns. Some of these may concern you directly. Or you may identify others as being similar to those of people you know and care about.

Different circumstances

Here is a selection of agony column letters. In all these letters personal circumstances led to problems with eating for the people concerned. You may be able to identify some issues that you have had experience of yourself. The letters bring home the fact that our diet is very closely connected with the rest of our lives.

Force of circumstances?

Read each letter again. What are the main circumstances which seem to have led to the problems about food?

You will probably have had no difficulty in spotting most of the following:

- changed social situation
- strained relationships
- money problems
- lack of competence in catering
- lack of knowledge about nutrition
- not conforming to manufacturers' ideas of what's normal
- state of mind – poor self-image, anxiety
- social status – living alone, being a single parent.

These things don't always cause people problems with their diets. But, as the letters show, they can get to be problems. They also show that it's possible to have to face several of these issues at the same time.

Now go through the list again. Which ones have affected you personally? Think back and write a few lines on a separate piece of paper about how these things affected your eating patterns.

Most of us have faced at least one of these at one time or another. It may not have caused a *problem* with our eating, but it may have altered our eating patterns, if only temporarily.

The rest of this topic looks in more detail at how some particular circumstances may affect eating patterns. Three groups of people have been chosen to help you explore this issue:

- single people
- elderly people
- teenagers

Some problems have been identified for each group. Remember, not everyone in that group has these problems *and* many of the problems could also apply to people in other groups.

The new guidelines for healthy eating need to be thought about in terms of people's lives. The advice to change to a healthier diet may stand a better chance of success if we acknowledge that everyone is an individual. Each one of us is involved in a unique situation.

Understanding what affects other people's eating may give *you* some insights into your own eating patterns.

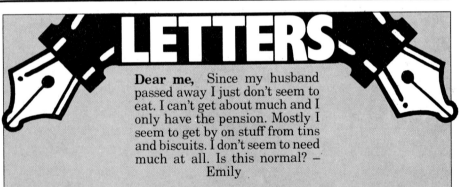

Dear me, Since my husband passed away I just don't seem to eat. I can't get about much and I only have the pension. Mostly I seem to get by on stuff from tins and biscuits. I don't seem to need much at all. Is this normal? – Emily

Dear me, Sally is our eldest. She is going through that terrible adolescent stage and has got very awkward about her food. She is rather plump and I know that the other children tease her. She is dreadfully self-conscious. I try to help her with her diet, but she thinks that it is me who made her fat. She hardly eats anything at home, but I know that her pocket money goes on sweets and crisps. Please tell me how I can help her. – Karen.

Dear me, I live alone. I love to cook, but the cost of food for one person is enormous. A small loaf only half the family size costs three-quarters the amount. Meat is sold in portions that are much too large. Surely this is unfair? I don't know how to cater for just myself. – Alex.

Dear me, I'm a single parent. I don't think anyone has any idea of how much skimping I have to do on other things to give my kids enough food to eat. And now I read about these new healthy eating ideas. I feel really guilty when I see things like this and think that I'm not giving them a good start in life. Have you got any suggestions about some basic diet that could help? – Chris.

Dear me, Our son, John, went away to University 18 months ago. In the first year he stayed at the hall of residence and got all his meals in. Now he has moved into a bedsitter. He can't even boil an egg for himself, but he won't listen to us. I'm afraid that he just lives on chips and beans. We don't want to seem like interfering parents but what can we do? – Lesley and Graham.

Single people

Living alone seems to be a very common experience. Our testers had lived alone for lots of reasons – they chose to; they were divorced; the partner was away from home; they were at college. One tester even regarded three years in the armed forces as living alone. And they all had something to say about their eating patterns . . .

"In the armed forces one had two choices, eat it or go without."

"I had one good meal a day in the staff canteen and didn't bother much in between."

"I used to live on cheese, apples and crispbreads — I was dieting all the time."

"Being four girls in a flat, we took it in turns to cook one good meal a day — a good time to get together to gossip."

What about you? Have you ever lived alone? If so, what did you eat? Did you:

- Take care to eat regular meals?
- Eat lots of your favourite snack foods?
- Eat whatever you could find in the cupboard?
- Eat a lot of takeaway food?
- Think about a healthy diet at all?

The problems they face

What sorts of issues do single people face that affect their eating patterns?

Read the following paragraphs. Which issues do you think only apply to single people? For each one try and think of a person from another group who might have similar problems.

Too busy? People who are busy both at work and at play may find cooking, shopping and eating healthily well down their list of priorities.

Too tired? Tired people coming home to an empty flat or bed-sit may just not be bothered. A pie at the pub at lunchtime may have to last the day.

No incentive? When you are feeding others – especially growing children – it seems more important to think of health. Single people may not have so much incentive to think about nutrition. When you've only got yourself to look after then you might not be so careful. You might not be worried about the monotony of a plateful of chips – or that you have had beans on toast every night for a week!

Single mothers

A study by the Maternity Alliance made disturbing reading. It showed what a single woman on supplementary benefit would need to spend on food if she was pregnant. The cost of sticking to the recommended hospital diet would be almost *half* of that supplementary benefit. This would leave the other half to pay for heating, lighting, clothing and all other costs! Poor diet during pregnancy can lead to low birth weight and abnormalities in the child. The women on supplementary benefit consumed less than the recommended amounts of Calories and many essential vitamins. Birth weights were lower for this group – more than one in ten babies were so light they needed special care.

Too little money? When single people are poor or unemployed then the problems multiply. To eat well on a small income requires more time and effort. Both unemployment and lack of cash can cause depression – and this wipes away any incentive to shop around or spend time on cooking. Lack of knowledge could add the final piece to an already bleak picture. A can of beans or cold spaghetti could be the day's main meal.

There are advantages. On the other hand single people do have control over their diet. Eating sensibly need not cost any more than any other sort of diet. It can even cost less. Many single people can succeed in making a healthy diet work without having to consider the needs or whims of others.

It's not only single people . . . Looking back at this section you may well have picked out the bit on unemployment and said that it doesn't just apply to single people! Or you may have come to the conclusion that being too busy to think about nutrition is not just a problem for single people. It may be for some, but you probably identified it as a problem for other people too. For example, a mum with three under-five-year-olds can also be too busy!

What other food issues can be a problem for single people? Do they apply to other people too? What are your ideas?

Elderly people

"Since my husband died, I can't be bothered with a lot of cooking. It doesn't seem worth it just for one. I'm not going to make a stew and eat it all by myself."

"We always used to eat well. Nowadays we've only got the pension so we can't afford much. We only eat meat when we have visitors or are round at my daughter's. We live on bread, jam and tea, just about. I suppose we could manage more if Alf gave up his pipe and I stopped bingo. But then you've got to have your pleasures haven't you?"

"The meals on wheels come twice a week. I don't always like the food but I eat what I can. I share my meat with the cat; sometimes I put a bit of food away to eat later. The rest of the week I don't eat much. I don't get about now and the boy who does my shopping doesn't come round every day."

"It's difficult you know, to buy just small amounts of food. You can buy two apples, of course, or one kipper, that's all right, but you can't buy less than half a pound of butter, and the bacon in our shop is only sold in half pound packets. Sometimes I throw food away because it's gone off by the time I get round to using it all."

The problems they face

Many elderly people live alone, they have little money and can't always get out to shop. Others find that changes in their families – death of a partner, children all grown up and living away from home – upset their routine. Their pattern of eating may have been established when catering for a family – changing to smaller meals with different quantities can be difficult.

Only one to cook for. When there is no-one else to cater for, people may not want to make elaborate meals, to try new foods or even to cook at all. Many elderly people made comments like *"It's not worth it"* or *"I can't be bothered with all that."* Perhaps many people make more effort when cooking for others.

Reduced income. Changes in buying power also count. A smaller income needs to be eked out. This may mean a change in the kinds of foods that can be bought. It can throw a lifetime's cooking and eating habits into confusion. Some elderly people may just not feel able to put effort into reviewing their diet on a lower income. Coming to terms with new foods and recipes may seem like too great a task. So their response may be cutting down on certain foods or cutting out others. The result can be an unhealthy diet.

Other demands on the money. With a small income some people may choose to sacrifice eating properly for other activities. The family pet is still around and now provides company. Unfortunately, it will only eat expensive tinned foods. Maybe spending on pleasures like bingo, beer or tobacco take priority over eating.

Loss of mobility. This brings other problems. It may be impossible to shop, so someone else has to do the shopping. People are used to looking for their own bargains in the shops. So having to plan meals and to write out a shopping list can seem quite alien. Not being able to walk far enough to search out the best buys may also mean budgeting problems. When helpers shop for an elderly person they may not always be careful in what they choose. A substitute for a food on the list may not be acceptable. Or if something is out of stock, or not bought at all, it can leave a gap in that week's menu.

Small appetite. Many elderly people also claim to lose their appetite or want to nibble at foods during the day rather than sitting down to meals. But just nibbling needs to be done with an eye to a healthy diet, too, or it may mean that they have fewer of the essential nutrients.

It's not only the elderly... Read through this section again. Can you pick out circumstances which relate solely to being elderly?

Clearly not all these difficulties are caused by being elderly as such. Changed social circumstances, the shock of the loss of a partner, or routines which are disrupted, can lead to eating patterns being altered for anyone. Loss of mobility may come not only from disablement, but from changes in transport arrangements. A lower income may lead to anyone eating smaller amounts of the same diet instead of choosing a different mix of foods.

Teenagers

"Not many kids round here have school dinners. Some people get sandwiches but most go to 'the chippie' or get crisps and coke."

"I don't like the stuff my mum makes. She likes things like stew and curry. I just want chips, beans, eggs, sausages — stuff like that."

"Things at home are pretty bad really. When I do go home to dinner my mum nags me and my dad has a go, so I stay away. Sometimes I just get chips."

"I want to watch my weight, but my mum thinks I'm stupid. She just won't get me the things I want like cottage cheese and salads. When she gives me a meal I just eat the vegetables and won't have the puddings. She cries and pleads with me. It's really silly."

The changing pattern

Recent research shows how children change their eating habits as they become teenagers. Many of them:

● Miss out meals – breakfasts and school dinners are often first to go.
● Just don't eat for long periods of time then fill up by bingeing.
● Dislike foods that are regarded as nourishing by their parents – they prefer chips, crisps, sweets, hamburgers, soft drinks and so on.
● Become diet conscious – especially to lose weight.

Peer group pressures. Food becomes influenced by peer group

pressure. Down on the street corner it's OK to tuck into chips. A wholemeal roll followed by an apple may not be seen as OK. Friends' approval is as important with food as anything else. Rebellion against authority can be shown at the family table as much as any other place.

Advertising pressures. Food advertising aimed especially at teenagers is big business. Look at specialist magazines for this age group. What kinds of foods are being promoted? Which television commercials are aimed at teenagers and what do they show? Chances are you will find a very limited range of foods – particularly snacks and soft drinks.

But diet foods figure in girls' magazines. Teenage girls are also big business. They spend billions on a very limited range of goods. Music, clothes, make-up, food and magazines are some top sellers.

Do you feel that health is considered much in the advertisements you have seen?

It's not only teenagers... Read the section about teenagers again. Some of the issues discussed demonstrate approaches which are positive. Taking control over your eating is one. Teenagers often use their eating as a way of asserting themselves, saying 'I'm me.' Eating is important in relationships and teenage rebellion over food is a striking example of it.

You may no longer be a teenager, and you may not be closely involved with one, but it might be worthwhile thinking again about the lessons they are learning... Do you have control over your eating? Are you influenced by those around you in regard to your food? Is food a bargaining point in your relationships? What about advertising pressures? Which teenage issues do you think relate to other age groups?

Choice and necessity?

In these three groups there's a varying degree of choice and necessity. You can't change the fact that you're elderly. You may choose to live alone. Even the 'can't be bothered' approach is something that does involve some choice. For example, an elderly man may say he hasn't got much of an appetite, but when he spends Sunday with his daughter and her family, he will happily demolish a three course meal! For teenagers it may seem that it is all a matter of choice – being offered regular 'proper' meals and rejecting them. But the pressure of this alternative lifestyle and the image a young person *wants* to project among friends are very strong forces indeed.

Other variations. You may know of, or be concerned with, other variations in patterns of eating. For each group there may well be 'special' features – vegetarians, immigrant groups who maintain the pattern of eating of the country they come from, or religious groups with special observances. But different patterns of eating are no excuse for not eating healthily.

Understanding the practical issues that different groups of people face over their eating may help you to think about the issues that concern you.

The cost of not being average

When it comes to food then it pays to be average. Shops sell most of their goods packed in average sizes. Caterers use average portions. Sizes calculated for the average family are more economical to buy – the typical foods bought by the average family tend to cost less too.

If you choose or happen not to be average then you will probably have to pay for it. Catering for one, being fussy about food or eating a special diet can cost money. And at the other end of the scale bulk buying facilities for large families are still few and far between. How is food sold? How well do your local shops cater for the non-average household?

Next time you are shopping look to see whether:

● pre-packed goods like bacon and cheese are available in single person sizes or large sizes – a quarter pound of bacon or cheese for example *or* 3 lbs
● all tinned goods are sold in small, or very large sizes
● bread, milk and spreads like margarine are available in small, or very large sizes
● special foods – sugar-free, salt-free, low-fat, gluten-free – are easily available
● frozen foods and prepared dishes are available in single servings.

If small sizes are available, check whether they cost more ounce-for-ounce than the average, regular or family sizes.

Practice does vary a lot from shop to shop. You will find that:

● some supermarkets do carry a lot of small sizes
● most pre-packed goods are large
● fresh foods sold loose – especially where you can help yourself – are less of a problem
● market stalls often use only set weights
● small shops may be willing to cater for single people and to get special goods, but they are generally more expensive shops anyway.

111

One more slimming diet?

Being on a slimming diet is a very recognisable eating pattern in Britain. Many thousands of us try to slim every year.

There seems to be no shortage of advice on how to slim. But there is little on how to keep the excess weight off. We are short of real help and support that works.

"I have been on many different slimming diets in the past and have always felt extremely hungry all the way through them. This has led me to be bad-tempered and listless. I have tried exercising at the same time. I have practically collapsed with hunger and weakness (shaking all over) and eventually had to have something sweet. All my slimming diets are successful — I lose weight, but my will power only works short-term (the thought of never being able to eat nice food again seems unbearable). I always put the weight back on in a few months or even weeks. Can dieting work?"

This is what one of our testers wrote about her experiences of slimming. Not very happy recollections. Why does slimming seem to be so difficult? What is there to be learned from the experience of eating that slimmers have?

Living off the fat of the land

Slimming is big business. If you haven't been on a weight reducing diet you may be surprised at what you can find.

Look in shops. You don't have to go to health food shops to find slimming foods. When you are next in your local supermarket look out for foods whose images and labels suggest that they are foods to help reduce your weight. Or for foods which are clearly labelled as:

- 'slimmer's' or 'slimming'
- 'low calorie'
- 'diet'.

For many of us 'diet' means slimming diet. In fact, the word diet really refers to all the foods that any individual eats.

Milk, bread, spreads, cheeses, yoghurts and soft drinks all have low Calorie versions that compete on the shelves with the regular products. Often they have something taken away – like the fat from skimmed milk – but they aren't usually any cheaper. You have to pay just as much for fewer Calories.

But it's not just slimming foods and the special products from the chemist's that take the would-be slender person's cash.

Look at magazines. Magazines, books, pamphlets, clubs all take their share. The specialist slimmers' magazines have captured a large share of the woman's magazine market. The more general woman's magazines carry a lot about slimming, fashion and food.

Take a look through any woman's magazine. You'll probably find fashion photos of slender women directly next to exotic and fattening recipes. Or next to glossy advertisements for slimming foods and products. Is this strange? Well, it's business and nobody wants to lose a steady market. How would the slimming product companies react if everyone got slim and stayed that way?

Who are the slimmers? In Britain one in three adults are overweight. In fact 39% of men are overweight and 32% of women. But far more women are on a slimming diet at any one time than men.

It is not surprising that more slimmers are women. Not because they are more overweight. It is more to do with the popular image of beauty being to do with slimness. If you want to be beautiful, be thin.

But why do so many of us fail either to lose the weight we'd wanted or to keep the weight we'd lost off? Some people seem to be on one slimming diet after another, and never seem to achieve the permanent result they desire.

Diets, diets, diets . . .

Have you ever tried to lose weight by going on a slimming diet? What happened? Take a look at these questions and jot down what you remember on a piece of paper.

- What slimming diet did you use?
- Did you set yourself a weight target?
- Did you achieve your target weight?
- Have you put any or all of the weight back on?
- Did you go on a binge once the weight was lost?

Why does it all go wrong?

Most people will have regained some weight. Some will have put it all back on again. Others will now weigh more. In her book, *Fat is a feminist issue*, Susie Orbach claims that 97% of dieters regain all of their weight. So what is wrong? Why can't we keep the weight we've lost off?

Lack of will power.   Could it be lack of will power? Well, if you've actually managed to slim and get to your target weight, do you really lack will power? It takes a lot of effort to overcome hunger pangs and to eat less than you want.

Greed.   Is it greed or gluttony? Not many people go out and gorge themselves after a diet. They just return to normal eating and many continue to be careful. After all, why ruin all that hard work? Besides your stomach may not want so much food after it has been on reduced rations for some time.

Slimming diets.   So is it the slimming diet itself? There is certainly plenty of choice available. Every year a new crop seems to reach the market. Some of the slimming diet books rapidly become bestsellers. So which is the best diet? Do any diets guarantee success?

Most slimming diets do the same thing. They give you a range of foods to eat that will reduce your intake of Calories. The high Calorie foods like cream, butter, fatty meats, sweets, cakes and sugary drinks are banned, or cut right down.

The popular 'fibre filler' diets work basically in the same way. The fibre will help to keep you regular – a big problem with some slimmers. It is the bulk which fills you up on a modest amount of Calories. This reduces your appetite for anything else.

Special single food diets – like eating just mangoes or bananas for example – do the same. And it really would be hard to eat more of your alloted daily amount of mango and banana – it would probably revolt you.

Some slimming diets are healthy, some may positively damage your health. But will the one that suits you best be successful?

Energy in ... energy out

Most people know that you get fat if you eat more food than you need. The surplus food energy is kept in reserve and stored as fat. Your body is a good manager. Not much is wasted. If it was left to your body then you would only eat when it needed you to. Instead it is your mind which tells you to eat – because it is mealtime, you fancy a bar of chocolate, you're bored ...

When you cut your Calories to fewer than your body needs then the body has to draw on its reserves of fat to make up the differences – or does it? Unfortunately, for slimmers, the picture isn't as simple as that.

Everyone an individual?

Different shapes.   Everyone is different. For one thing, we all have different body shapes. When you are in a crowd sometime, have a look around at the different people – you can easily check the differences. Take a look at people of the same sex who are within an acceptable weight range – you will find that their flesh is spread very differently over their bodies. Some people look lean and angular, others slim and willowy, yet others quite round.

Different lifestyles.   And then we have different lifestyles. Being in an active or inactive job isn't the whole picture. Some people rush around or run everywhere, others are languid, economising on their movements. Some people deliberately take a lot of exercise. Others walk from the house to the car and that's it. We all eat and drink at different times of the day: some people may have more meals and fewer snacks. Others may eat snacks all the time. Some of us take our time to eat and drink. Others bolt their food, or eat it on the run.

Ticking over

Different 'tick over' rates.   How our bodies work is very different too. Our basal metabolic rate, as it's called, determines how fast we burn up Calories when we are doing nothing. Even when you're just lazing about your basic bodily processes need to be fuelled to keep you alive. It's rather like a car just ticking over. If you don't need many Calories just to tick over, then there's some evidence you may be one of the people who are more likely to put on weight easily.

Some scientists now think certain people can speed up their basal metabolic (or tick over) rate if they take regular exercise. People with a high basal metabolic rate are not going to have so many spare Calories left over at the end of the day. It's these leftover Calories which are stored away as fatty tissue.

Some 'naturally thin' people have been found to have a 'safety valve' which enables them to get rid of a great many of these spare Calories as heat through their skin.

Counting the Calories

One of the main concerns that slimmers have had for many years has been Calories. Calories have become a way of life. Many slimmers know the Calorie content of every foodstuff they're likely to be offered and a lot of foods they'll probably never eat. They weigh themselves every week or every day on the bathroom scales. They weigh their food. They are concerned about whether a pound or half a pound has been lost. The whole process of slimming and all its associated tasks and rituals seems to take over. It gets to be a very complicated business and the actual object of the exercise gets lost in the whole 'slimming' way of life. Many people are understandably impatient for results and this can mean taking extreme measures which don't really take account of the real purpose of slimming either.

Crash diets

You probably know people who lose a lot of weight in a very short time. Perhaps you have tried this kind of diet yourself. Some slimming diets claim high targets – like 14 pounds in two weeks. You lose weight rapidly. But does it help and is it good for you?

Just losing pounds in weight is not the same as losing pounds of fat. When the body is starved of foods it has three main sources of energy to turn to:

- fat stored in the body
- glycogen stored in the muscles
- protein from the muscles themselves.

Emergency stores.   Stored fat gets turned into usable energy. But, unfortunately this process is slow and not very efficient. Fat is the body's long-term store.

Glycogen, on the other hand, is a high energy fuel that is easily burned. It is there to fuel bursts of short, intense activity – like sprinting or lifting a heavy object. When the body is looking for quickly available energy, glycogen is ideal. Glycogen also helps keep up the level of glucose in the blood to meet all our energy needs. You can lose some weight through burning up glycogen on a crash diet, but the body doesn't actually store very much glycogen at any one time. Since glycogen is stored with water in the body you can lose some weight by using up glycogen and releasing water by excreting it, so some of the lost weight is water.

Slowing down. Crash diets may also change your metabolic rate. Your body reacts to a sudden shortage of fuel from food by lowering your metabolic rate. The vital organs simply slow down their functions and get by on less energy. You begin to feel tired and listless. You won't feel like taking much exercise. And you'll probably feel cold. You need to rest. This lowers the amount of energy that you use anyway.

The result is that you get by on less so there may not be much demand on your energy reserves. Your ticking over rate drops – you need less energy to keep your bodily processes going.

Burning up muscle. For most people in any one day only a small amount of stored fat can be brought back into circulation to provide fuel. Very fit people will use more fat.

In any emergency – such as a crash diet or fast – fuel has to be got from something more easily available. This comes from the protein in our muscle. People on crash diets normally eat solids, whereas people on extreme fasting have only liquids. However, those fasting for religious reasons do usually have some form of solids in the day. So people on severe fasts may weaken their heart muscles and make heart problems more serious.

Diet and grow fat?

Slimming can cause problems when you put weight back on again. There is some evidence that you may end up fatter than you were before. A recent book, *Dieting makes you fat*, by Geoffrey Cannon and Hetty Einzig argues this theory.

Basically, someone on a weight reduction diet – and especially a crash dieter – is almost bound to put on weight when eating goes back to normal. *Dieting makes you fat*, put another way means that your body finally ends up with a higher proportion of fatty tissue in it. Fatty tissues need less energy to maintain them than do lean tissues (muscles).

Look at these diagrams which show proportions of fat and lean in the body.

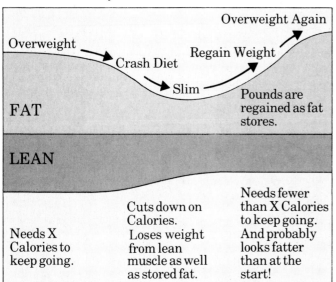

	Cuts down on Calories.	Needs fewer than X Calories to keep going.
Needs X Calories to keep going.	Loses weight from lean muscle as well as stored fat.	And probably looks fatter than at the start!

Some people think that the more a person goes through this cycle the higher the proportion of fat to lean tissue in the body becomes. And so fewer Calories are needed to maintain the same weight.

And the moral of the story?

If you have been on repeated dieting you can check part of this process. Measure your waistline, hips and thighs. Have they gained much on what they were before you started dieting? Is your weight more than it was before you started? It is likely that your measurements have increased more than your weight. Fat is not so heavy as muscle, so you will have more bulk pound for pound.

The moral is don't bother to go on a slimming diet until you find 'a once and for all' way of keeping it off. If you are to stay on your diet it should have a healthy balance of nutrients and give you a wide choice of enjoyable food. A once and for all way of controlling your weight will always include reasonable exercise.

What can be done?

If you want to lose weight and maintain your ideal weight then there may be a price. You will need to watch your weight for the rest of your life. You can start by changing to the current recommended guidelines for healthy eating. At least be overweight on a basically healthy diet. Then cut down even further on fats – some of them are bad for your heart too. Next cut down on sugary snacks and foods.

Watching your weight

- Don't bother about Calorie counting.
- Watch skirt or trouser waistbands as a way of telling you whether your weight is altering.
- Stick to your current diet for a month. Are your clothes getting tighter or looser?
- If you're overweight eat plenty of vegetables, fruit and whole grain foods. Cut down on fats and sugars until you start to lose weight, then persist.
- Take some sensible, regular exercise. You'll burn off a few Calories doing the exercise. But the big benefit is that is could help re-set your ticking over rate! It takes more Calories to keep a fit body ticking over.

Exercise. Take up an activity that you will enjoy – this will help you to stick to it. And don't do too much too soon. But you need to do it at least twice a week for 20-30 minutes. Eventually you should exercise hard enough to make yourself fairly breathless – but not gasping. Exercise needs to be a permanent fixture in your life. What exercise is effective? Look out for guides in magazines – these will help you to pace yourself.

> **Warning.** When you are unfit it can be dangerous to do too much exercise too quickly. Start very gently. Never do more than you think you can. If you are in any doubt at all, consult your doctor before you start a programme of exercise.

Slim, fit and healthy?

Everyone needs to decide how to achieve or maintain their target of being within the acceptable weight range. The message is that keeping slim, fit and healthy – in other words looking after yourself – is a life long task. And it can be an enjoyable one. It's OK to pay attention to maintaining your health. Feeling in charge, having control over yourself, makes many people feel quite good.

'Old style' slimming isn't really being in charge of yourself, it's letting Calorie counters, unhealthy wonder diets and the bathroom scales be in charge of your life!

Disordered eating

Many health and slimming magazines give 'acceptable weight for height' charts. You'll have heard of them, too, if you've ever tried to get your life insured.

The table below is a weight for height chart. You will see in it the acceptable weight band. It's OK to be somewhere in this band. If you are above, you would be classed as fat. If you are a lot above, obese.

A report on obesity by the Royal College of Physicians in 1983 stated that more than a third of adults in Great Britain were overweight. The medical evidence was that being overweight increases health risks. Many insurance companies would want a higher premium for life insurance if you were outside that weight range. Insurance cover might even be refused.

But there are people who are below the acceptable weight band. In Britain few people are actually starving through poverty, but some, for various reasons, drop far below the acceptable weight.

This topic looks at the dangers and problems of both under- and overweight. Some of these are connected with health. Some are to do with our feelings about our bodies. Extreme feelings about our weight and figure can result in eating problems. Eating patterns can become disordered. Then eating can become so irrational that it is a far worse problem than the weight itself.

Over the top

Being overweight can increase the risk of developing certain diseases – especially if there is a family history. The main health problems listed in the Royal College of Physicians' report include:

- coronary heart disease and strokes
- high blood pressure
- diabetes
- gall stones

But there are also mechanical troubles which can be connected with carrying too much weight, such as, tiredness, breathlessness, and wear and tear on the weight-bearing joints – the knees and hips.

Under the weight line

If it's a result of a healthy diet and a reasonable amount of exercise, then being mildly under ideal weight is fine for your health (for instance, up to five pounds). People in this band suffer less than average risk of the major diseases listed in the last section.

If someone is, or becomes, very much underweight the dangers are:

- Emaciation – this means a loss of muscle as well as body fat – literally wasting away.
- Lack of particular nutrients necessary for health. If a person gets very little food it's possible to drop below the minimum level of essential vitamins and trace elements.

An ideal diet

Food provides us with essential nutrients for growth and repair. But food also gives us the fuel that keeps our bodies supplied with energy. As far as *weight* is concerned everything is fine as long as the energy we get from our food is equal to the energy we use everyday. Too little food and the body turns to other sources of fuel, including fat and muscle. This would result in losing weight. A diet that supplies just enough energy to maintain an acceptable weight is ideal.

Lightweight, heavyweight?

Being seriously under- or overweight is unpleasant and unhealthy. So why do we get that way? The obvious

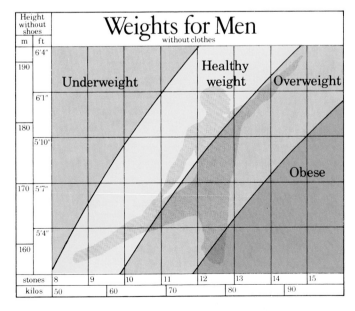

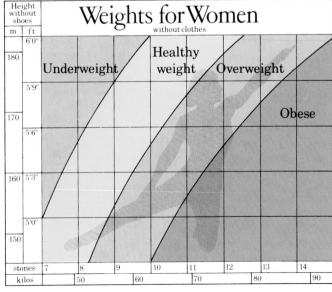

The turn of the century

Diana Dors, the 1950s

answer is because of the way that we eat. But many other factors may be the root cause.

Images of overweight. What kinds of pictures do you conjure up of people who are overweight? Do you have any of these images?

- fat and jolly
- motherly or fatherly
- puffing and panting
- tubs of lard
- greedy pigs
- unattractive lumps
- poor soul.

On a separate piece of paper write a few phrases that sum up what you tend to feel about very overweight people that you meet.

Images of underweight. And how do you feel about very underweight people? What about these images?

- sylphlike, model girl
- skeletal, all skin and bones
- pale and puny
- wasted away
- lean
- like a skinny kid.

Again write your own phrases down to describe how you feel about very underweight people.

A different weight. Now just imagine that you woke up one morning very much overweight or underweight – very different in weight from the weight you are now. How do you think people would react to you?

Our testers had a variety of answers. Some of their reactions on overweight were:

"I'd think I was having a nightmare."

"I'd hope that people would be sympathetic and want to help me."

"People would say it was because of our house move, my husband's job, think I had problems."

And on underweight:

"Friends would wonder if I was ill, offer me tasty delicacies."

"My husband would probably be pleased and be more sexually attracted to me."

Being overweight. And here are some comments from people who are or have been overweight.

"I just got fat when I was expecting Wayne. I must have put on two and a half stones. Everyone was fine then, they all looked at the baby not me. I just went on eating and putting on weight. After a while people began to stare and make comments. My husband said that I should lose weight and used to call me 'fatso' when he was in a temper. I just turned even more to food. It was a comfort. I could put up with insults with a cake or two inside me."

"You know that people talk about you. Kids in the street point and say, 'Look at that big fat woman'. I used to cry sometimes, it's just not fair if you're large."

"I can remember getting the family snaps back from holidays. I was so ashamed. I looked like a stranded whale. Everyone made jokes about sinking to the bottom or breaking deck chairs — it was awful."

"After a while you just stop caring. You ignore people and just get on."

Feelings

Feelings about our self-esteem and our body image are important in understanding why people get very fat or very thin.

For many people attractiveness is a more important reason to be slim than health reasons are. You don't look like the pictures in the magazines. It's hard to find nice, fashionable clothes that fit. When you thought of images of overweight and underweight people did you feel it was better to be thin than fat? Look back at your answers. One reason that many people think it's better to be slim is that it is fashionable to be thin.

Body image

What is an ideal figure? Opinions have varied over the years. Take a look at the pictures on this page. They represent ideas of female beauty portrayed at different periods of history. Many Victorian pin-ups, for example, show women that would be regarded as too fat to be fashionable nowadays.

116

Twiggy, the 1960s

Christie Brinkley, the 1980s

Today's fashion. The latest change in woman's ideal shape probably stems from the 1960s. A search for new fashion faces and images came up with Twiggy. Some people were genuinely horrified by such thinness – but it changed the face of fashion. Tall, long legged and slim became the order of the day. Is there a current fashion image for men? What does the ideal man look like nowadays?

Try looking round the shops to see how fashion clothes are cut. Look at the models used in shop windows. Look at the glossy, magazine images. The picture is the same for both. The image of fashion is powerful and the desire to look attractive can influence many people. Ask your friends if they are happy with their body shape.

Would you say that only women and girls are influenced by the power of these images? Is there an equally powerful attractive image for men too?

At any one time a vast number of people are trying to slim. Many of them are in pursuit of the ideal figure. But of those only a small minority will actually become sufferers from serious eating disorders. And their original reasons for slimming may well have been different from the majority of slimmers. The fact that a small minority of people do suffer from disordered eating patterns should not put other people off. Maintaining an acceptable weight is important for everyone.

Disordered eating patterns

Many people, especially women, are obsessed with food. For them eating has little to do with hunger or greed. In the book *Fat is a feminist issue* Susie Orbach describes compulsive eating as:

● feeling out of control around food, submerged by either dieting or gorging
● spending a good deal of time thinking and worrying about food and fatness
● scouring the latest diet for vital information
● feeling awful about yourself as someone who is out of control
● feeling awful about your body.

The compulsive eater thinks she should be slim. Being slim means conforming – and competing. Some compulsive eaters are driven to bingeing through anger, frustration, anxiety or boredom.

What about you? Put yourself in their shoes. Which of these reasons for eating given by compulsive eaters apply to you?

● *"I eat because I'm nervous or anxious and food is a comfort."*

● *"I reward myself with food. It's my real treat when I've worked hard or done well."*

● *"I'm not usually hungry at mealtimes. I eat to be part of the family."*

● *"When I've had a bad day I eat to cheer myself up."*

● *"If I'm bored and don't know what to do I just eat."*

● *"Feeling good makes me eat to celebrate."*

Most of us have done one or more of these at times – but every day? And do we feel guilty or bad about it?

For most people these signs of compulsive eating come and go. The trouble becomes real when they are constant, or only broken by periods of dieting. But compulsive eating and dieting can have more unpleasant signs.

Bulimia Nervosa

Compulsive eating and fear of putting on weight can mean Bulimia Nervosa.

A bulimia sufferer binges regularly. Food is an obsession. Mostly they eat vast quantities of almost any food. These are bought, prepared and hoarded in advance. So sufferers plan their bingeing, often clocking up huge food bills. A binge can last anything from 15 minutes to three weeks. It is usually done out of sight of other people. Food is not chewed much – usually stuffed in and swallowed.

Because the sufferer is concerned with diet and weight, binges are followed by bouts of vomiting, and the use of laxatives (which are purchased in large quantities) or slimming tablets.

Before a binge many bulimia sufferers feel anxious. They may have physical symptoms like sweaty palms and palpitations. Afterwards many have suicidal thoughts because of the overwhelming feeling of guilt.

Bulimia affects young women. The average age at which the condition starts is 17 years. It doesn't seem to affect any particular group in the community. Sufferers are either inside the normal weight range or above it.

Jane's experience. Jane, aged 32, admits to having suffered from bulimia since her days at a teacher training college.

"I went on a crash diet to lose half a stone. One thing I learned was about Calories and I began to use diet foods and only eat one meal a day. I don't know what came over me. I was so hungry that one day I skipped college and went on a spree. At the supermarket I just bought all my favourite foods and hid in my room and ate them before my flatmate got home. I felt so bad and bloated afterwards that I stuck my fingers down my throat and was sick. From then on I have used vomiting and senopod tablets to keep the weight off."

Jane's problem has led to the loss of her job, a marriage break-up and debt. It has also led to physical harm. Her gums and teeth have been worn away by stomach acids. Her voice is husky through persistent vomiting. Her bowels are sore and she has constipation if she doesn't keep up the laxative tablets. Often she is so sick and weak that she can't work. For six years she took sedatives for depression.

Help! Bulimia sufferers have to *want* to get help. At the very least they probably need information. For instance, they particularly need to know about taking a potassium supplement and about going for regular dental check-ups.

There are both medical and non-medical sources of help available.

Anorexia Nervosa

Another disordered eating pattern is Anorexia Nervosa. Here the control over bingeing and food intake is much stricter. The result is weight loss.

People who suffer from anorexia become severely emaciated with a very low body weight. They avoid food. Many sleep badly and are overactive.

Another feature of people suffering from anorexia is that they tend to cover up. They are secretive and fear discovery. This makes the disorder extremely difficult to detect. They develop as very good manipulators of people and often show extraordinary cunning in order to get their way.

Anorexia mainly affects women and especially teenage girls. Many are from the middle and upper classes.

Sally's story. Sally comes from a good home with caring, protective parents. At the age of 13 Sally was admitted to hospital semi-conscious. She was, at that time, more than 26 pounds under her ideal weight. Her bones were very prominent. She had been refusing food for the past four months. When she had been treated for the worst of the symptoms she continued to refuse food, saying that it would make her fat. It took three months of careful medical and psychiatric care before she was well enough to go home.

In Sally's case the problem appeared to be a sheer terror of becoming fat.

"I used to love eating. My mum and dad were always buying sweets. Mum is a good cook and we had three good meals a day. I suppose it was when I started to develop I noticed the fat all over me. I wanted to be thin, but the sweets and the meals were always there. At first I tried to diet, but I would always come back to the food and would give in and stuff myself. I sometimes felt so bad that I stuck my fingers down my throat or swallowed a load of Ex-lax. In the end I hated myself and the fat so much that I just stopped eating as much as possible. It upset my mum and there were rows. I think that they only made me even more determined to go on."

Theories about anorexia. Sally's situation is not unusual. But it is not one that explains every case of anorexia. Psychologists have given many possibilities:

- lack of self-confidence
- low self-esteem
- a need to feel perfect physically – as well as in other ways
- conflicts about becoming a woman with prospects of sex and pregnancy
- fear of growing up and possibly losing a place in the family
- a wish *not* to grow up into an adult with its expectations of a sexual life (anorexia halts the physical development and stops periods)
- to assert oneself by taking control over the body
- poor personal relationships.

People suffering from anorexia work to suppress natural feelings of hunger. After a while many say they never feel hungry. Others are always hungry but overcome these feelings. Food represents fat and weakness. It means giving in. They think that their weight would zoom on if they ate anything much at all.

Despite this people who are anorexic can be obsessed with food and cooking. They may binge on food from time-to-time. Usually this will be closely followed by self-induced vomiting or dosing with laxatives.

Help! People who suffer from anorexia nervosa, like those who suffer from bulimia nervosa, have to *want* to get help. Authority figures, parents, colleagues and so on, who seek help on behalf of people they label as having bulimia nervosa or anorexia nervosa, can very easily make matters worse.

Again, there are both medical and non-medical sources of help available.

Medical help

When disordered eating becomes acute a sufferer may need immediate medical help just to keep alive. Hospital treatments vary a great deal but all take time. Some are sympathetic, others aren't.

The overall need for people suffering from disordered eating patterns is to be more positive about themselves – to like themselves enough to take responsibility and not fear either themselves or others.

Much of the pattern of disordered eating is about a struggle or rebellion against authority of various kinds. An authoritarian approach to matters is unlikely to help in the long run.

Cry wolf

Anorexia nervosa and bulimia nervosa are now well-known illnesses. A lot of people have heard of them and may be alarmed by what they've heard.

Some people may have had very occasional, brief episodes of disordered eating patterns. Perhaps they feel that it is now acceptable to talk about such experiences in terms of these illnesses. In some groups of teenagers the claim of having had these illnesses may even provide them with an 'exotic past'. Such stories *do not* by any means imply that people are actually suffering from such diseases.

What can be done?

People with disordered eating patterns need help with seeking out information. They also need support to enable them to make changes in their own lives.

As with alcoholics and compulsive gamblers, the first step is for the person to admit that there *is* a serious problem. A lot of sufferers from eating disorders are girls still at home so the family can give support. But, many parents feel themselves to be responsible for what their teenagers eat. So if it comes to a show down parents may find it difficult to strike the right balance in helping their teenager to begin to seek out ways to change.

There are special programmes to help the sufferers change a pattern of what is basically self-destructive behaviour. These may involve sensitive discussions. Talking and working together over a long period of time may uncover the root causes of the problems and help sufferers to come to terms with them. Many programmes also include relaxation techniques which help with stress.

Good nutritional advice together with other forms of support can help. Disordered eaters often know a lot about food but mostly about slimming. Cutting Calories drastically may lead to a grossly unbalanced diet, lacking essential nutrients. Binge foods are often sugary and fatty, so they aren't likely to add up to a reasonable diet. A proper diet based on sound nutritional advice will give a good range of foods.

Many people who have disordered eating patterns *do* admit it to themselves – and then find the support they want. This then helps them to gain a more confident self-image. It is possible to allay fears and dispel some pressures that contribute to disordered eating. A positive way forward is for all those concerned to tackle the problem in partnership and to negotiate solutions together.

The meaning of meals

If you are to have a healthy diet then some knowledge of the current guidelines for healthy eating is going to be very useful to you. But eating means a lot more than nutrition. You have *learned* about food and eating – what is 'right', 'normal' or 'to be expected' – both in your everyday eating and on special occasions.

It's not just what you eat that's important, what you *think* about food and eating is important too. You might not be conscious of these thoughts most of the time, but if you want to change your diet, putting yourself in touch with them is useful.

This chapter helps you to look at the personal and social influences that lead you to eat the way that you do. In it you think about how what you've learned about food and eating affects your diet. You also look at eating out, entertaining guests, and at what these occasions mean to you.

First of all, though, you think about your reactions to all those pictures you see in cookery books and articles and at how your imagination gets to work on food!

Selling a dream

How do we use cookery books and articles? Do they give us instructions on how to prepare food or are they selling us a dream?

Sensual, rational and emotional appeals.

"I haven't got time for these glamorous cookery books. I want to know a recipe is simple and works."

On the face of it, cookery books and recipes are practical resources. We use them if we need a recipe for a special occasion, maybe to ring the changes in our everyday eating. But for many of us they feed our imagination too.

"I sent away for one cookbook. When it arrived I was spellbound. For two days I just pored over the pictures. In the six months since I've had it I don't think I've tried more than two of the recipes."

This topic helps you look at how you react to the images of food presented in published cookery books and articles. Once you've analysed your reactions you can think about how you can use cookery books to help you towards a healthy pattern of eating.

The appeal of recipes

Most of us don't come into contact with the starker facts of food preparation. For example, having to chase the main dish around the garden and getting it in the pot. However, the glossy illustrated recipes we look at are often far removed from our own experience.

What makes them appealing? One advertising agency's analysis of what makes food appeal to people can be used as a helpful starter. It puts the appeal of food into three categories: sensual, rational and emotional. Think about these categories in relation to cookery books and articles.

Sensual appeal. *"After all,"* said one famous cook, *"we eat food with our eyes before we taste it."* This view was proved by a group of hungry boys in a food colour test. They refused to eat some mashed potato coloured blue, even though the taste was the same.

Colour, shape, texture, sheen, garnish, lighting, how it's served – all these constitute sensual appeal. Pictures of food make us think, 'I'd like to eat that. It should taste good.' We are tempted by the *look* of the food to select, cook and eat it.

Rational appeal. This is suggested more by words than pictures. Food appeals because it is:

● cheap
● convenient – easy to buy, prepare, serve
● good for us – nutritious, slimming, healthful.

Emotional appeal. This is not to do with the food itself but what we associate it with. For example, other times, other places, other occasions, other people. Emotional appeal can be shown in recipes by:

● what the food is served on – fine china, old wooden bowls worn smooth with use
● what else appears in the picture – flowers, fruit, wine, table linen
● the lighting – sun, candlelight, dappled shade
● the setting – cottage kitchen, mediterranean villa
● the occasion – an idyllic picnic out of doors in the height of summer, sitting by the river where the wasps don't gather and you don't get grass in your sandwiches!

What appeals to you? Now look at some of your recipes, preferably ones with pictures too, and choose a few of them to analyse their 'appeal'. If you haven't got a collection of recipes then go through some magazines and cut out any cookery articles that appeal to you. You will find that many are highly illustrated. A great deal of skill and care has gone into the photographs. What sort of 'appeal' does the food have?

Make a chart like the one right to analyse the appeal of each picture. Make a list of your recipes and in the 'appeals' column write down 'sensual', 'rational' and 'emotional' in the order

of importance that you decide for each recipe. Then add any comments you want to make about the picture and recipe.

While you're looking at the pictures you may find it useful to think about the following questions:

- Does the food look near enough to touch? Do you feel as if you could reach out and actually eat it?
- Does it look real?
- What background is the food set against? Would it be displayed like this if someone actually had to eat it?
- What types of people would eat this food? Would they be like you?
- What sorts of occasions would people eat such food at?

Who reads the recipes?

When you are looking through your recipes you may well be looking at them from two points of view. You may be thinking about *eating* the food yourself. Or you may be thinking about *catering* for other people. Sometimes, of course, recipes will appeal to you both as an eater and a caterer.

Here are some people's reactions to recipes. Read through them and then go through your own recipes again. Which recipes do you read as a caterer, which recipes as an eater?

Old English apple pie. 'There are few more delicious puddings with its

filling of applies, dried fruit and spices.'

"Just the name reminds me of my mum's cooking," said Debbie. *"I could really eat that for old time's sake. My two kids have never had this sort of pie — it would be nice to make one just for once and share one of my childhood memories with them."*

This had an instant *emotional* appeal to Debbie as an eater. But she also felt as a caterer that she wanted to pass on the emotions about food too.

Oeufs Florentine. 'Eggs and spinach together make a very nutritious light supper dish.'

Mike's reaction was, *"That's another quick dish I can add to my list — it's easy to make and cheap too."* This had a *rational* appeal to Mike as a caterer.

Sharon's first reaction was to the *rational* appeal too, but as an eater – *"I'll try that — spinach is supposed to be good for me".*

Summer pudding. When Rita saw it the mouth-watering combination of summer fruits in this pudding had a *sensual* appeal for her as both caterer and eater. *"Imagine presenting that with strawberries piled round it as the finale to the meal! And imagine eating it, sinking your teeth into that fruit."*

RECIPE	APPEALS	COMMENTS
Seafood platter	Mainly sensual but also emotional	The colours made the food look really tempting - but it also seemed far away. The cottage style made it look so 'make believe'.

Setting the scene

Recipes with their pictures, also set scenes for us. Look at your recipes. How would the food look different on your dining table, on your everyday china, with the washing up waiting in the sink? Would a different scene be set?

Recipes also set scenes through the way that language is used.

The instructions. Are they impersonal? For example, '...cut tomatoes in half, place on baking sheet, season with salt and pepper...'. Or are they more like this one?

'This is a more complicated pie than most, but if you put it together carefully you will have a true aristocrat of pies. The artist in you will probably want to get into that magnificent crust, but first the filling...'

The writer. How does the writer present herself or himself? Are likes and dislikes clearly present in the text? 'If you are a sandwich enthusiast like me, on some occasions I think almost anything tastes better in a sandwich...'

Does the writer offer other aspects of her or his life for you to admire and copy, or even get annoyed about?
'...Our garden salad started in the spring as a nice and unassuming little salad. April turned to May and tender young peas appeared. In June avocados were plentiful, tomatoes beautiful and ourselves inspired...'

This piece is almost as fanciful as deliberately contrived cookery photography. If you're a 'no nonsense' cook it might well put you off the recipe!

Photographs don't lie?

Because our interest in the subject is so great, cookery books and articles are a major area of publishing. It is a highly specialised and developed area where the marketing people know a lot about making books and articles appeal to us.

Think of one of the most glamorous recipes you've found. Try and picture what it would look like if you cooked it. Would it look like the glossy photograph? One competent cook felt she wasn't so despondent any more and said, *"I've grown to accept that it won't turn out like the picture."*

What purpose does the picture serve? Is it a stimulus to get us to cook the food? Or is the act of looking at the picture simply satisfying in itself?

Perhaps we accept that the food we cook will not look like the food in the photograph. Even the ingredients we use will not look the same and our kitchens won't be so orderly. Maybe we accept that it is, in some ways, a fantasy. Do we secretly admit that the whole of food coverage in the media is a game in which we all participate? Perhaps we enjoy the fantasy in the same way that we enjoy soap operas or fiction? The producers certainly recognise that they are feeding our fantasy as much as our stomachs!

Of course it's not all fantasy. We do use our recipes too!

You and your recipes

How do you actually use your recipes?

Think about any recipes that you have used recently. What were they and why did you use them? Were any of the recipes new ones?

Where did the recipes come from?

A tried and trusted book ☐

A new book ☐

A friend ☐

Newspaper or magazine ☐

TV/radio programme ☐

Other ☐

Why did you use the recipes?

"I saw it and thought I would try it out" ☐

"I was looking for inspiration" ☐

"I couldn't remember exactly how to make this" ☐

"I had never cooked it before and needed instructions" ☐

What were the recipes for?

Main dishes ☐

Cakes ☐

Starters ☐

Puddings ☐

Bread or pastry ☐

Other ☐

Was the meal planned?

Did you plan in advance to use the recipes? ☐

Were they last minute decisions? ☐

Who ate the food that you cooked?

You ☐

Your immediate family ☐

Other relatives ☐

Guests ☐

Recipes over the years. Research in the use of recipes shows that in 1961, 92 per cent of English housewives interviewed said that they did 'plain English cooking'. Few used recipes for anything other than cakes or puddings. Only 15 per cent said that they used recipes for main dishes. By 1977, 49 per cent of housewives said they were using recipes for main dishes and for experimenting with new or unusual dishes.

In the two surveys the percentage of housewives, whose use of recipes at least sometimes, looked like this:

	1961	1977
Cakes	60%	69%
Puddings	40%	51%
Main dishes	15%	49%

Are your experiences different from the 1977 findings? What do you use your recipes for? Try asking your friends what kind of food they use recipes for.

The people who tested this topic all used recipes at some time – for cakes, puddings and main dishes – and more besides. The most common reason was for cooking special meals for guests. So new recipes tended to be used. All of the testers owned cookery books. The range was from four up to 60!

Collecting recipes

"I've got two boxes full of recipes and about forty books! They are all dirty and well used."

Most of us collect recipes and have a place in our home where we keep them. Apart from cookery books, you may have a folder or a drawer somewhere that is filled with cuttings or notes. Take a look in your collection and pick out some recipes that you have actually cooked. Looking at them again will probably bring back memories. No doubt some will be pleasant recollections of your successes, other memories of flops or dis-

asters. Apart from your own skill as a cook what makes the difference between recipes that work and those that don't?

Jot down your ideas on a separate piece of paper.

Recipes that worked had:
(ie. clear, step by step instructions)

Recipes that didn't work had:
(ie. ingredients wrong)

Cooking or contemplating?

What about the other recipes in your collection – the ones you haven't tried? Look at them again. Why did you collect them?

Listed below are what several people gave as their main reasons for collecting recipes, other than for immediate or regular use.

Take a look at a few recipes from your collection of books and cuttings. For each one make a note of which reasons (1 to 9) apply to you. Add any other reasons you have for collecting recipes.

Reasons for collecting recipes:

1 *"I might cook this one day. I'm being prepared by having a wide choice ready to hand."*

2 *"I'm interested in other cultures. I suppose I'm learning about the world through the recipes."*

3 *"I just enjoy it. I like the pictures."*

4 *"It's a substitute for eating. I don't get fat this way."*

5 *"It's not just the food, it's the way of life that goes with it — the china, the rooms, the places."*

6 *"It just made my mouth water."*

7 *"It is a really attractive dish that is healthy and economical too."*

8 *"This is the kind of recipe I'd use if I was the kind of cook I'd like to be."*

9 *"I'll try it out when I manage to get all the ingredients together."*

A number of our testers who did this activity admitted to having fantasies about being a 'supercook'. Most testers seemed to have some good, practical recipes mixed up with a pinch of fantasy. But have you ever thought of limiting your collection? You could have *"recipes where I don't think I'd be helping anyone on to a heart attack!"*, as one of our readers put it.

There's no reason why your collection of recipes shouldn't be both attractive and healthy too.

Fancy and healthy?

Fancy foods are for many of us appealing, and feeding our imagination is part of the appeal.

> The current guidelines for healthy eating recommend that we eat less fats, including less fatty meats, less sugar, less salt and more fibre rich foods.

There's absolutely no reason why these recommendations should get in the way of the *appeal* that cookery books and recipes have for you! To begin with fantasies don't have to be guilty ones, they can be fun. Fantasy won't spoil a healthy diet, especially if you're only 'eating with your eyes'.

When you look through recipes perhaps you could set about finding some healthy, fanciful recipes for meals that you would enjoy making and eating. If you are a recipe collector this is the perfect excuse!

● If you like fancy foods, and collect recipes in the hope of being a 'supercook', you can still put yourself through your culinary paces. Just use the guidelines to healthy eating to check your recipes.

● If you like fancifully presented food with a sensual appeal then the new guidelines are OK too. An exotic fruit salad, all black fruits, or green fruits, or a large piece of fruit scooped out with different fruits inside, are the dishes that dreams are made of anyway!

● If the appeal of recipes is emotional for you, then you can set your table and create your atmosphere with a healthy meal just as well.

● If you are approaching your recipes rationally then the guidelines are no problem. In fact, they're an advantage. They may give you some very specific things to look for and to avoid in recipes.

So perhaps you could set about finding some recipes that both conform to these guidelines and have the sort of appeal that you know you succumb to. That's if you have any intention of cooking them! If not, just carry on looking. Though maybe if you are getting on well with changes in your diet you may find your food fantasies are changing too.

"I used to go weak at the knees at the thought of a strawberry meringue and cream. Just looking at the recipe made my mouth water. Now it's recipes for fresh fruit salads. Mangoes have much the same effect that trifle used to have on me!"

Family traditions

'Recorded messages' are the powerful instructions given us in childhood, mainly by our parents, which guide us in our adult lives.

Imagine a young child being like a tape recorder with the record button pressed down and a blank tape recording everything. Straightforward 'don't eat that' messages are recorded, but also things which aren't really spelled out. 'What Mummy does' is enough for us to get the message.

Playback. When we're adult the taped messages are played back. Often we're not openly aware that we act on these messages. If we were asked maybe we'd call them family traditions, *"We've always done it like this in our family."* But quite often, we don't think about them. We 'got the message' as they say, when we were little and often we obey without thinking. Other times we disobey these messages and get a kick out of being naughty. Or we feel guilty and demoralised, but again without being really aware of what's going on.

Recorded messages about food get played over and over again when we are faced with making decisions about what to eat. They may sabotage the more rational, informed, adult decisions we may wish to make. If we listen more carefully to these recorded messages we can become more aware of the situations in which they are most likely to cause trouble.

But first we have to learn to spot the messages at all. Of course, many of the messages about food will be good ones. Best of all might be *"You can work out and choose for yourself what's best to eat"*, or, like one of our testers, *"be flexible"*, which gave her permission to change her mind in the light of new evidence and try out new things.

This good message wasn't just about food, but a whole way of life.

This topic focuses on the messages that make life difficult. However, we can consciously choose to retain or wipe out these messages. We can also record new messages. It's when we just go on using the old recorded messages without thinking about them that we don't feel in charge of our lives.

How do we get them?

To start with you may have some difficulty in remembering messages about food that you received when you were little. So, first of all, try listening to parents talking to their children about food, or better still feeding them. If you have children of your own listen to what you say and watch what you or your partner do when you're eating with your children or feeding them.

Messages about eating will certainly be passed on in these situations. Do the phrases or the behaviour used ring a bell? When you watch other people with their children you may not be familiar with the sorts of messages being passed on in their family.

However, if you find yourself reacting strongly then you are beginning to hear echoes of messages you've received in your childhood. For instance, *"Why does she force the poor, little thing to finish it all off? You can see by the way he threw it on the floor he didn't want it."* Were you encouraged to eat only until you'd satisfied your hunger? Or were you always told to finish it up and are now (rightly) rebelling against it?

Our messages

Each of us slowly builds up a set of messages that tell us what foods we should eat and how we should behave at meals. They guide us about what to eat to be 'good'. What's right for boys and girls and what weight and shape to be. There is almost always a powerful set of messages to remind us 'what people like us' eat. Again you may need to think about family traditions to unearth these. Finally, and perhaps most destructive, some messages we've got in the past may tell us that if we can't get love we can always settle for food.

'Good' and 'bad'

Many parents see eating 'well' or 'properly' as *good* behaviour. A good appetite or a poor one are subjects for comment: *"She doesn't seem to want her bottle." "I can't keep up with him. I have to use the bottle as well as my own milk ..."* We say of babies: *"She takes her feed well," "He was terrible — I had endless feeding problems with him."* Parents often complain about their toddlers' food fads and refusal to eat. Children are often told to, *"Eat it all up, so you'll grow big and strong."*

It's not just the quantity of food but the type of food that children eat that is a constant concern for most parents.

"Eat your vegetables, there's a good girl, and then you can have some pudding."

Children often seem to prefer foods that are treats, but not really very nutritious. And parents often give out strong messages about how they feel about this. Food is often given to children with conditions.

"You must eat your bread and butter before you can have some ice cream."

Thought and care often go into the preparation of a meal, yet children can be unappreciative. One reward they can give their parents is to eat it all with enthusiasm, 'one for Mummy, one for Daddy'. When the parent doesn't get the rewards then disappointment or annoyance can show.

"I cooked that especially for you," or *"Daddy won't be very pleased when he sees how little you've eaten."*

Your own messages. How have the messages about being 'good' and 'bad' filtered through to you as an adult? Think about some of the feelings you have about food now. If you are being a 'good' boy or girl what do you eat and how do you behave at mealtimes?

For the next few meals you have, make a list of what makes you feel that you're being 'good'. And then another list of what makes you feel 'bad' or naughty.

It may help you when you're doing this activity if you also watch how other people behave at mealtimes.

For instance, do you feel guilty if you don't clear your plate? Perhaps you find yourself thinking someone who leaves food is a finicky eater? Or perhaps you're the opposite, you always leave something on the side of your plate and feel that people who clear their plates are greedy? You feel you're good and they're naughty.

Here are Jo's two lists:
Good girl

Eat bread with my main meals, leave fat off meat, eat slowly, chewing a lot, put knife and fork down between mouthfuls, tackle chicken with knife and fork.

Bad girl

Clean gravy up with my bread, have second helpings, bolt my food, leave my vegetables, eat chicken with fingers.

Men's food, women's food

Parents also may send out messages about what may be appropriate for girls and boys (and men and women) to eat. These messages may not be given in so many words, but are conveyed by actions and behaviour. For instance, women often give their husbands larger portions than they themselves eat. There are foods which men are believed to prefer, or to need, particularly red meat like steak, and carbohydrates, like potatoes. Chicken or quiches or salads are often presented as more 'feminine' foods.

Messages to girls are often to do with behaving in certain ways. Girls may be encouraged to eat daintily. This means smaller portions, smaller bites and attention to table manners.

"Don't stuff your mouth full of potato like that — it's not very ladylike," is a message for girls. The same message may also mean *"It's all right for boys to 'tuck in' to all sorts of food, but not for girls."*

There are even messages about what to eat if you are out with a man. The most common seems to be 'don't eat too much'. Chocolates are often considered OK for a woman to eat, particularly if they are a gift from a man.

Your own messages. Look through this list. Put a tick by the items which you associate with women and a cross by ones you associate with men. Leave the item blank if you don't associate it with one sex or the other.

- Salad
- Steak
- Chicken
- Fancy cakes
- Black Magic chocolates
- Flora margarine
- Cottage cheese
- Cheddar
- Doorstep sandwiches
- Asking for seconds
- Finishing the dish off
- Just picking at food.

This should help you get started, in making your own list of men's food and women's food. Ask someone you know of the opposite sex to make a list of men's foods and women's foods too.

Now check your list and underline foods you tend to eat. Are they the ones you linked with your own sex? Are there any foods you don't eat because you think your sex doesn't eat them?

Think back to your parents' diets when you were little. Perhaps your father dismissed salad as 'women's food'. Perhaps your sister could always get away with picking at her food, but you had to get a 'decent meal' inside you?

Many women have received messages in childhood that imply 'men won't find you attractive if . . .' And for some women eating a lot of food comes to be seen as a good way of making sure that men won't find them attractive. As long as men don't find them attractive they won't have to explore their sexuality.

Shape and weight

"He's got a healthy appetite, just like his father." "All of our family are fatties — there's nothing wrong with having a bit of weight to throw around." "No son of mine drinks halves."

Children gain impressions very quickly of what the appropriate shape and size is for members of their family and their sex. If the mother is slim and petite, the daughter may be expected

125

to follow suit. But living up to 'the women in our family' messages can be very difficult if she has inherited genes for a large build from her father. In a family where there's a tradition of being well-covered, plenty of second helpings dished out to children will ensure that the family tradition is carried on.

Your own messages. What shape or weight is it OK for you to be? Perhaps it's OK for you to be overweight or big? One of our readers said *"One side of our family is small and fat, the other side tall and thin. Me? I'm tall and fat! When I'm fat it's all right for me to say I take after my mother's side of the family. But father always goes on at me about my weight, because he's the tall, thin one. But I suppose I choose to hear my mother's messages which are things like, 'No one on our side of the family's ever been thin.' Her views about shape and weight are the significant ones for me."*

People like us

Some of the things we say about our shape and weight could start off with 'people like us'. Saying this can give us a sense of identity.

Traditions of what a family eats together give a sense of belonging and they can be hard to break away from.

"We always had roast beef and Yorkshire pudding for Sunday lunch. It was years before I realised that as an adult with my own family that 'people like us' didn't have to have a big Sunday dinner if we didn't want to."

"Salt cod is what we always have at big family gatherings and celebrations. Now, of course, they say you shouldn't eat too much salted food."

"Bacon and eggs — that's a proper breakfast. We always had it. I know it's supposed to be bad for you but ..."

Sometimes it's not even a case of saying 'people like us eat so-and-so',

it's just when we're children that we 'record' the cooking habits and tastes for certain foods in our families. The chances are that your ideas about what makes a proper meal follow in the family traditions.

"Every evening we sat down to a cooked meal, like cottage pie or sausages and mash. We would start as soon as Dad got home from work."

"When I'm fed up, I cook myself latkes (potato pancakes) — they're very greasy and fattening, but my mother always used to give them to us as a treat."

Food instead of love

Everyone needs a lot of love. As children we are always demanding attention to reassure us about being loved. But parents are busy people ... and often use food as a distraction, or as a replacement for the attention they are not able to provide at that moment.

A child is too young to understand the pressures on its' parents. It just picks up the message *"You can't have love but you can have food"* in other words *"Don't bother me now, here's a biscuit."*

How do you respond? As adults we can treat or indulge ourselves with food when we feel in need of comfort or love and attention and we're not getting enough of it!

Some responses to childhood messages about food are very depressing and can make you think it's impossible to change. Do you ever find yourself in the following sort of situation?

You're tired, depressed – perhaps feeling lonely and unloved. So you eat because you've learned in childhood to settle for food instead of love and attention. You make a pig of yourself. Then you hate yourself for it and feel weak-willed and fat. You decide that if others knew how horrible you were they certainly wouldn't love you ... and the cycle starts again. So you have some more to eat ...

It's obvious that these sorts of messages that affect your eating are damaging. You don't feel good. Your comforter only brings you depression. But you *can* wipe the tape clean. You can learn new messages and break this vicious circle ... You don't have to live with these unhelpful messages all your life. Learning new positive messages is looked at later in the topic.

Obeying and disobeying

You may be lucky and have had nothing but supportive messages that are a blessing to you now. Your family traditions may be constructive and helpful to your eating as an adult. However, look back at the list of messages that you've built up as you've worked through previous sections. Which ones do you obey? And which ones do you now disobey? Either way how do they make you feel? For any of them do you:

Obey and feel good about it? Is this you being passive? Or do you feel good because you have openly considered the messages and adopted them as your own?

Obey but feel confused, depressed, fed up ...? This may be because you've been more or less blindly responding to recorded messages. Now you are more aware of them you can choose for yourself which you'll keep and which you'll replace with more positive messages.

Disobey and feel depressed? You *are* free to discard these messages. New messages can over-ride early messages and help you feel OK about what you decide to do.

Disobey and feel rebellious? It's a normal part of adolescence to question and rebel. Hopefully, this leads to us choosing our own values – and deciding on our own messages. Some people get stuck in this rebellion. Particularly if they find it exciting to rebel. However, almost every adult likes to rebel occasionally.

Responding to advice

We can listen to good advice about food. But when it comes to having to change everyday eating habits, the advice is harder to put into effect. How we respond to such advice will depend to some extent on:

- our early messages about eating
- whether we obey or disobey these messages and how we feel about what we do.

Rebelling against it

Have you felt like 'rebelling' and discarding the topics in this book?

They aim to provide you with information and to help you reach your own decisions. However, you've probably 'rebelled' against some of the things you've read, particularly if it seemed too prescriptive or bossy. If you have had this reaction stop and think about it. It may help you to examine your general reaction to advice such as this.

Would you react in the same way to advice from friends? What kind of rebellion would advice from your parents or in-laws provoke? After all, if you're still at odds with the person who gave you most advice or messages about food when you were young, then you'll probably find it difficult to accept advice about healthy eating from anyone.

What would be your reaction, for example, if a new message sounded like the same message your mum used to give you frequently?

"You sound just like my mother — she was always going on about eating your greens."

Maybe you are still in a state of open rebellion – *"I always had to finish my potatoes before I had any dessert. I hate potatoes and I'm not going to eat them."*

"One of the nice things about being grown up is that I don't have to do what my mother tells me! I don't have to be bossed around by other people either and that goes for the so-called food experts too."

Old messages and new advice

It's sometimes difficult to trace the messages that you have taken to heart and which have led to your current pattern of eating. But it is important to do so when you are finding a particular dietary change hard to accept

or carry out. This final section should help you see more clearly how your old messages may affect how you respond to the new dietary advice.

Here is a list of dietary changes recommended for Britain in the 1980s:

- Eat more fruit and vegetables.
- Eat more potatoes, bread (particularly brown bread), rice and pasta.
- Eat less fatty meats like beef, pork and lamb.
- Switch to chicken and turkey.
- Eat less butter, margarine, cream and hard cheeses.
- Switch to cottage and curd cheese, and skimmed milk.
- Cut down on fried food – fish and chips, roast potatoes, crisps, doughnuts, fried chicken, samosas, pakoras, spring rolls, etc.
- Cut down on sweet things – cakes, biscuits, sweets, chocolates, fizzy drinks, etc.
- Cut down on salty foods – salted peanuts, crisps, kippers, salt cod, olives, beef extracts, salt beef, etc.

Now consider each change and write down your answers to these questions.
1. How do I react to this recommendation? Does it seem to me to be good/bad/cranky/sensible...?
2. Does this recommendation conflict with my present eating habits? Would it be hard to make the change?

If the answer to both of these questions is 'Yes' then ask yourself the next questions.
3. Where did that eating habit start? Have I always, as far as I can remember, eaten like that? Should you find it hard to track down the message try asking yourself 'what would my parents think of this recommended change and of a diet which included that change?'

You will most probably find at least some of these changes conflict with your family's traditions. You may need to look seriously at the messages that you received as a child.

You may even find that problems lie in your own rebellion against messages. For example, someone who grew up with a well-balanced diet with parents insisting on potatoes, bread and vegetables may have rebelled and plumped for a 'steak and chips' diet as soon as they left their parents' home. Such a person won't find the new advice easy to follow.

Receiving new messages

In this topic you've thought of certain influences on your present eating habits. In particular you've thought about what messages led to those habits being formed and how, if *you* choose to change the message, you're well on the way to changing your behaviour.

Be positive about those helpful messages you want to retain. At the same time, think about possible changes to your diet. Make up some short, positive messages for yourself. And then help yourself by 'recording' them so they become part of your everyday life.

You could try the following:

Self talk. It's OK to talk to yourself. You can talk louder than whoever gave you the old messages! Keep saying to yourself, out loud if it's convenient, 'I'm the kind of person who eats...' (your new choice).

Written reminders. One place to put these is on the door of the fridge. Many slimming groups recommend doing this. Your notes can be about any changes you want to make towards a healthier diet. But keep them positive. Let them state the enjoyable foods you are going to choose to eat. Give up telling yourself all the things you must not do.

Get someone you trust to 'record' the message. Hearing someone you admire or someone you love ask you to make the change makes it more likely you'll 'record' it and take it to heart. It's often easier to make a change for someone else's sake.

The best message of all is 'It's OK to take care of myself.' That includes eating well. Taking care of yourself is a sign of loving yourself. Giving this message to yourself, or saying it again if you were lucky enough to have acquired it already, will free you to feel more in charge of your own life.

Some people find the 'take care of yourself' message hard to accept. Often they have feelings like 'I don't really count for much' or remember other people saying things like 'Who do you think you are?'

If anyone learns to feel this bad about themselves they are not going to care about whether they are eating a healthy diet. They may even feel eating an unhealthy diet is a suitable way of punishing themselves. There are books that explore these issues more widely. This approach is part of Transactional Analysis (T.A.), which is just one way of looking at how we get to be what we are and how we get on with people. T.A. books are easily available in ordinary book shops. There are also other books which look at 'eating messages'.

If it's your whole self rather than just your eating pattern that you don't feel good about you might consider joining a T.A. group. Many women's health groups take a similar line – look in your library, local paper or perhaps wholefood shop for details of local groups.

Catering and caring

For those who do it, the everyday catering at home can take a lot of time.
People approach the task in different ways and with different feelings.

Pain or pleasure?

Is the job of catering for a household largely pleasurable or something of a pain? Try the quiz below. Tick as many of the items in the list as you like. On a separate piece of paper add any ideas that you think are missing.

If you aren't a caterer for a household do the quiz based on what you have observed in your household. Then ask the person who caters to try the quiz.

Catering is a pleasure because:

It involves using creative skills. ☐

The finished product is 'visible'. ☐

Food can be presented artistically. ☐

Looking after others' nutritional needs is important. ☐

It's nice watching people enjoy the food that's been prepared. ☐

Receiving praise is a good feeling. ☐

Preparing food shows love and caring. ☐

Meals allow people to share and become closer. ☐

Catering is a pain because:

The work is messy and lonely. ☐

It is an endless chore – tedious and boring. ☐

It is so monotonous to cook every day. ☐

It's like being a galley slave or skivvy. ☐

It takes hours to prepare a decent meal and in a flash it's all gone. ☐

Everyone complains if it goes wrong, but you don't hear a thing when it's all right. ☐

It's really hard work to plan and prepare all of that food. ☐

You always seem to smell of cooking. ☐

A glance at the number of ticks and your other comments should tell you where the balance lies for you. On the whole the people who tried this quiz thought that there was more pleasure involved. Most of our testers agreed that the feeling of closeness at mealtimes was pleasurable. But testers who enjoyed catering still had feelings of drudgery.

But feelings can vary from one day or one meal to the next. For example, a compliment could boost your ego for days! Whatever your reaction, being the caterer *is* an important task. How you set about that task shows a lot about you, your attitude to food and your attitude to those you cater for.

If you live alone. If you have no one else to cater for but yourself, then some of the comments in the quiz won't apply to you. But aspects of your own catering can still be pleasurable or painful. 'Receiving praise is a good feeling' – but what if there is no one to give praise? Would you put 'there is no one to give praise' in the list of painful comments?

Think about catering just for yourself and add two comments which are pleasurable to you specifically, and two comments which are painful.

Yesterday's memories: today's meals. What would a typical family meal from your childhood have been like? You probably have mixed memories – some very happy occasions, others that were distinctly strained. How important was the preparation of food in your household routine? The importance you attach to preparing food and your attitudes to it may have been learned in childhood. Think about how meals were prepared and who prepared them. Whoever did most of the catering in your family when you were a child will have had a powerful effect upon you. They will have provided a model. And, whether you like it or not, it can affect the way you perform the role yourself – or how you react to another person performing it.

Preparing a meal

Think about the times when you produce a meal both for yourself and for others. In your mind, go through all the preparation. Try and picture yourself to see what you do. Use the following questions to help you think what you are like when you play the role of 'food preparer'.

● What are you usually thinking about – and feeling – as you prepare the meal?
● What is the expression on your face like?
● What are your movements like? Orderly, cross, quiet – what?
● How do you feel when you put the meal on the table?
● How do you *hope* the people eating the meal will behave?
● What do they actually say and do?
● How would you feel if you were eating alone, not with others?
● Do you feel satisfied with the whole job?

The picture most people gave was one of harassment. By the time the meal was served, the caterer was hot and bothered but trying hard not to show it. Mealtimes seemed to be spent with the caterer looking for signs of enjoyment, or otherwise, in the other people eating.

Meals and emotions

Strong emotions can be aroused by the preparation and eating of meals.

Withholding or giving love

This may be most obvious at meals for children. But it's often there in a less obvious form at other meals. Sometimes the caterer refuses to 'give' the person a meal. A naughty child is told,

"No supper for you — straight off to bed."

"If you want a meal, get it for yourself" is one way to get back at other people. Disapproval can be shown by a week of cold cuts and monotonous meals.

And what about giving love? What experiences have *you* had?

"I've cooked all of your favourites . . .",

"Here's your birthday surprise."

Think about times in the past when you've been offered specially 'loving' meals from members of your household. Have they always been pure pleasure? Have you sometimes felt – whether or not you really wanted it – that you had to eat it? Have you sometimes refused to eat – even though you were hungry? The amount of caring shown in a meal calls for a careful response if feelings aren't to be hurt. The special Mother's Day breakfast of cold tea and burnt toast needs a steady smile and a strong stomach to give the right reward! You can also say sorry with a meal.

"I've cooked it especially for you."

Pride and self-esteem

This is where the people who eat the meals have a vital role to play.

"What? You don't want any? But I've been slaving over a hot stove for hours ..."

Catering is a pleasure

Never mind that you are on a diet or don't feel hungry – it's the cook's love that is in that cake or casserole! Rejecting the food may be seen as rejecting the cook's love. As the caterer, something of you has gone into that meal – even if it's only fish fingers and baked beans that you've knocked up in a few minutes. Indifference or worse on the part of the eaters can have a dispiriting effect – totally out of proportion to the 'offence'.

'No, thanks.' The next few times you offer, or are offered, food, think about how both sides will feel if the reply to 'Go on, have another' is 'No, thanks'. These offers are 'pressures' that are difficult to refuse because they risk causing offence.

Refusing a meal. Make some notes about the experiences in your life that have involved the refusal of meals. Are there certain situations or people you find particularly difficult to refuse? Do you feel differently depending on whether you're giving or receiving the food?

A diplomatic touch can soften the blow of a refusal. Most caterers are looking for praise or some sign that their efforts are appreciated. A compliment helps.

"It really is lovely — but no more now thanks."

Holding the power

Many caterers don't consult the eaters about what they will serve. So sometimes there's an air of 'like it – or lump it' when meals are served up. With children this may be enforced with open threats like, *"Make sure there's nothing left on your plate."* For adults the pressure is usually more subtle. The caterer might announce that *"I like cooking and eating this meal"* or *"I think this food is healthy for us."* Doing good to the person who is to eat the meal gives the caterer a moral advantage. At least if you cater for yourself, you are in charge of what you end up eating.

A caterer is in a potentially powerful position. The power of preparing food is recognised in expressions like, 'If you don't like the heat, stay out of the kitchen!' or 'The way to a man's heart is through his stomach'.

And that potential power is often shown by the attempts of others to put the provider of food 'in their place'. Traditionally the caterer is the woman. Her power may be contested, her role undermined. Notice jokes and stories of angry husbands coming home and throwing their dinner at the fire. And what about the tongue-in-cheek expression 'Woman should be barefoot, pregnant and in the kitchen'?

129

Catering styles

There are many ways of approaching the task of catering. Read through these pictures of caterers that have been sketched out here. They are exaggerated descriptions, but each type contains more than a grain of truth! You may not fit neatly into just one category. Something out of several types may apply to you. Different situations could bring out different aspects of your catering personality. Underline any part of each description that you identify with.

Earth mother. Provides ample and constant supply of meals. Loves feeding the masses. Gets immense satisfaction from the task. Woe betide you if you refuse the food. Adores ritual meals – family reunions, christening parties, wedding breakfasts, funeral wakes. Favourite foods: home baked pies, cakes, huge casseroles.

Harassed cook. Too many to feed. Too little time. Too little organisation. Sees the task as fending off the hungry hordes. Likes quick, easily prepared meals. But often feels obliged to provide more complicated – and more harassing – meals. Favourite foods: fish fingers, baked beans, ready-to-heat pies, chips.

Martha the martyr. Loves the pain and effort involved. Does it all for love – and the people had better remember it. Internal (though sometimes out loud) talk goes... *"I've slaved all day... worked my fingers to the bone... spent more than I can afford...if there's not enough to go round, I'll do without... so eat my darling!"* You'd better – or else! Favourite foods: anything that is fiddly, takes hours to prepare or involves expensive ingredients or exhausting trips to the shops.

Nanny. Knows who is in control around here. Shows it. Produces good, wholesome meals at the proper time. Expects them to be eaten up – with good table manners. 'Nanny' knows best, of course. Favourite foods: plain meat and fish plus 'greens', bread and butter pudding.

Anxious Annie. *"Are they getting enough?"* is a key phrase. Their life is in her hands. Responsible for their health and responds to all dietary advice, regardless of source. Worries about balanced meals, enough vitamins. Works hard, does her best but is still worried about 'is it good enough?' Favourite dishes: dishes that some 'expert' has said are good for you.

Gourmet cook/cookery teacher. At a quick glance these two are not the same. But the key feature of them both is the deliberate acting of a part. *"Look at me, I'm being a good cook."* Does things right. Understands the processes, but may fall short on picking up feelings that go with preparing and eating meals. Feels good about his or her skills, therefore may not even notice responses of the consumers. Favourite foods: classic dishes, homemade mayonnaise.

Cookery hater. Always says hates cooking. Looks grim and resigned while doing it. Always exclaims couldn't care less what it's like or whether people eat or leave it. Often spends longer than necessary in the kitchen. Any praise is met by a casual *"Oh, it's nothing special"* or *"Something that I just knocked up"*, or *"Do you really think so?"* Favourite foods: none, they're all hard work.

Over-eager money manager. Budget always tight. Shopping involves continual search for bargains. Meals taste better if composed of reduced price goods. Sometimes shows startling originality in combinations of foods! Takes pride in managing on next to nothing. Favourite dishes: creative leftovers, food gleaned from hedgerows, stews that last a week.

What about you? When you've thought about these styles, write a few words about yourself as 'caterer'. Of course, this will be particularly important if you consider that none of the styles are like you. If you're not a caterer in your household then write a few words about what sort of caterer you might be, or could become. Which of the styles do you identify with most?

Changing to a healthier diet

With your style of catering. Think about the current guidelines for healthy eating together with your own particular style of catering. How easy or difficult would it be for you to cut down on fats, particularly saturated fats, sugars and salt – and at the same time to prepare more foods that are high in fibre?

What's your response? Think of the *strengths* in the catering in your household that would help to change to, or maintain, the new guidelines. And which feature of the catering might prove to be a *hindrance* in sticking to the new guidelines?

These might be such things as *"It's all such an effort"*. Or it might be more practical: *"I always love marinating things — I love to show that sort of care — we'll be able to have loads of beans and pulses."* Write down your own comments.

Men only?

You will have noticed that some of the catering types listed above have women's names. But, of course, both men and women carry out this role. If you want to imagine any of them as men then substitute, for example, 'Anxious Andy' for Annie. Can you identify any of the styles with the men in your household? Or, if you're a man, with your own style? Do the styles listed seem to be real, as far as you're concerned?

Men who live on their own demonstrate that it is possible for them to be perfectly good caterers. But are men in general brought up and encouraged to take catering seriously? Most girls learn the skills at home or school as a matter of course.

Knowing how to be a caterer can be difficult if you have not been 'prepared' from childhood. This applies to both men and women. But on the whole men seem to face more problems with catering.

Now read through the problems and advantages of learning to cater for people who have not been 'prepared' and see how much you think they apply to men specifically.

Problems.
• You may not expect to find catering rewarding.
• You can feel awkward about catering for others – because it is an unfamiliar role and you have no incentive to explore it further.
• Other people do not expect you to be good at cooking meals for yourself and others.
• You may lack the skills and the confidence to prepare a meal. (This can often be used as an excuse *not* to learn.)

Advantages.
• Because you are not so attached to the role of caterer you may be able to stand back and think about ways of changing styles of catering.
• Because you do not have a set style you probably find it easy to pick up tips from anyone.
• You might find that with no 'track record' to undo you can build new advice into your catering more readily.

Sharing the work. Some men enjoy catering and want to share in it. Most children want to learn how to do it or at least to imitate. How much is catering shared in your household?

Many women, even if they find continual catering irksome, don't want to let anyone else in on the act. They may enjoy the sense of power, even if they're not conscious of it. Or perhaps they only feel valued for exercising their skills as a caterer and so might feel useless if asked to share or relinquish that role. Sometimes they just get frustrated by the inept efforts of a 'learner' caterer. After all, many of the best cooks find it hard to teach and a kitchen needs to be an orderly place . . . then there is the sense of territory many women feel about *their* kitchens.

Someone else in your kitchen? If you're a woman and a caterer in your household how do you feel when other people do the cooking? Who do you let do the cooking? Do you keep an eye on what they are up to?

Stop for a while and sort out how you feel on these occasions. Sometimes it's a marvellous break. But how long do you go on feeling relieved of having to be in charge? Would you prefer only to have a 'guest' caterer occasionally? And what about other people in your household? How do they feel about shared catering? Do they prefer to be just 'guest' caterers too?

The overriding feeling of several of our woman testers was one of guilt. If they let someone else do the cooking they felt that they were failing in their duty as a wife or mother. Their expectations were all of being *the* family caterer. This can be taken to extremes.

Changes in style

Styles of catering are affected by other changes throughout your life. Changes will also affect whether or not you are the caterer. Remember that if you are single you can still be affected by changes – a new job, different friends, moving to a different part of the country, retiring.

Which parts of the pattern described below are familiar to you?

Leaving home. Leaving home and moving away can completely change catering habits. For many it's their first taste of the role. New habits and limitations will emerge. The young, single might want help. Friends may cook for each other.

Courtship. Both partners occasionally prepare special meals. At other times they eat out quite a lot.

Early marriage. Both working. Woman tends to do more, but they share a lot of the tasks involved in preparing meals.

Children. Now they have children and the woman does most, if not all, of the catering. It's far less of a pleasure, more of a chore.

Being single again. Couples do split up leaving either single parent families or people who are suddenly single again. Catering changes, any shared catering is outside the family.

The pattern for John and Kathy. Kathy talks about what catering means to her.

"I used to quite like cooking, but having so much to do at home with the children has killed a lot of the pleasure for me. I'd like to spend less time in the kitchen. John can cook — before we married, he used to cook for himself quite well. We've slipped into these roles, which I'm not so happy with, but don't know how to change."

There's no simple solution, but John and Kathy have looked at their changing roles and have given some thought to ways of easing the situation. Here are some things they could do:
• Organise a babysitter and eat out regularly – perhaps once a fortnight or once a month.
• Get in takeaway food occasionally.
• Share cooking in advance and freeze the food.
• Use more convenience foods.
• Negotiate to share roles. For instance, John could do all the cooking every Sunday.
• Specialise in simple dishes that are nutritious, but don't need a lot of preparation.
• Make a definite date to cook something special together.

All of these ideas ring the changes. They give changes of pace and variety to eating.

Changes to your diet. If you are planning changes to your diet why not sit back for a while and consider what changes in the roles of caterers and consumers in your household could help. After all, health should be a concern to everyone and it's a chance to learn.

Eating out

Most people eat out from time to time.
How can you get the best out of these occasions?

At home. You are in control if you are the caterer. You can eat healthily or not; you can eat as much or as little as you like. You can prepare a meal in the way you like and be more comfortable in your own surroundings. You can also eat well at an economic price.

Why eat out? The reasons are not hard to find:
• Other people do all the preparation, cooking and clearing up.
• You don't have to shop.
• You've got nothing to eat at home.
• It provides an opportunity for a social outing – eating becomes a social activity.
• You can feel good – you're going to indulge yourself.
• You can treat others, by choosing a special meal and paying the bill.
• You can try unusual or exotic dishes that you don't normally have.
• It can be enjoyable and fun!
• You go along because others expect you to – a business lunch . . . or someone asks you out.

It's an occasion

Think of the times that you have been out for a meal in the last few months. What sorts of occasions were they?

Special treats, like birthdays or anniversaries.

Get togethers with family or friends.

Celebrations, like parties or wedding receptions.

Business or work meal – maybe in a cafeteria, a restaurant or a pub.

Meals out by yourself – you couldn't be bothered to cook, or you were out shopping and hungry . . .

Spur of the moment trips out – you just decided on the spot to go out and eat.

Regular meals out – you like to eat out at least once a week, on work days you normally eat out at lunch time.

Are there any other times you might eat out? Jot them down on a separate piece of paper.

Think back to two of these occasions when you've eaten out. Choose one you enjoyed and one you didn't enjoy. Now use these questions to help you write about those events.
• Why did you decide to eat out on this occasion?

• Why did you decide to eat at that particular place, café, restaurant, etc.?
• What was good about the occasion?
• What was disappointing about the occasion?

What other people said. Testers who did this activity chose a wide variety of occasions. They wrote about everything from a snack pizza meal to a full blown dinner at a smart London restaurant. But it wasn't always the special foods or the special, planned occasions that were most enjoyed. Nor was it the quick, spontaneous meals that were least enjoyed. A whole range of reasons were given for enjoying or not enjoying meals.

"I enjoyed it because of the company."

"The food was good but it was ruined by the dirty tablecloth and the constant sniffing of the waiter."

"We were celebrating our wedding anniversary, the restaurant looked nice and the service was excellent. It just seemed very special."

"It wasn't particularly special but I was being treated."

"The food was meagre and expensive, the restaurant was crowded and you had to queue — a waste of money."

"What we really liked about the place was the fact that the toilets were clean. We had the children with us."

"The building was old, smelled musty and the toilets were just disgusting."

Very often the food eaten didn't fit exactly with ideas of a healthy diet. Celebrations usually have a lot of rich food. Not surprisingly, people didn't feel too bothered about this aspect of eating with the 'once in a blue moon' treats. The food was much more of a concern with regular meals, like pub or cafeteria lunches or other places where people ate out a lot.

All sorts of things can make or break the occasion. Below are some of the general factors testers pointed to.

Food. Was it to your taste, plentiful and at the right temperature? Was there anything wrong with it?

Surroundings. Did you feel at home or out of place? Was it clean, comfortable and suited to the occasion?

Atmosphere. Did the occasion seem pleasant and enjoyable? Was there any background music or other type of entertainment? Were there any annoyances like noise or smell? Did the staff make you feel small? Were you put off by a sea of cutlery in front of you?

People. Was the company good? Were you bored or out of your depth with the conversation?

Price. Did you feel that you got value for money? Was it too pricey? (People who were being treated often enjoyed the occasion, no matter what the food was like!)

Service. Was the service fast, polite and well timed? Were there problems with too little attention by staff or with fussing, over-attentive waiters?

What can you do?

Often planning in advance can help ensure that a meal out is pleasant and satisfactory. Sometimes people also need to use their wits to make the best of a situation when things don't seem to be going too well.

Look at the following case studies – the eating occasions are different. The first describes a *spontaneous* event. The second is one which was *planned* in advance. And the third describes an activity which has become a *regular* occurrence. In each case you can consider some possible strategies for dealing with issues that crop up.

Going along with the crowd

A spontaneous event. Eileen lives alone and is a quiet, retiring and thoughtful person. She is also rather overweight. Lately, she has been trying out a new diet for health reasons. After a stormy union meeting some workmates suggest going out for a meal together. Eileen is torn between accepting the invitation or going home. If she accepts she will have a chance to talk to one or two people she would like to know better, and be seen to be joining in a social event. But this may mean breaking her diet. Alternatively, she could go home to her lonely flat to eat a healthy meal and know that next time she may not be asked.

Strategies for Eileen. Eileen needs to balance the social gains she'll get from such an occasion with her strong views about diet.

● She could decide to blow her diet just for once. After all, it's important to her to socialise. So, she doesn't want to appear a 'pain' to her workmates by insisting on being different. She knows it's her regular diet that counts. The odd break in a good diet is less damaging to health than eating a doughnut every day.
● She may not find it possible to insist that they all eat in a 'health food' restaurant on this 'one off' occasion. But her own feelings about food *are* important. She could do the 'best she can' and look for the least unhealthy option on the menu. She could choose grilled meat rather than fried, white meat rather than red, fish rather than meat, or a salad, or a meal where the main ingredient is carbohydrate rather than meat – such as risotto and pasta dishes. If the outing becomes a regular event then she may be able to plan more in advance. She could suggest going to a restaurant that serves the sort of food she wants to eat.

Celebrating in style

A planned event. Mr Barnes, aged 45, used to eat out regularly in his youth, but now does so only occasionally. However, he and his wife do like to celebrate their wedding anniversary in style. This year they decide to try a new venue: the King's Hotel.

Mr Barnes' night out. Remembering meals of his youth, Mr Barnes forgets about the boiled chicken and grilled fish, which he eats at home, and the shellfish and pasta of his favourite restaurant. Instead he plumps for five courses with an aperitif, appropriate wines and after

dinner drinks. He is miserably aware of spending too much money. So, although he chooses five courses, he goes for the cheaper dishes that he doesn't really fancy so much.

Mr Barnes is up all night trying to digest his food. He's hung over all the next day and tries hard to avoid the pitying look in his wife's eye the following evening.

Mrs Barnes – the same night out. Mrs Barnes didn't want an aperitif so she paid a visit to the loo before the meal arrived. This gave her a chance to walk around and make herself feel comfortable. She asked the waiter to help her choose from the menu. He recommended the fish dish which she made her main course. She followed this with a really nice piece of fruit. Having made personal contact with her, the waiter made sure that everything was first class. It was an enjoyable change for him to make someone's evening rather than serving his 'seen it all' regulars. Mrs Barnes stuck with the first bottle of pleasant white wine her husband ordered and added a little mineral water to it later in the meal. She capped her meal with a piece of cheese – a type she'd never had before – and went home feeling she had celebrated in style.

The best strategies. No prizes for guessing who'd had the more enjoyable evening. Yet both of them were in the same restaurant, presented with all the same options. Mr Barnes allowed himself to be overwhelmed by the occasion. He was more concerned with his memories of what seemed right, rather than what was enjoyable. Mrs Barnes was concerned to do what was right by her own reckoning and went from strength to strength. Clearly Mrs Barnes' strategy was well worked out and satisfactory. Mr Barnes might have done better if he

too had:
● stuck to a modest meal
● not tried to 'impress'
● asked advice and 'wooed' waiters.

Enjoying your own company

A regular event. John Matthews is a retired journalist living in a provincial town. Divorced a few years ago, he has a wide circle of friends, but still spends a fair amount of time on his own. He's never enjoyed cooking, and since splitting up from his wife, has tended to snack or buy in a meagre range of convenience foods. After a period when he felt rather 'low' he decided to eat out more regularly. He had visited many of the restaurants in his area with friends but he found going alone a very different experience. At first, John felt that he stuck out like a sore thumb. It was no problem having to lunch out alone, but in the evening almost everyone was accompanied.

John's strategies. This is what he did to make eating out alone enjoyable.

● Initially, taking a newspaper to read, or some work to do – scribbling some notes for an article was the only way he could prevent himself feeling embarassed.
● He found that the choice of restaurant was important. Returning to the same restaurant several times helps. John timed his arrival with the slightly slack period in the evening.
● The seating arrangements made a difference – he always had the same table – in a quiet corner with a good view of everything that was going on.
● He got to know the staff. When he became a regular customer the waitresses recommended dishes, or reserved food for him that they knew he liked.

How to get what you want

Depending on the situation this can involve:
- Planning in advance – cutting down on the potential hazards before they arise, and anticipating anxieties.
- Being assertive – matching what you find against what you *want*.
- Making the best of things – accepting what you can't alter.

Planning in advance

Ask your friends where they eat, or choose places that have been recommended to you personally. It's always worth knowing tips about good eating places. Keep them in your head, or jot them down with a few notes so that you have them for future reference.

Look through recipe books, study menus, consult eating out guides. Research like this will always come in useful to help you select dishes from the menu and choose the right kind of restaurant.

It's a good idea to have some tried and tested places you know to be good. And it's useful to know which dishes in certain restaurants are always worth having. But it's also worth being a bit adventurous and sometimes trying out new places and new dishes.

Book in advance, particularly if it's a celebration like a birthday or anniversary that's important. Try to make personal contact with the manager and check out the arrangements beforehand.

Find out about all the details that you might tend to overlook. For example, will they hold your table if you are late? Are you expected to vacate the table at a certain time? What parking facilities are there? Do you have transport home? All these could spoil an otherwise pleasant experience if they go wrong.

Being assertive

When eating out be prepared to ask a lot of questions, and be firm about what you want. In this country, we tend to be very passive. We put up with inconvenience because we don't like to make a fuss.

Seating is important. If you don't like the table you're asked to sit at then insist on being moved. Even within your own group of people, feel able to make the choice to sit next to someone you like.

If the menu says your dish is served with 'chips and peas' and you'd rather have salad, or something else, then do ask. It's often possible to substitute one for the other. Restaurants are usually prepared to be flexible.

Don't feel obliged to eat more or spend more than you intended. Look at the size of the portions that other people are eating, or ask for more details. Some places won't let you have a starter and dessert, or just a main course. Their restrictions may mean that you won't be able to eat in the way you want to eat. So why not just avoid them in future? Better still – tell them why you won't be eating there again.

What helps? Being assertive needn't mean being unpleasant. It does help if you know your facts and your rights. If all else fails then complaining to the management may be necessary. It also helps to know your law – *Fair Deal,* which is a shopper's guide produced by the Office of Fair Trading, gives practical advice on complaining. It is available from HMSO offices. At least you might not have to foot the bill for a bad meal! If we don't say what we think, things will never improve.

Making the best of things

Remember meals out consist of more than food. Even if the meal is disappointing you can enjoy the company or the surroundings and try and forget the overcooked vegetables and undercooked sauce.

If it is the company that's suspect, savour every mouthful of your food. And watch what's going on at other tables – this is nearly always a worthwhile activity!

Getting it right

Planning what you will do reduces the chances of a real catastrophe. Having some strategies for meeting disappointments also helps. Most of us go back over the horrors of a disastrous meal and imagine what we would have done. Perhaps you might like to do this with your own most disastrous meals. What would you do or say in the same situation now?

It's also worth thinking of a meal that you really enjoyed. Consider what made it special. Concentrate on aspects other than the food. How can you make sure that you keep these qualities on other occasions? Choosing your company, the place to eat and the time carefully could make all the difference. Sort out what you really want from a meal out and make these your ground rules.

Entertaining

When we invite people to eat in our homes, we are creating a bond with them. We may also be showing them what we think of ourselves and them.

Most people invite guests to eat in their home at some time. The way we entertain might vary in formality depending on our guests and the occasion. And, of course, our enjoyment can vary too depending on how comfortable we feel. For most of us, the opening moments of a social occasion can be nerve-racking, however, when we get the guests, the food and the degree of formality or informality right – that's entertainment!

This topic helps you look at how you feel about entertaining guests, and at different sorts of occasions.

How would you react? Consider these situations which make different calls on your hospitality:

● A relative you hadn't seen for years, calling by for lunch on his way North.

● Your children's friends who want a picnic in the garden.

● A workman who is laying the ground floor carpet – it will take him most of the day and he has no lunch-box with him.

● A good friend of your husband/wife who comes for an evening meal.

First, how comfortable would you feel about providing food for each of these occasions? Try to put them in order from the most to the least comfortable. Next put a 1 next to the event you'd *most* enjoy providing hospitality for down through to 4 for the one you'd find *least* enjoyable. Your enjoyment will probably relate to whether you expect to feel comfortable or awkward.

Now make a few notes about what you imagine each of the four events would be like. What food would you offer? Would you feel obliged to make an effort for your guests or not? Would you spend money and time making things look nice? In the cases where you don't feel required to make an effort, why is that?

Go through the notes you have made and think about the level at which you pitched each event in your imagination. Was it very structured, was it formal, or was it casual?

Social occasions

How we do our entertaining says as much about what's going on as any words. We convey a lot to our guests by our actions and how we organise events.

You may want to organise an occasion in such a way that shows you are on close friendship terms with people. And that can be done in different ways. If you really like someone you may want to get out all your best china to show that you're prepared to put yourself out for them. On the other hand, you may feel that it's a compliment to your guests if your organisation says, 'Take me as I am.'

You can also arrange your entertaining of guests to show that you are aware that your relationship isn't an intimate one. For example, you might decide to go formal when entertaining your boss and her husband, to show that you respect her position. But on the other hand, not knowing someone very well may make you decide to pitch the event at a very casual level.

People have different ideas about just when to be formal and when to be informal. Whatever you decide it's clear that the amount of structure and formality you give to an event is significant. It tells your guests something about what you think of them.

A comfortable meal?

You can explore this idea by looking at three more situations.

Mrs Kendal's fund raising meeting. Mrs Kendal's just moved and, for the first time, it's her turn to host a group meeting of her national woman's organisation. She puts out tea, coffee and biscuits in the lounge. Then, at the last minute, she puts out sherry 'just in case' with bowls of crisps and nuts. No one takes her up on her offer of 'something a little stronger!' And when it's all over, she finds the crisps and nuts haven't been touched. Although *she's* nervously polished off those in the bowl next to her.

Visitors for tea. Mrs Kendal's friend Sally is home from Australia on a visit. Mrs Kendal hasn't met Sally's

husband or children, and is a little nervous about the tea. She puts out a big spread of sandwiches and cakes, beautifully laid out with her best china and table linen. Mrs Kendal and Sally talk non-stop. Sally's family love the traditional English tea and are impressed with the amount of trouble she's gone to. Mrs Kendal's own family keep passing through to have a chat and a sandwich.

Christmas dinner. Mrs Kendal's brother and his family come for Christmas dinner. They arrive through the back door and hang around the kitchen during the final preparations. For dinner they eat chestnut soup, turkey with cranberry sauce, Christmas pudding with brandy butter and Stilton cheese. There are no surprises for anyone – funny hats, crackers, port and cigars feature as always. The table looks beautiful, everyone's dressed up to the nines. Things are always done like this at Mrs Kendal's house at Christmas.

Different styles. In each case Mrs Kendal has done her entertaining differently.

At the fund raising meeting she knows it's an informal event, with not much to prepare. But she's embarrassed and nervous because she doesn't know her guests. After the event she looks at the uneaten crisps and nuts and thinks that she tried too

hard. *"Next time they'll have to take me as they find me!"*

When Sally comes to tea, she's slightly nervous, too. But it's important to her to show she cares about doing it right. The afternoon is very successful and everyone feels comfortable.

The Christmas dinner is very highly structured. Everyone knows what to expect. But it's all about family ties and the event finds Mrs Kendal completely at her ease.

Putting on a good show

In giving food, we offer a part of ourselves as well. All sorts of things affect the kind of display we put on.

How we were brought up to treat guests. Your own lifestyle may be very different from that of your parents. Yet the way they treated guests in your home when you were a child will have had an effect upon you.

As a child, you may have been taught that making conversation with your guests when they arrive is the most important way of welcoming them. But what if you are needed in the kitchen just then, to check the meal? You may feel a conflict about what you should do. Parents of a lively family may feel embarrassed if they were taught that formality was appropriate treatment for visitors.

Having boisterous and outspoken teenagers may suit day-to-day life, but be a source of worry when entertaining.

Of course, your parents' style of entertaining may be one you have always tried to copy. Perhaps you have felt under pressure to live up to it?

Going up in the world. Class differences are an obvious factor in the way guests are entertained in our society. People who have not stayed in the same social class as their parents, and have jumped a class or two in their own lifetime, may be particularly aware of this.

"The other day we went out for a meal at a doctor's house. My husband knows him through work. We had been sitting there for a while and I looked round at the table, candelabra, silver place settings, pure linen tablecloth and the first course beautifully served. I thought, that this was a far cry from when I was a child."

Times change. Economic and social changes have played their part. Houses are different, the huge kitchen of earlier times is just not a feature of most modern houses. Dining rooms and tables are smaller. So, entertaining seems to involve fewer people. For lots of people it also seems that plain English cooking is not acceptable these days. Meals need starters and a complicated main course to seem special. Thirty years ago, even a prosperous family would not have sat down to a supper of avocado pears, followed by an aubergine and pasta dish, with kiwi fruit for dessert. These days many people have tasted such exotic foods and eat them regularly.

People like us. We identify strongly with people who lead a similar lifestyle and have similar values to ourselves. This is particularly true of entertaining. People like us ... have to overfeed guests/use low-cholesterol ingredients/don't serve jam roly-poly and custard for pudding/would never serve frozen peas for guests/would never serve guests from fancy dishes put on the table and so on.

The need to spend money – or produce good food. If we invited people to a meal and then made it obvious that we had made no effort at all – or offered them a bowl of cereals at lunchtime – they would most probably feel a little insulted. We need to show our guests that we have made an effort on their behalf, because this makes it obvious that we value *them*. It also shows that *we* are capable of providing good food, that we have the means and skills needed to do so. Spending money or putting a lot of time, effort and imagination into the preparation of the food shows that we consider the occasion to be important.

When you entertain

How do all these things influence us when we entertain people? Extending hospitality can be greatly enjoyable. It can also be a strain. When we do find it a strain, it can be helpful to see what kinds of pressures we feel subjected to.

Different expectations. Below is a list of many of the sorts of expectations that people have about entertaining. Tick those that you feel are always true for you. Put a cross against those that don't apply to you at all. Put a question mark against those that sometimes apply to you.

Entertaining means:

● Being hospitable – friendly.
● Being warm, keeping conversation going, etc.
● Being friendly but polite and formal.
● Being relaxed and making guests feel relaxed.
● Being calm, cool and collected.
● Making sure the house is clean and tidy.
● Expecting good behaviour from others – children, spouse, etc.
● Showing you've made a special effort by the way the table is prepared.
● Spending more money than you normally would on food.
● Spending a lot of time on food preparation.
● Giving them what they're used to (don't serve Granny unfamiliar foods like aubergine).
● Never running out of food – having too much rather than too little.
● Making everything where possible (not shop bought).
● Presenting food well, so that it looks nice.
● Being present in the room most of the time once guests have arrived (rather than still be cooking, or seeing to the children).

When doing this exercise you may have felt that your answers depended on *who* you were entertaining. You may also have thought that a lot of the items on the list describe ideal situations and standards which very few of us live up to. None of the things listed are actually right or wrong in themselves. If you've got a lot of ticks then you probably have plenty to do and think about every time you have people to eat in your home.

Look again at your answers in the list. What gives you satisfaction and what is inappropriate or just too much strain? If you want to change some of your expectations, adopt new ones or get rid of some, there is no reason why you shouldn't. These are *your* standards of entertaining.

Breaking with tradition at Christmas

Changing the pattern

Sometimes you can feel stuck with a pattern of entertaining you don't feel happy about. You may decide you want to break with tradition. Or you may find yourself struggling to compete as to who can entertain most lavishly. Perhaps too, there are some occasions when you lose your nerve and you don't enjoy entertaining because you're unsure of what your guests expect?

Here are three examples of people who want to change their pattern.

Breaking with tradition

Mrs May has adopted a wholefood vegetarian diet which is low in fat and high in fibre. She has also eliminated a great amount of sugar and salt from her diet. Her brother and his family want to come for Christmas dinner as usual. They know about her new 'food fads' but don't expect her to make any changes to the marvellous traditional fare she usually serves up. What is she to do? Well, she could try one of these two plans.

Plan 1. She could go ahead and prepare what she had planned – an exotic Indonesian meal – with melon, ginger and brown rice, followed by fresh figs, dates and tangerines. She could make her usual beautiful table decoration and all the trimmings would be as they always were. Her brother would be likely to pull her leg about it, whilst eating as much as he decently could. And his wife would probably appreciate not putting on any extra weight – a problem for her every Christmas.

Plan 2. She could tell them what she plans to serve up. Then if they really felt that their celebration wouldn't be the same without the traditional food, they could bring their own turkey and the usual accompaniments. This would be a compromise, with each side accepting the needs of the other.

Competitive cooking

Jill and Geoff are a young professional couple. They alternate weekly meals at home with two close friends. The other couple are good cooks, and take a lot of interest in unusual foods. When Jill and Geoff eat at their house it's obvious that a great deal of thought, effort and expense has gone into the meal.

Jill is no mean cook herself, but after three months, she feels the whole thing has become unnecessarily competitive – the meals are getting bigger and grander every time.

How could this situation be altered?

Plan 1. The important thing about the meals is the enjoyment and friendship. What you eat needn't be so important. Jill could down-play the whole thing by serving up something very simple on the next occasion and see if any of the enjoyment is lost.

Plan 2. Jill and Geoff could actually make moves to restrict the more lavish displays and dishes of their friends. They could suggest a joint meal where they each provide a different course, or limit the amount spent on any one meal, or vary it by going out for a *cheap* meal occasionally. They could restrict the kind of food eaten by cutting out meat, or having different kinds of unusual dishes.

Ill at ease

Tricia is from a working class background and has lived away from home since she went to college.

She is now married to an architect, and still after many years, her mother is tense about catering for Tom – her husband – when the family come to stay. She worries endlessly about the kind of food to give to him, how the table should look and what it means when he leaves food on his plate.

Is there a way Tricia's mother could suffer less anxiety every time she has to entertain her son-in-law?

Plan 1. Tricia's mother could speak to her daughter about the kinds of food Tom likes and take some tips from her. She could try out a dish beforehand if it was unfamiliar to her and she was nervous about it.

Plan 2. She could go straight to the heart of the problem and ask him into her kitchen. Why not invite *him* to cook a meal, or help in the preparation, lay the table and so on? She must reassure herself too, that Tom, as a *good guest*, must take his hosts as he finds them. If he gives signs that he's being critical, then it's his problem.

How about you?

Do you feel under a lot of pressure on some occasions when you entertain? If it spoils for you what could be an enjoyable occasion, it might be useful to ask yourself what expectations you have and why. It may be possible to make things easier for yourself without upsetting your guests. For example, how about letting people see you as you are and taking you as they find you? If you'd like to have rhubarb crumble for pudding, why not? After all, this lets people get to know *you* better and gives you the security of cooking what you are happy with. Equally it's possible to create new ways of being hospitable to fit present day lifestyles and modern knowledge about healthy food.

You don't need to be lavish and spend a lot of money on food when you entertain in order to enjoy the social benefits of eating together. The more relaxed you are the easier it will be to enjoy the occasion.

Organising meals

Meals and snacks pace our days. For most of us they provide a routine. For many of us, too, they involve some organisation in planning and preparing for them.

How we go about organising food in our lives is an important consideration if we want to change to a healthier diet. We need to think about the strengths and weaknesses of our own style of organisation. And then we can begin to work out what changes we want to make for a healthier diet.

Of course, different people organise their eating in different ways. And it's worthwhile considering what we can learn from groups with various dietary preferences – for instance other nationalities and vegetarians.

This chapter helps you look at how you organise your eating. What do you mean by meals and snacks, how do you fit eating into your day, how do you plan your food? It asks you to think about how your style compares with other people's and how you adapt food to your own taste . . . So what effect does the way you organise your eating have on your diet?

Real meals

Our ideas about meals and snacks are quite similar to the rules of a game we know very well. We never give them a second thought until they're broken.

This topic looks at our understanding of meals and snacks and how this might affect attempts to change our eating patterns. If your store cupboard or refrigerator is well stocked you could stand by it and pick at a whole range of things and still ensure that you were having a healthy diet. However, eating involves a whole lot more than nutrition. Most of us get satisfaction from how foods are put together and presented, as well as from the basic components. Meals and snacks have meaning for us apart from just being food. They are often associated with various firm, but rarely spoken, beliefs.

We went to tea... Look at the following quotes. Which ones do you identify with in some way?

"We went to a buffet lunch to welcome friends home from abroad. It consisted of cheese sandwiches, egg sandwiches, luncheon meat sandwiches, shop sausage rolls, cheese and biscuits, small cakes and white wine. It was an uninteresting display of food and rather stodgy. A cup of coffee was only provided after several people had asked for it."

"We had soup and salad, a sensible, light meal because we'd eaten at midday. Then, of course, we had to have tinned fruit and ice cream when we were watching the television an hour later."

"After the good, nourishing soup, the pair of us sat there waiting for the main course. Our hostess offered cheese and biscuits and a bowl of fruit...and that was it!"

"I arrived to stay in the middle of a heatwave. My friend presented me with hot pie and mushy peas saying 'I thought you'd need a good, hot meal after your journey'. It was a bit like having a sauna."

"We went to Sunday tea expecting a meal—tea, sandwiches, fruit cake and biscuits at the very least. When we got there we found a cup of tea and a rich tea biscuit awaiting us."

Satisfied?

All these eating experiences refer to some kind of lack of satisfaction. Some of them are unsatisfying because people expected something different – for instance, a meal ought to contain a main course. Some of them are unsatisfying because some different food would have been appropriate.

A proper meal

One example of firm beliefs is the idea of a 'proper meal'. Our testers were asked the question, 'What is a proper meal?' They mostly defined it as meat or fish with more than one vegetable. Almost all of them also included a pudding or fruit or yoghurt as part of a proper meal. In a recent survey by the British Nutrition Foundation most of the people asked thought a proper meal was meat and two veg.

Many people have firm ideas about which foods are put together and in what order. For them this is part of the definition of what a meal is. One tester seems to have succeeded in changing her husband's firm ideas about meals.

"For the first 15 years of my marriage my husband did not consider a meal complete without a pudding. Now if he has anything it's yoghurt or fruit."

If it's a meal . . .

So what do you think a meal is? And what do you think the difference is between a meal and a snack?

Below is a list of phrases. Go through them and put an S by the phrases that you would apply to a snack, and an M by the phrases that you would apply to a meal. If you think some of them apply to both a snack *and* a meal, mark them with an S and an M. Leave a blank by any of the phrases that you don't think apply to either meals or snacks.

1. *" . . . I always sit at a table to eat."*

2. *" . . . I can eat it on my lap while watching television."*

3. *" . . . there would be several courses."*

4. *" . . . at least some of it would be cooked."*

5. *" . . . I would eat it in company."*

6. *" . . . I would use cutlery to eat it."*

7. *" . . . it would be accompanied by a hot drink."*

8. *" . . . it would contain some meat."*

9. *" . . . it would be OK if I ate it with my fingers."*

10. *" . . . some of it would be hot, some cold."*

11. *" . . . it would consist of a good balance of different foods."*

12. *" . . . it would fill me up."*

13. *" . . . it would have required more than a few minutes' preparation."*

14. *" . . . it would be a spontaneous event."*

15. *" . . . I would definitely be hungry."*

16. *" . . . it would be eaten at a specific time."*

When this activity was tested there was fairly strong agreement on the following:

1, 3, 6, 11, 13 and 16 apply to meals.
2, 7, 9, and 14 apply to snacks.

There was a lot of agreement that *"I would definitely be hungry"* (15) needn't necessarily apply to either meals or snacks. But it was considered that *"it would fill me up"* (12) applied equally to both meals and snacks. Opinion was very divided over the rest of the phrases – 4, 5, 8 and 10. Perhaps you think differently from our testers? There are no right or wrong answers in a matter of opinion. However, for you it's an important opinion, because it affects your eating patterns.

What's important?

Several factors may be important in helping you define what for you is a meal or a snack. Any or all of the following may be important to you:

- who you eat with
- when you eat
- where you eat
- how complicated or lengthy the preparation has been
- what sort of food it is
- how the food has been combined together
- whether the food is raw or cooked
- how much planning has gone into the event.

Changes in the pattern

By looking at what you understand a meal or a snack to be you can begin to build up a picture of what it might mean to change that pattern. At certain times in their lives, people do change their patterns of meals and snacks. The changes may be in the type or amount of food eaten, or a dif-

ferent balance of meals and snacks in the day. From a health point of view, as long as a reasonably nutritious diet is maintained overall it's OK. But for some people such changes make healthy eating difficult.

Changing circumstances

Look at the following instances:

"When my mother, who's 78, came to live with me I found that I started to eat several more meals a week than I used to. For instance, I would come in at lunchtime to have my snack of bread and cheese and would find that she'd made a salad, got pickles out and put a fruit pie in the oven. Then I found the dining table laid and we'd sit down to 'a meal'. In two months I put on four pounds in weight."

"After my husband died I found I had no inclination to either sit down to meals or even prepare them. I went through a phase when I wasn't eating very well at all. But even when I started to eat better I found I never got back my taste for meals. Now I have good, nourishing snacks. I never sit down at the dining table unless I have guests, whereas in 40 years of married life I don't suppose we ate more than a couple of dozen meals away from the table, except, of course, when we were out!"

"When I lived on my own I ate when I wanted — mainly snacks. Sometimes I'd go for days without getting anywhere near the dining table and I felt perfectly OK. When I was living with someone else I found myself being pressured into eating at the table, cooking meat and two veg., and getting very lethargic, fat and constipated."

"I have found that our eating habits have changed dramatically since we became parents. Instead of convenience foods when and where we wanted, we eat fresh meat and vegetables and sit down to our meals at the table with the children."

Why? Looking at these examples you can probably see what led to the changes. A mother wants to show her care for her daughter by getting 'real meals'. A widow no longer has anyone to care for except herself. She doesn't want this to be brought home to her by sitting at the table alone to eat meals. Having a family or living with someone can mean that new patterns of meals and snacks develop.

Changes in your life's circumstances may bring about changes in your eating patterns. Can you think of any changes in your life that led to you having a different pattern of eating meals and snacks?

141

Different patterns?

There are a whole set of new guidelines for healthy eating which recommend ways in which the nation might change its diet. They show that most of us eat too much fat, sugar and salt and not enough fibre.

Healthy eating. Making changes to our diet means thinking not only about what we eat but how we eat it and what this means in terms of our ideas about meals and snacks.

Below are some of the suggestions that are being made to help people move towards having a new and healthier diet.

● First, look at each suggestion and think what it would mean in terms of your own pattern of eating meals and snacks.

● Then tick on the scale how easy it would be to bring about these changes within your current set of ideas about meals and snacks.

● Finally, write down why you think it would be easy or difficult.

Cheryl's thoughts on these suggestions are shown in the chart below. You'll probably find it useful to jot down your answers in the same way on a separate piece of paper.

SUGGESTION	VERY EASY	QUITE EASY	QUITE DIFFICULT	VERY DIFFICULT	COMMENTS
Skimmed milk instead of whole milk.	✓				It doesn't affect my meals and snacks at all. It's just a straight acceptable substitute.
Sandwiches instead of meat and 2 veg.			✓		I wouldn't have sandwiches for a proper meal. But I might be prepared to have more sandwiches and call it a light meal, say, instead of meat and salads.
Fresh fruit instead of tinned fruit.				✓	I always look upon fresh fruit as something I eat between meals. Tinned fruit is a pudding. It would seem odd to substitute fresh fruit for it at meal times.
Meat and four veg. instead of meat and 2 veg.		✓			OK, but I'd have to cut down the quantities of each vegetable or I'd never get it all on the plate.
Small portion of meat instead of a lot.			✓		Not sure. OK in a casserole where there's a lot of other things floating around. But then I don't eat casseroles much.
Beans instead of meat.				✓	No. Beans are snacks to go on toast. I wouldn't replace meat as a main meal — most unsatisfying.
Cottage cheese instead of camembert.				✓	I only eat cheese at the end of a main meal. I'd never dream of eating cottage cheese on biscuits then.

142

Some changes are more threatening to Cheryl than others. Notice Cheryl's resistence to losing out on her meat ration. Some changes are really only going to be achieved effectively if you do take a new approach to eating. Again, notice Cheryl's comments that she'd have to cut down on each vegetable in order to get four on to the plate – she didn't consider eating either more vegetables overall, or less meat. That would have threatened her idea of what a proper meal was.

Our testers

Our testers had lots to say about this activity. Their remarks ranged from the delightful 'buy larger plates' for meat and four vegetables in a meal, to comments about what the suggested changes mean if you live in a family.

Eating with the family. One tester's view shows that you may want to alter your own ideas about meals and snacks but your children may be more resistent! Family traditions can be very strong. Here are some comments.

"Meat and four vegetables — could do this quite easily for myself and husband, but have difficulty in getting children to eat a lot of vegetables, as they do prefer meat at a meal."

"Beans instead of meat — have made homemade soup from a mixture of dried beans with added vegetables and found it extremely delicious and filling. The children, though, did not like it very much."

"Small portions of meat instead of large: yes, casseroles are useful — you can disguise all sorts of things and the children don't mind either."

"Often have sandwiches at lunchtime — especially one child and husband. Would be quite easy for us to do".

Meals mean meat! Testers also had some firm views about how beans and meat fitted into meals.

"Surely beans should be used as a vegetable and not as a substitute for meat/fish/cheese unless it's a snack?"

Several testers had the same comment – beans mean snacks. Beans are not an adequate replacement for meat in a meal, as far as they are concerned. The current guidelines recommend that we eat more fibre-rich food for a healthier diet. Beans and pulses are fibre-rich and also provide protein that's not wrapped up in saturated animal fats. You can use all sorts of beans, not just baked beans. If your reaction was like some of the ones outlined, then try looking at vegetarian cook books which show how to include beans as a central item in a dish and as a contribution to a meal.

What you could do

Check your chart and comments. You might well find that some changes don't threaten your basic ideas about what meals and snacks are. For instance:

● Whatever your pattern of meals and snacks, using skimmed milk doesn't threaten that pattern.
● Eating less salt doesn't threaten the patterns of meals and snacks either.

Use some imagination!

One of our readers, having read Cheryl's comments about implementing the guidelines for healthy eating, said *"She hasn't got much imagination, has she?"*

It's all a matter of finding satisfying ways of changing to the new guidelines. The satisfying part of a meal can be its structure with its different courses. Is this what you find satisfying about meals? What other features do you think are satisfying? For example, is it the way the food is put together? Is it the way that you eat the food (for instance, a pudding is a pudding because you eat it with a spoon)? Or is it that certain foods seem right to start or finish a meal?

Here are some further suggestions.

Sandwiches instead of meat and two veg. If you don't think sandwiches would satisfy you, how about sandwiches and a salad (say celery, apple and nuts). This is more like a meal – the sort of meal you might easily eat in a pub.

Fresh fruit instead of tinned fruit. Maybe one of the satisfying things about tinned fruit is that you eat it in a dish with a spoon – a proper pudding. If you think that, why not eat grapefruit or melon, or perhaps a fresh fruit salad, or sliced oranges and bananas in orange juice?

Meat and four veg instead of meat and two veg. Maybe if it was presented differently this would make a more manageable meal – for example, a curry and rice with three or four vegetables in different side dishes.

A small portion of meat. Casseroles aren't the only way of doing this. A large salad of chopped vegetables with small portions of meat may be an attractive alternative to a casserole.

Beans instead of meat. Chilli con carne is a good way of using more beans in a savoury dish.

Cottage cheese instead of camembert. You may not find cottage cheese satisfying to finish your meal. You could try something a little more exotic like skimmed milk cheese with garlic and herbs or cottage cheese with pineapple.

Oh no, I prefer snacks! If you're a snack person then check that snacking allows you to eat a good range of foods that match the new guidelines of less fats, less sugar, less salt and more fibre-rich food. Ready-made snacks may well be salty, or fatty or sugary. Can you get plenty of fibre-rich food in your snacks? Bread is one obvious answer. Can you think of others.?

Whatever people believe, it just isn't true that you have to have one proper meal a day. It's much more important to find a way of incorporating a good balance of healthy foods with a pattern of as many snacks and meals a day as suit you and your life.

The right time to eat

You don't have to eat three meals a day. The main thing is to find an eating routine that is convenient and enjoyable for you and right for your body.

Three good meals?

The various snacks and meals that you eat during the day should add up to a varied and well-balanced diet in total. But does the proportion of snacks to meals matter? And does it matter when and how you eat them? It is worth looking at your routine. What is satisfactory about it? What are the points of dissatisfaction? Certain eating patterns may lead to an unbalanced diet or having too much food. But in addition they may make people feel lethargic, rushed, over-hungry and so on.

It does seem that there's more flexibility in our eating routines. A recent British Nutrition Foundation survey on *Eating in the early 1980s* found a lot of variety in the numbers of meals and snacks that people have each day. Only two out of ten people have three meals a day. And four people out of ten have four or five snacks a day.

How do you pace your day with meals and snacks? Check *what sort of* eating you do *when*.

Fill in the chart below.
● Think about one recent ordinary weekday and one ordinary weekend day.
● Put one tick for *each* time you eat in the five listed periods of the day. In some boxes you may want to put more than one tick.
● To fill the chart in you'll need to think what you mean by a meal. You'll also need to think about other occasions when you eat but you don't consider what you've eaten is a meal. In the chart these columns are headed *non-meals*. Try and stick to the idea of a non-meal being 'less than a meal'. You may call your non-meals snacks, or a bite to eat and so on.

Now look at your ticks in the chart carefully and think about each of your eating events.

● Can you write down a reason why each eating event takes place like it does? For instance, if you ticked a meal for up to 8.45am on a weekday you might say something like, "I have a meal before leaving the house in the morning to set me up for the day."

Here is a comment from one of our testers on one weekday.

"Up to about 11.00am I drink tea without sugar because I am not hungry. About 11.00am I have a sandwich usually, or toast, sometimes muesli, to give me the energy to carry on."

● Also write a sentence about any of the eating events you've noted down that you consider are a problem for you. For instance, "We never eat till 10.00pm on a Saturday night and I always get indigestion" or "Sunday midday is a problem as my husband likes a meal before he drives back to London where he works during the week, whereas I like to eat my main meal in the evening."

When you thought about your pattern of non-meals and meals by filling in the chart and writing about it you probably considered some of the following things which our testers wrote.

Your own bodily reaction to food. *"Missing meals altogether is a problem for me — I get dizzy and bad tempered."*

Convenience. *"At the weekend especially on Sunday we get up late and eat a longish meal about 11.00am — a sort of brunch — and then we don't have to eat anything again till about 7.00pm."*

Enjoyment. *"I have a meal early evening after unwinding from work. I enjoy this most of all."*

Other people's needs. *"I always have a snack at midday as I cook a dinner when my husband comes home at 6.00pm."*

Preparation time. *"Although it's done in a second, a mid-morning cup of tea and biscuit is satisfying enough to keep me going till my midday meal."*

Social life. *"At weekends we plan eating round our social life, we get meals out of the way at midday and then have a very long afternoon of swimming or walking or some such activity."*

What other things did you consider about how your everyday eating routine works?

Finely tuned? Some people are finely tuned in their eating routines and notice alterations quickly. You probably know of people who rapidly become very cross and bad tempered if they can't eat at the 'right time'. Other people may miss a meal or snack and yet still forget to eat for hours. For instance, three people miss their normal early evening meal to go to the cinema. One complains about being hungry throughout the film and has to rush off and eat as soon as the film finishes. One makes do with a bag of popcorn and an ice cream during the performance. The third just doesn't bother to eat at all that evening, and starts again with breakfast the following day.

Individuals differ but it is important that you know what your comfortable range of eating is in your own routine. And, of course it's also important to consider the range that others will tolerate if you cater for a family or household.

	One weekday		One weekend day	
	Meal	Non-meal	Meal	Non-meal
Up to 8.45am				
8.46am – 11.45am				
11.46am – 15.45pm				
15.46pm – 20.45pm				
After 20.45pm				

TIME TO EAT

Regular as clockwork?

Unless your eating routine is as regular as clockwork you are probably aware that even in an ordinary average week or month there's variation in how you pace your eating on different days. Things happen to us in the normal course of events that can slightly change our routine. Think about how your eating

routine alters when:
● the weather is extremely hot or cold
● you are feeling on top of the world
● you are feeling under the weather
● you are feeling depressed.

In addition, many women find that their eating routine alters substantially over the course of their menstrual cycle.

And then there are bigger upheavals. Some of these might be when:

● you are on holiday eating at a hotel or catering for yourself when eating is under your control
● relatives or friends come to stay
● you are away on business
● you stay at someone else's house
● you go home to your parents
● you are home decorating and the household is completely disrupted.

So think now about some days when you might have said to someone 'That wasn't my normal pattern of eating'.

The same chart about when you eat meals and non-meals is given again below. This time fill it in for one *non-typical* weekday and one *non-typical* weekend day that you can easily remember.

Now do three things:
1. Check the chart against your average weekday's and weekend chart and consider how different it is from your average pattern.
2. Try to recall how you felt about your two non-typical days.
3. If you can remember several non-typical days that happened in a row think about those too. Did you find that you developed some kind of routine even though it wasn't your normal routine?

	One weekday		One weekend day	
	Meal	Non-meal	Meal	Non-meal
Up to 8.45am				
8.46am – 11.45am				
11.46am – 15.45pm				
15.46pm – 20.45pm				
After 20.45pm				

Go to work on an egg

One of the most famous advertising campaigns we've been subjected to in recent years was to 'go to work on an egg'. It highlights the significance of breakfast. How important is breakfast? There are no 'right' answers! But we offer these ideas to you to help you make up your mind for yourself.

● Physiologically you don't need breakfast provided you are used to not having it.

● Breakfast is now a meal that people eat independently ... if you're living with other people, is it a good way to start the day with four people all in different stages of preparing food and eating?

● Is the important thing about breakfast the mental preparation of the day rather than the physical lining of the stomach?

● Breakfast is a useful opportunity for eating several high fibre foods and so it does have nutritional significance.

● The English breakfast is famous. We are supposed to 'make a meal of it'. But is it actually a real part of our routine? The French don't make a meal of their breakfast!

Our testers.

"I enjoyed it in the caravan, eating exactly when we wanted."

"I went on a course and stayed at a hotel, where we had to sit down to meals at specific times. The balance and the quality of the food was good, but I ate too much and felt fat and over full the whole time. I didn't feel able to refuse the food — I suppose I didn't wish to appear finicky."

"A non-typical day and weekend doesn't make sense to me. The only time in any day that is typical to me is breakfast. My lunchtime and evening meal are flexible. It depends purely on how I feel. I dislike rigid time keeping."

"One Sunday when we were staying with friends, we had a large cooked breakfast and then took a picnic out with us. When we got home we had sandwiches. So we seemed to be eating bread and cakes most of the day".

And you? Looking at unusual days' eating should help you to think more fully about just what part routine plays in your eating patterns. Perhaps, like one of our testers, you are very flexible and don't have a firm routine. Perhaps you are one of the people who find that a familiar routine paces your day and eating so that you feel comfortable. Are there any aspects of your usual routine that you don't find satisfactory?

Routine – help or hindrance?

Timing

Our eating events certainly break up and structure our day for us. You might look upon them as punctuation marks. Think about whether sometimes you pause to eat at the wrong moment for your real convenience. There isn't a magical significance to eating lunch at 12.30pm or 1.00pm. The British Nutrition Foundation survey mentioned earlier in this topic pointed out that in any hour from 6.45 in the morning to midnight about a third of adults are eating or drinking something. If your meals and snacks don't seem to pace your day satisfactorily can you change some of the times you eat?

Control

For many people their eating routine may be controlled by other people. They may feel they are being 'fed' too much, or too little, too often or not often enough! Why is this? Family caterers often have fixed ideas about what should be eaten when. Whether it's a hotel or your mother you need to remember that daily routines of whatever sort are for your benefit as well as other people's. It's a long, hard struggle in some cases to convince people who cater for you. However, if you're uncomfortable with your eating routine this is an important question to tackle.

Hunger

Eating when we're hungry seems so obvious. But many of us never do it. We eat because it's 'the right time' regardless of whether our bodies are saying it's the right time. Do you actually ever get hungry – really hungry? If you can, try for a couple of days to eat only when you feel really hungry. Ignore your usual routine and try and put yourself in touch with when your body wants you to eat.

Order

When people's ordinary daily routine gets disrupted, then a firm *eating* routine can help matters. It can bring order to the day.

"When I was revising for my exams — I made myself stop and eat lunch and supper — both properly cooked. I never normally do this but I found it a very good way of breaking up the day without straying into the temptation of going to see friends."

"I went to stay with a friend a few weeks after her husband's death. I started to cook lunches and dinners for us both and though she had difficulty finishing them — or even starting them some days — I think it started to put a bit of order back into her life where it had just been chaotic for six weeks."

Health

Does your eating routine help or hinder you if you are aiming to follow the new guidelines for healthy eating?

If you are always rushing and snatching snacks are you eating too many fatty, sugary or salty foods?

Enjoyment

Eating the right food at the right time and right place can be a very enjoyable experience. Eating things you enjoy and feel hungry for when you want them is an attractive goal to aim for.

Why not examine your eating routine with an eye to doing two things:

● Alter parts of your eating routine which lead to discomfort, inconvenience, or maybe unhealthy foods.

● Include in your routine those things that you have found enjoyable when your routine has been disrupted.

This may seem to be rather a tall order. If so, then why not try to think of just one alteration in your routine that would make it more enjoyable.

To get you started here are some ideas that our testers had.

One thing that would be more enjoyable would be:

"All sitting down together at breakfast."

"To have 'brunch' at 10.30 — 11.00am instead of breakfast and lunch."

"To share meals with other people occasionally."

"To have more meals out."

"Perhaps to eat my main meal slightly later in the evening after the children have eaten their meal — sometimes to have a meal when I don't have to get up and down a number to times because of children needing drinks, hands wiping, etc!"

"To eat slightly earlier in the evening giving more time for leisure."

"To insist on eating my own food at my parents' and encourage them to share my eating pattern."

Styles of planning

If you want to introduce changes into your diet, you may need to look again at how to plan and prepare your food.

How does changing your diet affect your approach to planning and preparing food?

If you are concerned about your diet and decide to change to some of the current recommendations for healthy eating, you'll need to start considering some of the following:

● eat more green, leafy vegetables and fresh fruit
● eat more wholegrain, fibre-rich food
● eat more beans and pulses
● eat fewer fats in general and saturated fats in particular
● use skimmed milk instead of whole milk
● eat less salt
● eat less sugar.

Planning and food preparation are important to your diet. Both can influence the amount of success you have in carrying out changes such as those mentioned above.

What's your style?

People, of course, differ in the extent to which they plan and prepare their eating. How much planning goes into your meals and snacks?

For some people one visit to the supermarket provides enough bread, cereal, milk and food provisions to take a large family through seven days of eating. This may be on the basis that '12 hamburgers will be enough for four meals, six large tins of baked beans will provide accompanying vegetables for two meals plus a couple of snacks'. Other people think out a week's menus and then go out and buy accordingly. So how you decide to shop is one form of planning your eating. Whatever style of planning you adopt it's worthwhile looking at it to see whether you are doing the best you can for your diet.

When you know what your style is you may be able to build on its strengths and down play its weaknesses to help with changes that you want to make in your diet.

But someone else does it for me!

By now you may be saying, *"But I don't plan my eating or prepare it. Someone else does it for me."* For many people their experience of food is largely just sitting down and eating it. Nevertheless, if you're one of these people do work through this topic bearing the following questions in mind:

● What sort of planning goes on in your household? Do you know enough about it to be able to identify a style? If not find out.
● What do you reckon would be your style of planning if you were involved? On occasions when you had to cater for yourself what would you say your style was?
● What effects does the planning and preparation of food in *your* household have on your diet?
● What benefits would you gain if you contributed to the planning and preparation of food in your household? Remember, ignorance is no defence!

Identifying a style

Below are a whole series of statements about how different people plan their food.

● Read through them quickly and underline *any* phrases that seem to describe aspects of your planning style. You may want to underline phrases from several of the statements.
● Then go through them again and find the quote that, overall, is nearest to the style you use. On a separate piece of paper write down any particular differences between your style and the statement you've chosen.
● If you find nothing in any of the statements that's at all like what you do, then jot down a few sentences which you think *do* sum up your style.

"Before I do my weekly shopping I have a picture of every meal in my mind's eye."

"Before I do my weekly shopping I have a picture in my mind's eye of any special meals in the next week. Otherwise, I have a general list of food we get through every week — cereal, bread, chicken, potatoes, etc."

"I do a weekly shop for food supplies that I know will cover roughly what will get us through the week. I never think about particular meals. I just know from experience how much of the various basics we'll need."

"Each day or few days I think what I'd like to eat and then I go and buy — you know, say about enough food for three particular meals."

"I do a weekly shop, or even a monthly one if I'm really organised. And then every couple of days I go out and buy food stuffs for particular meals — to make the basic food supply more interesting."

"I tend to just go out and buy things for us when we've run out."

"I plan meals carefully and then have to keep going out and buying things because I haven't got half the ingredients in stock."

Food for meals. In some of the statements above the individuals concerned start from the idea of particular meals or eating events and plan from there. Others start from a more general idea of food they want to eat and then fit particular meals in as they go along.

When our testers did this activity the first two styles were identified with most. Several testers pointed out that their style could vary, for instance, having a special meal might mean moving from one's normal style altogether.

Timing? The statements also show a wide range of timing – from major, forward planning to responding to the needs of the present moment. How far in advance you plan is an important consideration if you want to change your eating patterns. If you decide you're going to be terribly well-organised and get everything in advance then you may find yourself with jaded vegetables, stale bread and meat that's seen better days. If you always respond at the last minute you could find yourself short of important staples that are one of the keys to a healthy eating routine. You may also find yourself paying more for your food.

Contradictions. Some of our testers underlined a number of phrases which seemed to be contradictory. Maybe you've done the same. If so, possibly your planning style varies depending on different circumstances in your life – this could even be something like winter and summer. Well planned, hot meals in winter and 'help yourself' in summer.

Planning, preparing, eating

For some people it's a long time from planning to eating food. Do you see yourself as a precise planner and organiser of food? Or do other events seem to overtake you?

Read through the list of questions below. Think about your honest response to them. Write 'Yes' or 'No' by the side of each one. You may think that some of the questions are insulting. Don't be put off.

Put a mark in the box by any of the questions that you do consider distasteful. This should help you get a clearer picture of how you see *yourself*. For instance, one of the questions is about whether things go rotten in your fridge. You might consider this to be a distasteful question that doesn't apply to you – so this will begin to tell you something about your style of planning.

1. Is there anything in your fridge that you haven't really got any idea what you're going to do with? ☐

2. Have you got any fruit or vegetables that you haven't got round to using which are looking a bit tired? ☐

3. Do you ever find that you have perishable food items that are past their date of using? ☐

4. Did you save anything that wasn't eaten at your last meal? ☐

5. If so, do you know how you are going to use it? ☐

6. Do you know now exactly what you're going to eat at your next meal or snack? ☐

7. Do you know how soon before the meal or snack you'll start preparing it? ☐

8. Does milk or yoghurt ever go off in your household? ☐

9. Do you feel annoyed if you've got any food left over at the end of a meal? ☐

10. Do you have items in your fridge, food cupboard, vegetable/fruit rack etc, that you or anyone in your household could just decide to eat *now* without it disrupting your future food plans? ☐

11. If someone dropped round unexpectedly at this moment could you give them a light meal? ☐

12. Do you ever prepare meals where you have to soak or marinate food well in advance? ☐

13. Do you find food you've forgotten about sometimes that's gone mouldy, stale and so on, in your refrigerator? ☐

How did you answer?

● If you answered 'Yes' to questions 4, 5, 6, 7, 9 and 12 then maybe you are a 'precise planner/preparer' with an eye to detail.

● If you answered 'Yes' to questions 10 and 11 then perhaps you are a 'general planner' who nevertheless matches plans and events quite well? These sorts of planning don't exclude each other.

● If you answered 'Yes' to questions 1, 2, 3, 8 and 13 you may be a 'precise planner' but there does seem to be a slight mismatch between your plans and your life!

We asked our testers for further ideas on what they thought being a general or precise planner meant. Here are some of their comments:

A general planner. This is someone who:
● has a reasonable idea of what they will eat and when – but can change their plans easily, adapt to change, and be prepared for surprises
● knows what basics are needed but supplements with extra shopping
● has a well-stocked cupboard and freezer and can always be relied upon to rustle up something
● knows what food is required for a week, but if faced with a bargain or special offer buys it and then thinks afterwards what can be done with it.

A precise planner. This is someone who:
● knows exactly what they will eat days in advance
● has everything worked out and doesn't do anything on the spur of the moment
● designs meals and doesn't deviate come hell or high water – inflexible!
● has each day's menu worked out for the whole week and shops accordingly.

Another one of our readers commented that she seemed to be bits of both types with a measure of 'food going off' thrown in! On the whole, most of our testers seemed to see general planning as a more flexible approach, pointing out that it allows you to be more adaptable.

The right system for you

Of course, planning and preparation merge into each other in some ways. You may plan your shopping carefully in order to avoid much actual preparation. You may plan and prepare food to deliberately give yourself 'leftovers'. As one person put it, *"I hate looking in the fridge and thinking 'no leftovers' — oh dear, now I've got to prepare everything from scratch"*. Or you may plan to avoid leftovers. *"I try never to get into a situation where I've got a lot of something that's got to be eaten today or it will spoil."*

Personal styles of planning that work can give you satisfaction in very different ways. For instance, you may be satisfied that you've used all the leftovers/that you haven't got any leftovers/that you've provided the best. People vary.

General planners – Janice

What does this mean if you want to make changes in your diet? Think about Janice's experience.

Janice is in her late 20s and lives alone. She saw herself largely as a

general planner and admitted that precise planning for her was likely to be doomed to failure.

"I'm organised enough to always have good, fresh bread, cereals, staples and that long-life skimmed milk in the house. None of these 'go off' within reason. Then I have a variety of individual helpings of several things in my small freezer plus attractive, tinned or frozen produce — mackerel, sweet corn, kidney beans, prawns and so on. They're the things that give my meals their individuality. It's absolutely useless my buying things like fresh meat and fish because I rarely get round to eating them. I used to buy them but they went off and I stopped. I never save leftovers for the same reason. Although, in fact, I try to gauge the amount I'll need at a meal or snack anyway.

"The same goes for planning tasty, vegetable casseroles, soaking beans, having a lot of vegetables. I know they're good for me, but what's the point of having good intentions if all you end up with is carrots that are so mouldy that it takes you five minutes to recognise what they are! As long as it's decent food I don't mind if it's thrown together."

Janice's forward thinking really amounts to intelligent shopping. She's worked out how her eating can be organised so at *the time of preparation* meals can be made quickly with no fuss.

Are you inclined to doing little preparation like Janice? If so, look at the guidelines for healthy eating again and you'll see that some of them can be achieved by merely buying your food carefully. Here are some examples:

● Apart from buying it, skimmed milk doesn't require any extra, forward planning. Neither does cutting down on salt, or spooned sugar or changing to polyunsaturated margarine.
● Less fat meat and less of it can mean less planning and preparation too. Buying more expensive, leaner cuts means not having to bash it with a mallet and only having to cook it for 45 minutes instead of the three hours cheaper meat requires.
● More fresh fruit instead of elaborate desserts can mean avoiding preparation of cooked sweets altogether.
● Changing to oven-ready chips instead of deep-fried chips means less fat, and no more preparation.

• Canned kidney beans are expensive, but they're instant and you don't have to think in advance to soak them for hours.

Some warning points.
• Omelettes, sausages, bacon and deep-fried chips may be quick but they're high in fat.
• If you choose not to serve leftovers then be careful not to finish everything off automatically just to get rid of it.
• Have you considered freezing leftovers? That way you don't have to eat them till you choose to. They don't stare accusingly at you from the fridge every time you open it.
• Check labels and ingredients of ready prepared food that you can eat instantly. Take care you're not providing yourself with too much saturated fat, sugar and salt. Also check the 'eat by' date.

Precise planners – Mary

Now compare Mary's approach with Janice's.
"I enjoy planning and preparing our week's food. I don't mind meals taking time to prepare and I always search until I get what I want when I go shopping for my food. I don't keep vast supplies of anything in the house and try to keep a fairly rapid turnover of food. I shop every couple of days. Consequently we have, I suppose, a quite elaborate and varied diet, though I wouldn't say an expensive one. I've got a slow cooker and a pressure cooker, and we like casseroles and eat a lot of them. We also have salads with lots of chopped vegetables.

"I generally prepare most meals with an eye to the next meal, doing double batches of some things and often making enough of certain things to have cold the next day."

Janice and Mary are chalk and cheese. Mary is able to use her style to introduce the new guidelines for healthy eating to her family. But with a different approach.
• You can take advantage of forward planning to do things, like soaking a variety of beans and pulses in advance.
• With frequent shopping you can use vegetables and fruit in tip top condition, providing a variety at all meals.
• You can prepare batches of things and get into a sort of rota system. Prepare beans today – half today, half tomorrow. Prepare rice tomorrow – half then, half the next day, and so on.
• With the idea that a meal can have leftovers you can prepare larger portions with an eye on the next day.

Problems for precise planners? Precise planners may give themselves time to devote to food. Healthy eating should be no problem. However:
• If you see yourself as being like Mary it's probably worthwhile asking yourself whether you sometimes devote more time to food planning and preparation than you want to.
• Do other things get rushed and missed out on?
• And how adaptable is your planning to what one of our testers called 'surprises'?

And your style? You may not see yourself as either a Janice or a Mary. But whatever your style is, you need to be aware of it if you want to change to different eating habits. So here are some more ideas to help you think about planning and preparing your food.
• Change your whole style of planning. This may be difficult but it is possible. It involves a strong commitment to changing your eating patterns.
• Get an overall weekly pattern of planning that largely cuts out individual planning sessions.
• Get someone else to do some of your planning.
• Cut out much planning and preparing by eating only one family meal together a day and leaving everybody to fend for themselves at other times of the day. (Lots of people already have independent breakfasts.)
• Share preparation of food with other people in the house. Use preparation time as a time to talk to family members.
• Don't get obsessed with planning. If you're really tired when you get in from work send your family out for a takeaway or let them serve themselves from an easily prepared stock of foods. One of our readers said, *"I have a ready-made list of suggestions for them pinned onto a cupboard ready for when I go 'on strike'"*.
• Arrange a system where a group of friends regularly eat together with a rota of one person planning and preparing (major preparations when it's your turn but very relaxing when it's not).
• Capitalise on an interest in planning by working out a weekly menu that closely sticks to the healthy eating guidelines.

Most of our testers seemed prepared to have a go at several of these suggestions. The last three were most popular. Which ones do you think you'd be prepared to give a try?

Vegetarianism as a way of life

Why do people become vegetarians?
What are the benefits and drawbacks?

This topic does not aim to convert you to vegetarianism. But we are advised to eat less fatty meat and more vegetables – in order to avoid too much saturated fat and get more fibre. So we may all have something to learn from how vegetarians plan their meals.

What does being a vegetarian mean? It can mean:
- Abstaining from eating the flesh of any animal including fish and birds.
- Eating no food whatsoever of animal origin including milk, cheese and eggs. These vegetarians are called vegans.
- Eating a wholefood diet – mainly wholegrain and seasonal vegetables with occasional fish, shellfish and fruit.

Where do you stand?

Dave: *"It's all lentils and leaden nut cutlets. I'd never do it."*

Susan: *"Last year I took a conscious decision not to buy meat. Sometimes I eat it if I'm offered it. I dare say about once or twice a month."*

Carla: *"Beards and sandals. They're just hippies by another name."*

Alan: *"My parents were vegetarians. I've never eaten meat in my life. The thought of doing so has never entered my head. I just don't think of it as a problem."*

Rachel: *"I just started to go off meat and eventually I found it completely revolting."*

George Bernard Shaw: *"Animals are my friends ... and I don't eat my friends."*

Where do you stand in regard to vegetarianism? Do you think it's cranky – all fruit, nuts and ethics – respecting the animal kingdom and the earth's resources? Or is it no different from other individual dietary preferences?

Talk to friends and colleagues about vegetarianism. Air your views and listen to what others have to say. You might even try saying you're thinking of becoming a vegetarian and see other people's reactions. To some people it is completely incomprehensible that anyone should actually wish to forego meat and fish. *"What on earth do they eat? They can't be healthy!"*

Different viewpoints? Look at the line below which labels various views. Ask your friends their views. Put your initials and those of others you have asked at the points on the line that apply. If all the initials are clustered round one area, anyone in your group of friends who adopted a very different style of eating might well come in for some lively criticism!

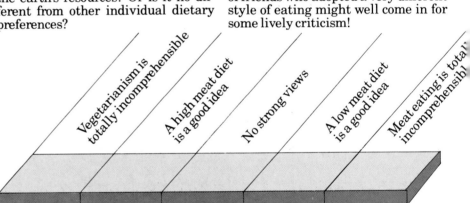

If you're not a vegetarian think about what strong pro-meat eating views would sound like to vegetarians or people inclined towards vegetarianism. How would a vegetarian view statements like *"You want to get some good red meat inside 'em"*, or *"Sundays wouldn't be Sundays without a leg of lamb."*? How would your friends respond to you saying *"I think I'll go back to eating chicken — after all, it's low in saturated fat so it isn't actually unhealthy to eat it."* What reasons did you find for people's views about vegetarianism?

Our testers. They gave a variety of comments. One criticised vegan friends who had a leather upholstered car. Another said *"The number of people who associate vegetarianism with 'hippies', communes and flared jeans is very annoying."* Most testers found that the majority of their friends seemed to think *"We all need meat."*

Why do people become vegetarians?

There seem to be three main reasons for this. Some people just don't like the taste of meat. But others are deeply committed to a non-meat diet.

Health reasons. Some people identify with vegetarianism as helping various health problems. Others who are already healthy simply want to hold on to it and make the best of their health. For them, to avoid disease is not enough.

Ethical reasons. Many people turn to vegetarianism because they are concerned about animal welfare and

about ecology. They object to the exploitation of animals. Many are prepared to eat milk and eggs, things which animals produce without being killed. 'Live and let live' sums up the views of many vegetarians.

Many vegetarians are concerned about the destruction of the earth's resources in pursuit of high farming profits. One argument you might have heard is – animals are fattened up on grain that could itself feed many more people than the meat does. You read statistics like 10lb of grain produces 1lb of beef. So, if we cut out the beef, there would be 9lb more grain to feed the starving nations. On the other hand, you'll hear people say that many animals are grazed on marginal land that isn't suitable for crops ... And that animals feed on types of grain that humans don't like ... And that cattle cake is made out of *waste* products of oil seed. So there wouldn't be much extra useable grain available if people stopped eating meat.

Ethics *are* involved, but there aren't simple solutions. It's not just a matter of redistributing the surplus grain that could be produced. The starving nations might not traditionally eat this type of grain. And this does nothing to improve their life in the long run. It's probably more important to think about how foreign aid could be used to improve their agriculture and to breed higher yielding varieties of the foods they do like.

Remember, informed decisions come from looking at all sides of the story. This is a path that many people have taken on their way to becoming vegetarians.

Religious and cultural reasons. For many hundreds of years, large groups of people in India and the Far East have been vegetarians. Religious commitment to vegetarianism is often based on not harming God's other creatures. In other cases, certain cultural groups choose not to eat meat – and because of their high status other groups copy them.

Meat eaters

Consider now why people are meat eaters. If you eat meat, ask yourself the following questions. If you don't eat meat, ask a friend or a colleague who does.

● How often do you eat it?
● Why do you eat it?
● Do you have good associations with meat eating?
● Would anything make you give it up?
● Is there anything you dislike about it?

Many meat eaters have taken no conscious decision to eat meat.

They've always done it. Although it's worth noting that as meat eaters we also avoid certain meats. Most people in this country take exception to eating horse, or rat, or snake!

Many Western vegetarians have taken a conscious decision about not eating meat. This tends to focus the attention on eating patterns. If you carry on eating meat that's fine as long as you focus your attention on how to do it, so as to eat healthily. If you are considering changing to the current guidelines for healthy eating, you will really need to think carefully about your meat eating. A moderate diet based on the new guidelines for healthy eating would mean smaller portions of lean meat, switching to chicken and turkey more often, getting more of your protein from vegetable sources.

Reading about the conscious decision-making many vegetarians are involved with, may help you think about issues related to changing your eating patterns – even if you don't intend to become a vegetarian.

A healthier diet?

Vegetarian diets can be cheap and healthy. It has been claimed that the diet is healthy because meat is *not* eaten. But the actual benefit is more likely to be a positive one. The benefit comes from the healthy balance of foods that are eaten. Indeed it's only the vegetarians who eat a widely varied, well-balanced, non-meat diet that do reap the full benefits.

Those vegetarians who eat lots of cheese, milk and eggs have an unhealthy diet. Such a diet is high in fat which increases the risks of developing heart disease and strokes.

There's some evidence that compared with those on an average diet which includes meat, vegetarians on a healthy high-fibre, low-fat diet have a lower risk of developing:
● Coronary heart disease and stroke because of lower cholesterol levels in their blood. High cholesterol levels are linked to eating a diet high in saturated fats which come mainly from meat and dairy products.
● Bowel disorders such as constipation, diverticulitis and cancer of the colon, because of higher fibre intake. A South of England study showed that vegetarians eat about twice as much fibre a day as non-vegetarians (41.5 grams a day as against 21.4 grams).
● Disorders related to obesity. Fibre fills you up more and you eat less fat so you are less likely to end up with too many calories and so become overweight. But maybe a vegetarian also takes more exercise?
● Damaged walls of the blood vessels because of the high vitamin C intake from fruit and vegetables.

An altogether healthier lifestyle?

Linking the vegetarian diet to improved health benefits isn't straightforward. As well as eating a non-meat diet many vegetarians are altogether more health conscious. They take better care of themselves in other ways. So they may exercise more, smoke less and pay more attention to keeping their weight down and to avoiding stress. It's difficult to separate out and just measure the effects of the non-meat diet on their health.

How do people get on as vegetarians?

People approach vegetarianism in many different ways:

Michael is 40 and eats fish sometimes and meat very occasionally. He's been a vegetarian for 12 years. He started in his teens because of a bowel disorder. He feels and looks much better than he ever used to. When he started, he found adapting to the diet difficult. He feels, even now, he eats too many dairy products. His family accept his vegetarianism and cater for it, but his wife has the occasional go at him, saying he can't be getting all the goodness out of food he needs. Whenever he gets a cold, she looks knowing and says, "You see!"

Rachel is 26 and has been a vegetarian since her teens. She found meat revolting. She had to start buying it for the family when her mother had a lengthy illness. Now she says she'd be physically sick if she had to eat it. She says she doesn't really feel any healthier, but feels good in herself because she's eating according to her beliefs. At 15 she was the only vegetarian in the family. It was a problem. Her mother was annoyed at having to do separate catering and Rachel got a perpetual diet of omelettes which she felt couldn't have done her health any good. Now she has no difficulties at home or anywhere else. The breakthrough came when the family saw she was serious about it. She managed to convince them that a vegetarian diet can include plenty of protein, and that meat isn't the only food containing protein!

Alan is 59 and a life-long vegetarian. He has never eaten meat or fish. He's the son of life-long vegetarians. He's serious about his health and pays attention to food, exercise and lifestyle. When he's away from home he finds getting the right food difficult and often takes his own.

Friends and family accept his regime. Colleagues at work think he's puritanical and cranky.

Maureen is 35 and a vegan. She followed a vegan diet during two of her three pregnancies. The children never took it for granted that eating dead flesh was a normal part of life. She and her husband didn't tell the children about their unusual diet until one of them enquired what meat was when looking in a butcher's window. Maureen watches the family's diet carefully and is well informed about the balance required. She is careful to make sure they get enough Vitamin B12 and feels happy that her family leads a healthy life feeding entirely on plants. As she puts it, "It seems to be a contribution we can make towards a more humane world."

Pros and cons

There are benefits and drawbacks for these four people whose styles of vegetarianism are very different. You probably detected their reasons and the extent to which their zeal for vegetarianism varied. What are the problems that might beset them?

● For a solitary vegetarian in a family (and for a new and uninformed vegetarian) there may be the problem of turning from a diet with meat to one that is still high in saturated fats – because it has a lot of cheese and eggs. Grains and pulses could provide the protein and don't come with animal fats.
● For vegetarians eating out there are also problems of the proverbial omelette or cheese salad as the only vegetarian offering. This is possibly OK for one meal but no joke on a fortnight's holiday. Vegetarians *have* to try hard in order to avoid being driven mad by tedium when eating out. It's also important for them to safeguard their health by avoiding too much dairy produce and too many eggs.
● Buying vegetarian food can be a problem. Fruit and vegetables are heavy to carry home and need to be bought often for freshness.
● There has been concern in the medical profession about some vegetarian diets. Some are healthy; others are not. There are problems if the variety of food in the diet is extremely restricted which may happen through choice or ignorance. It's important to have a wide variety of food for all the necessary proteins, vitamins and minerals we need. An ordinary vegetarian diet is likely to be OK in this respect. Extreme diets, for instance, only brown rice or diets of fruit alone can have dire effects.
● There is also concern about vegans

who are people who eat no dairy produce at all. Plant foods do not contain vitamin B12 and are a poor source of riboflavin. Both of these vitamins are needed for blood formation – a deficiency of these nutrients may lead to anaemia. Many vegans are knowledgeable about what they are doing and advice is available from the Vegan Society. The shortfall can be made up from supplements added to food little and often . . . There are occasional problems of inadequate energy intake in vegan infants. Their food tends to be bulky but they don't have big enough stomachs to be able to eat the large volume of food required to give enough of the essential nutrients.
● Anaemia is quite often reported amongst Asians living in the UK on a restricted diet of boiled white rice, vegetables and milk. Milk should provide B12 but it's destroyed by the custom of boiling it for a long time.

Most of these problems come down to lack of knowledge either on the part of vegetarians or other people. It can be difficult to maintain a satisfactory vegetarian diet in the face of other people's lack of knowledge.

Changing your diet?

You may not wish to become a committed vegetarian.

> However, current guidelines for healthy eating suggest eating less fats, particularly saturated fats, and more fibre with wholefood cereals, beans, fruit and vegetables.

You could use some vegetarian strategies to help you in this. Meat is often a dominating factor in a meal, everything else is subservient to it. If you're serious about healthy eating your cooking need not follow this pattern of a main course centred on a large lump of meat.

● The American MR FIT healthy heart programme suggests choosing at least two or three main meals a week based on vegetable protein sources. It also recommends that the daily allowance of lean meat, fish, poultry and low fat cheese should together form no more than 6ozs. Try weighing this quantity out to get some idea of how little this really is!
● A main course can use meat to flavour it but be composed of a majority of vegetables.
● Several vegetable dishes can be served at once like a buffet.
● Using less meat doesn't mean having to use more dairy produce. Wholegrain cereals, beans and pulses, fruit and vegetables all contribute to a healthy diet with plenty of variety.

Other cultures, other cuisines

We seem to welcome dishes from all over the world and adapt them to our taste.
But how much do we consider our health when we make these adaptations?

Traditional fare?

If you are eating out, how much of the food that you choose is typically British? Looking at the foods we choose when we eat out or buy takeaways is revealing. This menu (left) came from a country pub advertising traditional pub grub. You'd expect it to be typically British but is it?

The Ploughman's lunch is nearest to a traditional British snack. But the way it is now served came from a publicity campaign in the 1960's when the trimmings were added.

A mixed bunch. What is left on the menu is a real mixture – Italian salami and pizza, French bread and pâté, Danish cheese, American club sandwiches and Indian curry. Ham-burgers started off as German. They were adapted by the Americans and changed to their present form. They have been spread worldwide by a business with a Scottish name. Chilli con carne was adapted from a Mexican dish in Texas. Today such dishes are eaten in homes all over Britain. Some you may even think of as being British.

A quick snack. Snack foods have changed greatly in recent times. Whereas once dishes like fish 'n' chips, faggots, jellied eels and pease pudding were common, today a much bigger choice of food is available. A snack menu tends to be international – beefburgers, fried chicken, pancake rolls, pizzas, kebabs, tortillas. Even the local chip shop probably serves curry or Chinese-style pancake rolls.

155

Here, there and everywhere

How does foreign food come to be so much part of our culture?

- Foreign travel is cheaper now. Many people have been on foreign holidays and trips. They like what they have eaten and when they get back they look the recipes up.
- Immigrants and visitors bring a varied cuisine to Britain. By opening restaurants and specialist food shops, they offer a wider choice of foods.
- Ingredients can now be easily and cheaply imported so that it is easier to try new and exotic recipes, with beautiful photographs and well-tested instructions. Having tried a certain foreign dish people can then go and buy specialist cookery books.
- Television cookery programmes and series often deal with foreign cuisines and produce cookery books to go with the series.
- There is a huge demand for glossy cookery books. They have many appeals – new recipes to ring the changes, photographs to feed our imagination, dreams of a different lifestyle.
- Family traditions and lifestyles have changed – a lot of families have no one with the time to cook elaborate meals. Foods that are easy to prepare yet are tasty seem to catch on quickly.
- Eating out presents us with a great variety of restaurants. This means that it is easy to experience a wide range of exotic foods.

From meat and veg to risotto

You may have experienced changes in your life that have given you the opportunity to try out food from different countries.

In a study of infant feeding habits people were asked to think about changes in their diet and the reasons for these changes. You might try asking yourself the same questions. Thinking about your childhood memories of food will help you to understand something about how lifestyles have changed.

- What was your diet like as a child? What was a typical meal? Can you remember trying new foods as a child?
- What happened to your diet when you left home?
- What changed or influenced what you ate?

Here is an extract from one interview. How does it compare with your experience?

"Looking back on it, the food we ate as a family was good, bland and ordinary. There were a lot of filling foods like steamed puddings and not much fruit. Danish Blue was the only foreign cheese we ever had ... I remember when yoghurt first came out I thought it tasted fantastic. Of course, you don't think anything of yoghurts nowadays do you?"

"When I went to college that was the really big change. I shared a flat and we would cook together. It was then that I learned most of the cooking that I do now ... casseroles, risottos, sauces, peppers, coleslaw and mushrooms were all new to me ... And then we'd go out for meals in town and there were a lot of Chinese and Indian restaurants and others like Greek and Italian."

Our testers. All our testers found these questions helped them think about how their diet had changed.

Here are some of their comments:

"In the post-war years, a wider selection of food-stuffs gradually became available — bananas were particularly memorable."

"I tried macaroni cheese for the first time when I was 11 and away at camp. It was horrible (but I like it now)."

"We were friendly with an Italian family and took it in turns to have meals at each others' houses."

"When I left home, I ate out more often, depending on the state of my finances or boyfriends' finances! We found Chinese and Italian food tasty and reasonably priced."

Several of the testers, like the person in the interview, mentioned the impact of yoghurt 'in small glass jars'. Green peppers, aubergines and courgettes also seem to have been a revelation to several of them when they left their parental home.

Influences on you. Maybe you have been influenced in similar ways. Read through the following questions and put a tick in the box if your answer is 'Yes'.

Have you tried new dishes abroad and then cooked them at home? ☐

Have you cooked a new exotic looking dish when guests were coming? ☐

Have you eaten with friends who have served new dishes that you now make or buy? ☐

Have you bought new kinds of ingredients that you liked the look of and tried recipes using them? ☐

Have you copied a new dish from a television cookery programme? ☐

Have you enjoyed a new dish when eating out and copied it at home? ☐

Have you spotted 'new' vegetables and fruits in shops that led you to trying new recipes? ☐

Adopt and adapt

You may have made changes to your diet. But it isn't likely that the dishes that you have added to it are exactly as they are served in their original country. There are plenty of reasons why we alter recipes. When we adopt a new dish we adapt it to our taste. This doesn't always make the dish more healthy. Take the story of Mrs London's dessert for example. While you are reading the account think about whether the dish was improved from a health point of view or not.

Mrs London's dessert. The Londons went to Majorca for a holiday. One striking feature of the buffet meals there was their exotic presentation. Mrs London was particularly impressed by one starter. Soft fruits were served in half a melon scooped out like a bowl – one for each person.

Friends who have eaten with the Londons have commented on the 'Majorcan pudding'. It is basically the starter that Mrs London liked at the hotel, but it has changed. Firstly, she thought all that fruit would be a bit strange at the start of a meal so it has become a dessert. Secondly, the fruits have changed. The melon isn't the same type as the ones in Spain and some of the original fruits in the filling were too expensive. Fruits that were easily available looked just as good. Lastly, Mrs London has added sugar. *"It makes the dish sweeter like a dessert should be!"*

This sort of process happens with many new foods and dishes that we take a fancy to:

● We add extra flavours that we prefer.
● We substitute ingredients when the original ones are difficult to get or are expensive.
● We build the dishes into the structure of our meals. They are served as a particular course or as a snack.

Are you an explorer?

What dishes have you discovered? Think of the foods that you have added to your diet, especially those you cook at home. How did you come by them?

Have you adapted the way in which the dish is served to suit your tastes? Below Jill has made a chart showing various dishes, where she discovered them, and how she adapted them. Do the same for some of the dishes you have discovered.

Dish	Where you discovered it	Adaptations
Beef curry	Indian restaurant	Much less oil, less chilli and other spices. I use a ready-made curry powder which doesn't taste the same. I think that I serve less rice but I'm not sure.
Coq au vin	Television cookery lesson	I use the same recipe but I use onion instead of shallots and large mushrooms not buttons. I serve it with potatoes or rice.

Spaghetti UK!

When it comes to main meals there are quite clear trends in what we like and how we adapt.

Bob and Sandie loved eating out at their local Italian pizza and spaghetti house. So, when they went on holiday to Italy to stay at a small family hotel, they looked forward to a real treat. They were quite shocked by what they found.

"The spaghetti bolognese we had for starters was huge! But there was only a tiny dollop of sauce. We could hardly eat it. Pizzas were the same — all dough and very little topping. Vegetables and salads were drenched in olive oil."

At home in Italy. Italians eat pasta to fill them up. Meat is expensive so main course portions tend to be small. Home cooked pasta dishes get their flavour from the freshness of the ingredients – especially herbs. Little mince is used, but it is very lean and finely ground. The freshly cooked pasta is usually served with an elaborate salad – again very fresh.

In the restaurant. The restaurant in Italy follows the same pattern but its ingredients may not be so fresh or the cooking as careful. Sometimes food sits around, cooked before it is served – after all they're cooking for 30 people. A lot of seasoning is added to compensate.

A British Italian restaurant. Bob and Sandie's local Italian restaurant knows the British taste. Their spaghetti, herbs and vegetables are not fresh, but their customers don't seem to notice. The sauce has more tomato and onion to pad it out. When they serve it up they use a lot less spaghetti and a lot more sauce. Salads are typically English – lettuce, cucumber and tomato with a choice of dressings. Little olive oil is used because it is expensive.

At Sandie's mother's. Sandie's mum also makes spaghetti bolognese sometimes, when they visit. She uses a lot more mince, and it is more fatty. Tomatoes are tinned and the herbs not fresh. The onion is fried in a blended vegetable oil. A beef stock cube completes the ingredients. It is much saltier and meatier than the Italian version.

It's a long step from home cooking in Italy to home cooking in Britain! The spaghetti dish has been considerably adapted by the time it's on the table at Sandie's mother's house.

From a nutritional point of view the adapted dish has changed in several ways:

• It has less carbohydrate.

• It has much more protein.
• It has more saturated fat from the mince and blended cooking oil.
• It has much more salt – including some from the stock cube. This has replaced fresh herbs as the main flavour enhancer.

Adopt, adapt and survive

If you consider your health as well as your tastebuds then you may need to look again at the ways in which you adopt and adapt.

Do you eat more of the highly flavoured sauces than the staple? Do you choose dishes because they are salty, sugary or have lots of meat in them? Do you cut down on some of the original staple foods like pasta, rice, beans or potatoes? Do you add foods like chips that are high in fats?

To check that you really are making healthy adaptations to these dishes takes time and effort, but you can use rules of thumb.

• Use plenty of staple foods – rice, beans, bread, pasta, potatoes.
• Use plenty of vegetables.
• Keep meat portions small.
• Don't add much salt or sugar to recipes or to the cooked dish.
• Find out how the particular dish would be eaten as part of a large meal in the original country. The overall meal may be well balanced. See if you can adopt more of that meal. Check some foreign cookery books which explain what dishes are served together in that culture.

Old cuisines, new country?

Adopting and adapting foods to achieve a satisfying diet are problems facing different cultural groups in our society. How easy do people coming to Britain find it to adjust their diet?

There are many specialist food shops all over the country. These meet the needs of particular groups, but can all of the right foods be easily obtained?

Moving in

Vietnamese boat people who came to Britain were originally housed in large groups. A study of one of these communities shows clearly how the people were able to adapt. Traditionally, the Vietnamese people ate a lot of rice and some meat, fish and vegetables. Sauces were another key feature providing flavour and some nourishment. Most of the necessary ingredients could be bought in this country. What is more, their diet is cheaper than its British equivalent.

The rice, their staple food, proved to be a problem. Vietnamese rice had six times as much calcium and nearly four times the iron as the rice they found over here. So their diet was deficient – especially in calcium. In Britain we get most of our calcium from milk and dairy produce. Plenty of milk was offered to the Vietnamese people, but it is not a part of their usual diet and many of them cannot digest it.

Other problems. Similar problems occur with other groups. Asians who come to live in Britain are at greater risk of rickets here than in their country of origin. This is due to a deficiency of Vitamin D. The majority of Vitamin D comes from the action of sunlight on the skin – very little Vitamin D is found in the foods Asians traditionally eat. The weather in this country makes them wrap up so that little skin is exposed to the sun – and customarily Asian women stay indoors and keep mostly covered up too.

Margarine is one food which is fortified with Vitamin D, but using margarine instead of butter to make ghee for cooking is not acceptable to all. A chappati flour with a vitamin supplement is made but isn't easily available. Very often a vitamin supplement is the only practical answer.

Religious laws

Some British food may break religious and ethnic laws and customs.
• Muslims and Jews should only eat meat which has been correctly slaughtered according to specific customs. The method of slaughtering conflicts with some local bye-laws, so meat is not always readily available.
• Rastafarians will not eat fresh fruit and vegetables which have been treated with pesticides and artificial fertilizers. Their kind of food is not usually available in supermarkets.
• Hindus should not eat beef. Muslims and Jews should not eat pork. This doesn't just mean that they avoid those meats. They must avoid dishes that they suspect contain disguised fragments of these meats or that have been cooked in animal fats.
• Many people totally reject meat for both religious and moral reasons.

If all this gives you the impression that almost no British foods are acceptable to people from different cultures it is not so. Various studies of different groups have shown that immigrants, particularly the children, quickly take to certain foods – soft drinks, crisps, sweets and pastries. The trouble is that such foods often contain lots of sugar, fats or salt.

The question that immigrants face is just the same as for any of us – how to achieve a good, balanced diet, that they enjoy eating.

Shopping for food

We all have to shop for food at one time or another and have our own patterns of shopping. And it's no use thinking we can make radical changes in our eating patterns without also considering the way we shop.

If the food in your home helps you maintain a healthy diet then you're OK. The topic *'Back to basics'* asks you to look at your food stores and at how you can develop a shopping list for such stores that contribute to a healthy diet.

'The shopper's world' asks you to look at your own shopping style and its strengths and weaknesses in relation to buying food. It helps you to think about how you can build on your strengths to achieve a weekly shopping basket of healthier foods.

'Food is a moral subject' and *'Finding a voice'* both ask you to consider the extent to which wider political, economic, social and moral issues about food concern you and whether you want to take any action about such issues.

159

Back to basics

A little time and effort spent at home thinking about what foods are best for your health, convenience and enjoyment can lead to more successful shopping.

Most of us don't live hand to mouth. We keep some supplies of basic food stuffs in the house. For some people these supplies are extensive, for others they're sparse. It's all to do with the styles of planning we adopt with regard to our food. Whatever the quantity of stored food you possess it can be a contribution to healthy eating. Knowing what purpose you want your stores to serve is useful when you think about your shopping list.

Your stores

What you've got in your store cupboard and the other stocks of food in your home can be pretty revealing.

If someone looked in your store cupboard, fridge and freezer would they get a clear picture of the sort of diet you eat? Would they get the impression that you eat a healthy diet? Would they get some idea about the sort of food preparation that generally goes on in your household? Of course, if you eat out a lot or eat mainly perishable food your store cupboard will probably reflect this by being quite empty!

Make a check of all the food that you have in your cupboards and on your shelves. Don't forget dry stores such as beans and cereals, tinned and packet foods, and such things as condiments, herbs and flavourings. Now look at all the items and think about the following things:

● What would you say the *turnover rate* was for your stores? How often do you replace the various items? Obviously, the ones that you replace often will be things that you use frequently. Are such things as salt and sugar regular items in your shopping list? Are dried beans and herbs years old?
● Do you know *how old* some of your stores are? Dry stores and tinned and packet goods do have a reasonable shelf life, but apart from anything else, things that you've had for years and years aren't likely to be a central part of your diet. *Why are they there?*
● Why did you buy the various items? Many of them are going to be things that you do use. But you'll probably be able to look at some of them and say 'I bought that because I remember I read it was good for me' or 'I bought the pulses because I decided I'd start eating more vegetable protein but I never quite got round to it'.

One of our readers found custard powder that had gone solid, herbs that had price labels in old money and a strawberry ice cream sauce that she recalled having in a flat she lived in ten years ago. What about you? How much do your stores actually indicate what you really eat? And how much are they a record of good intentions in the past?

If you are the main person who buys the food in your household:

Promise yourself that you'll throw out things that you never use and that you won't buy replacements for them.

Promise yourself you'll use stores to work for you and not just to fill up shelf space.

And if you are thinking of changing to the new guidelines for healthy eating – less fat, sugar and salt and more fibre –

Promise yourself that you'll build a set of food stores that you can use for a healthy diet.

If you don't buy the food in your household, looking at the store cupboards should have been a useful exercise even so. Do they reflect the kind of diet you want? If you are trying

to change to a healthier diet how does what's in your store cupboards help?

Look back at the *promises* suggested. While it may be expensive to buy things that are never used, it's more worrying to buy things that are used but are not a helpful contribution to a healthy diet.

If your diet is important to you, you need to be involved in decisions about it.
● How much do you contribute to the planning and buying of your basic food stores?
● How much do you just accept what's put in front of you, regardless of whether it's what you want?
● How much do you talk to the person or people doing the catering in your household about food and what you want to eat?
● How much could the store cupboard stocks be expanded with items that you are prepared to take responsibility for in getting food together in your house?

Unless you and the person catering in your household are in absolute agreement about the diet you want, then you too may need to make some promises about what *you* are going to do about basic foodstuffs that help your diet on.

Here are some suggestions for you:

Promise yourself you'll talk to the caterer in your household about how she or he uses the store cupboards.

Promise yourself that you'll make suggestions about additions to the store cupboard that will be useful for a healthy diet.

Promise yourself that you'll offer to take responsibility for certain items you'd like to see in the store cupboard, that the caterer in your household doesn't like or won't prepare.

Stores for health

Once you've got rid of your museum pieces you should have the space to create a store cupboard that can contribute to a healthy and interesting diet. If you've kept your promise to yourself to get rid of useless items, what you have left now in your store cupboard should be items you actually do use fairly frequently.

Building up stores. Choose foods you know you'll use. Before you buy an item for your store cupboard think *how* you are going to use it? Are you going to have the time to soak beans and so on? Do you have recipes that you'll be able to use an item for?

Expand your stores slowly, even one item at a time. Maybe you could buy small sizes to begin with until you're sure each item is actually going to contribute to your pattern of eating.

Dry stores for health. Building up dry stores can give you a wide variety of staples to include in your diet. Many fibre-rich foods can be stored – pulses, beans, peas, lentils, wholegrain flours, brown rice, cereals, nuts and so on. Remember too that a garden shed which is cold and dry is a good place for storing sacks of vegetables, like potatoes and onions. Often you may have to use a bit of foresight, soaking things in advance for instance. But if you can build them into your pattern of eating all these fibre-rich foods are useful stores to have – increasing the variety of your diet no end.

For health you could cut down on dry stores such as salt and sugar. For variety you could have more herbs, spices and nuts which can all make your diet more interesting.

Bulk buying? You may want to consider a bulk-buying scheme for dry stores where a group of people decide to buy food in bulk and share it out.

This is not to make a profit at resale – but each member of the group benefits from the savings that can be made from buying large quantities. If you do join or start such a scheme, remember there's time and effort often involved. But members will usually share jobs in the scheme.

Tinned and packet foods for health? Buying tinned and packet food saves on time and effort. Many people find convenience foods pleasant. If you're not keen on soaking beans and pulses you can buy tinned versions which save you time.

With tinned and packet foods you can build up stores that provide you with complete meals or snacks – these can be real time savers.

Tinned produce can also give you a wide variety of vegetables all year round – this adds plenty of variety to your diet.

Do look at labels on tins and packets and watch out for added salt and sugar. Some manufacturers now produce tinned fruit and vegetables containing no added sugar or salt.

Check occasionally that you're getting through your tins and packets of food. If you aren't, then your choices may be suspect! Perhaps you could make a note for yourself – write the date you purchased each item on its' label.

Making a start. So now make out a list of what you'd like to add to your food stores. Building these stores up needn't be something which makes your weekly shopping more of a chore. Once you've found a shop that stocks salt-free tinned vegetables you could decide to purchase a stock every few weeks, or even months and be done with it. But remember to try them out on a small scale for a few weeks first or you may find yourself with more museum pieces again!

Think about whether you want your stores just to supplement fresh food, or whether you want to be able to build a store of foods that can provide you with complete meals and snacks.

Not everything that goes into freezers is helpful for a healthy diet!

Frozen foods for health?

Another store of foods that many people keep are frozen. Freezers can save time and effort too, but do they fit in with healthy eating? The answer is, it depends what you put into them!

Having a freezer, or fridge-freezer, can increase your options for healthy eating a lot and give you flexibility in your catering and eating patterns.

However you do have to buy the freezer, stock it and run it. And it's probably wise to insure the goods. So deciding to go in for one deserves some thought – it's not quite like having purchased a bag of wholemeal flour you never used!

Ready frozen foods. Choose frozen foods sensibly with these things in mind:
● Frozen vegetables and fruits have more vitamins than tinned versions and many fresh versions.
● Frozen fruit and vegetables do not generally have added salt.
● Frozen fruit often has less or no added sugar.
● Frozen fruit and vegetables are reliable. In weeks when all the fresh fruit and vegetables look jaded they are an easy attractive alternative.
● You can buy larger cheaper packs of all sorts of frozen foods.

It's also worth remembering that frozen food is prepared and stored under very hygienic conditions – more so than loose food and usually more than home cooking. Also, increasing numbers of fridges and freezers have played a part in reducing cases of food poisoning.

Freezing your own. Freezing your own food gives you the sort of variety *you* want in your diet. It also gives variety to your catering and eating.
● You can store 'fresh' raw portions of the sorts of foods you want to eat more of. For instance, a whole chicken cut into small portions, small portions of lean mince, fresh pasta and so on.
● You can freeze your own fruit and vegetables for out of season occasions.
● You can cook large quantities of healthy food all at one go and freeze

162

unused portions.
- You can freeze leftovers.
- You can reorganise your time – cooking when you've got plenty of time ready for occasions when you've got very little time.

Buying and running a freezer. You need the capital to buy a freezer, or be able to keep up repayments.

You need the right freezer for your household. Many take up a lot of space. Fridge-freezers may be the answer for small houses.

Running costs are higher than people think. You need to stock it and that might mean quite a lot of money in one go. Freezers waste electricity if they are not full. It's worth remembering that taking up the space with polystyrene or cardboard boxes will prevent this.

Freezers do not often go wrong. So repair bills aren't high. But, if you have a lot of food in your freezer then it's worth taking out insurance. Power cuts, for example, could cause problems.

★★★★★

Foods cannot be frozen indefinitely, as most people are well aware. But not many people know the exact freezer life of particular foods. Fish, for instance, won't keep as long as some other foods. Before you freeze things you should find out how long they should be kept for.

Storing skills

However you store your food you need to remember the following:
- Be aware of the 'sell by', 'use by' dates and make sure that the shelf life of tinned and frozen goods is reasonable.
- Make sure that you have the right 'star' rating for frozen foods. The packets should tell you how long the goods will last in your freezer.
- Choose storage space you have easy access to, then you won't forget about some of your stores. In fact, they need to be somewhere where they are a constant reminder to you.

Retrieval

Hopefully, your stores are an accurate reflection of part of your diet. But also, less obviously, they reflect your catering style – or they should do! There's no point in having a superbly equipped, dry store of beans and pulses if you never get round to soaking the food so you can use it.

So your stores should also reflect the amount of planning you are prepared

to do with your catering.

How instantly do you want to be able to turn your various stored foods into edible food? Do you want it generally to be a matter of a tin opener and five minutes' cooking? Does food need marinating, thawing, dehydrating? In other words, what amount of advance planning is required for your stores?

How fast? Think for a moment about preparing a meal or a snack *now.*

How long would it be before you could get a meal on the table from your stores and freezer? If you look on your stores as being extras to your diet, how long would they take to prepare if they were going to be part of a meal consisting mainly of fresh food?

How much are you put off using various items from your food stores by the time or effort they take to prepare? Perhaps you can begin to think about getting a balance in your stores – some dry stores that only take a few minutes, some food that can be cooked from frozen, with other parts of your stores that you know take time but you don't mind about.

Speeding things up. There are some ways round advance planning. For example, you could use:
- pressure cookers
- slow cookers
- microwave ovens.

These can help speed up cooking or thawing times. They can also help you use time more flexibly. It depends on how instantly you want to eat your food. Cutting this advance planning aspect out of your catering also depends on how much money you're prepared to invest.

Of course, in addition to speeding up your catering, freezers and microwaves enable you to buy prepared meals and snacks that you can serve up very quickly.

Time and effort

Knowing your stores and how they can work for you can be very useful when you think about your diet. So think now about how you can use this knowledge to get the best results.

Look at your stores again and make a chart like the one below and fill in the stores in the various boxes. Remember we aren't talking about a *long preparation time* because of a complicated recipe, but only in terms of the time it takes – from the time you get foods out of the cupboard or freezer until you can cook them or eat them.

Think also about how you could alter the situation if you find that it's difficult for you to 'get at' your stores easily! Read the previous section again about 'speeding things up'.

When you've done this you'll have a record of stores you can mix and match according to the times they take you to get them ready.

You can use your chart to help you build up your stores some more by increasing the items in each time band so you've got a variety of foods to mix and match.

What does this mean for shopping? If you've had a serious reorganisation of your ideas about food stores then you need to think about how your shopping can best accommodate your new ideas. You could try the following:
- Do a separate shop for stores every few weeks. You can buy largish quantities occasionally.
- Keep a running list of stores you need and add them to your usual shopping list.
- Concentrate on one set of stores at a time – buying tinned goods this month, dry stores the next and so on.
- Concentrate on the time element – buying stores that only take a few minutes to prepare this week or month, things that take longer next month.
- Decide that once a month or so, you'll go round a few of your favourite food shops and see what's available, checking out new things to add to your stores that will help you with the diet you want.

This topic should have helped you to think about your food stores in some detail. It should also be useful for you in planning your shopping lists for healthy eating. Shopping for stores may not be something you'll want to do very often, so when you do, it is worth knowing you're going to get the best results!

	Instantly prepared	Long preparation time (e.g. needs thawing or soaking).
Quick and easy — (eg little or no cooking)	tins of all sorts dried fruit fish fingers	ready-prepared frozen desserts frozen fruits
Requires more effort (e.g. cooking time involved).	brown rice wholemeal pasta	frozen stewing beef chick peas beans and pulses

The shopper's world

Healthy eating doesn't start at the table. It's influenced by the way you shop for your food and what you are able to buy.

Going shopping for food is something which everyone does at some time in their lives. For many women in this country it is one of their most frequent and important domestic activities.

Shopping can have an enjoyable *social* purpose – meeting friends, going for coffee, and exchanging news and views. You can see what's new in the High Street and what's happening generally. It keeps you in touch with your locality. It provides you with a reason for getting out and about and makes you feel part of what's going on. These things are important aspects of shopping.

It's worth remembering, too, that meeting people and knowing what's going on can help you make choices about what food to buy. You get on a grapevine, you spot signs in windows, you discover new shops. This can be an important part of your shopping expeditions!

What do people want?

The assumption has often been that shoppers are almost wholly concerned with the lowest possible prices. This has resulted in what has been called the 'High Street War' with stores competing with each other to knock another 1p or 2p off the prices of the goods sold by their competitors.

However this has not always been to the advantage of customers or shopkeepers. It has ignored many of the other factors which shoppers have stated in opinion polls are important to them.

It's not just the cost. Market research has shown that customers are not always concerned with the bargain offers, or being lured into shops by the prospect of 5p off a certain brand. Many people are suspicious of cut prices because they do not always know what the normal price is and so cannot compare them.

So, despite the fact that the cost of food *is* important to most people, it has to be weighed against other things – such as time, convenience, pleasant surroundings, and a choice of food that can contribute to a healthy diet. And often people are willing to pay a little more to satisfy these needs.

What's important to you when you're shopping for food?

Look at the chart below and for each item tick the column which describes your feelings about whether it is important or not important.

What did you tick on the list? The items on the list broke down into four different groups divided up with lines in the chart.

- The food itself – quality and variety.
- Money – prices and savings to be made.
- Enjoyment – services and facilities.
- Convenience – easy access and suitable opening hours.

Look back at the items that you ticked as important. Was there a pattern in your ticks? Perhaps you had more ticks in one category than the others? If so, this should give you a clear indication of just what your priorities are in shopping for food. Did you think of anything else that was important to you? Which category did it fall into?

Of course, considering various items on the list as important and being satisfied with what you find are two different things.

A question of balance. It's all about balancing your ideals against your circumstances. In reality you have to find as good a match as possible between:

- what's available in your locality
- what's possible given your lifestyle and finances
- what's important to you.

Largely it's a matter of compromise. But there may be ways of getting more of the foods you want from your shopping trips. There may also be ways of eliminating some of the things you don't like about shopping.

Next time you go to the shops give each shop a rating for *each* of the four

	Important	Not important
Range and variety of foods available A good choice of healthy foods Quality goods available Special foods sold – like delicatessen or wholefoods		
Prices Bargain offers, frequent cut prices Bulk-buying savers Own brands		
Nice atmosphere in shop Cleanliness/hygiene Not too many people Small queues Personal service/friendly assistants Design and decor of building		
Close to home or work Near to other shops you go to Convenient opening hours Late night opening or Sunday opening		

categories. Use a scale from one for 'absolutely awful' to ten for 'terrific'.

How do they line up? Are you generally satisfied?

Want some changes?

Of course, the best of all worlds is to find the food you want at the price you want, in enjoyable and convenient surroundings. But if that doesn't seem to be your experience of shopping for food what can you do?

Perhaps you can capitalise on some of the things you find satisfactory. For instance, one very useful rule of thumb is to make regular use of shops where staff can give you help about which foods are healthy.

Try asking the assistants or managers which products are low fat, low or no sugar, low or no salt, for example. Do they know? Will they be prepared to order goods for you or look around for special brands? A good shopkeeper/manager/assistant can save you a lot of legwork. Many of the large supermarkets are proud of their reputations for good quality food and do take their customers' views seriously. Other customers at the shop might also be interested in the same products as you so there may be an incentive for the shop to experiment with some healthier products.

Some of the changes you can bring about may well be by influencing shops to stock food you want to buy. You can make your views known.

However, some of the changes you may want to make might have more to do with you and your own style of shopping.

What kind of shopper are you?

Your experience of shopping won't be solely determined by what's in the shops. You bring your personality and tastes to the shops – and these aspects are important too.

Look at the lists in the following paragraphs – underline anything that you recognise as being an important part of your own shopping style.

Money. I look at prices in various shops/I compare prices of different brands of the same product in one shop/I calculate unit costs of the products/I don't look at prices because it's too time-consuming/I always buy particular brands regardless/I always buy the best quality regardless.

I always cost out my shopping lists and make sure I have enough money/I know roughly how much it's going to cost/I don't know what I'm going to buy until I've been round the shops/I don't look at costs/I spend what I have.

I always look for bargains, bulk buys, special offers, coupons etc./I keep to my normal brands regardless of special offers/I distrust special offers, bargains/I sometimes get bargains depending on how I feel.

I usually pay cash/pay by cheque/credit card for large amounts/I budget for food for the week in advance/I never put aside an exact amount for food, it varies from week to week.

Planning strategies. I always make lists/I rush in and grab a few things/I plan some things, but leave the rest for when I get to the shops/I never make lists, but keep it in my head.

I plan a route through the town or shopping centre/I always know what shops I'm going to in advance/I like trying the variety of different shops/I decide when I get there and have a chance to look around.

I will only use shops within walking distance/bus ride/with car park/I just go and see what it's like.

The health aspects of food. I know the food I like and I never look at any of the other shelves/I spend a lot of time browsing around and seeing new brands of things that are in/I've got an open mind when I get there and choose food I fancy/Healthy food is my main consideration/I try and buy healthy food but get tempted and succumb on other counters to fatty, sugary and salty foods/As long as it's good quality I don't worry too much about whether it's healthy or not/I'd go a long way, out of my way even, looking for healthy food.

What's your style?

Looking at the statements you've underlined will give you some idea of your 'profile' as a food shopper. There are quite marked differences in the way people shop. Think of an older relative you know well. Would they have underlined different statements in the exercise above? If your partner was to do more of the shopping, would he or she do it very differently?

Are there ways you could change your shopping style to better suit your needs?

Your style with money. If you like to shop around and compare prices you can spend a lot of time going backwards and forwards, getting different items in different shops. This is both tiring and time consuming. Is it worth it? You may feel it is because you resent paying more than is absolutely necessary or feel you have no other choice. Or you may decide that your time could be more satisfyingly spent doing something else – the savings are not adequate compensation for your exhaustion and bad temper.

You may pay by cheque because it is easier, but perhaps this way you find that you always spend more than you meant to? You tend to splash out on 'little extras' when you have a cheque book with you, because somehow it's unlike 'real' money... It's not like having £15 in your purse and not being able to spend a penny more.

Your style with planning. You may be a person who tends to plan in advance or one who gets 'bits and pieces' as the need arises during the week. If you do this it might be worth making a list of what you spend shopping over the period of a week – then compare it to working out a weekly shop planning in advance. Is it more costly doing it your way? Or do you prefer the spontaneity of shopping as you do, and accept that it may cost you more?

Your style with shopping for food. And what about food? After all, this topic is about shopping for food. If you've decided to change to the new guidelines for healthy eating – less fats, sugar and salt and more fibre – it's worthwhile considering just how you can best serve your purposes.

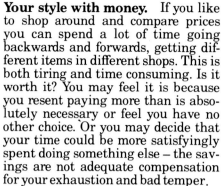

Temptation? Most of us are going to succumb to temptation in the shops at one time or another. The odd treat isn't really much to worry about. But if week after week your shopping basket is full of high-fat, high-sugar, high-salt foods and little fibre you have a problem if you are trying to build up a healthier diet.

Thinking about your style of shopping you may detect certain characteristics that tend to define you as a 'planner' or an 'impulse buyer'. Below are a series of cartoons. Look at them and see whether you identify anything that's like your own style.

THE IMPULSE BUYER

School fête | Check out at supermarket

Delicatessen | Back home

THE PLANNER

Greengrocer | Butcher

Kitchen table | Supermarket

Research has shown that people who have lists and plan their shopping do tend to spend the amount on shopping that they intended, whereas impulse or spontaneous shoppers tend to spend more.

A healthy diet and a healthy budget?

Is it possible to buy foods that fit in with your plans for a healthy diet and still keep within your budget? Eating healthily needn't cost the earth if you plan carefully.

Marjorie is a good manager. *"I have four children. That's six mouths to feed on a low income. When I look at the cost of all that lean meat and expensive vegetables and fruit I just don't know what to do. Things like low-salt foods just cost a fortune. My local health food shop has it all, but I can't afford to buy it week in, week out."*

Marjorie keeps her family well fed on a low income. Over the years her diet and her shopping habits have built up into a predictable pattern. Economy dishes mean lots of cheap cuts of meat, giant packs of bacon, eggs and plenty of sliced bread. When she examined her diet in the light of the new guidelines for healthy eating she found:
- more saturated fats than she needed
- more sugar than she needed
- much more salt than she needed
- fibre not too bad, *but* in need of a little more (they eat plenty of bread, baked beans, potatoes and some rice and pasta).

Some changes were easy to make. Using a wholemeal loaf; using semi-skimmed milk; switching to a margarine high in polyunsaturated fats, for example. Other food changes were more a problem of cost rather than that her family wouldn't eat them. Lean meat, fresh fruit, more vegetables all meant changes in the family budget for each week.

Advice. A nutritionist looked at her diet and her budget and came up with these suggestions.
- Use more chicken, and smaller pieces of lean meat. These fit in with the stews and casseroles that Marjorie likes to make but saves money because chicken's cheaper anyway and lean meat needs less trimming, draining and less cooking. They give much less fat.
- Spend less money on biscuits, cakes and jam and instead buy more fresh fruit and things like high-fibre breakfast cereals. These are all good snacks and are lower in sugar and fats and higher in fibre.
- Buy potatoes, rice and pasta in bulk and use these as the basis of many dishes. Where, for example, a stew would normally have a couple of potatoes in it, now put in more.

She recommended more detailed changes but the overall message was 'Changing your shopping habits gives you variety and costs less.'

Look before you buy. For Marjorie the first job is to look carefully at the way she shops and at the kind of things that she fills her trolley up with at the supermarket. Selecting healthier foods means keeping a careful check on labels and asking the shopkeeper for lower fat/sugar/salt products. It doesn't need to mean a weekly trip to expensive health food stores.

How you shop. Your style of shopping can help you towards a healthier diet. Whatever your approach to planning or money you can capitalise on it. As you check through the following suggestions you'll probably recognise underlying styles of planning and using money.

When you've read them, go back to the activity about what kind of shopper you are. Look again at what you've underlined and see if you can come up with a way that the various aspects of *your own style* could help you with a healthy diet. For instance:

● If you're a bargain hunter make your target nutritional bargains – lean meat, low-fat cheese, fruit and vegetables – that you can use in cooking.

● If you're an impulse buyer then you can take advantage of foods you see and fancy that can help make your healthier diet interesting and fun. You're the sort of person who'll be prepared to try all sorts of things out.

● If you're prepared to walk from one end of the town to the other, why not make it in aid of healthy foods rather than 1p off?

Money isn't everything in shopping. You may value your time and your health before everything. However, most people have to work to a budget. Using your shopping skills to advantage can help you to eat well and still keep costs down.

Read labels

Our labelling laws need improving. The ingredients – the meat, gravy, vegetables or whatever – must be listed in order of decreasing weight. So the ingredient of which there is most by weight is listed first. But the actual amounts need not be given.

At the moment the nutrients – the fats, proteins, sugars, complex starchy carbohydrates and fibre, vitamins and mineral salts in the food need not be given. Any extra added nutrients must be labelled. Health educators want to see nutrient labelling introduced so that people can be more aware of how much fat, sugar, salt and fibre they are eating.

Some products volunteer nutrient labelling. They usually only tell you about their good points. You will see foods labelled 'high in polyunsaturates', 'sugar-reduced', 'no added salt', 'low-salt' or 'fibre-rich'.

Products made in the USA and some European countries will give the detailed nutrient information that is required by law in these countries.

At the time this book was written the government was reconsidering the labelling laws. At the moment, important information – such as fat content – is not required to be labelled. And some information that is given can be quite misleading.

For example, meat products, like sausages, may give their meat content as 'beef' or 'pork'. Many consumers believe that this refers to lean meat. But, in fact, the required definition of 'meat' may include the percentage of fat normally found in the animal. So such a 'meat' product may include, in some cases, up to 60% fat.

New regulations are expected to require the total amount of fat in the product to be declared. Ideally the saturated fats – which can be bad for your heart – should be labelled separately. However, pressure from the meat marketing and milk boards, whose products would show up badly with this type of labelling may prevent the labelling of saturated fats to be required by law.

Misleading labels. Watch out for these four types:
● 'Mixed vegetable oils' – these trade on the general consumer's belief that vegetable as opposed to animal fats are good for you. Not so: some vegetable fats – coconut and palm oil – are saturated fats like the animal fats. Coconut and palm oil are cheaper than the polyunsaturated fats eg., corn oil, sunflower oil, and are much used in pastry, cakes and biscuits. The ingredient list could conceal them under the misleading label of 'mixed vegetable oils'.
● 'Added bran' – which you don't need. Adding bran is not the same as eating a wide range of naturally fibre-rich foods.
● 'Low or reduced sugar' – this may be true. However since manufacturers need only count the sucrose when labelling 'sugar', check that the sucrose sugar has not been replaced by another sugar such as glucose, glucose syrups or honey.
● Additives – chemicals added to foods to improve their colour, flavour, texture or shelf life must be labelled. But in many cases, only the official E number needs to be given. To check out what these mean you need to get *Look at the label*, a booklet by the Ministry of Agriculture, Fisheries and Food. But this booklet only gives the chemical names of the substances, so you may not be much wiser. Sometimes the full chemical name is given on the label. Many of these additives have been well tested and/or used for many years. But this is a complex area that needs constant reviewing. It's also an area where scare stories may be used by the popular press. The more additives like polyphosphates, emulsifiers, preservatives and colourings there are, the more likely it is that the product is highly processed. Such products also often contain cheap fillers – such as saturated fats – to give bulk, and flavour enhancers such as sugar, salt and monosodium glutamate.

INGREDIENTS: FARINE DE FROMENT, GRAISSES VEGETALES (AU MINIMUM L'UN DES CORPS GRAS SUIVANTS: HUILE DE PALME, HUILE DE COPRAH, HUILE DE COPRAH HYDROGENEE, HUILES DE PALMISTE ET DE SOJA PARTIELLEMENT HYDROGENEES), FROMAGE, POUDRE A LEVER (BICARBONATE D'AMMONIUM ET DE SODIUM, E 450A), EPICES, SUCRE, PLANTES AROMATIQUES, AROMES NATURELS ET ARTIFICIELS.

INGREDIENTS: WHEATFLOUR, VEGETABLE FAT (CONTAINS AT LEAST ONE OF THE FOLLOWING: PALM OIL, COCONUT OIL, HYDROGENATED COCONUT OIL, PARTIALLY HYDROGENATED PALMKERNEL AND SOYA BEAN OILS), CHEESE, RAISING AGENT (AMMONIUM- AND SODIUM BICARBONATE, E 450A), SPICES, SUGAR, HERBS, NATURAL AND ARTIFICIAL FLAVOURINGS. REG. PENNA. DEPT. OF AGR.

BESTANDTEILE: WEIZENMEHL, PFLANZLICHES FETT, KASE, BACKTRIEBMITTEL (AMMONIUM- UND NATRIUMBIKARBONAT, DI-NATRIUMPYROPHOSPHAT), GEWURZE, ZUCKER, KRAUTER, NATURLICHE UND KUNSTLICHE AROMEN. KUHL UND TROCKEN LAGERN. HERGESTELLT IN HOLLAND. KONINKLIJKE VERKADE FABRIEKEN B.V. ZAANDAM-HOLLAND   75 g ℮

原材料：小麦粉，植物性油脂，チーズ，膨張剤（炭酸水素ナトリウム及び重炭酸ナトリウム，ピロリン酸水素ナトリウム），香辛料，砂糖，香料植物，自然及び人工風味加工

輸入業者：宝商事株式会社東京都千代田区鍛冶町1-9-19

Royal Verkade Factories Ltd.
Ζάανταμ, Ολλανδία.

How much information do you need on a label?

Food is a moral subject

*Have you ever decided – "I won't buy that food.
I'm unhappy about how it's produced"?*

Moral issues

From a moral point of view we may need to consider the following:

• The resources of the planet we live on.
• The short- and long-term effects of our farming techniques on the balance of nature.
• The quality of life of the animals that we rear for food.
• The production and promotion of foods which make it difficult for us to choose a healthy diet.
• The working conditions of those who labour in the production of food.
• The way in which meeting the food needs of the wealthy nations may actually contribute to the inadequate diets of those in poorer countries.

"I went shopping..."

...and in my basket I put

• some Granny Smith apples from South Africa
• some English bacon
• some chocolate made from cocoa beans from West Africa
• some dates from Israel
• some eggs from a battery chicken farm.

On moral grounds – would you object to putting any of these in your basket?

Some people do. One of our testers said that one or more of his family objected to all of these – and this was just a start! Other items in the long list of food from our testers included butter, tea, coffee, sugar, chicken, veal, pheasant – and anything from South Africa, Israel or Chile.

Make your own list of foods that you wouldn't put in your basket. Add your reasons, as well. If you don't feel strongly about any foods try asking some neighbours or workmates what they think. But be prepared for some heated arguments.

Pros and cons

When discussing these moral issues people tend to take up extreme positions – either for or against them. Both sides also tend to offer simplistic solutions to the problems.

The moral questions and problems attached to food and its production are actually vast and complex. There are often good arguments for and against certain approaches. So, it can be difficult for the average consumer wondering what to buy for dinner that night to work out what his or her moral position is.

This topic can only start you thinking a little more deeply about these issues. It also suggests some ways in which you can make your opinions heard more effectively. But moral issues are always about values and opinions. So it's also possible for two people to have deeply held – but opposite – convictions on most of these matters.

Be warned! One person may find this topic fascinating and want to find out much more. But another may decide that 'life is too short to worry about all this – and anyway I've more important things to worry about!'

Food and health

Consider whether you think the following issues related to food and health have moral implications.

- The British food industry puts money into research and advertising to promote the very foods which doctors maintain may harm our health – high in sugars and saturated fats.
- Animals may be injected with artificial hormones to increase the yield and quality of their meat. There are regulations controlling this, particularly how close to slaughter this may be done. However, it is difficult to keep strict checks on how long after the injections the animals are killed.
- DDT, a potentially harmful insecticide now banned in Europe and America, is still widely used in the Third World. Other pesticides and weedkillers are frequently used for crop-spraying in Europe and America. The yield is improved but there is a danger of residues being left in the harvest if they are sprayed near this time. There may be very little risk where just the seed – or grain – is harvested. But with vegetables, where a large part of the plant is eaten, the risk may be greater. Market gardeners make particularly frequent use of sprays.

Recent reports (1984) on the chemical residue levels in vegetables have been worrying. The government is now expected to bring in legislation to control spraying on all crops. At the moment there is only a voluntary code of practice that cannot be enforced.

Agricultural workers are particularly at risk, as are other people in the area, when crops are sprayed.

Farming and the balance of nature

Modern farming practices often upset the delicately balanced ecology in which a wide range of plants and animals live together.

- Insecticides kill harmless butterflies and ladybirds as well as the insect pests.
- Chemicals which are sprayed on the plants and insects may not be broken down and so accumulate in the bodies of the animals which eat them. In turn, they are passed on – along the biological food chain to the animals, which eat them.
- Some pesticides are also harmful to the much needed worms, which maintain the structure and fertility of the soil.
- To make the harvesting of grain crops easier, many hedgerows and copses have been rooted out to provide very large fields. There are then no suitable habitats for hedgerow and woodland plants, animals and birds.
- Marsh land is drained to bring more land into farming. This destroys the habitat of rare plants and birds.
- Putting a wide area down to a single crop and cutting out the hedges and copses which provide wind breaks makes soil erosion, from rain and wind, more likely. The fertile top soil can be swept away.

Animal rights

Many people feel it is unacceptable to eat meat when it is possible to eat well on vegetable proteins without killing animals. Others will eat some kinds of meat but not others. For instance, some people will not eat veal because they feel that intensive farming methods are unacceptable. Eggs from battery hens may not be acceptable because of the conditions the hens are reared in.

Food for thought. If we are breeding animals or fish merely to consume them, need we be concerned about the conditions in which they live?

If the answer to this is 'yes' then do intensive methods of rearing chickens, calves and pigs for the market really take into consideration, to any degree, the quality of existence of those creatures? Does there, also, need to be more openness about what happens when they are slaughtered?

Economics and human rights

Products of various companies. Avoiding products of companies, which are known not to pay a living wage, is an economic response to what is seen to be an immoral situation. For example, there has been considerable publicity about some tea companies who exploit their plantation workers.

Cash crops. Along similar lines, you might avoid products made from Third World cash crops like cocoa, coffee or peanuts. Using land for cash crops ruins the traditional pattern of subsistence farming where the people can feed themselves. Today, with so much land used for such crops, many Third World countries have to import much of their food.

There is, however, another side to this argument. Subsistence farmers are not wealthy enough to pay taxes. But a taxation system is needed to raise money to provide roads, schools, hospitals, pure water supplies and sewerage systems. Encouraging the sale of cash crops overseas does build up wealth, some of which, via taxes is used to benefit the whole community.

Food and politics

Political regimes. Many people have strongly held views about political regimes in different countries – that their human rights record is not as it should be, that sectors of the population are being repressed or exploited. One tactic people often adopt is to avoid buying goods of that country and thus avoid supporting the regime. Sometimes it's the politics of the food industry itself – rather than the whole government – that is objected to.

CAP. There are now widespread objections to the EEC's Common Agricultural Policy (CAP). At a consumer level we hear of the British objecting to having to allow French Golden Delicious apples on to their markets. And the French object to the entry of British lamb. There is a more substantial moral objection to the CAP that's little realised as yet. It makes its decisions for economic and political reasons and pays little regard to the health of the consumers. It still encourages increased production and promotion of dairy products and meats high in saturated fats that may damage our health.

Reviewing your shopping

Now you've read more about those moral issues you may want to think again about what you'll choose to buy.

Do this after you've done your next main food shopping. Put all the food on a table. For each question below check through all the foods *one at a time*.

For example, with question 1 put all those items to which you object in a pile on one side. Make a list of these foods and call it 'List one'.

Repeat the whole process for each question so that you will end up with six lists. Some foods may turn up on several lists.

1 Do I object – for any reason – to the politics of the country where this food comes from?

2 Do I object to the politics and economics of the way in which this food was produced?

3 Am I concerned that my health might be at risk if I eat this product?

4 Has anyone else's health been put at risk during the farming or production of this food?

5 Has anyone who contributed towards producing this food (right up to the point where I bought it) been economically exploited?

6 *If it contains meat, eggs or dairy products* – am I happy with the way in which the animals have been reared and slaughtered?

Some foods you won't have been sure about. You may wish to find out more about these. But at least let's start with those you are concerned about.

What next? Work through each list and decide what you will do next time. Will you:

● buy the same food from a different acceptable source?
● choose an alternative, but similar food, that is acceptable?
● do without it?
● decide that, despite your reservations, other reasons must take priority – and buy it?

Options for action

Consumer action

This 'shopping review' will have helped you decide what *you* will or will not buy. But you may not see individual action as the right or the only action that needs to be taken.

Many of us may feel powerless to do anything that can influence the wider course of events. But it is possible to put pressure, when we feel able and where possible, on those who do have the power to influence the processes of food production.

These options will be different for each individual. The following quotations reflect some of the possible

responses to these moral issues.

Chris. *"Well, I don't know a lot about it — but quite honestly I don't want to be made to feel guilty everytime I open my mouth and swallow something. I think it's up to governments really. It's enough for me to think of something different to give the family every night that doesn't cost the earth, without worrying about things like politics and world hunger."*

Sheila. *"I'd like to be a vegetarian for moral reasons, but I like meat too much. But I have cut down on it and only have it a couple of times a week."*

Sam. *"If there's two brands of a product that I want and one's got colouring and additives and the other hasn't, I get the one that hasn't, although, sometimes there's not a choice. I buy the straight, simple, orange juices."*

Ronny. *"I have strong political beliefs and I boycott all South African goods."*

Monica. *"I have written letters of complaint to manufacturers and supermarket managers. Sometimes you wonder if it's worthwhile, although I am always pleased I've done it at the time. I suppose I could tackle my MP about things I feel are important but it's a case of having the time and*

energy. When you do make a written complaint you usually get told 'most of our customers are satisfied — we get very few complaints.' I don't think people are satisfied, they just accept things and don't complain."

Mike. *"I am conscious of the gap between rich and poor nations. But this doesn't really influence the way I eat, which is much more related to the cost of food, what's available, what I fancy eating. But I do send a monthly cheque to one of the Overseas Aid Organisations — I suppose that's my way of doing what I can."*

Speak up?

As a nation we tend to be passive and apathetic about raising our voices in complaint – or even in constructive suggestions. Yet manufacturers state that they want to know what consumers think and they can't act unless we tell them what we think. It does take time and energy, but you may feel better for it. There are several different ways of 'finding a voice' – it's worth thinking about what you want to do and say.

What, if anything, would you most like to comment on to the manager of your local foodstore? And – to the directors of a food company? What's stopping you from writing to them?

Join a pressure group?

You could join a pressure group that campaigns to persuade the government to change its food policies. Or perhaps some organisation to which you already belong would wish to make its opinions on these food issues known to the government? The Department of Health has said, recently, that it wants to know what information the consumer would like to see on food labels.

There are powerful sectors of the food industry who don't want to have to label, for example, the saturated fat content of their products. Yet how is the consumer to follow the advice to cut down particularly hard on saturated fats without such information on the label?

Food additives are another area in which the consumer is kept in the dark. There have been many claims that food allergies are linked to certain of these additives.

Certainly, the long-term effects on health of some of these additives are not known. In the States, for example, Saccharin may be added to food but they must carry the label 'This product contains Saccharin which has been determined to cause cancer in laboratory animals'! What would you want to see on labels about additives – so that you can choose whether or not to buy the product?

We have to rely on the government to provide certain safeguards governing the foods we consume. The government must take responsibility for ensuring that conditions for workers in factories are satisfactory, and that methods of rearing and killing animals are humane. A realistic overseas aid budget also needs to be set.

What change, if any, would you most like to see the government make? Through which groups could you bring pressure to bear on the government?

Boycott the goods?

You can refuse to buy food from countries whose politics or food production policies you disagree with. The argument for boycotting on the part of individuals goes like this, *"In a small way I can show that I do not condone what's going on in that country. Economic sanctions are an effective way of putting pressure on foreign governments. And I feel better — I've made my protest."*

The argument against boycotting is that such action on the part of individuals is rarely effective. If governments apply the same economic sanctions rigidly then this *can* have more effect. But this is much harder to achieve.

Boycotting goods *may* actually further oppress those the action is supposed to help. Those at the bottom of the ladder suffer adverse effects before those at the top.

What, if anything, do you now plan to do about boycotting certain foods?

Finding a voice

The voice of the consumer can range from one quiet voice making its owner feel better, to the collective voice campaigning through many channels.

This topic traces various ways that you might use your voice as a consumer.

Your voice

While you're doing your food shopping you're probably familiar with feelings of occasional dissatisfaction. What you want isn't there, things are labelled inadequately, sizes of food are inappropriate, you're not happy with food for moral reasons.

Make a list of anything that's annoyed you in your food shopping in the past month or so. Think also about the following questions:

● What went on inside your head on each occasion?
● Did you say anything to anyone? . . . at home? . . . at work? . . . at the shop? . . . elsewhere?
● Did you take any action? For instance, did you shop elsewhere, write to the food chain, and so on?

You may have used your voice:
1   to make yourself feel better
2   to lodge a complaint
3   to bring about a change.

Most of us get no further than 1, or if we're really provoked, 2. This is fine so long as we can buy basically what we need or want. But if this isn't possible, what then?

Using your voice

A need for change?

If your week's shopping for food isn't wholly satisfying you may see a need for change if:

● You find it difficult or expensive to buy the sort of food you want to bring your diet in line with the new guidelines for healthy eating – less fats, sugar and salt, more fibre.
● You feel that being single/elderly/ having special dietary requirements, and so on, you aren't being catered for properly.
● You object to some of the food that's on offer for moral or political reasons.

Need for change → motivation

Whether you do anything about this need for change will depend on your motivation. Mary felt that changes to the current guidelines were very worthwhile, but she only changed the parts of her diet where it could be done easily. When John's father died of a heart attack at 62, John was highly motivated to cut down on fats. Annie will never buy Cape fruit because of apartheid. Margaret shares her views on apartheid, but buys Cape apples if they look good.

Fear of ill-health, concern for our children's teeth, the need to feel well, look good, enjoy being alive, coupled with an understanding of the effect of diet, all affect motivation. And people's motivation varies.

Need for change → motivation → voice

Ann Dixon worried about the effect of sugar on her children's teeth. Her kids wanted the sweets temptingly displayed at child level at the supermarket checkout. She wouldn't buy them. Embarrassing battles followed.

Angrily, she wrote to the manager. He invited her for a discussion. He

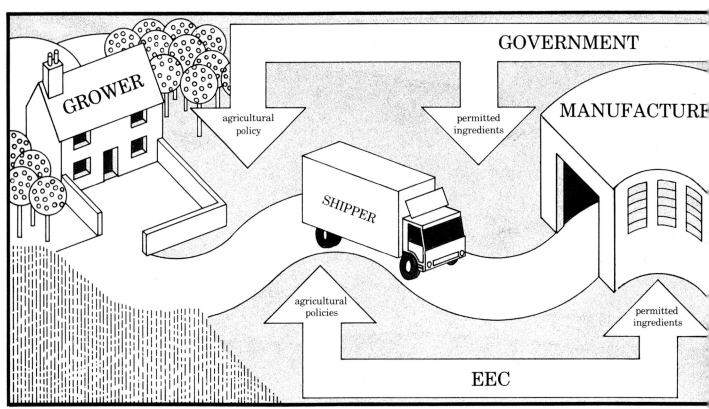

justified the display on the grounds that the store offered choice. *"Displaying sweets to children was provocation not choice,"* said Ann. *"Choice would mean having one check-out without a sweet display."* He said he would present her view to the company.

Ann went home feeling better. But a year later sweets were still there, at child level, next to the checkout. Nothing had changed.

Ann Dixon found a voice. Which of these needs did her voice meet?

To protect her children's teeth. ☐

To make her shopping with kids easier. ☐

To let off steam. ☐

To let other people know her views. ☐

To change store policy on sweet displays. ☐

Why do you think she failed to change policy?

She complained to the wrong person. ☐

She didn't follow her complaint through. ☐

She should have got other people to help. ☐

What else might she have done to meet her needs?

Well, perhaps she could have used her voice differently. Perhaps she could have campaigned in some other way.

Towards change. Our testers were asked about the extent to which they'd be willing to work for a change. Here are some of their comments:

"I think I might feel as though I were being a bit 'overboard' about things, considered neurotic or something!"

"Prefer to adjust my own habits than campaign, so I shop where I can get things. I haven't experienced serious problems so I've got no motivation to campaign."

"I am very tentative about putting my ideas over to other people."

"I have difficulty in whipping up any enthusiasm that lasts long enough to do anything about campaigning."

"Too utterly embarrassing!"

You may feel that your own voice is not one you want to raise very loudly. However, it's worthwhile remembering that we all use our voices as consumers in many ways already. We all know the voice of complaint. Here are some others which sometimes we're not so aware of.

● The very food we buy speaks volumes about our views. What we do buy is as much of a 'voice' as what we say.
● When we don't buy things, because we don't like them or because we disapprove, we use another sort of 'voice'.
● In telling our friends things like 'That muesli's all sugar!'... 'I never buy fruit from South Africa', we use another voice.
● We also use a voice to recommend – 'Did you know Jackson's sell sugar-reduced jam?'

Some people, though, are motivated to use their voices more publicly. How can this be done most effectively?

A voice in the wilderness?

If you want your voice to do more than let off steam then you need to know:

● how to get help to pursue your case
● exactly who needs to be tackled
● how to tackle them.

You may know at the start who needs to be tackled. However, most of our food reaches us through a long food chain – which involves actions and decisions by many people. This ranges from the people who grow the raw materials right through to you with your decision to buy or not.

Where on the chain...? Knowing which bit of a long food chain to tackle can be difficult. A long food chain looks something like the one below. Of course it can be short too like market gardener to consumer.

Ann Dixon complained to the shop; perhaps she should have complained to the retail chain as well. But the problem was about the shop. So, she saw no point in going any further along the chain than the retail shop. Knowing how far along the chain to go is quite a skill. This can result in bringing about change more effectively.

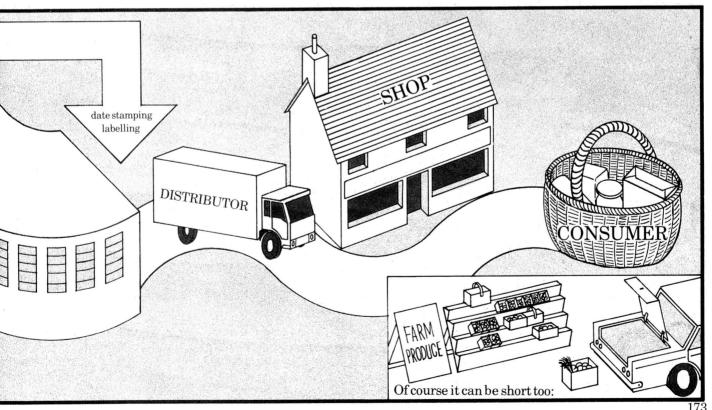

date stamping labelling

DISTRIBUTOR

SHOP

CONSUMER

FARM PRODUCE

Of course it can be short too:

When you think what other agencies affect the food chain, knowing *who* to complain to becomes even more of a problem.

So sometimes you may want to get help not only to pursue your case, but also to find out who you need to tackle.

You may decide that your voice stands a better chance of being heard if you team up with other people. And even if you are campaigning on your own, of course, they can help too. For instance:

People you know. Talking things through with people we know helps us decide what to do, and feel better. It also informs them. Effective action can start here.

Groups and associations. There may already be a group near you with an interest in your problem. Use your local Citizens' Advice Bureau to find out. Such groups might be consumer groups who campaign locally and nationally for better services and shops. Or, perhaps, health interest groups, persuading food manufacturers to improve products that will aid groups at special risk and also the community generally. For instance, the Coronary Prevention Group persuaded St Ivel to put nutritional information on all their products. They have also succeeded in getting a big retail chain to do the same. And the Coeliac Society – for people who can't digest gluten – got Boots to put gluten labelling on all their products.

It may be environmental or ecological groups of various sorts – for instance, Friends of the Earth – concerned with what is grown, how we grow it and the effects of this on the planet.

An advantage of such organisations is that they all have publicity networks and can make themselves heard. They are also familiar with where the problems in the food chain lie.

Media and influential people. One big powerful well-known voice has a lot of effect, especially via television and the media, like *You and yours* and *The food programme.* Local newspapers and television and radio programmes can also be useful.

Information and back-up

There are other sources of information and back-up to use too.

Trading standards officers help if you're sold short weight.

Environmental health officers prevent sale of unfit food, control quality of food sold, control food preparation, places and methods, control how food is labelled and described.

Consumer advice centres can be found in a number of local authorities. There may be one near you.

Health education officers have a responsibility to educate the public on matters of health. They can help you with facts and tactics.

Community health councils are the consumer voice on the National Health Services and may be able to help you with campaigns.

All of these sources of support and advice can be very helpful. Together with skills you can develop yourself, they can help you make your voice effective. As you read the last section of this topic think about where it would be useful to have such back-up.

Getting on with it

Preparing your case. You should:
- know your facts
- know what you want to happen
- make sure you're speaking to the right person; be civil; take into account that the person you're speaking to may feel threatened and angry.
- avoid apologies and aggression
- be assertive
- don't be deflected – stick to your point
- make sure your suggestion is feasible – suggesting one sweet-free checkout is more likely to get results than suggesting a sweet-free shop.

Acting out the encounter. This is a useful thing to do with a friend before hand – it can be helpful and is fun too. Start with brief notes. You can use the list above to guide you both. You can use several imaginary situations to help you practice. For instance:
- Persuade your local supermarket to change to sugarless yoghurt.
- Encourage a local baker to put less salt in his wholemeal bread.
- Get the catering manager at work to use more fresh vegetables.

Choosing the right channels. It's important to approach the right people – through the correct channels and at the right level.

You've identified your target. You know what you want to say. Whom do you say it to?
- Aim as high as you can.
- Don't be fobbed off, it pays to persevere.
- Find out if there is an already established route for the consumer's voice.

For instance, some companies have procedures for handling complaints which might be of help to you. Some have Consumer Affairs employees whose job is to present consumer needs and get the company to react

positively. Some have consumer panels. Or there may be issues about which you're so concerned you want to speak to central government, perhaps the EEC. Do this via your MP, reachable by letter, monthly constituency surgery, or personal visit.

Writing a letter. It makes a meeting more productive if you write first stating your needs. Be brief, to the point and well-informed. Ann Dixon's letter said this:-

60 Portland Road
Runcorn
Cheshire
12th March 1985.

Dear Manager,

I write to you after an awkward scene with my two year old at the checkout sweet display in your store.

Research shows conclusively the link between sweet eating and tooth decay in children (currently at epidemic proportions).

Your company is well known for the concern that it has with its customers' well being. This is why I shop with you. The display of sweets at small child level goes right against this policy and upsets many people.

I would like to meet to discuss this matter.

Yours faithfully,

Ann Dixon

Ann Dixon.

The way forward?

Any one change you want to bring about may be achieved by several different routes. The suggestions already made may have given you some ideas.

What you choose to do will depend on your motivation and the ways of using your voice that you find most satisfactory and successful.

It is useful to monitor your own progress:
- assess the current situation
- work to bring about a change
- assess the success of what you've done.

Not all of the changes you might want to bring about need necessarily involve confronting people face to face. You may, like the tester mentioned earlier, decide to adjust your own behaviour when you've assessed the situation. Actions as well as words help you to speak out.

Any change that makes you feel that as a consumer of food you are getting a better deal is all to the good. You can make your voice heard at all sorts of levels and you can get pay offs at all sorts of levels too. Think about what you are prepared to do.

A different pattern

You may be like most of us in that you eat too much fat, sugar and salt and not enough fibre. However it's not enough to say we all need to cut down. We need to know how our diet comes to be like it is, why we follow the patterns that we do and then perhaps we can alter them.

As you have worked through this book you should have found out for yourself what the significant things are in *your* life that shape your pattern of eating.

You may have discovered significant elements in your pattern of eating that reach back to childhood – family traditions may have affected your style of planning for food, how you organise your eating during the day and so on. You're probably aware that your own pattern of eating, though unique, bears some relationship to national or regional trends. And that food is about a lot more than eating – having as it does social, political, economical and moral implications.

This chapter helps you to think about a plan of action for a healthy diet. You should be able to use what you have found out about your eating patterns earlier in the book to help you make your plan one that really works *for you*.

Before you read through this chapter flick through the earlier pages of the book again to remind you of what you now know about your pattern of eating.

And remember, you can have a different pattern of eating if you want to!

Good advice

There's certainly plenty of advice on diet and health available.
Whose advice do you accept? Having accepted it – how easy do you find it
to act on good advice?

Nutritionists, the media and health food shops place great emphasis on dietary advice. Though they don't, of course, all give the same advice. Then there's also the opinions of your workmates, neighbours and family.

Quite often your opinion of all this advice will be affected by who said it and how they said it. But you may not be sure which advice is good. And your beliefs and experience will colour how you see this advice.

This topic will help you look at:

- who is giving the advice
- what affects whether or not you will accept it
- how likely you are to act on the good advice you do accept.

'Good advice' – who says?

The next four sections look at some of the sources of advice about nutrition. After you've read each section, think about one piece of advice that you've heard from that source. In your note book jot down a few lines answering the following questions about each of the four pieces of advice you've thought of.

- How likely is it that this piece of advice is good?
- What are my reactions to this piece of advice?
- How relevant is this piece of advice to my life?
- Would this advice be easy to put into practice?

The experts

If you're looking for good advice, what expert nutritionists say would seem to be a good starting point. But, however much a group of such experts agree there's nearly always at least one expert who disagrees.

Disagreements between scientists – in any field – provide the essential spur for additional research. This provides additional evidence so that theories are confirmed or modified. While there is any shred of doubt it's important for scientific research that someone should speak up.

Unfortunately, it's impossible to reach absolute certainty about most nutritional advice. Exact repeatable experiments can seldom be done on groups of human beings. Many nutritionists would now agree that advice can only be based on a mounting collection of evidence and reach the best possible consensus they can before offering dietary advice.

We tend to hear a great deal about the experts who disagree with the new advice. That's usually because the media don't want to go on repeating the consensus opinion. That becomes boring. But anything that stirs up the argument – or rates as 'bad news' – attracts an audience and is therefore newsworthy! When they are interviewed by journalists these experts, naturally, put over their view with a great deal of fervour.

Indeed, when interviewed, many nutritionists emphasise only their field of research and play down the importance of others. Listening to one you might decide fibre is *the* most important item in your diet. Another would convince you to spend all your energy cutting out sugar. A third might worry you so much about salt that you forget to worry about saturated fats! Or, if you listened to all three, you might decide to ignore them all because they seem to be talking at cross purposes.

It's better to settle for the NACNE (National Advisory Committee on Nutrition Education) and COMA (Diet and Cardiovascular Disease, presented by the DHSS) reports' long awaited and widely accepted recommendations. However, both these reports emphasise that, although they embody the best advice available today, they expect to have regular reviews to up-date and make more exact recommendations.

From their research findings nutritionists can make general recommendations about the nutrients in our diet. By now you should be very familiar with the new guidelines for healthy eating. For example – cut down on saturated fats by 50%. For individual advice about what *you* should do, in terms of which actual foods to cut down on and by how much, you would need to seek the help of a dietician. Indeed you can ask your GP to refer you to one. But there aren't many dieticians and most have a heavy workload. You may need to be your own dietician!

What have you heard? Check the four questions at the start of 'Good advice – who says?' for some piece of advice from an expert that you have recently come across.

The media

Nutritionists publish their research findings in scientific journals. Their writing is full of technical terms and written in a cautious style that makes it difficult to understand.

Most of us cannot seek advice from our own dietician so we tend to rely on the media to translate what the experts say. We take our advice from the media – the television and radio programmes, the newspaper and magazine articles.

In turning scientific research papers into plain English simplifications tend to be made. To 'sell' the news item the journalist may seek to sensationalise it.

No wonder the headline *Fat Kills* upsets the expert author of the long, carefully argued paper that links an increased risk of coronary heart disease (in certain susceptible groups of people) with high levels of saturated fat intake! Such a headline can also frighten or irritate the ordinary readers, so that they reject it.

However, by keeping an eye on the media you can get some useful ideas about what is of current concern to nutritionists.

Also, by paying attention to the media you can get a clearer idea about what actually concerns *you* about nutrition. What articles or television programmes make you sit up and pay attention? What do you talk about the next day to your friends and colleagues? What have you come across recently? Check through the four questions at the start of 'Good advice – who says?'

Health food 'experts'

If you're interested in eating a healthy diet you may think 'health foods' by their very name would be a starting point. But in radio and TV programmes these 'health foods' are often discussed as unnecessary, expensive or in some cases bogus. So what basis is there for the confidence many people have in them?

Something missing? Nutrition is such a complicated subject that it's easy to feel we are forgetting to make sure we get enough of all the vitamins or the many mineral salts we need. Perhaps *to be on the safe side* we'd better take them in tablet form as a supplement to our diet?

The NACNE report states firmly that we don't need to worry about our diet in such detail. If we pay attention to the main recommendations the minor details will automatically be taken care of. We can remain healthy by eating a wide variety of foods that together provide us with the balance of nutrients – fats, sugar and fibre – that NACNE recommends. Such a varied diet will also provide enough vitamins and mineral salts. There is no need for ordinary people to take dietary supplements.

'Faith' foods. Some people have great faith in health foods. They firmly believe they feel better after taking them. This confidence goes beyond scientific evidence.

Again many people will believe that if someone they admire recommends the health food then it must be good for them. This recommendation may come from a well-known beauty, a sports personality or a lively 80-year-old. Or it may come from a loved and trusted relative. Such personal recommendations count for much more in people's minds than the cautious comments from health experts. Real people also speak louder than statistics!

It seems to be little or no use to explain that if you feel better after taking the 'health food' it *may* not be direct cause and effect. Something else, that occurred at the same time may have made you better. Or – although the 'health food' had no scientifically measurable effect on your body – your mind may well have worked the improvement on your health.

One way this strong link between mind and body becomes clear is in drug trials, when some patients are given harmless identical tablets – called placebos – which they believe to be the real drug. In these cases some of the patients taking the placebos show the same, expected improvement as do those taking the real drug.

What's your position? Think through the four questions at the start of 'Good advice – who says?' Next time you have the chance to visit a health food shop try making two lists of the 'health foods'.

● List 1 – of those that claim to provide something you may be missing out on.
● List 2 – those which you are recommended to by famous people and/or with overtones of magical cures.

The shop will probably sell ordinary healthy foods too! Such as cereals and beans, dried fruit and nuts, yoghurts and 'high in polyunsaturates' margarine. Providing they have no added bran, vitamins or 'magical ingredients' which unnecessarily increase their prices these are fine.

Finally try to sum up what attracts you to or puts you off certain health foods.

Friends and friends of friends!

There is another source of advice – people you know and talk to. Everyone has tales to tell and advice to offer. Some of this advice may be good. It may be from people who pay attention to the field of nutrition and know the current guidelines for healthy eating. Other advice may have a grain of truth in it. Or – it may have been good advice twenty years ago.

People often pass on information and advice from TV and radio programmes, or newspapers and magazines. Or from their doctor or health visitor – or just a friend 'who knows'. These messages can get distorted as they are passed along. Rather like the game of Chinese

whispers! Our testers confirmed this. Their accounts of what they had heard in recent TV programmes against video-tapes of the original programmes showed that there was often some distortion. And studies, which check what patients claim their doctors tell them against tape recordings of the actual interviews, again show how the listeners often only hear what they want to hear.

How do you see it?

Reading through the various sources of advice you may have thought of some examples that didn't actually seem to have any real significance for you. Whatever its source quite a lot of advice may well just go over your head. Hearing advice and even believing it to be true doesn't always lead to action. Lots of people find that they only take notice of advice if it's relevant to their lives now. You've probably had the experience of seeing print leap up off the page because the advice that's offered concerns you *now*. If you are concerned about an issue, then whether you hear a casual acquaintance talk about it, or seek your doctor's advice, you find yourself paying a lot of attention!

I'd really like to know ... Can you think of any times in the past couple of years when you would have liked guidance about a health issue or better still advice about nutrition? This might have been about, say, weaning a baby, coping with an allergy, a sudden outbreak of spotty skin.

● Did you seek advice from anyone?
● If so, who?
● Did you follow up advice?

Try and remember who you talked to about the issue. You may well find that you sounded out a number of people. Perhaps you rejected some of the advice you were offered. Taking advice instead of just hearing it is quite a complex process.

Accepting advice

Even soundly based good advice may not be acceptable to us. Many people hold beliefs and attitudes about nutrition that almost 'give them permission' to carry on as normal whatever the advice they're given. A recent British Nutrition Foundation survey on eating said:

"Most people seem to eat what they enjoy, and would only change if something drastic happened to them — and sometimes not even then."

Following are the four attitudes that they found were very widespread. Tick which of these you hold. Then look at

the beliefs that might lie behind these statements and think which of these you accept.
● It's important to have one proper meal a day.
● Eat what you like.
● Moderation in all things.
● If you feel fine your diet's OK.

It's important to have one proper meal a day. This might mean you believe:
a It's important for the children – but it doesn't matter so much for adults.
b It's an important time for the family to get together.
c 'Proper' means a cooked, hot meal.
d Snacks can't be as good for you as proper meals.

Eat what you like. This might mean you believe:
a You should eat, drink and be merry.
b Everyone's different – you can't make general rules about what's healthy or unhealthy.
c People don't have to eat foods they don't like the taste of.
d A little of what *you fancy* does you good.
e When it comes to food – variety is the spice of life.

Moderation in all things. This might mean you believe:
a No food is an absolute 'baddie' or 'goodie'.
b A *little* of what you fancy does you good.
c If I stick to this my diet's bound to be well balanced.
d Moderate portions and a moderate amount overall.
e Each food in moderation but plenty of food overall.

If you feel fine your diet's OK. This might mean you believe:
a I'm fit and full of energy so my diet must be OK.
b I'm not fat so my diet must be OK.
c As long as I've got a good appetite I'm OK.
d Stop worrying about your diet and get on with life.
e Food experts only make you worried – I ignore them.

These four commonly held attitudes will affect how we respond to dietary advice. Behind some of them are the strong beliefs about 'the old ways are the good ways'. Some of them emphasise that you should avoid worrying about your health and get on with enjoying life.

No wonder that if these attitudes are held, health education tends to fall on deaf ears! Any advice that challenges clearly held beliefs is likely to be ignored. Or if it is accepted will be found to be difficult to put it into practice. The deeply held beliefs are likely to be more powerful when it comes to everyday decisions.

When you hear new dietary advice it's important to check out whether it seems to conflict with your attitudes and beliefs. Particularly if you hear yourself saying *"Nothing you — or anyone else — can say will make me believe that . . ."* or *"I don't care what they say I still believe that . . ."*

However, if you are the kind of person who tends to say things like this you won't find what this topic has to say acceptable!

Rejecting good advice

As you will probably have thought on many occasions while reading this book it also seems to be particularly difficult to accept dietary advice:

● If you are told the diet, *on which you feel healthy,* is unhealthy. The immediate evidence of how healthy you feel – far outweighs the long-term 'invisible' threat. This, of course, is particularly true for teenagers, many of whom seem to act as though they believe they will live for ever.

● If you know individuals who have lived to a ripe old age on a so-called unhealthy diet. This anecdotal evidence outweighs cold explanations and statistics. And those who die prematurely on the same diet were unidentified or have been forgotten.

● If you don't know how to make the recommended changes or can see many obstacles to putting it into practice. Some people find such a situation very uncomfortable and may reject or forget the advice.

● If you find illness and death are very frightening. Your mind – again without you fully realising it – may keep you well away from any topic that heightens these fears.

Responding to advice

There is a common pattern in the way that people respond to something that requires them to take action. Look at the 'freeze, fight or flight' diagram below and compare your reactions with the various paths shown.

You may like to look at the diagram several times – each time thinking about a piece of advice that has come to your attention. If you can't think of several pieces of nutritional advice choose other areas of your life where you've recently received advice.

If you've tried the diagram out using several pieces of advice that you've received, perhaps you can see some pattern to your responses?

Do you tend to see yourself as powerless in the face of good advice? Or maybe you 'show willing' but tackle things in such an ineffective way you know in the back of your mind that you won't really have to do them? If either of these is the case you FREEZE.

It may well be that many people find themselves 'freezing' because in the past even their best laid 'action plans' have failed.

Maybe you dismiss advice, or never get round to doing anything at all? In other words do you take FLIGHT? If so, look back through this topic and check if anything you have learned might suggest why you find it difficult to accept good advice.

And what about FIGHT? It's true that 'nothing succeeds like success'. Making your next 'action plans' more likely to succeed is dealt with next.

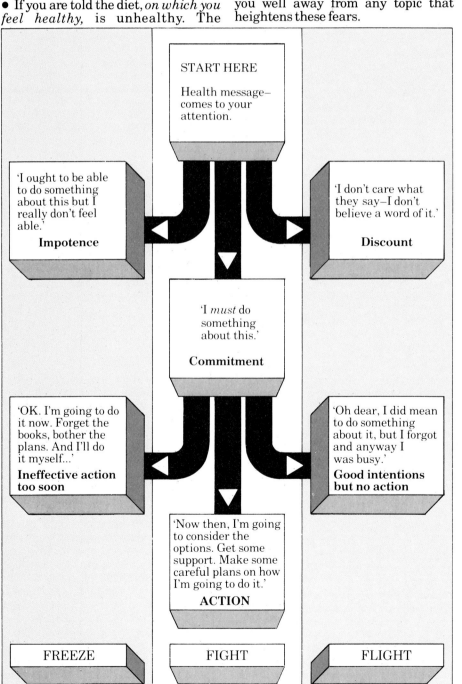

START HERE

Health message– comes to your attention.

'I ought to be able to do something about this but I really don't feel able.'

Impotence

'I don't care what they say–I don't believe a word of it.'

Discount

'I *must* do something about this.'

Commitment

'OK. I'm going to do it now. Forget the books, bother the plans. And I'll do it myself...'

Ineffective action too soon

'Oh dear, I did mean to do something about it, but I forgot and anyway I was busy.'

Good intentions but no action

'Now then, I'm going to consider the options. Get some support. Make some careful plans on how I'm going to do it.'

ACTION

FREEZE

FIGHT

FLIGHT

Reason to feel 'impotent'

Some of our testers felt 'impotent' about cutting down on fats. They didn't know how much fat they were eating or what best to cut down. There should soon be labelling that will reveal just how much fat is in such products as pies, pastries, cakes, biscuits, cheeses, sausages and meat spreads. It will then be easier to make changes.

At the moment you may also be justified in feeling 'impotent' about cutting right down on salt. You can cut down on what you add at the table or in cooking. But you will still get more than you need from manufactured foods. Fortunately, as experiences in America have shown, it can be quite easy for manufacturers to cut down on salt once they are convinced of the public demand for this. A major chain of family chemists are doing pioneer work in Britain by marketing their own brand of certain lower salt sauces, flavourings and vegetables.

Action plans

It's easy to make good resolutions. But not so easy to put them into practice. If you are to succeed you need some well thought out action plans.

The average British diet is now known to be unhealthy. So most of us have changes we should make. Some may be quite easy, others may mean changing the habits of a lifetime. However, if too many changes are too drastic then old habits will probably return before long.

Good resolutions

Have you made New Year's resolutions in the past? Which ones have you kept and which have dropped by the wayside?

Is there one resolution you make most years but can't keep up? Or have there been major resolutions that you still feel upset about not having kept? The chances are that in these cases you did have a strong motivation to make the change. But you shouldn't be labelling yourself a failure or weak willed if you haven't stuck to them. You may well not have succeeded because you did not know enough about the skills of making effective action plans.

The resolutions first to be broken may have involved major changes. After all, it's not so hard to resolve to paint the bedroom or change your appearance. A little hard work and it's done.

It's much more difficult to stop annoying habits or cut out some pleasure that you know is harmful to you. It becomes stressful ... These activities prove to be more important to you than you may have realised.

Changes seem to be most difficult to make and keep up when they:

- involve long established ways or habits
- mean giving up something pleasurable
- go against long-held or strongly-held beliefs
- don't provide immediate results and rewards
- involve inconvenience, expense or hard work
- involve other people who may not share your motivation.

If any or all these apply to changes you want to make you will need to do extra careful pre-planning. Then you can anticipate possible problems and work out strategies to cope with them.

Changing your diet

What you have read so far has probably helped you to think of the changes you need or want to make to your diet. The NACNE and COMA reports recommend cutting down on fats, sugar and salt and eating more fibre-rich foods. What does this mean for you? To remind you here is Tom's New Year's resolution list for a healthier diet. Is it over optimistic though?

Resolutions for a better diet in the New Year:
- Eat less dairy foods – cut out cream; use semi-skimmed or skimmed milk; use a polyunsaturated spread instead of butter; fry with unsaturated vegetable oil (corn or sunflower); use low-fat cheese like Brie or cottage cheese or the newer low-fat Cheddar-type cheeses.
- Cut down on fat meats, especially bacon and red meats; switch to chicken.
- Eat more fish.
- Grill instead of frying foods.
- Don't add salt to food in cooking or at the table; avoid salty foods.
- Cut down on cakes, biscuits and sweets; don't add sugar in tea.
- Eat more fibre-rich foods – wholemeal bread, rice, peas, beans, lentils, pasta, potatoes and fresh fruit and vegetables.

You may already have made some of the changes. You may still be thinking about other changes. By now, too, you'll probably also be aware of the different scales of some of the changes for you as an individual. Make a list of changes you feel you *ought* to make.

Wanting to change

You've made a list of changes you *ought* to make. Now you need to move on one step to committing yourself to making the changes. Many of us carry around in our heads a long list of 'oughts'. But if we were honest we would have to admit there is little chance of us putting them into practice. We have probably never sat down and produced a plan of action. To do so would be the sure sign that the 'I ought to' has changed to 'I will'!

To make this commitment you need to be sure of what is motivating you to

want to change. Being clear about the rewards that you expect is important.

So what sort of rewards will you expect and look for? Some diets have obvious benefits. Slimming, for example, has a visible reward. You should look better and feel more confident in your appearance. Eating more fibre-rich foods can provide dramatic relief for constipation.

Does the kind of healthy eating that you have in mind have a reward?

Our testers' motivations tended to fall into one or more of the following three categories.

Improving your chances of avoiding certain diseases and disorders. There can be no certainties: no promises of definitely avoiding developing the disease. But the recommended new healthier diet will improve your chances and make you less likely to have:

- dental decay
- bowel disorders – constipation, piles, diverticulitis, gall stones and cancer of the bowel
- coronary heart disease and strokes
- high blood pressure
- obesity – and the extra health risks that come with it.

Avoiding a premature death. Of course, some people do want to do everything possible to live as long as possible. But more of our testers emphasised that they wanted to minimise their risk of dying prematurely of a heart attack in their forties, fifties or early sixties.

Feeling more in charge of their health. Many testers mentioned that they wanted to take care of themselves. They felt more confident when they were doing all they could – in the light of present evidence – to maintain their health.

Some of our testers who had already made the changes pointed out that although these long-term rewards have been their original motivation, they soon found many shorter-term rewards that encouraged them to keep on. These included:

- Discovering the varied and real flavours of food after salt was cut down on.
- Enjoying being able to eat more fibre-rich foods which are usually bulky, without gaining weight.

On the balloons: *Eat more fibre* · *Cut down on fats* · *Eat more fish* · *Eat less dairy products* · *Don't add salt* · *Cut down on cakes* · *Don't so m...*

- Appreciating their 'treats' when they had them, at times when they didn't stick to the rules.
- Finding they didn't enjoy their old 'treats' so much, so resisting temptation was easier. They particularly mentioned losing an appetite for cream cakes after they had been on a low-fat diet.
- Discovering new 'treats'. The fruit section in large supermarkets provided most of these – mangoes, paw-paws, fresh pineapple, etc. Or venison – instead of fattier beef, pork or lamb – when eating out in expensive restaurants.
- Discovering the new diet can cost less. Once you have cut down on expensive meat and dairy products the savings soon add up.
- Enjoying the increased interest and compliments from family and friends when they prepared new dishes.
- Working out that they could still eat moderate amounts of their 'favourites' – however unwise their nutrient content – if they balanced things out over all.

You do need to anticipate and work out how to reduce the problems changing your diet may involve. But it's not helpful just to keep focussing on the problems. Be sure to make a note too of the rewards *you* anticipate as you make the changes, and the rewards you discover as you go on.

Where will you start?

Go back to the list of changes you felt you ought to make. Now you've thought about what motivates you to want to change put a star (*) beside those you want to make now. Put two stars beside the really important ones. You may have several items with stars on your list.

Next, put a tick beside those starred changes you think would be fairly easy to make and put a cross against those that would be difficult to make.

So now you've rated the changes by how motivated you are to make them and how easy or difficult it would be to make them.

Start with those that have **✔. Put these at the top of a new list headed 'Priorities list'.

Would you prefer to tackle the ** × or *✔ items next? Most of our testers preferred the ** × because they felt their motivation would carry them through the extra planning the difficult changes would involve. Now finally add, in whichever order you prefer, these remaining starred items to your 'Priorities list'.

You will now have a final list in order of priority of the changes you want to make. We suggest you start at the top and make the changes one at a time. The danger with making them all at once is that you will become confused and swamped by all these changes and soon end up saying 'to hell with it' and giving up.

With the best will in the world . . .

Take the case of Liz. She is a nutritionist and has tried to make changes to her diet which were lasting.

Liz and her husband James had been trying to eat more healthily for some time, particularly since the births of their two young children. They ate wholemeal bread and brown rice and sauces and pastry with much less fat. The children were rarely allowed sweets, but did have the occasional biscuit or cake. Then one day James suggested they cut down their salt intake as well. That day at tea time Liz was opening a jar of fish paste for the children's sandwiches when she saw on the label that not only was there salt but a number of other additives in the jar. It was the end of the day, she was tired, the children were hungry and she suddenly exploded with anger and frustration – jam was sugar, a yeast extract spread was salty, the baby couldn't chew tomato or cucumber yet, cheese was fatty, cottage cheese, ham and meat paste were salty and an egg had to be cooked – there seemed to be nothing she could easily put in the sandwiches that wasn't somehow 'unhealthy'. That day the children had jam sandwiches (and thoroughly enjoyed themselves) and in the evening James came home to a po-faced wife with a greasy pile of sausage and chips.

Liz's story illustrates several dilemmas which face her and probably many other people who cook.

- She found the responsibility of making sure her family ate well a bit much at times.
- The meals she prepared had to be liked or they wouldn't be eaten.
- She had the monotony of preparing up to four meals a day – breakfast, children's midday meal, children's tea, husband's evening meal.
- She wanted meals she could prepare quickly and with little fuss.
- She had to rely on foods that were readily available either in the store cupboard or in the shops.
- She often felt tired, so trying to think what to prepare was difficult.

So even changes which seem possible at the outset may become difficult in practice. When you are planning, especially for a lot of changes, it is not always easy to imagine just what your diet will be like. After all, you will be hoping to keep to the new diet, possibly for the rest of your life.

Maybe one of Liz's problems is that too many changes all at once just piled on the pressure. Too many steps at a time mean that there are no habits to fall back on that aren't suspect! You no sooner find a food that is low in fat than it turns out to be salty!

One of our testers pointed out that if Liz involved her husband in putting their decisions into practice by preparing some of the meals himself, this would make the changes easier to cope with. The practical involvement of all concerned in the change avoids one person becoming the scapegoat if the plan fails or proves difficult to implement. You've probably come to the conclusion yourself that changes to your eating habits involve other things. Your family, your shopping, your personal style of doing things, the way you organise your day – it's important to consider all of these even when you are thinking of making even the most *practical* of changes. Look back through this book and think about which topics you might have suggested to Liz that would help her on this very difficult day.

Making a plan

Hold off! Don't start the change tomorrow. If you want to make a change that will stand you in good stead for the rest of your life you need to do your homework first. For any one change you may need to work through this list of questions:

- What do I need to find out?
- Who do I need to discuss it with?
- How can I break the change down into small steps?
- What might be the pitfalls?
- How will I know if I've succeeded?

In order to be able to answer the last question, it should be the first one you think about.

The worked example in the next section is how Tom planned to cut down on salt. But you will need to work out how this applies – in your circumstances – to the changes you want to make.

Checking you've succeeded

'Cut down on . . .' or 'Eat more of . . .' is too vague. What could you measure that will give you a check on how well you are progressing? And how much will be enough – what is your target?

Tom decided he might keep a count of how often he added salt to his meals. Maybe he could aim to give added salt up completely.

He reviewed his present diet and decided to cut down on certain salty foods. He had bacon three times a week, pickles whenever he had cold meat or cheese, and crisps or salted peanuts when he watched TV or went to a pub. He could keep a record of whenever he ate these to keep a check on how well he was doing.

Getting going? Tom started by looking at the labels on the food already in his store cupboards. Then he had a good look at the alternative brands available in the shops. For example, he found that the food section of one large chemist had a range of low-salt sauces – so that would make one of his changes easier. He also found his pub stocked unsalted raisins and nuts.

For your change do you need to do the following:
- Find out more about the medical evidence for the nutritional advice? This would help you be more committed to making the change.
- Read the labels more carefully on the foods you buy?
- Survey your local shops to find out what choices you have?

Other people

Will your changes affect any one other than just yourself? If so what are their reactions likely to be? Will they need to change their own habits or their attitudes to you in any way? For example, might they regard you as cranky? Will you need to convince them that you are serious?

Negotiation. If you also want to get other people to make the change involve them, and get their acceptance, as soon as possible. They will

Step 1. *Start Jan 6th*
Add less salt at table
Make a note each time I add salt. Keep my own salt cellar and weigh it each Sunday to see how much I've used. Ask the family to tell me if I'm adding salt heavily or without noticing.

need help and encouragement too if they are to share the courage of your convictions. How can you explain changes in terms that they will understand? After all, if you need motivation and rewards to stick to changes think of the encouragement that they will need. For instance, an elderly relative may be more co-operative if the benefits of a high-fibre diet for constipation are spelt out.

Tom's wife, Jill, didn't feel she would benefit from cutting down on salt. She wasn't too keen on cutting down on the salt she added during cooking. So, to begin with, Tom decided to concentrate on the easier changes of cutting down on what he added at the table and on salty sauces, pickles and snacks. After a while Jill offered a compromise – if he would cook more of the meals they would cut down on the salt added during the cooking. Provided, too, that he didn't nag if she topped up the salt in her portions at the table.

Sounds trivial? Far from it – it's these everyday negotiations that need attention, and pay dividends!

Sabotage? Might anyone in your circle 'sabotage' your good intentions? How can you challenge this?

"I know you're cutting down on salty food but we'll have to have a Chinese takeaway (most dishes are salty) because ... it's too late to start cooking, ... I'm tired, ... there's nothing in the house." (Tom's wife.)
"We always have kippers when you come home for Saturday tea." (Tom's mother.)
"I've bought you salt and vinegar crisps — that's OK isn't it?" (Friend at pub.)
"These bacon pieces were much cheaper than chicken joints so ..." (Tom's wife.)

When planning your change. Take time to think of as many examples as possible – however trivial or way out – of situations you may have to face. Having predicted as many as possible, plan *now* how you would handle each of them. By the time the situations arise it's often too late to do much about them. But if you plan ahead you should be able to work out how to avoid hurting other people's feelings, or ending up with nothing to eat.

Tom realised he had to explain to his mother exactly why he wanted to cut down on salt. He also reminded her, well in advance, that he'd rather have fresh herrings or mackerel at Saturday tea times.

He and Jill spent some time working out what ingredients to keep handy for cheap, less salty meals – so that Tom could take his share in cooking. For example, chilli con carne can be prepared quickly using a tin of kidney beans. And the chilli pepper and herbs give a good flavour even if no salt is added. Tom agreed to pick up a Tandoori grilled chicken from an Indian takeaway on his way home when they were really stuck.

When his friends assumed he would eat salty snacks he decided to learn to say, *"No thanks, I've cut down on salt,"* – in a non-aggressive way!

Step 3. *Start Jan 20th*
Cut down on bacon
Only eat bacon once a week instead of three or four times. Keep a note of what I choose to eat instead. Decide this in advance: baked beans on toast? *But* watch the fat eg. sausages.

Support. It isn't all problems. You'll often be able to get support. Perhaps someone close to you, who also cares about your health, will give you moral support – even if they don't want to make the change themselves. Also you may find others who do want to make the same change. You might share shopping and cooking to save time and money. And exchange practical tips and information as well as moral support.

One of Tom's workmates kept him supplied with homemade chutney with much less salt in it. Tom stocked up with a wholesale pack of mixed nuts and dried fruits from a wholefood store which he took to work and shared out with his mates.

Small, measurable steps

This way you don't get swamped. And succeeding with each small step is a short-term reward in itself. You'll gain confidence and keep up your motivation this way.

Here's where you start thinking about measuring or counting how much and how often you eat certain foods.

Incidentally it's much more easy to encourage people to eat more rather than less food! So if you are making cutting down changes try to make definite decisions as to what you will eat instead. For example, if you want to cut down on beef or lamb you will need to count how often you eat it. But also keep a record of the number of times you eat chicken, fish or a bean (pulse) based dish instead.

Checking up on success

Your records which show you can actually measure how well you have succeeded are, in themselves, a rewarding encouragement to keep on with the changes.

A part of Tom's step-by-step plan and record are shown here. Each Friday he decided the next step he would add to the changes in his diet. Then on the Saturday he could buy anything special he needed. On Sundays he began to put the new step into practice. Once he had got going he also reviewed on Sundays how he'd got on with the new step and whether he wanted to alter his plans. He checked, too, to see if some of the earlier steps were now a matter of habit to him and didn't need watching anymore.

How could you adapt this type of plan to provide a check on how well you are succeeding with your changes?

Incidentally, when a whole family is making changes, taking turns to choose what the new step will be helps to keep up motivation.

Step 2. *Start Jan 13th*
Switch to fruit and nut snacks
Note how many times I've chosen fruit and nuts instead of salty snacks like peanuts or crisps. Visit wholefood shop to stock up. Ask at pub.

Review Step 2
It's going quite well, but I think I'm eating too many nuts!

Review Step 1
I seem to need a lot of reminding – but it's going well. I can't seem to face a boiled egg without salt.

Review Step 1
I've actually started to notice how salty meals can be. I salted something by mistake and it tasted awful.

Putting it into practice

Most people do at least some cooking. And many people regularly have to cook for others. Do you need to review your approach to preparing meals?

It can be quite a challenge to the cook to have to prepare meals that match up to the new, healthier diet. Preparing the new meals may seem more time-consuming or difficult. But this is likely to be because you're used to your old ways and don't have to give them much thought. You may be almost an 'automatic cook'!

But you may find this challenge adds new interest to your cooking. This topic suggests three strategies you might explore:

- re-organise your kitchen
- choose new dishes
- learn how to adapt recipes.

Re-organise your kitchen

On your new diet you will probably be storing and preparing more vegetables and fruit, and dried goods such as rice, beans and pasta. You'll be trying to avoid frying, or at least keeping the fat used to a minimum. And probably doing more steaming. You may be experimenting with new recipes too.

To make all this easier check through the following list and tick all those which you haven't got but would like.

Sharp vegetable knife that feels good in the hand. ☐

Knife sharpener – sharp knives are quicker and safer than blunt ones. ☐

Stiff brush for cleaning potatoes and carrots. ☐

Big chopping board. ☐

New vegetable racks – preferably in a cool place. ☐

More storage jars for pulses, rice, dried fruit and nuts. ☐

Pressure cooker – speeds things up, especially cooking dried pulses. ☐

Vegetable steamer – perhaps with dividers for cooking several vegetables at once. ☐

Wok – for quick stir-frying using a minimum of fat. ☐

Non-stick frying pan with lid – for dry frying – food cooks in its' own juice. ☐

Roasting rack – to hold meat above dish – so fat drips off. ☐

Special bin for vegetable waste to put on compost heap, if you have a garden. ☐

Plastic recipe stand – if you're trying new dishes. ☐

Pinboard on kitchen wall – for pictures of new foods, recipes, commitment statements, contracts you've made with yourself, jokes, cartoons. ☐

Weighing scales. ☐

Measuring cups and jug. ☐

Liquidiser – particularly useful when making vegetable soups. ☐

Food processor – for rapid chopping, grating and mincing. ☐

Good value? Some of our testers were adamant that one good, sharp knife was all they needed. Others sang the praises of their food processors. Don't rush into buying expensive items if you know they don't suit your style of cooking. Will they save you time – or do they take time to assemble and clean? Will you use them once or twice and then will they be unused but occupy valuable storage space? You may not find that you need to weigh and measure for recipes once you've 'got your eye in'. But at the start, weighing and measuring might, among other things, make you feel that you're really getting down to tackling the job.

You'll need weighing scales, too, if you are weighing and measuring as part of keeping a record of the changes you are making in your diet.

Ready to hand? When you've got hold of the tools you want, keep them at hand – near enough to see and use easily. Putting something at the back of a cupboard or on a high shelf will not encourage you to use it.

Storing food in a hot, possibly steamy, kitchen can be a problem. Provided they are in airtight containers dried foods will be fine. But watch out for and discard any food that becomes mouldy. Bread easily becomes mouldy. So too do breakfast cereals if they are left open – particularly 'natural' products with no added preservatives. Low-sugar jams and low-salt chutneys should be kept in the fridge once opened – high levels of sugar and salt prevent the growth of moulds. Dried pulses can also become mouldy easily if steam gets to them.

Fresh fruits and vegetables are bulky. You may not be able to keep these readily to hand as they need a well-ventilated, cool storage place. They may have to be kept outside or in an outdoor shed if you need to store more than you will use in one or two days. Small amounts can be kept in the bottom section of the fridge. In the long run you will probably get better value for money if you can start off with top quality fruit and vegetables.

Choose new dishes

A British Nutrition Foundation survey in 1982 showed that in most households the same old meals were eaten week after week. Cooks felt bad about this but unable to change because of budgets, fixed habits and general lack of interest on the part of other eaters.

If you and those for whom you cook like to stick with the old favourites then you may wish to skip this section! However, it does seem that most cooks at least dream of preparing new dishes! With the promised health benefits in mind you may now be more motivated to try them out. And if it's your family who hold back, you may be able to get them interested by involving them more in choosing and preparing the dishes.

Finding new recipes

Our testers said they were most likely to give up on their new resolutions when they ran out of ideas of what to serve. If this is a problem for you here are some ideas:

● You could get hold of some new cookery books. You may be able to borrow them from a friend or the library to see if you like them.
Look out for those that claim their recipes match up to the new low-fat, high-fibre targets. Or, for example, those on cooking for a healthy heart. Vegetarian cookery books are good – provided the recipes don't use a lot of cream cheese and eggs. Have a look, too, at Mediterranean cookery. Many of these recipes use vegetable oils instead of butter or lard. And the quantity of oil can often be cut down.
● Collect recipes from magazines and newspapers so that you build up a range of recipes. Keep any particularly enticing ones pinned up in the kitchen until you've a chance to try them. Check them over when making your shopping list in case they have ingredients you need to buy specially.
● Consider enrolling at a cookery class. A basic one if you're not sure of skills. Or any type that's in line with the new guidelines for healthy eating. Our testers found several on 'high-fibre cookery', an 'Indian vegetarian course' and 'Japanese cookery for beginners'.

Trying new dishes

Which of these strategies appeal to you?

● **Try a foreign food night.** Eat out or fetch a takeaway meal. Or ask your friends for recipes they have tried.

● **Serve food the Chinese way.** Several small dishes – including some new ones – from which people can help themselves.

● **Prepare the new dish together.** When you know most of the family will be together, agree in advance to prepare and eat a new dish. Or invite one or two friends around to do this.

● **Share the entertaining.** If you're entertaining close friends suggest each person brings a part of the meal in line with healthy eating. You could divide the labour in the same way if you've got a large family. Or take it in turns to prepare a new, healthier dish.

Adapting recipes

Recipes aren't sacred. Try inventing new recipes or adapting old ones.

Old family favourites may be able to be adapted to make them more healthy. Basic cookery processes can be changed slightly so that they don't involve frying or so much fat, white flour or sugar or salt.

Check list for change

When you are working out how to adapt recipes bear in mind the following possibilities:

● Can you substitute wholemeal flour for some or all of the white flour?
● Can you substitute polyunsaturated margarine or oils for the butter, lard or suet?
● Can you halve the amount of sugar? Could you substitute dried fruit to provide sweetness?
● Does it still taste OK with little or no salt? Could you substitute herbs or spices to improve flavour?
● If you make your own bread, experiment to see how little salt you need. You may find you also need to use less yeast.
● Can you use semi-skimmed or skimmed milk instead of whole milk?
● Can you add single cream, or full or low fat yoghurts, instead of double cream?
● Can you grill rather than fry at certain stages?
● Can you leave out the 'browning in fat' stage?
● Can you cool a meat dish at some stage so you can drain off the fat?
● Have you tried thickening sauces in casseroles by adding pureed or mashed potatoes, or carrots?
● Have you tried thickening sauces and gravy with cornflour instead of starting with flour and fat? (Mix the cornflour with a little cold water, add to the hot sauce or gravy and bring to the boil.)
● Can you substitute root vegetables or pulses for some of the meat in casseroles, pies and stews?

Food	Easy to prepare	Changes to make the new dish 'healthier'
Chicken casserole	Yes	Can make it lower in fat by removing skin. Could use less chicken but add a tin of butter beans.
Shepherd's pie	Yes	Try draining off all the fat after the first stage of browning the mince. Try minced chicken and vegetables.
Fried egg and bacon	Yes	Grill bacon and scramble eggs. Have one or the other plus baked beans or grilled tomatoes.
Roast beef, Yorkshire pudding and roast potatoes and carrots	Not particularly	Roast meat on rack. Trim off fat when carving. Have jacket potatoes. Leave out Yorkshire pudding. Have a second green vegetable.

Family favourites

You'll already have thought about how you view recipes in *'Selling a dream'* and you've looked at how to sort out the health features of various dishes in *'Other cultures, other cuisines'*. Try applying the same critical eye to everyday favourites.

Think of four dishes you *really* enjoy – do this with other household members if you don't live alone. Go through the list and make a chart like the one on the previous page. Note whether each dish is easy to prepare, and whether by cooking it you'll be in line with the new guidelines for healthy eating. Consider whether there are any changes you could make to reduce the amount of fat, sugar and salt or increase the fibre.

Once you've practiced adapting old favourites in this way try getting into the habit of questioning each recipe you use. When you see new recipes ask yourself if you could have worked out a healthier recipe than the one the 'cookery expert' has given. You will very often find you can! And if you *can*, then do it.

Same function: different ingredient

We tend to put butter on toast because of the taste. To many people margarine doesn't taste as good. In sandwiches, however, the butter is there as a lubricant – to make the bread easier to swallow; as a waterproofer – to stop the bread becoming soggy, and as a glue – to help the filling and the bread stick together. In a sandwich the taste of the butter is less important and skimmed milk cheese or chopped tomato or chutney can equally well perform the other functions. It's useful to think of the *function* a food has for you before looking for a substitute. Some other changes, bearing the function of the ingredient in mind, are shown in the chart, below.

Start	Function	Small change	Big change
Butter	When used as a spread, rather than for its taste	Polyunsaturated margarine	Low fat, skimmed milk cheese spread
Cream (single 21% fat, double 48% fat, whipped 35% fat)	To decorate, make food easier to swallow, and give a mellow taste	Custard (4% fat) Whole milk yoghurt (4.5% fat) Ice cream (6% fat) Cream mixed with yoghurt	Low fat yoghurt (1% fat) Custard made with skimmed milk (1% fat)
Cream cheese (47% fat)	To give creamy texture in some recipes	Cheese spread (23% fat)	Cottage or skimmed milk cheese (0-4% fat) Low fat soft cheese 'Shape' (8% fat)
Whole milk	As a drink, or a liquid in sauces and other recipes	Fresh semi skimmed milk	Fresh skimmed milk
Cheddar cheese (33% fat)	To provide flavour in recipes.	Camembert Edam Processed (23% fat)	Low fat hard cheese 'Shape' (16.5% fat)
Mayonnaise (79% fat)	To make food easier to swallow and extra flavour	⅓ mayonnaise ⅔ plain yoghurt	Yoghurt with garlic or lemon and chives (1-2% fat)
Stewed beef	Main protein providing ingredient in stew, casseroles and pies	⅔ beef ⅓ beans	⅓ beef, ⅓ beans, ⅓ root vegetables plus hunk of bread
Lard or dripping	For frying to seal in flavour, make food look attractive and easy to swallow	Polyunsaturated vegetable oil (eg., corn oil or sunflower oil)	Simmer vegetables or meat in stock and add a dash of oil to the cooking liquor if necessary
Luncheon meat (27% fat)	Ready cooked, easy to serve	Corned beef (12% fat)	Ready cooked chicken with skin removed (4-7% fat)
Sausage roll (36% fat) Pork pie (27% fat)	Easy to hold, ready cooked and filling	Cornish pasty (21% fat)	Pizza (11.5% fat) Beefburger in a bun (10% fat)

Catering for the masses

Cooking healthy meals for family and friends can be quite a challenge. Imagine then what it's like trying to provide a healthy diet for hundreds of people each day!

Nutritional needs may not take top priority when it comes to cooking for very large numbers day in and day out.

We all eat institutional food at some time in our lives – for example, in the works' canteen, in hospital, at school, at a conference, at college or in the armed forces. Standards are often below what nutritionists recommend for health. When we only eat one meal a day in an institution it may not be a problem because we can restore the balance by what we eat at other meals. Even so, if it is the main meal of the day, and it's difficult or we're not inclined to pay special attention to our other meals we can easily end up with a high fat and sugar and low-fibre diet.

Two vulnerable groups of people are hospital patients and school children. One in five of us will spend some time in a hospital during our lifetime. And we all go to school! School children, above all, should be set the example of a healthy diet.

What are the meals like?

Schooldays. You've almost certainly had experience of mass catering at an early age. What were your school dinners like? Try talking to a friend, or your partner, or children, or a school teacher about school dinners. Most people are quite emotional about this subject... the foods you loved, the foods you hated, the way the food was dished out, leftovers, table monitors, custard, gristle and sago pudding!

You may even have had off-putting names for certain dishes. How about these for sago pudding? – Fishes' eyes, frogs' eyes, fishes' eyes in glue, frog spawn, wallpaper paste, baby food, snot goggles and bogey occy.

However, despite the names, several of our older testers enjoyed their school food. It was more often the queueing, pushing and shoving, limited choice and messy tables that put them off their dinners.

Recent experiences. Now you've remembered school meals which are institutional eating in their full glory think about the extent to which people you know eat in institutions.

Choose three people from family and close friends. Jot down the extent to which they eat institutional meals if you know. If you don't know, ask them... Is it daily, occasionally, or do they do things like go to conferences for the short periods of time they have institutional meals? Ask them if they have ever lived full time in an institution.

There are many varying experiences. Ask the three people you've chosen which of their institutional eating experiences they've enjoyed and which they've hated, and why. The answers, of course, won't necessarily be based on health grounds!

Here are some examples from our testers:

Conference catering (hotels, universities, colleges) – *"My husband attends conferences and courses and is* usually served three large meals per day. After three to five days of this excess eating it takes a couple of days of lighter meals for him to recover. However, he usually enjoys the food."

A maternity hospital – "As I'm vegetarian I couldn't find enough dishes to choose. I was always hungry. But the other women were hungry too. Their husbands used to bring them in Kentucky Chicken and pizzas in the evenings."

At college – "It was always an exciting part of the day, wondering who would be there, whether you'd get to sit next to someone interesting, or whether you'd be cornered by a real bore."

Hospital – "The meals were old and tired. They'd been overcooked in the first place and then kept warm for ages. One morning I heard one of the nurses say — 'Don't go asking them all if they want eggs — there won't be any for us'"!

Why are they like that?

What are the reasons that you think lie behind good and bad institutional meals that you have eaten? For example, do you think caterers were unimaginative, costings were too low, equipment old fashioned or the service was bad because of poor staffing?

Consumers' needs and wishes

There may be a conflict here. Do you give people what is nutritionally good for them? Or do you give priority to providing what you are sure they will eat?

Some institutions still prepare a 'no choice' meal assuming that everyone will be hungry enough or suitably grateful and eat it all up. Some hospitals are providing a diet that matches up to the new recommendations for healthy eating and which also allows some choice.

The institutions' responsibilities

What do institutions see as their responsibility with regard to food? To whom does their responsibility lie – consumers, staff, pay masters, higher authorities? Do they see their roles as to feed consumers healthily, to dictate choice, to offer choice, to pander to unhealthy tastes . . .?

The school meals service is an excellent case study for this question.

It had its origins before the First World War in the need to provide meals for undernourished children. During the Second World War it expanded to supplement the austere diet of individual food rations. It was further developed in the post-war period as part of family welfare provision. During these times the school meals service was subsidised. And the emphasis was on sound nutrition.

Recently policies have changed. Now it has to pay its own way. It can't afford to provide food that will be wasted. Today with a cost-conscious cafeteria system chips are top of the bill. Most of the customers are satisfied, but the items of food are often fatty, sugary or salty.

Very few schools offer nutritional guidance as to what to choose. However, the hospitals adopting new food policies may do so. For example, in a hospital in Hackney, menus say on them that wholemeal bread is provided because it is better for health. Sugar and white bread is also provided, but patients are told they should ask for it if they require it.

In Stockport, hospitals hand out a leaflet explaining their menus, for patients and staff alike, which give people a chance to choose what they like. It says – "So we're inviting you to try some of the more healthy foods included on our menus. You may be able to use some of the ideas later when you go home." It goes on to explain how and why they have modified their menus.

Caterer's knowledge and skills

Knowing about nutrition is only part of the job. We asked an NHS mental hospital caterer what he did. And here is the list he made out:

● Survey patients' needs via staff surveys.
● Survey staff needs re serving, quantities, etc.
● Draw up 'balanced diet' offering variation and choice.
● Relate this to cost limits.
● Produce menus.
● Transfer these on to three week 'order blocks'.
● Oversee contracts for food suppliers.
● Ensure food delivered on time.
● Oversee kitchen in all its aspects.
● Ensure time between cooking and serving as short as possible.

Surprising he had any time to devote to nutrition at all! In any case, cater-

ers who've learned old fashioned views may use them when they draw up menus. Afterall, the most up-to-date nutritional views are not necessarily always taught in the training of caterers. Caterers need to be kept up-to-date and this is one of the things the individual consumer, local health authorities and the Health Education Service can take initiatives about.

Costs

The issue of costs seems to be in the fore front of everyone's minds and some caterers would claim that you can't keep costs down – let alone make savings – if you are to provide nutritionally sound meals.

This has been proved not to be true. Hospital costing is often scrutinised to check its cost effectiveness. Stockport, for example, has facts and figures to prove the savings it has made. A saving of £11,000 in a year was made in one hospital just by switching from whole milk to semi-skimmed milk. In 1983/84, the first full year following implementation of the new food policy in this hospital, a 15% reduction in spending was achieved, – a total saving of £67,000. And this was despite them offering a wider choice of food to patients!

What food is available

Since labour costs are high many institutions prefer to buy in partially prepared or pre-cooked food. Their choice will be limited and they may have little say over the nutritional content of the recipe.

For instance, one national supermarket chain sells semi-prepared dough for caterers to make into bread. One caterer asked for semi-prepared wholemeal dough. The chain did oblige but it took them six weeks to adjust their system to be able to cope with this new demand.

However, those responsible for institutional catering are in big business and do have buying power. As an increasing number of health authorities have begun to show, institutional caterers can demand certain nutritional standards from those who tender for their contracts.

How it's prepared

Cooking in bulk can be difficult. Vegetables can easily be overcooked and soggy. Fried food – which can't be done in huge batches may sit around soaking up fat.

And, where the customers don't come to a canteen near the kitchen, distributing the food can be difficult.

In large hospitals a food train, of heated cabinets, may set out from the kitchen up to an hour before the meals will reach the patients in their beds.

Where there is a choice, dishes not chosen may need storing and re-using in different meals on the next day.

How it's served

How food is served is important. Food talks! Sometimes it says 'this meal is here simply to fill you up.' Sometimes it says, 'I'm offering this meal to you because I care for you.' Such messages come across in several ways.

What does the way the food is served tell you? What do you like or dislike about:

● a self-service cafeteria?
● queueing at a hatch?
● one person serves and hands out to a small group?
● food put on plates in a kitchen and then distributed by servers?

What about where the food is served? Do you enjoy your meal in a loud, noisy and crowded room? Or is it important to you that the room should be peaceful, quiet and well-lit? The atmosphere of the room is important. But how food is cleared away is important too. Does everyone reach the same stage in the meal at the same time, or are other peoples' leftovers being scraped into slop buckets as you start on your soup? Do you have to move ash trays or a shredded paper cup off the table to put your meal on it? No wonder, it sometimes takes a strong stomach to eat institutional food.

Next time . . .

If and when you next have to eat institutional food, review the experience by checking through the following questions. You might like to think about how you would describe your experience in a letter to a friend, or if you were interviewed for local radio.

If you were eating in a hospital your local community health council would like to hear of your experiences – try to cover the good as well as the unsatisfactory points.

Remember, don't just think about the food in terms of how good it is nutritionally – think about the whole experience.

● Was the food nutritious?
● Was it attractive?
● Was there variety?
● Was there enough?
● Was there a choice?
● Was the food hot (if it was supposed to be), cold or what?
● If there was a menu, was it truthful?

● Was the service good or bad?
● How long did it take you to get your food?
● Was the atmosphere where you ate pleasant/unpleasant?
● Did anything put you off your food?

Making the best of it.
● Make the best of what's on offer with sensible choices.
● If you are in hospital – operations and lying in bed can make your bowels less effective – you're more likely to become constipated. So find out if medical advice permits you extra fibre. Then see if the nursing and catering staff can supplement the fibre in your hospital diet. If not, and if it's OK to have more fibre, consider having some wholemeal bread and fruit brought in.
● If you're at a conference or in a refectory don't overeat just because you've paid for it. Keep your normal eating patterns very much in mind.
● Make requests and complaints, not just about the food itself, but consider service, environments, atmosphere. If you have to complain, use your own good experiences, or examples of food practice you've heard of, to make positive suggestions as to what you would like to have.

An official 'health and food policy'

Some health authorities have an official food policy that is undoubtedly an example of good practice. Find out from your local community health council if your local health authority has a healthy eating policy. If there is such a policy they will let you see a copy of it. If not you might like to ask for a copy of the one from Stockport health authority or from other progressive authorities.

This policy commits the health authority to pursuing a wide range of changes throughout their community. It includes reviewing and improving the food served in institutional settings. It calls for collaboration between widely separated workers, cooks, catering managers, nurses, teachers, health education officers, dieticians, clinicians and so on.

They base their policy on essentially the same nutritional advice that is given in the NACNE and COMA reports which set out the new guidelines for healthy eating. Often there's material developed to help people pursue these policies. Maybe you can introduce it at your institution.

'Food and health policy': Stockport health authority. Here is an extract from this policy's summary of recommendations.

The implementation of such a 'food policy' involves careful planning and evaluation. After all the principles are easy to follow. More difficult is the detail ie., day-to-day meals in institutions. All health authorities are short of money and have to give careful account of how effectively they use it. In some cases – as in the Stockport hospital quoted earlier – financial savings can be made at the same time. With Stockport's overall food policy they intend to measure the policy's progress in terms of:

- improvements in the population's knowledge about diet and health
- changes in the community's purchasing and food preparation habits
- co-operation from the food and catering industry
- a reduction of the diseases associated with diet, *over a period of time.*

Hospital meals

Most health authorities with a 'food policy' begin by putting it into practice on their home patch. They review what they serve to patients and staff in their own hospitals.

Ideally, they should end up offering a choice of food that encourages a healthy choice. After all, no one has the 'right' or 'responsibility' to force people to eat healthy food! Indeed some would argue that when you're ill in hospital, and everything in your life seems to be changing, you need the comfort of familiar food. However – and again Stockport is quoted – most

patients have been shown to welcome the chance to try out new, healthier dishes.

What would you choose? Below is an example of a menu from one hospital which has adopted a new food policy. In many hospitals today patients can choose in advance what they want to eat. And if they wish can get advice as to what to choose. What would *you* choose from the sample menu? What would be your reasons for your choice? What would you want more advice about? Would the menu enable you to have a healthy diet?

A national food policy?

Ideally, the government should take the lead directly in developing a national food policy. Instead they are encouraging local health authorities to devise their own policies. This, of course, leads to a very patchy response across the nation.

You may be lucky but if your health authority doesn't have a formal 'food policy' you should consider making your opinion heard through a local interest group. Community health councils, College of Health groups, Women's Institute, the National Housewives' Register, Parent-teacher associations – and many others – are playing a part in asking for better provision for helping people make healthy food choices. Encourage your local groups to make their opinions and needs known to community dieticians and the community physicians.

AFFIX	NAME
DIET LABEL	
HERE	
	WARD

PLEASE TICK APPROPRIATE BOX
Select only ONE item from each Section

1	
2	Clear soup
3	Tomato soup
4	Grilled fillet of fish
5	Poached fish in parsley sauce
6	Brisket of beef salad
7	Cottage pie
8	Chipped potatoes
9	Creamed potatoes
10	
11	Peas – marrowfat
12	Mixed veg
13	Tapioca pudding
14	Ice cream
15	Fresh fruit
16	Creme caramel
17	Cheese & biscuits
18	
19	
20	

AFFIX	NAME
DIET LABEL	
HERE	
	WARD

PLEASE TICK APPROPRIATE BOX
Select only ONE item from each Section

1	Boiled gammon
2	Spaghetti bolognaise
3	Meat salad
4	Egg & cress sandwich (white)
5	Egg & cress sandwich (wholemeal)
6	Creamed potatoes
7	
8	Ice cream
9	Jam sponge sandwich
10	Blancmange
11	
12	
13	White bread
14	Wholemeal bread
15	Polyunsaturated margarine
16	Butter
17	
	SOFT MEAL
18	Spaghetti bolognaise
20	

AFFIX	NAME
DIET LABEL	
HERE	
	WARD

PLEASE TICK APPROPRIATE BOX
Select only ONE item from each Section, making sure you choose either a Continental OR a Cooked Breakfast – NOT both.

1	Fruit juice
2	Porridge
3	Branflakes
4	Cornflakes
5	Scrambled egg
6	
7	
8	Tomatoes
9	Baked beans
10	OR **CONTINENTAL BREAKFAST**
	Wholemeal roll, butter, marmalade
11	White bread
12	Wholemeal bread
13	Polyunsaturated margarine
14	Butter
15	Marmalade
	SOFT MEAL ONLY
16	Scrambled egg

Read on

This guide lists books and organisations that you may find useful having worked through the topics in Patterns of Eating.

Useful books

Several of the following books have been mentioned in specific chapters and will provide additional reading for that part of the book. However, the books in this list will give a useful context for the whole of *Patterns of Eating*. Thinking about just one aspect of food will inevitably lead you onto many other food issues – it's a bit like eating from a buffet table, one thing leads to another!

Whatever you choose to browse through will most likely reflect a particular area of interest for you, or your need for further information. Remember also to look at the book references given by authors of books you follow up from this list – these books will most likely be relevant too.

- **Bombers and mash – The domestic front 1939-45.** Raynes Minns (1980). *Virago.*
The Second World War crops up time and time again in material about food trends in Britain. (See *'A different diet'*).
- **Diet 2000.** Dr Alan Maryon-Davis with Jane Thomas (1984). *Pan.*
'Putting it into practice' is helped by practical information presented in a very unthreatening way. (See *'A different pattern'*).
- **Dieting makes you fat.** Geoffrey Cannon and Hetty Einzig (1983). *Century.*
A paperback version is also available (1984). *Sphere.*
This book discusses popular, current theories about body weight. (See *'A different diet'*).
- **Fat is a feminist issue** and **Fat is a feminist issue 2.** Susie Orbach (1979 and 1984). *Hamlyn paperbacks.*
Examines social and psychological aspects of body image and weight control. Second book has detailed suggestions on how to overcome such personal problems. (See *'A different diet'*).
- **Food for beginners.** Susan George and Nigel Paige (1982). *Writers and Readers Publishing.*
When people think about the moral implications of food they tend to have some very strongly held views. Reading other people's views, with which you may not agree, is part of developing your own. (See *'Shopping for food'*).
- **Glutton for punishment.** Louise Roche (1984). *Pan.*
This book gives a personal account of a serious disordered eating pattern. (See *'A different diet'*).

- **I'm OK, you're OK.** Thomas Harris (1973). *Pan.*
An introduction to transactional analysis. (See *'The meaning of meals'*).
- **E for additives.** Maurice Hanssen with Jill Marsden (1984). *Thorsons.*
A comprehensive guide to additives in food – their use and potential adverse effects. (See *'Shopping for food'*).
- **The good health guide.** From the Open University short course 'Health choices' (1980). *Harper and Row.*
When you are thinking about a healthy diet it is also useful to consider other aspects of health, such as drinking, smoking, getting fit, work and health, stress and emotions. (Mainly *'A different diet'* and *'A different pattern'*, but is useful for any further action plants.)
- **The making of the modern British diet.** Derek Oddy and Derek Miller (1976). *Croom Helm.*
Clearly the national history of our diet is significant when it comes to what we eat now. (See *'A different diet'*).

On the book shelves. You will find a vast range of cookery books, which are too numerous to mention, that give useful reading for *The meaning of meals'* and *'Organising meals'*. Don't forget to look out for cookery books of different cultures.

Going through a variety of recipes will help you to get a better idea about how you view meals and snacks in our culture. This will provide you with a springboard on how you view your own eating.

Don't swamp yourself with reading cookery books! It's important that you enjoy them but also that you look at them critically. *The meaning of meals'* and *'Organising meals'* should help you to view cookery books with a critical eye.

Local resources

- If you are not a regular visitor to your library you may be pleasantly surprised to see exhibitions, displays of the work of local organisations, comprehensive arrays of useful pamphlets and lists of addresses of sources of help and information.
- Find out what's available from your local community workshop if you have one. Local writers' groups often produce pamphlets on the history of the local area – frequently this will include domestic arrangements and eating patterns. Such additional literature, together with books from your library, will increase your awareness of 'patterns of eating'.

Helpful organisations

- **The Health Education Council (HEC)**
78 New Oxford Street
London W1A 1AH
- **The Scottish Health Education Group (SHEG)**
Woodburn House
Canaan Lane
Edinburgh EH10 4SG
- **The Consumers' Association**
14 Buckingham Street
London WC2N 6DS
The HEC and SHEG publish a range of leaflets, booklets, charts and posters associated with health, some of which are free. Write to them for their publication list.
- **The Vegetarian Society**
53 Marloes Road
Kensington
London W8 6LA
- **The Vegan Society Ltd.**
47 Highlands Road
Leatherhead
Surrey
- **Anorexic Aid**
11 Priory Centre
High Wycombe
Bucks
Anorexic Aid offers help and advice for both anorexia nervosa and bulimia nervosa. Look out for any self-help groups in your area (you could start by asking at your local library, community or health centre).

Reports and surveys

- **NACNE Report** (Sept 1983). A discussion paper on nutritional guidelines for health education in Britain. Prepared for the National Advisory Committee on Nutrition Education by an ad hoc working party under the chairmanship of Professor W P T James. Available free from the Health Education Council.
- **COMA Report – Diet and Cardio-vascular Disease** (1984). Committee on Medical Aspects of Food Policy. Department of Health and Social Security (DHSS), Report on Health and Social Subjects. No. 28, HMSO.
- **Eating in the early 1980s** – attitudes and behaviour: main findings January 1984. Prepared for the British Nutrition Foundation by MRB International Ltd, London.

Picture credits

Anthony Blake Photo Library: pp 155, 185.
Marion Blight: pp 78, 79.
Gerard Browne: pp 5, 27, 40, 43, 59, 75, 122/3.
Mel Calman: p 16.
Colour Library International: p 134.
The Coronary Prevention Group: p 17.
Ken Cox: pp 26, 64/5, 166.
Richard Downer: pp 156/7.
Farmers' Weekly: p 168.
Chris Forsey: p 140.
John Fraser: pp 100, 102, 104, 176, 181.
Richard & Sally Greenhills: pp 22, 35.
Hulton Picture Library: p 101.
John Ireland: pp 12/3, 51, 62, 80, 130, 162, 188.
Keystone: p 106.
Simon McBride: p 187.
John Melville: pp 7, 11, 33, 36, 37, 38, 56/7, 58, 60/1, 67, 72, 73,
      74, 76, 81, 83, 97, 99, 103, 109, 110, 112, 119, 120, 121, 129,
      135, 138, 139, 142, 143, 146, 149, 159, 160/1, 165, 175, 182.
Elaine Mills: pp 69, 136/7, 150, 151.
Popperfoto: p 133.
Bill Prosser: p 70.
Rex Features: pp 116, 117.
David Shepherd: pp 44, 45, 52, 54, 84, 86, 89, 92, 152/3.
Topham: p 117.
Vision International: p 32.
Woolston Design: pp 4, 6, 8/9, 15, 17, 18, 21, 24, 28, 29, 30, 32, 46,
      47, 49, 71, 94, 114, 115, 121, 145, 170/1, 172/3, 179, 184.
Woman's Own: p 88.
Joe Wright: pp 25, 77, 124, 125, 126.
Zefa: p 14.

Figures quoted in this book are taken
from previously published sources. The
Open University and the publishers
have made every effort to check these
figures but cannot be held responsible
for any inaccuracies. Main source of
numerical information: *McCance and
Widdowson's The Composition of Foods*
(HMSO).